THE BASIC WAYS OF KNOWING

The Basic Ways of Knowing

An In- depth Study of
Kumārila's Contribution to Indian Epistemology

GOVARDHAN P. BHATT
M.A., Ph.D.

Foreword
T.R.V MURTI

SINCE 1901
MOTILAL BANARSIDASS
PUBLISHING HOUSE

3rd Reprint: Delhi, ***2026***
First Edition: Delhi, 1962

Also available at:
MOTILAL BANARSIDASS PUBLISHING HOUSE

- 4637/20, F-2, Hari Sadan, First Floor, Ansari Road, Darya Ganj Delhi–110 002 *Tel.*: (+91-11) 4559 7999
- 1st Floor, 1/2 Rathnavilas Road, Basvanagudi, Next to Pai Vista Convention Hall, South End Circle, Bengaluru–560004 (India) *Tel.*: +91-80-41275911

ISBN: 978-93-5760-482-6 (Hardcover)
ISBN: 978-93-5760-472-7 (Peperback)

Printed & Published by
Rajendra P Jain *for*
Motilal Banarsidass Publishing House
A-44, Naraina Industrial Area, Phase I, New Delhi–110 028 (INDIA)
Email: naraina@mlbd.in Website: www.mlbd.in
Tel.: (+91-11) 4751 1592

TO THE SACRED MEMORY OF

My Dear Parents

WHOM GOD WILLED TO END UP

THEIR EARTHLY SOJOURN TOO EARLY

FOREWORD

The contribution of Kumārila Bhaṭṭa and his School to Indian philosophical thought is not in any way inferior to that of Dignāga, Śaṅkara or Bhartṛhari. In fact, the entire Advaita Vedānta epistemology is based on the Bhāṭṭa School (*vyavahāre bhaṭṭanayaḥ*); its theory of language and mode of interpretation of scriptural texts are closely modelled on that of the Mīmāṃsā. Kumārila's *magnum opus*, the *Śloka-Vārttika*, is a landmark in the development of Indian thought. Kumārila, as a realist and empiricist belonging to the *ātmavāda*-tradition, develops his characteristic standpoint by a sustained and deep criticism, all along the line, of the Buddhistic doctines of *anātmavāda*, of momentariness, denial of the Universal (*sāmānya*), and advocacy of *apohavāda* (Negative Theory of Meaning), of the Idealistic denial of the external object (*nirālambanavāda*) etc. The *Śloka-Vārttika* is a lucid and penetrating critical work presented in delightful language.

In contrast to Śaṅkara who does not evince any deep or first-hand acquaintance with the Buddhist schools, Kumārila's knowledge of Buddhist thought is direct, authentic, comprehensive and profound. Śāntarakṣita and Kamalaśīla quote profusely (about 150 *ślokas*) from the *Śloka-Vārttika* which refutes the Buddhistic contention of Personal Omniscience (*sārvajña*). So do the Jaina philosophers.

Kumārila's stand is that of an eminently reasonable advocacy of a realistic and empirical philosophy: in some respects, it is much superior to that of the Nyāya-Vaiśeṣika. It steers clear of the Buddhist Devil who denies the reality of Substance (permanent underlying locus of qualities and action), of the Whole (*avayavī*), of the Universal (*jāti, sāmānya*) on the one hand, and the Deep Sea of the Advaita Vedānta which denies the ultimate reality of the *dharma* (qualities etc.) and the Parts and the Particular. Kumārila accepts the reality of both the Permanent and the Momentary, of Substance and its Predicates (Qualities and Action), of the Whole as well as its Parts, and of the Universal and the Particular; he is committed to a middle standpoint close to commonsense and ordinary language. Dr. Bhatt makes a brief reference to this characteristic stand especially on page 387 of his book. We should be deeply thankful to Dr. Bhatt for giving us *Epistemology of the Bhāṭṭa School of Pūrva Mīmāṃsā** based on a deep and comprehensive study of Kumārila and his School.

Primarily concerned in interpreting the Vedic texts, as inculcating ritual religion, the Mīmāṃsā is led on to questions of Reality and Knowledge in support of its contentions. It formulated the doctrine of the Self-validity (*Svataḥ-prāmāṇya*) of all knowledge, including the Verbal Testimony of the Scriptures, because any other position is not plausible, and is even ureasonable. The factors which engender knowledge are the only necessary and sufficient conditions which also constitute its validity. No extra or external considerations such as correspondence, coherence or successful activity are required. Each knowledge is also known as valid the moment the knowledge occurs (*jñaptau prāmāṇyaṃ svataḥ*). Invalidity (*aprāmāṇya*) is caused by the presence of alien factors, alien to knowledge, and is detected later (*aprāmāṇyaṃ parataḥ*). This view and the untenability of other views is demonstrated by detailed and subtle analysis by the author in Chapters III and IV of the book.

The Mīmāṃsā goes on to consider modes of knowledge other than *Śabda* (Verbal Testimony), because it is interested in pointing out that Perception, Inference etc. cannot give us knowledge of the Super-sensuous Dharma, the performance of ritualistic and ceremonial acts (*yajña*) leading to *svarga* (the heaven) and other UNSEEN or *adṛṣṭa* results; by their very nature they are precluded from leading us to these results.

Its realistic attitude is also the consequence of its conception of Dharma. The Mīmāṃsā finds that the investigation of Dharma involves metaphysical and epistemological issues about the nature of the Self, nature of Karma and its result. It is committed to a form of Realism. As Kumārila says in the *Śloka-Vārttika* (*Nirālambanavāda*, 3-4):

*The original title of this work—Author

Karmabhyaḥ phalasambandhaḥ pāralaukyaihalaukikaḥ /
Sarvam ityādy ayuktaṃ syād artha-śūnyāsu buddhiṣu //
Tasmād dharmārthibhiḥ pūrvaṃ pramāṇair lokasammataiḥ /
Arthasya sadasadbhāve yatnaḥ kāryaḥ kriyāṃ prati //

The *Kāśikā* thereon says clearly that the entire business of the Mīmāṃsā is based on the assumption of the existence of external objects (sarvo hy ayaṃ mīmāṃsā-prapañco bāhyārthāśraya eva). It is thus opposed to the Advaita Vedānta stand of relegating the performance of ritualistic ceremonies (*yajña*) to *vyavahāra*, a lower order of reality. The Mīmāṃsā does not therefore favour two levels of reality, *paramārtha* and *vyavahāra*. Thus the Mīmāṃsā is led either to deny illusion and the illusory object entirely (the Prābhākara position of *Viveka-akhyāti*, the Non-apprehension of Difference between two Knowledges and their respective objects), or the more reasonable stand of Kumārila that only the *relation* between two real separate objects is false and non-existent (*Viparītakhyāti*). The Mīmāṃsā cannot countenance the Advaita theory of *Anirvacanīyakhyāti* which means the acceptance of an apparent (illusory) content, with the experience of such content also being unique and illusory. All these topics are admirably well-treated by Dr. Bhatt in his work under consideration.

The most significant contribution of the Mīmāṃsā, especially of the Bhāṭṭa School, is with regard to its conception of Language and Verbal Knowledge. There was never a time when Language and linguistic activities were absent; they are beginningless and eternal (*Śabda-nityatva-vāda*). The Impersonality of Scripture (*Vedāpauruṣeyavāda*) is also the necessary consequence of this doctrine. That the Semantical Rules of Syntax and Interpretation also do not need any person, is also to be accepted. That Action or the Verb is the Principal Meaning of the Sentence is also a special Mīmāṃsā doctrine.

As indicated before, the Mīmāṃsā schools undertake a consideration of the *Pramāṇas* (Sources of Valid Knowledge) to show that Knowledge of Dharma (Ritual Religion) cannot be got from sources other than Scripture (*Śabda*). This does not mean that its investigation of Perception (*Pratyakṣa*), *Anumāna* (Inference), *Upamāna* (Analogy), *Śabda*, *Arthāpatti* (Presumption) and

Anupalabdhi (Conscious Non-apprehension) is scrappy or inadequate. The Bhāṭṭa School holds that all human knowledge falls under one of the six kinds enumerated above, neither more nor less. It therefore comes into clash not only with the Buddhists who accept two mutually exclusive and exhaustive knowledges (Perception and Inference) based on two disparate objects (the *Śvalakṣaṇa* and the *Sāmānya-lakṣaṇa*)—*mānadvaividhyam meyadvaividhyāt*, but also with the Sāṃkhya who accepts only three sources (*Pratyakṣa*, *Anumāna* and *Śabda*) and the Nyāya which accepts four along with *Upamāna* and the Prābhākara who accepts *Arthāpatti* (Presumption) but does not accept *Anupalabdhi*. The burden is to show that there is no knowledge or object which could not be brought under any one of the six kinds; nor could we do with less, without reasonable propriety.

The justification for accepting the above stated six kinds of knowledge and objective content is that we are led to them by distinct (although not absolutely exclusive) modes of apprehending them. The Buddhistic (Dignāgian) conception of *Pratyakṣa* as the apprehension of the Unique Particular (*Svalakṣaṇa*) and the *Svalakṣaṇa* as given only in *Pratyakṣa* is actually an extreme type of *Nirvikalpa Pratyakṣa* and rules out the *Savikalpa* as *Pratyakṣa*, because the *Savikalpa* involves mental construction and is therefore not confined to the strictly given (*na sannihitamātra-viṣayam*). For the Bhāṭṭa and other realists, the *Savikalpa* is the principal type of *Pratyakṣa*; they choose to ignore or slur over the *a priori* functioning of the mind and its *saṃskāras* at work in forming the *savikalpa*. The Realists consider Substance and its Predicates, the Whole and the Parts and the Universal and the Particular as equally and directly given and perceived.

The Buddhist is equally perverse in denying Verbal Testimony as giving fresh and unknown access to entities; it is only an index or outward expression of *Vikalpas*, our internal thought. He denies that the Word can reveal anything not known before; of course it is incapable of revealing to us the transcendent reality. The Buddhist doctrine is akin to Logical Positivism and the Linguistic Philosophers of the Wittgensteinian School. It also therefore advocates a Negative Theory of Meaning (*Apohavāda*). This is clearly wrong, because for most of our information we depend upon hearsay or verbal communication from others, not on our own thoughts. For the Mīmāṃsā and the Vedānta there is an added reason that with regard to the Supersensuous or the Transcendent Dharma or Brahman, *Śabda* is the only Source of Knowledge.

The Nyāya is rather naive in reducing *Arthāpatti* to a kind of Inference (the *Kevala-vyatireki* type); because in *arthāpatti* we do not start with a ready-made major premise (*vyāpti*), but we frame one to explain an apparently odd situation. In fact, most of our scientific and philosophical generalisations are nothing but *arthāpatti*. Nor is his attempt to subsume *Anupalabdhi* (Conscious Non-apprehension) under *Pratyakṣa* more convincing. For, we have to remember the thing absent and try to perceive and know it by other means and as this does not lead to any apprehension, we conclude that the thing in question does not exist or is absent. For instance, a person who denies the existence of God does not make the assertion only on the non-availability of perception, but necessarily of all other modes of knowledge open to human beings:

Pramāṇapañcakaṃ yatra vasturūpe na jāyate /
Vastusattāvabodhārthaṃ tatrābhāvapramāṇatā //
[*Śloka-Vārttika*, *Abhāvaprāmāṇyavāda*, 1]

The non-availability of all the five sources of positive knowledge itself serves as a means to negative conclusions. There is no other way to make negative assertions. Therefore, any knowledge of absence or negation involves a well-defined process; there cannot be a direct perception of absence, as the Nyāya wrongly holds.

The topic of *Pramāṇa* and *Prameya* (the whole extent of Theory of Knowledge) is a fascinating enquiry, and there are many, many sophisticated issues involved. I invite the reader to go through the main body of the excellent work of Dr. Bhatt and enjoy the way he has treated every detail and has brought out its subtle implications. This is a commendable performance.

If I have any criticism to offer it is that his treatment of *Śabda* is not comprehensive, or even adequate. Dr. Bhatt should have brought out the full implications of the Beginninglessness (*Nityatva*) of the Word and the Impersonality of the Scripture and even of Language. He should have refuted the Convention-Theory of

Language (*Saṅketa* theory) advocated by the Nyāya School. That language is underived and that the word is a form and is thus distinct from its material embodiment, sound (*dhvani*), are established by the Mīmāṃsā theory of the Eternality of the Word (*śabda-nityatva-vāda*). Words and their relation with meaning are eternal, underived and impersonal (*autpattikastu śabdasyārthena sambandhaḥ tasya jñānam upadeśo'vyatirekaścārthe'nupalabdhe tat pramāṇam Bādarāyaṇasyānapekṣatvāt—Mīmāṃsā Sūtras* I.1.5). It may be thought that we give names to persons and thus initiate new conventions, and that the same logic should be applied to other words also. They too were the result of convention (*saṅketa*), and where human convention is not available, recourse may be had to divine convention. Against this view, the Mīmāṃsā argues rightly that the relation between the word and the meaning is not an arbitrary convention, established by man or even by God either now or in the past. We do not have record of any such convention. Convention itself presupposes language, which is sought to be derived from convention. To make convention, words have to be used and understood by persons participating in the convention. This is to use language. And language itself is sought to be derived from language. This is clearly circular. Invoking God does not help either. How could God make known his intentions, his conventions between words and their meanings, to persons who did not use language already? And if they had already been using language, God's convention does not obviously initiate language. However far back we may push the beginning of convention, we would still find language preceding it. An absolute beginning of language is untenable. Linguistic usage is continuous. This is a doctrine which the Mīmāṃsā shares with the School of Grammar (*Vaiyākaraṇa*). But it is unlike the Grammar School which takes Language as a Whole Impartite Sentence primarily (*Akhaṇḍa-Vākya-Sphoṭa*), while the breaking of it into individual words and syllables is only a convenient abstraction. This is a device meant for pedagogical purposes. The Mīmāṃsā, as a realist and empiricist, is committed to a kind of atomism and pluralism in language (*varṇā eva śabdaḥ*); it considers the sentence as a real combination of letters and words, under the guidance of some syntactic rules.

The Mīmāṃsā conception of the Impersonality of Vedic Texts (*Apauruṣeya-vāda*) and their interpretation as not involving any reference to the intention of the speaker or writer (*Tātparya = Vaktur icchā*) in construing a sentence are also to be emphasized. The Mīmāṃsā also takes the Verb or Action as the principal and substantive part of the sentence, a doctrine which it shares with the Grammar School.

These points deserve to be stressed in any consideration of *Śabda* (Verbal Knowledge). Even in elementary text-books of Nyāya, like the *Bhāṣā-Pariccheda* or *Tarka-Saṃgraha*, mention is usually made that *Āsatti, Yogyatā, Ākāṅkṣā* and *Tātparya-jñāna* are the necessary factors in construing a sentence. The Nyāya is also insistent upon taking the Noun (Nominative) as the principal part of the sentence.

Dr. Bhatt's treatment of the subject is not at all uncritical. As an instance of this, I may draw attention of the reader to his consideration of the peculiar Bhāṭṭa conception of JÑĀTATĀ (Cognizedness) of Knowledge. "Kumārila's keen intellect rightly grasped the root idea from which Idealism grew. The Idealist assumed that cognition must be known before an object is known. He took it as a self-evident truth. Kumārila proved the untenability of this notion. He went further ahead and proved that cognition is never known directly, because it is a formless and fleeting entity. Cognition is not even self-aware. Its existence is rather presumed to explain the fact of object-manifestation. In this connection Kumārila put forward a unique theory of cognizedness." (p. 413) "...knowledge must presuppose some kind of activity belonging to the subject, which consists in attending and actively responding to the influences produced on the subject by the objects in the environment. But an activity is generally conceived as producing some perceptible and tangible results on objects, while in the case of cognition no such results are observed. The mistake of the Bhāṭṭas consists in placing cognition on the same footing as other voluntary activities. They thought that cognition produced cognizedness in objects exactly as cooking produced cookedness in rice. But while cookedness is a visible and tangible result, cognizedness is not. And there is no ground to suppose that cognizedness is a very subtle and invisible result, because in that case the cognizer himself could not perceive it. Of course, when a man has already known an object, he happens to experience a feeling of familiarity when he is face to face with it on a second occasion. But this feeling does not reside in the object; it resides in the knowing subject." (p. 65). "Cognizedness is said to be directly cognized while cognition is said to be inferred. But in that case a new cognizedness will be generated in the first cognizedness and so on leading to infinite regress." (p. 69). "Knowledge is a unique phenomenon and cannot be brought under any of the usual categories of substance, quality, relation and action. Knowledge may be knowledge of a substance, of a quality, of a relation, or of an action; but it is neither a substance, nor a quality, nor a relation, nor an action." (p. 67). There are some other places where this doctrine is criticized.

Dr. Bhatt's eminent work amply proves that there is no neutral or completely objective, disinterested epistemology. Every system of philosophy is committed to an ultimate metaphysics or a conception of Self, Object, Reality, Relation, Knowledge and Causation etc., whether this is consciously expressed or is merely pre-supposed. The theory of knowledge of any system is merely the overt drawing out of the implications of its metaphysics with regard to knowledge. This is evident from the way the Buddhist radically differs in his theory of knowledge from that of others- And also it is proved by the fact that the Bhāṭṭas differ from the Nyāya, Prābhākara, and the Advaita Vedānta.

In dealing with the Bhāṭṭa epistemology, Dr. Bhatt compares and contrasts this position on various issues with not only other Indian schools but also with some of the European Philosophers like Reid, Hume and Kant. In a sense it is an exercise in Comparative Philosophy. This is inevitable, as otherwise, the position of the Bhāṭṭa school cannot be clarified and brought out in depth.

Epistemology of the Bhāṭṭa School of Pūrva Mīmāṃsā is based on a close study of the original Sanskrit works down the ages, from Kumārila's *Śloka-Vārttika*, its Commentaries and sub-commentaries, as well as the works of Prabhākara and the Nyāya Schools. Dr. Bhatt has also consulted the modern literature on the subject, especially Dr. Ganganath Jha's works. In the result, he has given us a well-constructed, lucidly presented, definitive work on the subject. This is a noteworthy contribution to Indian philosophical thought.

Varanasi T.R.V. Murti

ACKNOWLEDGEMENTS

It is my pious and pleasant duty to express my indebtedness to all those who have contributed in any way to the completion and publication of this work. It is not possible to name all the authors whose works have benefited me. Those who have been quoted or criticized have obviously contributed to and stimulated my thinking and I am indebted to them. Out of those Dr. Ganganath Jha stands apart and deserves a special mention for having dedicated his life to the interpretation and translation of the basic texts of most of the systems of Indian Philosophy. He was the pioneer in the special field of Pūrva Mīmāṃsā and having produced the first thesis was, as a matter of fact, my predecessor. I should also utilize this opportunity for offering my heart-felt apologies to the great sage for the unpleasant act of criticizing his views on a few very important fundamentals.

In the second place, I should be grateful to all those scholars who have appreciated my work and encouraged me by their carefully considered and judicious comments. Again, it is not possible to name all but those who have since departed certainly have a claim to be mentioned by name. It is very sad that Dr. B. L. Atreya and Dr. Jadunath Sinha whose names occur in the Preface are no more with us. I was fortunate to have had a long association with them and their memories still haunt me. Mm. Pt. Gopinath Kaviraj and Prof. T. M. P. Mahadevan have passed away recently. I should also name Dr. B. G. Tiwari who passed away long ago and shortly after publishing his most encouraging appreciation in the *Darshan International*. I should also mention Prof. P. S. Naidu who if alive, as I would very much wish, must be around ninety-five. One of the great men was Prof. D. D. Vadekar whom we unfortunately lost in March, 1985. His contribution to the philosophical literature in Marathi is unique and immense. In addition to being a talented philosopher he was full of human virtues and I am deeply indebted to him for his generous appreciation of my work.

To Prof. T. R. V. Murti, who too, to our great loss and sorrow, has passed away, I am especially grateful for the valuable Foreword that he has very kindly contributed to this edition of the book—a great honour, perhaps not so well deserved. As a matter of fact, he has put me under perpetual indebtedness by this generous act of his. Prof. Murti was really a giant among contemporary Indian thinkers and his readiness to write the Foreword alone speaks a lot. It may however be mentioned that it was not so easy to get this Foreword. A considerable amount of worry was caused by some cunning worldling to the peace-loving philosopher and he found himself mentally too much upset to be able to concentrate properly. I had to wait for more than a year but the waiting at last ended with a pleasant relief to my mind when I got the amply rewarding Foreword which really deserved the waiting. As the great poet has said:

क्लेशः फलेन हि पुनर्नवतां विधत्ते । [*Kumārasambhava* V. 86]

[Suffering refreshes the spirits on the attainment of the desired object.]

It would not be fair on my part if I fail to mention my niece Lakshmi and daughters Anita and Namita who did many odd jobs and have thus earned lots of my good wishes and blessings.

Lastly, I am very much obliged to my friend Lali Babu, a partner of Messrs Motilal Banarsidass, who readily accepted to take over the publication of this revised edition, and also to the senior partner Prakash ji, two big names in the trade.

Vijaya Dashami
October 20, 1988
Delhi

G. P. BHATT

PREFACE

Kumārila is one of the brightest luminaries in the sky of ancient Indian thought. Yet, strangely enough, we do not find a work devoted exclusively to Kumārila and his school. Dr. Ganganath Jha was the first scholar to produce a systematic work on Mīmāṃsā, but instead of Kumārila he selected Prabhākara, a less known exponent of Mīmāṃsā, for his doctoral thesis. Dr. Jha's latest work *Pūrva-Mīmāṃsā in its Sources* is a work of wider scope and gives the views of Śabara, Prabhākara, Kumārila and Murārimiśra on all the philosophical and Mīmāṃsā topics. However, the major portions of this work and the earlier one, viz., *The Prabhākara School of Pūrva-Mīmāṃsā*, are devoted to the Mīmāṃsā topics proper which have now lost the philosophical importance that they formerly had. In *The Prabhākara School of Pūrva-Mīmāṃsā* Prabhākara's epistemological and philosophical doctrines have been discussed in about a hundred pages only and in *Pūrva-Mīmāṃsā in its Sources* Dr. Jha summarizes the philosophical and epistemological views of the Mīmāṃsā thinkers in 165 pages. Both the works are of a descriptive and non-critical nature. There are two other important works in English on the Mīmāṃsā system, viz., Keith's *Karma Mīmāṃsā* and Pashupati Nath Shastri's *Introduction to Pūrva-Mīmāṃsā*. But these are very brief and merely introductory. Thus a critical, comparative and elaborate work was still needed and the present work is an humble attempt to fulfill this need.

The logic of Nyāya, the categories of Vaiśeṣika, the cosmology of Sāṅkhya, the metaphysics of Advaita Vedānta and the ethics of the *Gītā* are outstanding contributions that India made to philosophical thought and the epistemology of Kumārila ranks with them. But while there are elaborate works on the epistemologies of Nyāya, Vedānta, Rāmānuja etc., there is none on the epistemology of Kumārila. The present work contains a detailed, critical and comparative account of Kumārila's epistemology. The theories of other schools also have been discussed at length in their proper places. The treatment of the subject is based on a first-hand study of Sanskrit texts.

This work was approved by the Banaras Hindu University for the award of the degree of Doctor of Philosophy in 1956.

I am very much indebted to Dr. B. L. Atreya, M.A., D. Litt. under whose supervision this work was completed. Dr. Jadunath Sinha, M.A., Ph.D. has been a constant source of inspiration to me. I express my sincere thanks to him.

I am conscious of many shortcomings in this work. However, to repeat what Kumārila himself has aptly said,

> आगमप्रवणश्चाहं नापवाद्यः स्खलन्नपि ।
> न हि सद्वर्त्मना गच्छन् स्खलितेष्वप्यपोद्यते ॥

[SV, Intro. to Sūtra 1, Verse 7]

[Reverencing the scripture as I do, let none reproach me, should I err in my exposition. He who goes by the right path need not be censured, even if he slips occasionally.]

G.P. Bhatt

CONTENTS

PART II
SOURCES OF VALID KNOWLEDGE

ABBREVIATIONS

BG	*Bhagavadgītā*
BR	*Bṛhatī* of Prabhākara (Published with SB and RV by Madras University)
GB	*Gauḍapāda's Bhāṣya* on SK
KK	*Kāśikā* of Sucaritamiśra (Trivandrum)
MM	*Mānameyodaya* of Nārāyaṇa (Adyar)
MS	*Pūrva-Mīmāṃsā Sūtra*-s of Jaimini
NA	*Nyāyāvatāra* of Siddhasenadivākara
NB	*Nyāyabindu* of Dharmakīrti (St. Petersburg)
NBT	*Nyāyabinduṭīkā* of Dharmottara (St. Petersburg)
NK	*Nyāyakandalī* of Śrīdhara (Vizianagram)
NKu	*Nyāyakusumāñjali* of Udayana
NM	*Nyāyamañjarī* of Jayanta (Vizianagram)
NP	*Nyāyapraveśa* of Diṅnāga (Gaekwad)
NR	*Nyāyaratnākara* of Pārthasārathi (Chowkhamba)
NRM	*Nyāyaratnamālā* of Pārthasārathi (Chowkhamba)
NS	*Nyāya Sūtra*-s of Gautama
NTV	*Nītitattvāvirbhāva* of Cidānanda (Trivandrum)
NV	*Nyayavārtika* of Uddyotakara
PDS	*Padārthadharmasaṅgraha* of Praśastapāda (Vizianagram)
PMS	*Parīkṣāmukhasūtra* of Māṇikyanandī
PNT	*Pramāṇanayatattvālokālaṅkāra* of Vādi Deva Sūri
PP	*Prakaraṇapañcikā* of Śālikanātha (Chowkhamba)
PS	*Pramāṇasamuccaya* of Diṅnāga
RV	*Ṛjuvimalā* of Śālikanātha
SB	Śabara's *Bhāṣya* on MS
SBBS	Śaṅkara's *Bhāṣya* on *Brahma Sūtra*-s
SBMU	Śaṅkara's *Bhāṣya* on *Māṇḍūkya Upaniṣad*
SBTU	Śaṅkara's *Bhāṣya* on *Taittirīya Upaniṣad*
SC	*Siddhāntacandrikā* of Rāmakṛṣṇa (Nirnaya Sagar)
SD	*Śāstradīpikā* of Pārthasārathi (Nirnaya Sagar)
SDS	*Sarvadarśanasaṅgraha* of Mādhavācārya
SK	*Sāṅkhya Kārikā* of Īśvarakṛṣṇa

SM	*Siddhāntamuktāvali* of Viśvanātha (Nirnaya Sagar)
STK	*Sāṅkhyatattvakaumudī* of Vācaspati
SV	*Ślokavārtika* of Kumārila (Chowkhamba)
TH	*Tattvasaṅgraha* of Śāntarakṣita (Gaekwad)
TPS	*Tattvopaplavasiṃha* of Jayarāśi (Gaekwad)
TR	*Tārkikarakṣā* of Varadarāja
TS	*Tarkasaṅgraha* of Annambhaṭṭa
TSR	*Tantrasiddhāntaratnāvali* by Cinnasvāmī Śāstrī
TT	*Tātparyaṭīkā* of Umbeka (Madras University)
VB	Vātsyāyana's *Bhāṣya* on NS
VP	*Vedāntaparibhāṣā* of Dharmarājādhvarīndra
VS	*Vaiśeṣika Sūtra*-s of Kaṇāda
Va	*Vākyapadīya* of Bhartṛhari (Banaras)

THE BASIC WAYS OF KNOWING:

AN IN-DEPTH STUDY OF KUMĀRILA'S CONTRIBUTION TO INDIAN EPISTEMOLOGY

CHAPTER I

INTRODUCTION

Kumārila Bhaṭṭa, though less spoken of than Śaṅkara in the modern histories of Indian Philosophy, is no less important as a system-builder. He deserves the same place in epistemology as Śaṅkara does in metaphysics. Both flourished in the same age and had a common foe. Both had the same interest, viz., the revival of Vedic learning. Their aim was to save the orthodox tradition from the Buddhist onslaught, and their victory was the victory of wisdom over 'erroneous philosophies' and 'perverted morality'. In a way Kumārila's work is more important than that of Śaṅkara. Kumārila had more contacts with the Buddhists and more outstanding victories in debates over such strong rivals as Dharmakīrti and others. He was a greater dialectician as is amply testified by the subtle, rich, original, and elaborate chain of arguments of the *Ślokavārtika*. He seems to possess a deeper understanding and a more extensive knowledge of the rival philosophies. Śaṅkara's work was complementary to Kumārila's. Kumārila purged the diseased Indian mind of the 'poison' of Buddhism and Śaṅkara re-constructed the tissues by giving a saner outlook. Kumārila's work was foundational. He took up the problem of validity and tried to establish the validity of Vedic knowledge. Śaṅkara gave a more consistent and appealing interpretation of the Scriptures, absorbing the best that was there in Buddhism, and thus erected a lofty structure on the firm foundation laid down by Kumārila.

The fact that there is no definite chronology and that most of the ancient Sanskrit works on philosophy and epistemology are now lost, makes it difficult to appreciate Kumārila's contribution duly. Prior to Kumārila a very high stage had already been reached in the development of logical doctrines, but both before and after Kumārila logic was treated mainly as an art of debate rather than a science of reasoning. The basic epistemological problems of the nature of knowledge, the relation of knowledge to reality, and the nature and criterion of truth and error were given a cursory treatment, though the problem of the sources of knowledge was considered at some length. The Buddhist thinkers like Diṅnāga and Dharmakīrti could not do full justice to these problems due to their biased outlook. Kumārila gave a more serious, impartial and detailed treatment to these problems for the first time, and from his time onwards till a few centuries back a discussion of these problems is found to be an essential feature of every important work on philosophy.

Kumārila was primarily a Mīmāṃsaka and secondarily an epistemologist, though his work on epistemology is of a more far-reaching value than his work on Mīmāṃsā proper. The aphorisms of Jaimini are concerned with Vedic ritualism and they hardly contain any philosophy. Śabara wrote a very lucid commentary on these aphorisms, which superseded all the previous commentaries. Kumārila wrote his *Ślokavārtika* on the Tarkapāda section of Śabara's commentary and *Tantravārtika* and *Ṭupṭīkā* on the rest. The *Ślokavārtika* is an extensive epistemological work in verses and is a fine specimen of the erudition, profundity and fertility of its author's intellect. Its criticisms of the rival theories are devastating. Kumārila's theories, particularly those of the inferability of the cognitive act and of the self-validity of knowledge, provide a strong stimulus to later discussions and his followers have put forth a vigorous defence of his theories against the opposition offered by the other schools of thought. The earliest extant commentary on the *Ślokavārtika* is the *Tātparyaṭīkā* by Umbeka.[1] Next comes the *Kāśikā* commentary by Sucaritamiśra and the last is the *Nyāyaratnākara* by Pārthasārathi. Of these three commentators Pārthasārathi is the most consistent and gifted thinker. He has also written an independent commentary named *Śāstradīpikā* on Śabara's *Bhāṣya* and an independent treatise named *Nyāyaratnamālā* discussing some important epistemological and Mīmāṃsā topics. He has ably defended Kumārila's views and has offered unassailable arguments particularly against the Prābhākara school of Pūrva Mīmāṃsā. Two later works on Kumārila's school, popularly known as the Bhāṭṭa school, are the *Nītitattvāvirbhāva* by Cidānanda and the *Mānameyodaya*, a joint work by Nārāyaṇa

1. Dr. C. Kunhan Raja has refuted Umbeka's identity with Maṇḍana and Bhavabhūti in his Introduction to *Tātparyaṭīkā*.

Bhaṭṭa and Nārāyaṇa Paṇḍita. The latter is a summary of the former in an easy style. There are other works also on the Bhāṭṭa school, but they concentrate their attention on the Mīmāṃsā topics proper. Rāmakṛṣṇa's *Yuktisnehaprapūraṇī-Siddhānta-Candrikā* is a valuable commentary on the Tarkapāda section of the *Śāstradīpikā*[2].

Another school of Pūrva Mīmāṃsā was started by Prabhākara who is now supposed to be earlier than Kumārila by a majority of scholars. Prabhākara wrote a commentary named *Bṛhatī* on Śabara's *Bhāṣya.* According to some scholars, eg., Dr. Jha, Prabhākara's interpretation of the *Bhāṣya* is more faithful than that of Kumārila. But so far as the Tarkapāda section of the *Bṛhatī* is concerned, we cannot subscribe to this opinion. On many occasions he has given forced interpretations and has even twisted the *Bhāṣya* texts in order to suit his own views. His style is very cumbersome and very difficult to follow without the commentary. Prabhākara, however, was a more original thinker thanKumārila and he will always be remembered as the author of a peculiar theory of knowledge known as *Tripuṭīpratyakṣavāda* or the theory of triple perception and a theory of error known as *Vivekākhyātivāda.* Prabhākara's work has been commented upon by Śālikanātha. Śālikanātha's commentary is known as *Ṛjuvimalāpañcikā.* He also wrote *Prakaraṇapañcikā* which is an independent treatise on the Prābhākara school. Śālikanātha was a first-rate scholar like Pārthasārathi and the reputation that Prabhākara enjoyed among scholars was mainly due to him.

The Bhāṭṭa school had a steady growth from Kumārila to Cidānanda. The commentators did not merely repeat what had already been said. Each one puts forth a stronger defence and fights against the rival theorists with sharper weapons. The toughest enemy that Kumārila had to fight with was Buddhism. The two main pillars of Buddhism, the doctrines of subjectivism and momentariness, crumbled down under the pressure of his relentless logic. In the days of the commentators Buddhism had lost all its force; yet there were other rivals, for example, the Prābhākaras.

2. An exhaustive list of Mīmāṃsā thinkers togeher with a critical account of their dates, works and personal histories is given by V.A.R. Shastri in his Introduction to *Tattvabindu* and by Dr. Umesha Mishra in his *Mīmāṃsā-Kusumāñjali*, appended to Jha's *Pūrva Mīmāṃsā in Its Sources.*

Pārthasārathi accorded the same treatment to Prabhākara as Kumārila accorded to the Buddhists. In the post-Kumārila period Pārthasārathi has been the greatest Mīmāṃsaka. His genius was recognized by his rivals also. Philosophers of other schools have frequently quoted Kumārila to support their own views; and similarly Pārthasārathi's *Nyāyaratnamālā* has been commented upon by Rāmānujācārya, a follower of Prabhākara.

The contributions of Kumārila and his followers are many. They introduced novel theories and novel criticisms of older and contemporary theories. In the following chapters we will discuss them in relation to the other systems of Indian thought and point out their merits and demerits. Before closing this introduction we may pass a few general remarks on Kumārila. Kumārila has a dual attitude. In the matters of Dharma, i.e., matters pertaining to the other world, his attitude is that of rationalized faith, and in secular matters it is that of reason. He is a thorough-going empiricist and a defender of common-sense. Common-sense believes in the reality of the external world and a plurality of subjects and the capacity of our senses to reveal things in their true character. Kumārila accepts the evidence of our senses, though not uncritically. The data of our senses forms the warp and woof of our very existence; realism is the presupposition of all human discourse and social intercourse, and if we want to have a specific label for Kumārila's realism there can perhaps be no better choice than *existential realism.*

PART I

KNOWLEDGE, TRUTH AND ERROR

अथातो प्रमाजिज्ञासा

CHAPTER II

THE NATURE OF KNOWLEDGE

2.1. *Knowledge and the Self*

Knowledge is the basis of all practical activities. The function of knowledge is to illuminate things other than itself.[1] Knowledge inherently refers to an object that is known and it always belongs to a subject that knows. There can be no knowledge existing independently by itself without implying a knower and a thing known. Knowledge is a self-transcending property of the self. It reveals certain objects to the self which has certain ends in view. It urges the self to act with regard to the objects thus revealed. The knowing activity helps the self in fulfilling its practical purposes. The self appropriates or avoids objects in accordance with the character of the objects that is revealed to it by the act of cognition. The self is essentially a spiritual substance. It is the abode of intelligence (*caitanyāśraya*). Intelligence or sentience is an essential property of the self, which differentiates it from the material substances. Desire, aversion, effort, pleasure, pain and cognition are the specific properties of the self. These can never belong to matter which is non-intelligent. Intelligence implies consciousness, purpose and the capacity of adapting means to ends. No intelligent being acts without some end in view. However dull a man may be, he always indulges in action with some conscious purpose.[2] Intelligence is the capacity of the self to 'enjoy'[3], which implies desire, cognition and effort. Thus the self is essentially a purposive entity and sentience is its inseparable property.[4] Teleological activity of man is of two kinds: one aims at one's own worldly well-being (*abhyudaya*) and the other at one's transcendental good (*niḥśreyasa*). Specific desires, cognition etc. continue so long as the

1. प्रतीतिः वस्त्वन्तरप्रकाशस्वभावा । NR on SV, *Nīrālambanavāda*, 44.
2. प्रयोजनमनुद्दिश्य न मन्दोऽपि प्रवर्तते । SV, *Sambandhākṣepaparihāra*, 55.
3. Ibid., 100.
4. SV, *Ātmavāda*, 26.

transcendental purpose, the super-mundane freedom, is not achieved. But as soon as the self attains its ultimate purpose it is no longer in need of its specific properties. Thus in the state of release the self discontinues its specific properties, but it is never divested of its intelligence which ever afterwards resides in it in a potential form.

According to the Nyāya system cognition and the other specific properties are only accidental to the self, which it acquires during its worldly existence when it comes to be joined to *manas* and sense-organs. Cognition, accordingly, is a quality of the psycho-physical organism: it belongs to the mind-body complex, while the mind, the body and the self individually are essentially non-sentient; the body when disjoined from the self is inert and the self in the state of release, divested of the body, acquires its natural form of a pure substance devoid of cognition, pleasure, pain, desire etc. Thus according to Nyāya and also to Prabhākara the self is essentially a pure substance and cognition is one of its adventitious qualities which come and go without affecting its essential nature.

According to Kumārila, on the other hand, sentience is the very essence of the self-substance, which cannot be taken away without at the same time taking away its selfhood. Specific cognitions come and go (*āgamāpāyinau*) without making any difference to the spiritual character of the self, but intelligence ever continues in all its changing states. Consciousness is the very core of selfhood. Cognition may not be there in the absence of objects to be cognized, but the capacity to cognize can never be taken away from the self. Pārthasārathi says:

> At no time is there any cessation of that which constitutes the cognitive potency of the cognizer. That potency is really indestructible. In the state of release there is no second to serve as means of cognizing, like the eye etc., or any cognizable object such as colour etc., which would have rendered cognition possible. It is, however, a fact that in that state the visible world does exist in its own right, but still in that state it loses its cognizability, so that it does no exist as being fit to be seen. Hence, because of the privation of the distinct instrument the Ātman does not perceive in that state and not because

> of the privation of potency. As for potency, at no time is it absent.[5]

Thus specific cognitions arise occasionally when the sense-organs are active; and when they are not functioning, as in deep sleep or in the state of trance, there is no cognition. But in that state, though the self is devoid of the awareness of objects, it is not devoid of the cognitive potency. Similarly, in the state of release too there is no object-consciousness because the self has done away with the apparatus of cognition, still the cognitive potency is not lost in that state. Summing up his view of release Pārthasārathi says:

> Having abandoned its adventitious properties, viz., cognition, pleasure, pain, desire, aversion, effort or volition, merit, demerit and impression, the self abides in its natural purity in which the cognitive potency, existence and substance-ness etc. persist.[6]

Pārthasārathi's conception of release is that it is a state of total unconsciousness. Not that object consciousness alone is lost in the state of release, even self-consciousness is lost, because *manas* and the other sense-organs are lost due to the exhaustion of all the *karma*-s and its connection with the world is severed. When Pārthasārathi talks of 'the persistence of cognitive potency', what he means is that consciousness remains in the state of potentiality and it never becomes kinetic. Anticipating the objection 'why *jñāna* does not arise in the state of release if the potency exists', Pārthasārathi says:

> Even the self cannot know itself without the means. It is well-known that in the state of mundane existence the self cognizes through the *manas*, and the relation with the *manas* does not exist in the case of one who is freed. Hence by which means could the self know itself? Hence the absence of self-knowledge is evident in one who is emancipated and it has been pointed out by the *Śruti* that only the potency to cognize does reside

5. SD, p. 128.
6. Ibid., p. 130.

in the self. Therefore, release is accompanied neither by *jñāna* nor by *ānanda*.[7]

But this does not seem to be what is exactly meant by Kumārila when he says that "the self never loses *caitanya*"[8] and that "the self is of the nature of consciousness."[9] If in the transcendental state, which is the realization of the highest and the most cherished end of life and which comes after the most strenuous effort of innumerable births and for whose sake the common pleasures of mundane life are denied by the self to itself, even the contentment of realizedness is not experienced, then any attempt to achieve this state defeats its own end. If such a state is achieved at all the self is a loser rather than a gainer. The cognitive potency is said to be indestructible. But if it cannot make the self conscious of its own state even, it is as good as non-existent. The self which loses all forms of consciousness in release and is incapable of enjoying its contentment of having realized its highest aim in spite of the cognitive potency which is said to persist, does not fare better than the Naiyāyika's self which becomes as inert as a stone. To say that the cognitive potency remains while the self has become absolutely incapable to cognize, is as ridiculous as to say that a man retains his power of locomotion while his limbs have become totally paralysed for ever. A potency which cannot enable one to act is really 'impotency'. A potency has meaning when its possessor, though not always doing the act of which it is the potency, actually does it whenever he chooses. So what Kumārila intends by the phrase *jñānaśaktisvabhāva* seems to be that the self is naturally equipped with the power of cognition or consciousness, but during the state of release, because the *summum bonum* of life has been achieved by the self, it no more feels the need of cognizing objects as there is no more dealing with the objective world. Otherwise, if the self is supposed to be essentially an unconscious substance, consciousness accruing to it as a result of its conjunction with *manas* as an adventitious property, the distinction between self and matter becomes meaningless.

7. Ibid., p. 128.
8. SV, *Ātmavāda*, 26.
9. Ibid., 73.

The Bhāṭṭa view as represented by Sucaritamiśra, Cidānanda and Nārāyaṇa seems to be more satisfactory. According to Sucaritamiśra[10] consciousness is the inherent property of the self. In release too the self is not divested of consciousness. Consciousness or the cognitive power (*citiśakti*) is inseparable from the self and when it is not tinged with object-forms it has the self as its object, because cognition can never be without an object to be cognized. *Manas*, which is the instrument of cognition, is eternal and the self remains conjoined to it even in the state of release. Nor can it be said that in that case object-cognition too will persist in the state of release, because *manas* is always dependent on the external sense-organs for object-cognition and they are destroyed with the body. Moreover, object-cognitions are the sources of pleasure and pain which are the result of *karma* and *karma* is totally destroyed in release, but self-consciousness is never a source of pleasure or pain. So, just as substance-ness (*dravyatva*) and all-pervasiveness (*vibhutva*) are not given up during release, so self-consciousness too is never given up. Thus according to Sucaritamiśra consciousness, though it is born of the *manas*-self conjunction, is eternal and indestructible.

According to Prabhākara self-consciousness is not an independent form of cognition; it is involved in every cognition which always apprehends itself, the (cognized) object and the self; and in the state of release the self becomes unconscious, because then there is no awareness of objects due to the absence of sense-organs which are the cause of cognition; on the cessation of object-cognition the self ceases to be aware of itself and remains in the state of pure existence like the inert ether. This view will be further examined in a separate section. Here it is enough to refer to the remark made by Sucaritamiśra in this connection: The sense-organs or the body or cognition are not the knowing subject; it is the self that is the knower and it can in no case and at no time be devoid of knowership.[11]

2.2. *The Act Theory of Knowledge*

So far it is plain that cognition, according to the Bhāṭṭa school, is the distinctive feature of the spritual substance called the soul

10. KK on SV, *Śūnyavāda*, 70.
11. Ibid.

and is its inseparable possession, eternally abiding in it as its substrate. Now the question arises as to what the essential nature of cognition is. Is it a substance or a quality, a relation or an action, or something different from these?

According to the Sāṅkhya system *Puruṣa* or self is immutable and conscious; it is neither a knower, nor a doer, nor an enjoyer; it is the pure light of consciousness. Cognition, pleasure, pain etc. belong to *Buddhi* which is an evolute of the material and unconscious principle called *Prakṛti*. *Puruṣa* is a pure subject (*draṣṭā*) and an absolutely inactive principle, while *Prakṛti* is unconscious and active. What we call knowledge or cognition is a mode (*vṛtti*) of the material *Buddhi* which transforms itself in the shape of the object that is cognized. *Buddhi* being in the proximity of *Puruṣa* reflects his light in it and thus becomes intelligized and falsely appears to be the knower of the object. Knowledge is a substantial transformation of the unconscious *Buddhi* and the conscious *Puruṣa* by itself is absolutely inactive, but, due to a beginningless confusion or indiscrimination (*aviveka*) which results in the intelligizing of *Buddhi* and activizing of *Puruṣa*, the phenomenon of cognition arises as a hybrid. In fact *Puruṣa* can never be the knower, though it is conscious, because knowing implies change and *Puruṣa* is absolutely changeless; and *Buddhi* can never be the knower, though it is mutable, because it is material and unconscious. Thus the cognitive phenomenon, according to Sāṅkhya, is rooted in a beginningless confusion and the *summum bonum* of life consists in the rooting out of this confusion.

According to the Vedānta of Śaṅkara too, all empirical behaviour is based on an illegitimate superimposition of the ego on the non-ego and *vice versa*, while the ultimate reality is one, undifferenced being which is existence-consciousness-bliss. Consciousness is the very stuff which constitutes existence. "Existence is consciousness; consciousness is existence; there is absolutely no difference between the two".[12] This seeming world of experience is nothing but an illusory fabrication of *Māyā* which, being neither absolutely real nor absolutely unreal, is indescribable, while the ontological reality is a characterless, differenceless unity. Consciousness is the very essence of reality as

12. सत्तैव बोधः बोध एव च सत्ता, नानयोः परस्परव्यावृत्तिरस्ति । SBBS, 3.2.21.

illumination is that of the sun or heat that of fire[13]. "The vision of the Absolute Reality is devoid of the distinction of knowledge, known and knower."[14]

Both of these views, the Sāṅkhya as well as the Vedānta, are erroneous. They are opposed to common experience. The Sāṅkhya says that the self is a pure subject or seer. But there can never be a seer without an object that is seen and the process of seeing. To say that the self is conscious and, at the same time, that it is conscious of nothing is self-contradictory. Consciousness is always seen to be the consciousness of something which is other than the consciousness. Cognition is an act whose subject is the self, whose object is the thing of which the self is aware and whose instrument is the sense-organs. The act of awareness presupposes all these distinct factors. The Vedāntic theory that Reality is a subject-object-less consciousness, tries to abolish the distinction which is given in experience and is never annulled. The possibility of cognition presupposes the difference of the cognizer and the cognized. Knowledge is impossible in a world which is a homogeneous, differenceless unity. It is self-contradictory to assert that there is only one self-identical reality and that it is conscious, because the concept of consciousness presupposes the distinction of that which is conscious and that of which there is consciousness.[15]

The Sāṅkhya view that knowledge is a substantive mode of matter makes knowledge material. But knowledge is not a material product. It is the activity of a non-material substance which is the self. Knowledge is an act of the conscious subject which manifests material and other objects to him. Matter has a form and is extended in space, but knowledge cannot be conceived as having a form and extension. Knowledge is formless (*nirākāra*) and has no size or extension. A material substance is the abode of qualities and size and is the material cause of other things, but knowledge is quality-less and sizeless and can never be the material cause of anything. Therefore, it is not a substance at all. The Vedāntic equation between thought and reality is contradictory

13. यत्तु ब्रह्मणो विज्ञानं तत्सवितृप्रकाशवदग्न्युष्णत्ववच्च ब्रह्मस्वरूपाव्यतिरिक्तं स्वरूपमेव तत् । SBTU, 2.1.

14. ज्ञानज्ञेयज्ञातृभेदरहितं परमार्थतत्त्वदर्शनम् । SBMU, 4 1.

15. भेदाश्रयत्वाद् ग्राह्यग्राहकभावस्य । KK on SV, *Śūnyavāda*, 63.

to facts of experience. Reality is wider than experience. Cognition is a fact among facts and there are facts which are never cognized. The Vedāntic philosophy of Śaṅkara reduces everything to *Ātman* and identifies *Ātman* with knowledge. But this is absolutely unfounded. Knowledge is not identical with existence; it is the awareness of existence. Awareness of an object is the manifestation (*prakāśa*) of the object which exists in its own right. Thought simply discovers things, it does not create them. Sucaritamiśra says: "'To exist' does not mean to exist as an object of consciousness"[16] Things are produced and have existence independently of consciousness. The Vedāntin says that *Ātman* is consciousness. But consciousness is momentary while *Ātman* is a permanent entity. A permanent and eternal entity can never be identical with fleeting cognitions. Pārthasārathi says:

> The thing whose nature is to manifest some other object beyond itself and which when present does indeed manifest some object... this is termed *vijñāna* in ordinary parlance. But this is not a rule that whenever the self is present the manifestation of objects does necessarily take place, since during deep sleep the self persists but there is no manifestation of objects. Therefore, the self is not cognition. It may be said by the Vedāntin that the self, though it is of the nature of illumination, does not do so because of the absence of auxiliaries. True, but then that auxiliary is no other than what is termed *jñāna* which invariably reveals a distinct object when it is present.[17]

Cognition is that which necessarily manifests on object; the self does not necessarily manifest objects; therefore the self is not cognition.[18] Thus the self is not knowledge but knower and the reality is not knowledge but the object of knowledge. Knowledge does not constitute reality; it is the revelation of reality. If

16. न धीविषयभावः सत्ता किन्तु सामान्यमुत्तरकालभावि तद्वताम् । KK on SV *Śūnya.*, 64.

17. SD, p. 129.

18. यस्मिस्तु सति प्रकाशत एवार्थान्तरं तज्ज्ञानशब्दवाच्यं, ज्ञायते अनेनेत्यर्थकरणात्, न चात्मनि सति किंचिदन्यत् प्रकाशते, अतः न ज्ञानरूपत्वमात्मनः । SC, p. 129. Cp. also NTV, p. 213.

the Vedāntin means by knowledge something other than what is ordinarily understood by the term 'knowledge', he is not at all justified, because that which is knowledge and at the same time is not an apprehension of some object is quite inconceivable.[19] Moreover, knowledge cannot be a substantive thing, because a substance exists in its own right without referring to anything beyond itself, while knowledge always refers to something beyond itself.

We have already referred to the Nyāya view of the nature of cognition. According to Nyāya cognition is a quality of soul. The Vaiśeṣika system, whose classification of categories is generally accepted by all, includes cognition under the category of quality. Cognition is a specific quality of soul. But it is not considered to be an essential quality, as the soul can be without cognition. In release cognition is supposed to be non-existent and in empirical life too there are such states as deep sleep, swoon and trance in which there is no cognition. Thus cognition is only a temporary quality of soul and is generated under particular conditions, viz., when soul, *manas*, sense-organs and some object have a simultaneous mutual contact. The quality of cognition arises out of a fourfold contact and is related to the soul by way of *samavāya* or the relation of inherence. It can be perceived through inner perception (*mānasa pratyakṣa*) just as the blueness of an object is perceived through vision. Some Naiyāyikas, for example Jayanta Bhaṭṭa, severely criticise the act theory of knowledge so vigorously propounded by the Bhāṭṭa.

There is apparently some inconsistency in the views of the followers of Kumārila about the nature of knowledge. All commentators and independent writers of the Bhāṭṭa school are unanimous in holding that cognition is an act of soul, but at the same time most of them include cognition in the category of quality instead of that of action (*karma*). Cidānanda and Nārāyaṇa say that cognition is one of the specific qualities of soul.[20] Kumārila himself, apparently with some ambiguity, says that cognition is a *dharma* or property of soul.[21] Pārthasārathi emphatically remarks

19. न चार्थविगतेरन्यद्रूपं ज्ञानस्य युज्यते । SV, *Ātma*., 66.

20. बुद्धिसुखदुःखेच्छाद्वेषप्रयत्ना आत्मविशेषगुणाः । MM, p. 248; NTV, p. 212.

21. SV, *Nirālambanavāda*, 47.

that cognition is a transitive act of soul which produces a result in its object just as the act of cooking produces cookedness in rice[22], and in the same work he enumerates cognition as one of the nine specific properties (*dharma*) of soul.[23] It is Sucaritamiśra alone who has raised the question, as we shall see, about the legitimacy of calling cognition an 'act' and at the same time including it in the class of qualities. Pārthasārathi's statement that knowledge is a temporary property of soul, appears to be a terminological lapse due to the habit of using Nyāya terms. Pārthasārathi uses the term *Ātma-dharma* in common with Kumārila and the use of this term may be justified to some extent as we shall try to do just now. But while Kumārila uses the term rarely and only in connection with cognition, Pārthasārathi applies it equally to cognition, pleasure, pain etc. The influence of Nyāya on the style and views of the later writers of practically all the schools is obvious and Cidānanda and Nārāyaṇa cannot be an exception to this. But it is strange that Pārthasārathi who seems to be the greatest exponent of Kumārila's theories, should have been so careless in the above respect. Now Kumārila and Pārthasārathi use the term *dharma* while the Nyāya-Vaiśeṣika writers use *guṇa*. *Guṇa* exactly means a quality or attribute in the sense in which blueness is one when we say about something that it is 'blue'. But *dharma* may denote a quality, a function or an action, that is, anything that can belong to something. Burning is a *dharma* of fire, though it does not belong to it in the same way as redness belongs to it. Burning is an action of fire on combustible things, while redness is its quality. The term 'property' is an exact equivalent of the term *dharma*. So cognition is an occasional act of soul which results in the manifestation of objects. Though cognition is not exactly like pleasure, pain etc. which too are mentioned as the 'properties' of soul, because the former refers to objects while the latter have no such reference, still all of them are the properties of soul in the sense that they belong to it. However, it should be borne in mind that cognition cannot be given the same status as is given to pleasure, pain etc., because the former does not characterize soul in the same way in which the latter do.

22. ज्ञानक्रिया हि सकर्मिका... SD, p. 56.
23. Ibid., p. 130.

Let us here refer to Prabhākara's view by the way. Prabhākara in his commentary on the *Bhāṣya* of Śabara emphatically says that *jñāna* is an act of soul and is inferred as all other actions are inferred.[24] But, as we shall show towards the end of the chapter, by *jñāna* he does not mean cognition, but the contact of soul with *manas*, and what others mean by *jñāna*, i.e. manifestation of objects, he calls *saṃvit* which is held to be an attribute of soul. According to Śālikanātha, a follower of Prabhākara, cognition is one of the nine ephemeral attributes of soul. Thus he is in agreement with Nyāya-Vaiśeṣika except that while the latter hold all these attributes to be mentally perceptible, the former holds cognition to be self-manifesting and the rest to be cognisable through mental perception.[25]

According to the Bhāṭṭa cognition cannot be a quality. Qualities exist in objects without referring to anything beyond themselves. A quality is an intransitive property of an object, while in activity we find a transition from one to an other. Cognition cannot be a quality, because in it there is inherently a reference to something beyond. Cognition is a self-transcending act of soul, because it necessarily implies ar 'other' which is cognized. To cognize an object is to have a mental approach to it. In cognition there is an ideal acquisition (*prāpti*) of some object. This ideal acquisition cannot be explained otherwise than on the basis of some activity on the part of the cognizing soul. The sense-organs or their activity alone cannot explain it, because during sleep there are sense-organs but no awareness of objects and in the state of absent-mindedness the senses are active without giving knowledge. The contact between soul and *manas* too is common in all forms of knowing and as such it cannot by itself explain specific apprehension of objects. Therefore, it is some specific activity of soul that is directed upon an object that alone can explain its ideal acquisition and this activity is nothing but cognition:

> There must necessarily be some form of action inhering in the soul, which is implied in such expression as 'I know' and is termed

24. Action, according to Prabhākara, is imperceptible.

25. PP, p. 149.

> 'knowledge' or 'cognition' in which an object is made the accusative of apprehension.[26]

Thus in the act of cognition an object is apprehended or ideally acquired by the self. It may be objected that in cognition an object is not acquired but revealed. True, but to whom is it revealed? If to none, then how can the difference between the practical activity of two persons with reference to the same object be explained? It is observed that one person appropriates an object, eg. a coin on the ground, while a second does not. If the object is revealed to none, then what makes the difference in the overt behaviour of the two persons? Certainly such discrimination is not observed in the case of a forest-fire which shines in an unknown place but is revealed to none. Therefore, it must be the cognitive act by which an object is apprehended that can explain the said difference. The knowability of an object cannot be possible unless it is made the accusative of the act of cognition.[27]

Now, if cognition is an act, why, asks Sucaritamiśra, is it generally included in the list of qualities? Moreover, an act is always some form of physical movement (*spanda*) which cannot be possible in the case of soul which is supposed to be a non-material and all-pervading substance. Sucaritamiśra answers that cognition which naturally occurs in the form 'I know' can be nothing but an act.[28] The evidence of direct experience, which is never contradicted, cannot be ignored. The quality-theory goes against a directly experienced fact. We directly know cognition to be an act whose subject (*kartā*) is the self and whose accusative (*karma*) is the cognized object. Knowing is certainly not a physical act involving overt muscular movements, still it does not cease to be an act on that account. Kumārila says:

> We do not hold motion to be the only form of action as held by the Vaiśeṣika; all that is expressed by a verbal root (*dhātvartha*) is an action.[29]

26. अस्ति कश्चिदात्मसमवायी ज्ञानसंवेदनादिपदपर्यायवाच्यो जानातिधातूपादानः क्रियाभेदो यस्मिन्नर्थानां प्राप्तिकर्मता । KK, Part II, p. 123.
27. न चाप्रमाकर्मणः प्रमेयता सम्भवति । Ibid.
28. बुध्यत इत्यादिभ्यश्च शब्देभ्यः क्रियाप्रत्यय एवोपजायमानो दृश्यते । Ibid.
29. SV, *Ātma.*, 74-75.

Again he says that the self is the agent of an action by virtue of its power of determination (*saṅkalpa-śakti*).[30]

We have so far described three theories of knowledge, viz., the substance theory, the quality theory and the act theory, and we have also seen the grounds on which the first two theories are rejected and the third accepted by the Bhāṭṭa school. Now there is a fourth theory too which is known as relation theory and is held by many prominent philosophers of today. The critical realists say that knowledge is a relation among three terms viz., a mind, an object and a datum. According to C.D. Broad and G.E. Moore knowledge is a two-term relation between a knowing mind and a known object. Alexander says that knowledge is a relation of 'compresence' between the act of mind and the object. According to the American neo-realists knowledge is a relation not between a knowing subject and a known object but between two objects. These theories do not explain the nature of knowledge. There is no doubt that in the act of knowing a subject and an object come to be related together. But this subject-object relation does not constitute knowledge: it is rather the result of the cognitive act. When one thing acts upon another thing in a particular way, then alone is a relation generated between them. Kumārila says that there is nowhere a relation which is not based on some action on the part of some agent; the agent-action relationship is the basis of all relations.[31] Thus like all relations the subject-object relation too presupposes some action of the agent of knowing on the known object, which is called cognition. Pārthasārathi says:

> Without an occasional cause (in the form of some action) there cannot arise the subject-object relation between the self and the object and that occasional cause is known by the term 'cognition'.[32]

One is ever engaged in some form of cognitive activity. At any moment he is either cognizing objects which lie in the field of vision, audition etc., or thinking about objects distant in place

30. Ibid., 83.
31. न क्रियाकर्तृसम्बन्धादृते सम्बन्धनं क्वचित् । SV, *Śabda*, 69.
32. SD, p.56.

and time, or imagining something. So long as one is awake cognitive activity goes on constantly like a stream. But this stream is occasionally interrupted by periods of inactivity. The self lapses into a state of apparent unconsciousness when it is in deep sleep or under the influence of some drugs. During these states cognitive activity is arrested but it reappears when the self returns to normal waking condition. Now, what becomes of the cognitive activity when the self is not actually cognizing or thinking or imagining ? Of course, it is not totally destroyed then; otherwise its reappearance would become inexplicable. According to Nyāya the self loses its connection with *manas* in these states. But the quality theory cannot explain these lapses satisfactorily. According to Kumārila *jñāna* is a capacity (*yogyatā*), potency (*śakti*), or faculty and the self is its abode. Sucaritamiśra holds that potency is an independent category. According to Nārāyaṇa it is a special form of quality and this explains the reason of his assertion that cognition is a specific quality of the self. Cognition is an act but in the form of the eternal potency of the self to cognize it is a quality. *Śakti* is an invisible entity and remains in a dormant state so long as it does not express itself in action, but when it is aroused it invariably assumes the form of an action. When a particular faculty is dormant the self is inactive in that respect and when it is functioning the self becomes active. A quality, on the other hand, either exists in some substance or does not exist. It does not imply action. A quality characterizes an object passively. It is not an active aspect of things. We cannot conceive how a quality, eg. cognition (according to Nyāya), would characterize the self when it is nonexistent, as during dreamless sleep, but we can conceive how a potency would do so in that state. That the quality of cognition is occasionally non-existent in the self and at the same time it differentiates it from the material substances, is unintelligible. Kumārila's conception of cognition as a potency is better than that of Nyāya which conceives it as a quality. According to Kumārila cognition is ultimately neither a substance, nor a quality, nor a relation, nor an action, but a potency of the self which is expressed in specific acts of awareness of objects. Specific object-cognitions are occasional acts of the self but cognition as its permanent and unique possession is a potency.

2.3. *Knowledge and Reality*

The relation between knowledge and object is that of the manifester and the manifested. In an act of cognition there is an object that is revealed, a self to whom it is revealed and lastly, the fact of revelation itself. All these three factors are distinct from each other, because they are clearly distinguishable. The objects exist independently in the external world. Thought does not constitute their being. Their being known is an event that occurs occasionally and it does not affect their nature and existence. The cognizer too exists in its own right. The self is not always cognizing objects. The act of cognizing is a feature that characterizes it at certain times. But whenever it takes place it always relates the self to some object which is known by it. Thus in an act of knowing some object is the accusative and the self is the nominative. In an act of apprehension, say 'this is blue', what is apprehended is 'this' which appears to be 'blue'. Cognition in this case manifests an external object 'this' directly to the self. It is the 'blue' object as it exists in reality that is the content of knowledge here and though it is revealed through a specific act, the act itself is not its own content.

The Bhāṭṭa is an upholder of direct realism. He believes in the independent existence of external objects. He maintains that in perception external objects directly become the content of consciousness. In this respect his theory is opposed to the epistemological dualism of the Sautrāntika Buddhist who is an upholder of representationism and to the subjective idealism of the Yogācāra Buddhist. The Bhāṭṭa theory is opposed to the Prābhākara and Nyāya realism too. But it is mainly the Yogācāra against whom the most of the Bhāṭṭa polemic is directed. Kumārila develops his direct realism in his controversy with the Yogācāra.

Though the Buddhists differ among themselves regarding epistemological questions as much as they differ from the orthodox schools yet they form a fairly homogeneous group among themselves due to some common basic metaphysical tenets which seem revolutionary in the context of orthodox systems. One such tenet is the Buddhist conception of reality as a perpetual flux. The criterion of reality for the Buddhists is causal efficiency (*arthakriyākāritva*). The real produces effects and that which produces effects is real. Reality is change and what does not change is unreal. Therefore, all that is real is momentary. The doctrine of momentariness is the logical outcome of the Buddhist criterion of reality. Hence, according to Buddhism all real objects, that appear to be stable, are actually in ceaseless flux. The self is not an eternal, unchanging entity, but a continuous series of cognitions or ideas. An apparently stable object is actually a series of object-moments. The basic conception that there is no permanent, self-identical self but a series of ideas, each giving rise to the next and a similar conception of what we call an enduring object, make a fundamental difference between the Sautrāntika representationism and the representationism of old Nyāya, between the direct realism of Kumārila and that of the Vaibhāṣika, between the Yogācāra theory of self-luminousness of cognition and that held by Prabhākara and Śaṅkara. The different matrices or systems to which an identical looking concept belongs generally make a lot of difference. As there is no permanent soul according to Buddhism, it is the momentary cognition that cognizes itself (Yogācāra) or an external object-moment (Vaibhāṣika) or the antecedent cognition that gave rise to it (some Buddhists according to KK and Vaibhāṣika according to NR on SV, *Sūnya.*, 130). All the Buddhists eliminate the distinction of the cognizing soul and cognition; they identify the cognizer with cognition. But according to the orthodox systems this distinction is a fact of experience and cannot, therefore, be eliminated. Thus according to the Sautrāntika cognition directly knows itself or its predecessor, while according to the old Nyāya the soul directly knows a cognition. According to the Vaibhāṣika a cognition directly knows an external object-moment while according to the orthodox form of presentationism the soul directly knows an external object. According to the Sautrāntika and the Vaibhāṣika knowledge is a two-term relation; but according to the orthodox realists it may be a two-term or a three-term relation and the soul and the object are necessarily two of the relata. According to the Yogācāra knowledge does not imply any relation: Cognition is the only reality which illusorily appears to be differentiated into the cognizer, the cognized and cognition.[33] The Yogācāra dispenses with the

33. Cf. अविभागो हि बुद्धयात्मा विपर्यासितदर्शनैः ।
ग्राह्यग्राहकसंवित्तिभेदवानिव लक्ष्यते ॥

knowing self and the world of knowable objects, which are the presuppositions of cognition and he postulates the reality of cognition alone. The Yogācāra does not feel the need of a substratum for his 'cognition'. This theory runs counter to the deepest convictions of mankind and destroys the very root of all practical activity. So, naturally it received the severest treatment at the hand of Kumārila. Unless the independent reality of matter and mind is established it is futile to talk of knowledge itself, to say the least of the relation between knowledge and objects or between knower and known. We can have divergence of opinions about the nature of cognitive relation, the manner in which cognition originates and the criteria of truth and error only when knowledge is established as a fact which in turn depends on the existence of a knowing mind and a known object, and it is only then that we can try to think out the right solution of epistemological questions. A relation presupposes some form of duality; but when the Yogācāra reduces everything to cognition the talk of any relation whatsoever becomes non-sensical. This is why Kumārila has devoted the largest portion of his life and work to the refutation of the Yogācāra. Below we give the arguments of the Yogācāra.

2.4. *The Yogācāra Subjective Idealism*

The subjectivism of the Yogācāra goes further than its modern version propounded by Berkeley. Berkeley believes in a plurality of minds which are enduring, substantial, and independently real. He also allows some objectivism when he ascribes his ideas of perception to an external source in the form of a Super-mind or God. But he does not believe in an independent existence of objects corresponding to ideas. The Yogācāra, on the other hand, is an out-and-out subjectivist. He does not believe in anything other than the non-substantial ideas except when he is under the compulsion of his adversary's arguments. He argues that ideas or cognitions are powerless to know anything other than themselves. The apparent reference to external objects is a mere illusion. The following is in brief Kumārila's exposition of the Yogācāra position:—

It is a fact of experience that something is cognized as having a shape. That which is cognized and that which has a shape are not different, because there is no consciousness of their differentiating properties. Therefore, they are not two things but one. Now the question arises as to what it is that is cognized with a shape. Is it an external object or the cognition itself? If it is an external object, the postulation of cognition becomes necessary for the establishment of its existence, because cognition is the sole proof of the existence of anything; otherwise anything, be it real or unreal, will come to have existence. Thus by the realist the existence of cognition has to be postulated for the existence of an external object. Now, that cognition exists cannot be proved except through cognition. So the realist has to admit that cognition cognizes itself because there can be no cognizer in addition to cognition. But it has already been pointed out that only one thing with a shape is cognized. Therefore, it must be the cognition alone that is apprehended and consequently the postulation of an external object becomes unnecessary, because there is no proof of its existence. The notions of externality and internality too are groundless. Something is said to be external in relation to some other thing that is internal and *vice versa*. But when it has been proved that there is no duality and that cognition is the sole reality, all these relative notions become inapplicable.[34]

The realist will say that the postulation of external objects is necessary to explain the diversity of cognitions: We are conscious of cognitions having different shapes and this is not possible unless an independent existence of external objects is granted. But this realist contention is involved in unsurmountable difficulties. We, on the other hand, says the Yogācāra, offer a simpler solution. In our theory, though the real character of cognition is pure, yet in this beginningless world there is an accumulation of diverse impressions (*vāsanā*) produced by foregoing cognitions and through these impressions cognition comes to appear in the various shapes of blue, yellow etc. tinged with the character of the cognizer and the cognized which appear as if they were quite apart from the cognition itself. Cognition gives rise to impression and impression again to cognition. The reciprocal causality of cognition and impression is beginningless like that of seed and

34. SV, *Śūnya.*, 6-14.

sprout and consequently there is no logical fault in our theory. The assumption of a diversity of impressions is certainly simpler than that of objects. We assume only the reality of cognition and explain its diversity by assuming a diversity of impressions, whereas the realist has to assume cognition, impression and an external object. The postulation of cognition having different forms is simpler than the postulation of external objects having different forms. For the realist, on the other hand, even after postulating external objects the postulation of cognition having different forms and that of impressions to explain memory and dreams becomes necessary and thus he introduces complexity in his theory.

Unless such forms of cognition as 'blue' etc. are established the cognition, which is naturally pure, is incapable of presenting particular objects. In the absence of difference in cognition no difference in the cognized can be established and in the absence of such forms of cognition as 'blue' etc. all cognitions would be identical. Thus for the establishment of the objects of different shapes it must be granted that cognition too has different shapes. For a discrimination among objects cognitions whose difference is not cognized are not sufficient and the difference among cognitions cannot be known except through their having different shapes. By the mere existence of cognition an object, eg. 'blue', cannot be ascertained. Therefore 'blue' etc. which are apprehended are forms of cognition and not of objects. The forms of objects are neither directly apprehended nor is there any other proof of their existence. So far as the diversity of forms is concerned it is equally well explained by postulating *vāsanā*. Hence, according to the law of parsimony (*lāghava-nyāya*) the assumption of external objects is superfluous.

If the form belongs to an external object and not to cognition, there will be a difference between the object and the cognition and hence the latter will not be able to illuminate the former. But in our theory illumination is possible because we hold that the form and the cognition are identical. Cognizability cannot be possible otherwise than on the basis of identity between the cognition and the cognized. If the relation between the two is supposed to be that of difference there can be no cognizability. The realist assumes the two to be different. But how can any relation be possible between two different things ? And if an object can be cognized in spite of the absence of a relation, then everything will be cognized by every cognition and omniscience will be the result. The realist may say that identity is not the only relation but causality too is a relation and it is this that holds between the cognized object and the corresponding cognition: the external object is the cause of generating cognition. But causality cannot constitute cognizability, for, then the eye which is held to be a cause of cognition by the realist will be cognizable. The realist may say that the eye is not cognizable, because, though it is a cause of visual cognition, it is not capable of imprinting its shape on cognition and that causality together with the capability to impart a form to cognition is what constitutes cognizability. This too is incorrect, because there is no proof that an external object imparts its form to cognition; and if this is held to explain the variety of cognitions, it is unnecessary as we have already offered a simpler explanation. Similarity too cannot constitute cognizability, because in this case an object which is not in contact with the eye will also be cognizable. If similarity and causality, both are held to constitute cognizability, then in a continuous series of cognitions of blue, for example, the antecedent cognition which is similar to as well as the cause of the consequent cognition will be cognizable to the latter. Moreover, is the similarity held to be partial or complete ? If it is partial, then, everything being partially similar to cognition in being momentary will be cognized by every cognition. If the similarity is held to be complete, then, as the cognizable object is unconscious, the corresponding cognition too will become unconscious, i.e., it will cease to be a cognition.[35] Therefore, there is no cognizable object other than cognition, and no second cognition of a cognition; cognition devoid of apprehender and apprehended object shines forth by itself.[36]

The form that is cognized belongs to cognition, because cognition is held even by the realist to be the means of revealing the

35. Cf. एकदेशेन सारूप्ये सर्वः स्यात् सर्ववेदकः ।
सर्वात्मना तु सारूप्ये ज्ञानमज्ञानतां व्रजेत् ॥

36. Cf. नान्योऽनुभाव्यो बुद्धयास्ति तस्या नानुभवोऽपरः ।
ग्राह्यग्राहकवैधुर्यात् स्वयं सैव प्रकाशते ॥

so-called external objects which lack self-luminosity. Objects are not self-revealing, because they may exist and yet may remain unknown. The difference between an object and a cognition is that while the former depends on something else to reveal itself the latter is self-revealing. The object to be known cannot be ascertained unless the corresponding cognition is known. A cognition is like a lamp which manifests objects and simultaneously manifests itself. How can an external object be apprehended if the apprehension itself is not apprehended ?[37] Therefore, a cognition must be apprehended as soon as it is born. All are agreed in holding that cognition must arise prior to the apprehension of object, for that which is not yet existent cannot be the means of knowing an object. The existent things are sometimes cognized and sometimes not. When they are not cognized it is because either a manifester is absent, as, when it is dark and there is no light, or there is some obstacle, as, when an object happens to be behind a wall. But in the case of a cognition which is born there is neither the absence of a manifester, nor the presence of an obstacle, because it is self-manifesting. Therefore, cognition, which is accepted to appear prior to object, must either be apprehended then and there or must not be apprehended at all. If it is held that cognition is known subsequently to the object, what peculiarity does it acquire later which was not in it previously so that it was not known at the time of its birth ? If it is said that the peculiarity is the birth of a second cognition having the first as its object, we do not admit this, because an object which is not luminous may wait for its manifestation by some light, but a cognition which is naturally luminous cannot wait. Therefore, a cognition does not stand in need of a second cognition. And if it is insisted that it depends on a second cognition, then the second too, being a cognition, will depend on a third one and so on *ad infinitum*, so that the whole life will be exhausted by a series of cognitions having a single thing for its object and there will never be a knowledge of any other thing. It is a matter of common experience that we recollect an object as having been known by us, and, as no recollection of an unexperienced thing is possible, we must have had a direct experience

37. Cf. अप्रत्यक्षोपलम्भस्य नार्थदृष्टिः प्रसिध्यति ।

of cognition too when the object was experienced in the past. Moreover, our cognitions of past and future objects cannot be explained except on the ground that what is cognized there is the cognition with a form, because in these cases the objects are absent and an absent object cannot impart its form to cognition. It is not only in the case of past and future objects that cognition is cognized as having a form. Even in the case of the cognitions of present objects we find people saying like 'this object is blue because I have a cognition of that form'. This is a clear indication of the fact that it is only after the apprehension of cognition that objects are apprehended. And when it is established that a cognition is apprehended, it is also established that the apprehended form must belong to it, because the apprehension of a thing devoid of form is impossible. It has been already stated that no two forms, one belonging to cognition and the other to object, are seen but one only, which must belong to cognition. Therefore, an external object is not cognized at all and consequently it is non-existent.

2.5. *Yogācāra criticism of representationism and other allied theories*:

There are some realists, viz., the Sautrāntikas, who hold that a cognition is directly apprehended as having a form but the form belongs to an external object and appears to be superimposed upon cognition. They think that the form of an external object is reflected upon cognition. But this is wrong. That a property of an external object leaving its abode enters cognition is inconceivable. The form which is directly known to be a property of cognition cannot reasonably be supposed to be the property of an external object. The representationist says that the form of the external object need not leave its abode, yet just as the moon is reflected on the surface of water, so the form of an object is reflected on cognition. But there is no proof for such an assertion. We ascertain the image shining on the surface of water as belonging to the moon, because we have observed the moon in the sky and the imageless water independently of each other and we can also compare the moon and the image reflected on water at present. But we can never observe a cognition without form, nor can we ever know the form of an external object independently of cognition. And even if the reflection theory be accepted in the case of visual perception, it can never be applicable to auditory and the other forms of perception. It is quite impossible to conceive a reflection of sound, taste, touch or smell. It may be said that the image of object is not reflected on cognition but while the form actually belongs to object it is by mistake attributed to cognition because of its extreme proximity. But this is wrong. How can it be said that it is a mistake when it is universal and even a single person is not found who is not mistaken? Moreover, why should it not be said that the form belongs to cognition but is wrongly attributed to an external object by foolish persons?

Some hold that the form is neither a property of cognition nor of object but is an entirely new phenomenon produced by the contact of a formless cognition and a formless object, just as redness is produced by the contact of lime and turmeric which are not red. This theory also is untenable because there can be no contact of cognition and object which are located in different places. Moreover, a novel form can be produced only by the contact of two material things while cognition is non-material. Again, the assertion that form is a property of contact can be possible only when the existence of a formless object, a formless cognition and their contact is known and established on independent grounds. But here the object is not known otherwise than through cognition; it is known neither before nor after cognition and what is known is never known as devoid of form. Therefore the contact theory cannot be supported.

According to the Buddhist realist, if the contact of cognition and object is not admitted the variety of cognition cannot be explained. Cognition is a caused phenomenon. It depends on four conditions, viz., the dominant condition (*adhipati-pratyaya*) e.g. the eye, the auxiliary condition, e.g. light (*sahakāri-pratyaya*), the immediately antecedent cognition (*samanantara-pratyaya*) and the basic condition, i.e. the object (*ālambana-pratyaya*). A sense-organ cannot be the cause of the diversity of cognition, because it is a common condition of many cognitions, as, when we have many visual cognitions whose dominant condition is the same eye. Similarly, a mere auxiliary condition, e.g. light, cannot be the cause of such diversity. An antecedent cognition too cannot explain the diversity of cognitions, because different cognitions are seen to follow the same antecedent cognition at different times, for instance, sometimes there is an awareness of a cow and sometimes of a horse immediately after the cognition of an elephant. If there were no other cause than a preceding cognition there would be a series of cognitions of 'elephant' following it. Thus the present 'elephant'-form of cognition points to some uncommon condition which can be no other than the contact with an external object. But, the Yogācāra says, there is no direct experience of this variety of cognitions being caused by contact with objects so that there can be no surity that the said contact is the only explanation. Moreover, those who say that the cognized form is the property of contact while cognition and object are formless, cannot account for the origination of the form and thus to account for the diversity of forms becomes difficult for them. A new colour, e.g. red, is seen to originate from the contact of two coloured objects, e.g. the white lime and the yellow turmeric. But when cognition and objects are held to be colourless, how can a variety of colours originate from their contact? And if it be accepted that a different thing can originate from a different cause, then a variety of forms also can originate from a single antecedent cognition. Hence there is no need to stick to the object-contact theory. Moreover, this theory fails in the case of memory, inference, dream and illusion. In these cases forms are seen but there is no contact with objects. The realist also accepts *vāsanā* (impression) to be the cause of the variety of forms in such cases. Then, why should he give it up while explaining the variety of perceptions?

The representationist Sautrāntika explains the multiform character of cognition by presuming the existence of external objects which, according to him, are multiform and not formless, and he defines cognizability as causality of an object together with its capability to impart its form to cognition. But how will the Sautrāntika explain the appearance of an object as belonging to the present when actually, according to the above definition of cognizability, the object which is held to be the cause of its cognition is past? The explanation offered by the Sautrāntika is that what is manifested as present is the form of the cognition while the object as the source of this form is known through inference. But if this be the case then all object-cognitions become of one kind only, viz., inferential, and thus the difference between perception and inference becomes non-existent. The Sautrāntika says that though the external objects are not perceived in the strict sense of the term, still the traditional distinction of perception and inference may be justified thus: In the so-called perception of objects the object directly transfers its shape to cognition while in inference it does so indirectly. When 'fire' directly gives its shape to cognition it is said to be perceived, but when 'smoke' gives its shape directly to cognition and subsequently the idea of 'fire' arises due to its invariable association with the idea of 'smoke' then 'fire' is said to be inferred. When, however, an object does not transfer its shape to cognition either directly or indirectly, then it is said to be uncognizable. Thus, the term perception in the sense of direct apprehension really applies to the self-cognition of a cognition alone, while an external object is always inferred from the shape of cognition; but in a secondary sense an object is 'perceived' when it is the direct cause of the shape of cognition and it is inferred when it is the indirect cause. The Yogācāra says that if this is so then at the present moment the object is not apprehended but the cognition only. Hence there is no evidence for the existence of external objects.[38]

If the form that is cognized is a property of an external object, as the realist says, then the different contrary and contradictory forms that are revealed to many observers at the same time or to one observer at different times as belonging to the same object cannot be explained, because the object which is one cannot have more than one form. The body of the same woman appears as a corpse to an ascetic while at the same time it appears as an object of sexual pleasure to an amorous person and as a lump of flesh to a carnivorous animal. Now, if the cognized form belongs to an external object, why does not a single form appear to all these three observers or if all the three forms really belong to the woman why does each observer not see all of them together? Therefore, these forms do not really belong to the woman, but they are mere creations of psychical dispositions (*vāsanā*) and thus we can safely generalize that external objects do not really

38. एवं च तस्यैवायमाकार इति निष्प्रमाणकोऽर्थः । SD, p. 52.

exist but they are mere thought-forms. The same conclusion is reached by a consideration of the properties of length, shortness etc. which are simultaneously attributed to the same thing by different persons. Similarly when a jar is called 'a substance', 'a thing' and 'made of clay' at the same time it is evident that the object is really non-existent, because different properties contradict the oneness of the object. According to the subjectivist's theory, on the other hand, as the cognitions of different individuals are different there can be no contradiction. Therefore, the realist has to accept that cognition assumes different forms under the influence of *vāsanā*. And when this is once admitted the realist may postulate external objects as imitating the forms of cognition, which will be superfluous as has been shown, but the assumption of cognition imitating the forms of objects can never be justified.

2.6. *Criticism of 'epistemological parallelism'*

Cidānanda[39] refers to a theory which may be termed as 'epistemological parallelism', and ascribes it to the Vaibhāṣika. According to this theory there is no causal or any other type of relation between cognition and the corresponding object though both are equally real and belong to the same moment of time. Cognizability is defined as consisting in the object being produced by the same antecedent conditions which produce the corresponding cognition. Probably Cidānanda has in mind the view of Vasubandhu, the author of *Abhidharmakośa*, who was a Vaibhāṣika in the beginning, then became a Sautrāntika and finally became a Vijñānavādin.[40] According to Vasubandhu "the cosmic mind (*ālayavijñāna*) transforms itself, on the one hand, into different subjects, and into different objects, on the other".[41] Thus the Vaibhāṣika view is that the object is not the cause of its cognition, as the Sautrāntika holds, because on the Sautrāntika view the presented character of the object cannot be explained and if the Sautrāntika tries to explain it by maintaining that the object being the cause of its cognition endures till the appearance of the cognition, he violates the basic principle of Buddhism

39. NTV, pp. 117-18.
40. Cp. Sinha: Jadunath, *A History of Indian Philosophy*, Vol. II, p. 349.
41. Ibid., p. 377.

viz., the momentariness of all existence, while the Vaibhāṣika position is perfectly consistent with this principle. The cognition and the object are two contemporaneous moments of two parallel series born of the same causes. This view, according to the idealist, is no improvement upon the Sautrāntika view. It is certainly true to the doctrine of momentariness but the other difficulties remain the same. When the Vaibhāṣika says that the object, e.g. a 'red apple', is produced by the same antecedent conditions that give rise to the corresponding visual cognition, then the cognizability of its sweet taste is a product of the same conditions which produce the visual cognition and the colour of the apple. Moreover, the eye is one of the conditions of the visual cognition of the 'apple', but no sane person can say that it is also a condition of the 'apple' as is assumed by this theory. Again, this theory cannot explain the cognizability of past and future objects which, we definitely know, are not brought to existence when we cognize them.

2.7. *Kumārila's Refutation of Subjective Idealism*

2.7.1. *Cognition cannot be both the cognizer and the cognized:*

When the idealist says that one single cognition is the cognizer as well as the cognized, is it the identity of action and accusative or of instrumental and accusative or of nominative and accusative that is intended? Whatever his intention may be there is no instance of any of these identities. We always find the nominative, the accusative, the instrumental and the action to be distinct from one another. For example, the action of cooking does not cook itself or cutting does not cut itself; the finger-tip does not touch itself or the point of a needle does not penetrate itself; nor can anyone touch his finger-tip by the same finger-tip. Thus, since there is no instance of the above-mentioned identities anywhere, the case of cognition cognizing itself cannot be proved. If the idealist says that by the identity of the cognizer and the cognized he means the self-revelatory character of cognition which accordingly does not stand in need of an illuminator, then, too, it may be asked, to whom is it revealed? The idealist does not recognize a self other than the momentary cognition. Thus, then, if the momentary cognition reveals itself to itself, it must take such form as 'I am blue' instead of 'this is blue'. But we find that a cognition always appears as pointing to 'this' which is other than itself. The functioning of cognition is directed outwards (*parāgvṛtti*) and not inwards (*pratyagvṛtti*) as the idealist theory implies. Therefore the identity of the cognizer and the cognized is impossible.[42]

The idealist may point to 'fire' as an instance in support of his theory. We do recognize the self-illuminating character of fire because it is of the nature of light and does not require a second light to illuminate it and so far there is no disagreement between us. But illumination is not equivalent to cognition. The light that illuminates itself does not cognize itself, because it is always cognized by a conscious individual through his sense-organs e.g. the eyes which serve as the illuminator of the light. The eye too is not cognized through itself as it is not its own illuminator; it is cognized by a distinct cognition which is of the nature of *arthāpatti* or presumption. A man does not directly know his sense-organs. They are rather presumed to exist and operate upon the objects of perception because of the otherwise inexplicable nature of specific cognitions. Similarly, cognition also is not directly revealed but is known through a second cognition as will be shown later on. Thus fire being a means of revealing objects at night, may be called the cognizer (in the sense of the instrumental) with reference to them, but with reference to it the eye is the cognizer; with reference to the eye a cognition is the cognizer and with reference to the cognition a subsequent cognition is the cognizer, so that there is no instance of the identity of the cognizer and the cognized. Therefore the means and the object of cognition are always different and the nominative of cognition, viz., the self is distinct from these.

In the case of the self too there is no identity of the nominative with the accusative. Though the self is its own cognizer and there is no second cognizer of it, still this case is not parallel to that of the cognition which, according to the idealist, is indivisible and differenceless, because we admit some difference in the self in the form of a property, viz., cognition and in that of a substance. The self has a duality of forms while keeping its unitary character intact, but the idealist does not recognize any real difference

42. NR on SV, *Śūnya.*, 64.

in cognition. When the self is in contact with *manas* which is in contact with a sense-organ which in turn is in contact with an object, there arises in it the property of cognition which is somehow different from the self. In the form of this property the self is the cognizer and in the form of a substance which it has in common with other substances, e.g. the earth etc. it is the cognized. But the Buddhist does not admit any duality such as that of substance and property in cognition. It may be said that we too do not admit any absolute difference between the cognizer and the cognized in the case of the self. Certainly so, but total difference is not observed anywhere. Even between a jar and a fire which are the manifested and the manifester, we do not admit an absolute difference as they too are somehow identical in the form of substances. Some difference between the manifester and the manifested is desirable according to our theory and it is not wanting in the case of the self. But, then, the Buddhist says, how do you explain ego-consciousness in the form of 'I' while maintaining that the functioning of cognition is always directed outwards? Śabara has truly said that in 'I' consciousness the cognition is directed inwards. But the property of cognition by itself is not the cognizer. It is the self qualified by this property that is the cognizer and the notion of 'I' refers not to cognition alone but to the self qualified by cognition. Thus, though the cognizing property of the self and the cognized substance of it are somehow different, yet the two are fundamentally one and because the I-notion refers to this fundamental unity of the nominative and the accusative of 'I know' the inward functioning in ego-cognition does not conflict with our view. In self-consciousness the 'I' refers to the nominative of cognition and it is explicitly different from object-consciousness in which the reference is to the object 'this' which the idealist cannot explain. The agent of cognition is directly revealed in ego-consciousness, but cognition is never revealed directly. In 'this is blue' only the accusative of cognition is revealed, neither the nominative nor the instrumental nor the act itself. Therefore, the self-revelatory character of cognition cannot be established at all.

Ignoring the direct evidence of experience the idealist sticks to his baseless theory that cognition cognizes itself and not an external object. But why should he be so much prejudiced against the existence of external objects? The idealist contention is that in 'this is blue' the consciousness is of cognition alone and the notion of 'this-ness' or externality is illusorily caused by *vāsanā* just as according to the Mīmāṃsaka the notion of egohood with regard to the body is caused by ignorance. But this is wrong. Our consciousness alone is the basis of making distinction between things and consciousness by its very appearance reveals objects as external. If the idealist can maintain that consciousness has cognition for its object in spite of the empirical fact that it has an external thing for its object, why should we not make the contrary assertion that consciousness has an external thing for its object even if the fact be just the opposite? It is wrong to reject the appearance of 'otherness' in cognition as illusory in the absence of a contradicting experience. Moreover the *vāsanā* to which the agency of causing the illusion of externality is ascribed by the idealist can be nothing but an impression left on the soul by previous cognitions. These impressions are deposited in the soul which is not recognized by the Buddhist. Cognition which is momentary cannot be the substratum of impression. Thus when the *vāsanā* itself is not established, how can it have the power of causing any illusion?[43]

The idealist holds that the cognition and the cognized are identical, but in that case the consciousness of anyone of these would bring about the consciousness of two forms which is never seen. When the form of the cognized object is apprehended the form of cognition is never apprehended, and conversely when sometimes the 'form' of cognition is apprehended the form of the object is not apprehended. Sometimes, it is seen that a previous cognition is remembered but the object that was cognized is forgotten. Therefore, from the non-concomitance of cognition and object it must be concluded that they are distinct from each other and not identical as the idealist says.[44]

The idealist says that the self-luminous nature of cognition is inferred from recollection. After the cognition of an object, for example, a jar, we have its recollection in the form 'I know

43. KK on SV, *Śūnya.*, 72.
44. SV, *Śūnya.*, 83-85.

the jar'. If the primary cognition of the jar did not reveal itself while revealing its object viz., the jar, this recollection becomes inexplicable. We can have no recollection of anything which was never experienced. If a cognition is not self-manifesting the recollections that we have subsequently of the object will be of the form 'there is a jar' and not of such form as 'I know the jar'; and thus however much we may recollect there will be absolutely no difference among the successive recollections of the same object. But actually we do find a difference in the successive recollections, for example, among 'I know the jar', 'I know that I know the jar' and so on. The difference among these is quite plain. In 'I know the jar' the form of the jar and the form of its primary cognition is recollected. In 'I know that I know the jar' the form of the jar, the form of its primary cognition and the form of the first recollective cognition is remembered. Thus the first recollective cognition proves that the primary cognition of the jar revealed itself simultaneously with the jar and the second recollective cognition proves that while recollecting the jar and the primary cognition the first recollective cognition revealed itself too.[45]

This is refuted as follows: We do not find a gradual accumulation of forms in successive recollections as the idealist says. There is only one form that is revealed in all these so-called recollections and it is of the object, viz., the jar. What have been called by the idealist 'recollections' are not really recollections. They are as primary as the cognition of the jar in the form 'this is a jar.' They differ from the latter in being appropriated by the self. And such reflective cognitions do not as a rule follow an object-cognition invariably. A reflective cognition takes place only when there is a curiosity about the cause of object-consciousness. When after we have had the cognition of an object we sometimes try to explain the cognizedness of the object, we become aware of the corresponding cognition through *arthāpatti* and thus we have such consciousness as 'I know the jar'. This awareness is quite apart from the awareness of the object and has no form. In this is included the recalled form of the jar as well as the primary consciousness of the formless cognition of

45. Ibid., 110-14.

the jar which belonged to a past moment. Again, when we have a fresh curiosity about the cause of this second awareness it is independently known through *arthāpatti* resulting in the form of a fresh cognition 'I know that I know the jar'. It will be said that if a cognition is cognized as formless, then such common assertions as 'the object is blue because I have a cognition of that form' become inexplicable. But, though there are such assertions yet they do not prove that cognition has some form. 'Blue', 'yellow' etc. are forms of objects while the cognition itself is neither blue nor yellow but formless. If a cognition had a form it would never be described in terms of the forms of objects.[46] Therefore, though cognitions by themselves are formless, yet their difference is established by the difference of cognized objects and there is no need of postulating a form for cognition for that purpose.[47] Moreover, a cognition may or may not have a form but it can never be self-revealing in nature. The idealist has said that the self-revealing nature of cognition is inferred from recollection, but as he resolves a cognition into a perception of itself he cannot legitimately have a recourse to inference. The division of cognitions into perception and inference is based upon the independent existence of external objects. Some objects are known directly and some indirectly and consequently some cognitions are perceptual and some inferential. But when the very existence of external objects has been denied their direct or indirect knowledge becomes impossible. Hence the idealist cannot talk of inference at all.[48]

2.7.2. *A cognition cannot apprehend either a part of itself or another cognition antecedent to or simultaneous with it*:

It has been demonstrated that one indivisible cognition cannot be the apprehender as well as the apprehended. Now the idealist may say that cognition is one but it is divided into two parts, one apprehending the other, so that there is no need of an external object in the form of that which is apprehended. But if the idealist recognizes in this way the difference of the apprehender from the

46. KK on Ibid., 115-18.
47. Ibid., 116.
48. Ibid., 12

apprehended he gives up his own theory and embraces our own. If the idealist says that the apprehending and apprehended parts, though different, are yet identical in the form of the cognition which thus divides itself into them, while according to the realist the apprehending cognition and the apprehended object are not the parts of one and the same thing, then we reply that he thus embraces the Sāṅkhya theory of difference and non-difference (*bhinnābhinnatva*) renouncing his own theory of absolute identity. In criticising the definitions of cognizability offered by others who allow a difference between the cognition and the cognized object the idealist has proved himself to be the upholder of absolute identity and now by allowing some difference between the apprehending and apprehended parts of cognition he contradicts his own theory.[49]

Some Buddhists (the Vaibhāṣikas according to NR) accept that there is a difference between the apprehender and the apprehended but they deny the existence of an object external to cognition because, according to them, a cognition always apprehends another cognition antecedent to it and 'this' in 'this is blue' refers not to an external object but to this antecedent cognition. This is wrong. There is no proof that the apprehended and the apprehender are both cognitions as there is no character common to both and the Buddhist does not recognize a universal like 'cognition-ness' common to and apart from many individual cognitions. According to the Buddhist a universal is nothing but the negation of the opposite (*apoha*). But as cognition is the only reality, its opposite, viz., non-cognition cannot be real, so that its negation cannot be conceived and consequently the universal 'cognition-ness' too becomes inconceivable. Therefore, the character of cognition cannot belong equally to the apprehender and the apprehended. It can belong to only one of them. And thus when the difference between the apprehender and the apprehended has been established, nothing more is desired. As for the relation of apprehender and apprehended between a subsequent and an antecedent cognition, we say that it is not possible because cognitions are momentary and when the subsequent cognition appears the antecedent one has vanished totally,

49. Ibid., 122-24.

so that it cannot be the object of the former. Hence, when a past cognition cannot be the object of a present one it must be an external entity which is the object of the latter. If it is said that the two cognitions, viz., the apprehending one and the apprehended one, are simultaneous, then too their relation cannot be explained, because the cognized object is supposed to be the cause of the cognition and causality implies sequence and dependence, while the said cognitions are simultaneous and independent.[50]

Now, the Mīmāṃsaka too may be asked as to how he can explain the causal relation between the cognitive act and the cognized object. To this Pārthasārathi answers:

> For us the effect is not the apprehending cognition nor is the cause the apprehended object; on the contrary, we recognize the apprehending cognition as the cause and the apprehended object as the effect. To explain: The cognitive act produces a result called manifestedness or cognizedness and as this result inheres in the object this latter becomes the accusative of the act and this accusative character of the object constitutes its cognizability. Thus as the result inhering in the object is not simultaneous with the act of cognition, there is no difficulty in their being the effect and the cause respectively.[51]

This sort of causal relation is not possible in the case of two simultaneous cognitions, nor in the case of two successive cognitions in which the consequent one is held to be the apprehender of the antecedent one.

If the Buddhist says that an antecedent cognition will be the object of a consequent one through imparting its potency or *vāsanā* to the latter which will thus become its effect, then too it cannot be acceptable, because an antecedent cognition having been destroyed as soon as it was born without leaving any trace behind (*niranvaya-vināśa*) cannot be conceived as leaving anything to its successor. Moreover, in that case the cognized object will be past just as in memory the object remembered is a past one and thus the presented character of the object of perception

50. Ibid., 130-50.
51. NR on SV, *Śūnya.*, 151-54.

will be inexplicable. In memory the impression of a past experience is revived and the object is always cognized as belonging to the past, while in perception the object is always cognized as belonging to the present without being contradicted by any subsequent experience. As for *vāsanā*, it is not possible for the Buddhist who holds cognition to be the only reality and it has already been said that the *vāsanā* can have no substratum in the form of cognition as the past and the future cognitions are totally non-existent now and the present one is no sooner born than destroyed and the Buddhist does not recognize any enduring entity in the form of a soul except a continuous series of discrete and momentary cognitions which could have served as the required substratum. The Buddhist may say that in dreams the objects which appear as present are really past, and similarly in perception too the object though apparently present may actually be a past one, so that the realist's contention that memory is always tinged with the character of pastness becomes untenable. The reply is that in dreams past objects do appear as present but it is due to some peculiar abnormal factors operating during sleep and the dream objects are always rejected as illusory on waking, while objects perceived during waking state are never rejected as illusory. Hence a past thing cannot be the object of a present perception. And even if the past be accepted as the basis of the present perception, there is no proof that it is a past cognition and not a past object.[52]

2.7.3. *The law of parsimony and the law of simultaneous apprehension do not favour idealism*:

The idealist claims truth for his theory on the ground of simplicity. He says that his theory is simpler than the realist's theory because it eliminates the external object which is unnecessarily presumed by realists. But this is wrong. The external object is not presumed, it is directly experienced. The external object whose reality is vouched for by direct experience cannot be eliminated to suit an ill-conceived theory. The Buddhist rejects the external object as unnecessary on the basis of his theory that cognition and object are apprehended simultaneously

52. Ibid., 156-63.

which again he bases on his groundless assumption that cognition which is a means must be apprehended prior to or simultaneously with the object of which it is the means. But cognition and object are not apprehended simultaneously; the object is apprehended directly while cognition is not apprehended at all, though its existence is presumed subsequently through *arthāpatti*. A cognition does appear first but it is not the first to be apprehended. Hence the law of simultaneous apprehension is not applicable in this case. It is not necessary that the means be apprehended first in order that the object may be apprehended, because the means may not be apprehended due to the absence of a suitable *pramāṇa* just as we see in the case of the eye which is the means of seeing an object but itself remains unseen at the time. That cognition cannot apprehend itself has already been proved and although it is true that when it originates there is no obstacle in the way of apprehending it, yet, because a suitable cognition that would serve as a means of apprehending it does not arise at the time, it remains unapprehended till later on a second cognition of the nature of *arthāpatti* appears to explain the cognizedness of the object. Cognition has the function of revealing an external object but is powerless to reveal itself. Just as the eye has the power of manifesting external objects but this power is restricted to the manifestation of colour alone, so the power of cognition is restricted to the manifestation of objects alone and thus it cannot manifest itself.[53]

The Buddhist says that recollection which immediately follows a cognition in such forms as 'I know the jar' cannot be explained if cognition was not cognized with the object. But this is wrong. What is remembered is the object and not the cognition; the cognition is known indirectly through *arthāpatti* as the means of object-consciousness. People do say 'the object is blue because my cognition appears in that form'; but this does not show that cognition is known prior to the object. Actually what happens is that when after cognizing an object as blue one comes to have some doubt about it or is questioned by someone else he confidently asserts that the object is blue and in the attempt of seeking its proof he becomes conscious of his cognition.[54]

53. Ibid., 179-86.
54. Ibid., 199, 226-27.

2.7.4. *The variety of forms is quite consistent with the unity of an object*:

The Buddhist idealist says that, because many different and contradictory forms cannot belong to a single object, the cognized form must be the form of cognition. But this is wrong. The woman cited by the idealist in favour of his view possesses all the three said forms, viz., that of a corpse, of a beautiful maid and of a lump of flesh. But the ascetic recognizes only the first form on account of his aversion of all objects that tend to tempt him towards worldly enjoyment. The amorous man recognizes the second form alone because of the predominance of sex instinct in him. And the carnivorous animal accustomed to flesh-eating recognizes her only as a palatable lump of flesh. Thus, though an object may possess various forms and properties, still their mere existence in the object does not assure that all of them will be recognized by everyone at once. The dominant disposition of an individual, his habitual modes of thought and action and his permanent and temporary interests determine what form or property of an object he will discover at a particular moment. The cognition of a form depends on the object as well as the subjective state of the observer. His predispositions and interests of the moment help him in attending to that aspect of a thing which harmonizes with them. But subjective conditions alone are not responsible for the cognition of a particular form. However lustful a man may be he never sees a jar as a beautiful woman. However hungry a dog may be he cannot perceive a stone as a lump of flesh. Therefore, the existence of multiple forms is not at all incompatible with the unity of the object.

The apparently contradictory forms of an object eg., length, shortness etc. can be easily reconciled. When an object is cognized as longer than a second one it is not at the same time cognized as shorter than the same object but is cognized so in comparison with a third object. So the existence of length and shortness in the same object at the same time in comparison with different objects is quite conceivable. There would have been a real contradiction if the same object could be conceived long as well as short without any relation to other objects. On the basis of experience we attribute one or more forms to a single object and there is no rule that one object must be of one form alone. A jar at once owns the properties of being a substance and of being made of clay, but an observer conceives it in one form or the other according to the name that he is reminded of at the moment. Thus subjective factors determine the observation of a particular form or property, though the object may possess many forms, just as the colour alone of a thing is seen when the eye is in contact with it, though the object also possesses a taste, an odour, a touch etc. at the same time.[55] Hence the cognized form belongs to an external object and not to cognition.

Pārthasārathi adds the following remarks against the idealist. In non-cognition (*ajñāna*) absence of cognition is apprehended. The absence of cognition cannot be a form of cognition because they are mutually exclusive. Similarly, in the cognition 'this is the same thing' some durable entity is apprehended while cognition is momentary. Durability cannot be the form of that which is momentary. Likewise, in the perception of various co-existing things various forms are collectively apprehended while cognition cannot have more than one form. Therefore, these are not the forms of cognition but of something else which is different from cognition. The object of inference is something mediate but cognition is always known to be immediate. How can mediacy and immediacy co-exist as identical with cognition? Therefore whether durability of objects or their having many forms etc. is tenable or not, this much is proved that cognition apprehends things external to it and not itself. The idealist denies external objects on the ground of the identity of the cognizer and the cognized and says that the notion of externality is illusory. But when someone asserts that there are no external objects it is certain that he has somehow been cognizing external things. Negation of only that is possible which has been previously occupying one's mind. This clearly shows that the notion of externality is primary in our experience and its negation is only an after-thought. But what is primary in our experience cannot be denied by inference.[56]

2.7.5. *There is no means to prove the unreality of external objects*:

There is no means of valid knowledge which can prove the unreality of external objects. Perception which reveals external

55. Ibid., 215-24.
56. SD, pp. 55-56.

objects directly contradicts the idealist theory instead of supporting it. Inference depends on perception. The universal premise of an inference is derived as an empirical generalization from a direct experience of external objects and as such it cannot prove the non-existence of external objects. The idealist arguing in support of his theory brings forward the following argument: "All waking cognitions are devoid of external objects, because they are cognitions like the cognitions in a dream." Kumārila points out several logical fallacies in this argument in the *Nirālambana-vāda* section of the *Vārtika* and puts forward a counter-argument as follows:

> The cognition of external objects in the waking state is valid, because it is not contradicted by subsequent experience, like the cognition of the falsehood of dreams.[57]

If the idealist denies the truth of this argument he will have to admit the validity of dream-cognition and thus he will contradict his own premise that all cognitions are false. Hence inference cannot prove the non-existence of external objects. Moreover, an argument is employed when there is a discourser (*vādī*) who employs the argument and an opponent (*prativādī*) against whom it is employed. Thus in the very attempt to prove his thesis by inference the idealist presupposes the independent existence of the realist whom he cognizes as external to him, which contradicts his theory that all cognitions apprehend themselves and not any external object.[58] Scriptural authority (*āgama*) too presupposes the reality of the external world. Religious instruction is impossible unless there is a preceptor and a pupil, both independently real. The Buddha himself has instructed people to follow his way of salvation. Moral and religious considerations demand a belief in the reality of external objects. If everything were unreal there would be no meaning in striving to attain heaven or release. Waking cognitions cannot have the same status as dream-cognitions.

It cannot be for the pleasures of a dream that people engage

57. SV, *Nirālambana*, 76-80.
58. Ibid., 70-71.

in the performance of duty. Dream coming to a man spontaneously during sleep, the learned would only lie down quietly instead of performing sacrifices when desirous of obtaining real results.[59]

Upamāna too cannot prove the idealist's theory. It has already been pointed out that there is no instance which can illustrate the identity of an action, its nominative and its accusative. *Arthāpatti* reconciles an apparent inconsistency between two *pramāṇas*. It proves the independent existence of external objects, otherwise the variety of cognitions cannot be explained. Negation (*anupalabdhi*) proves the reality of the external world by negating subjective idealism. The idealist's assertion that even if there be an external object it cannot be perceived because it is an aggregate of atoms which are invisible, is false. When it has been proved that cognition cannot cognize itself the idealist is forced on logical ground to accept that cognition cognizes an external object. As regards the constitution of an object we do not necessarily follow the Vaiśeṣika theory of atomism which is merely an hypothesis and as such may be given up if it conflicts with the reality of external objects.[60]

2.8. *The Relation of Cognition to its Object: The Theory of Cognizedness*

Kumārila says that identity cannot be the relation betweeen cognition and the cognized object; it is the relation of *viṣayatā* that subsists between them.[61] According to KK and NR *Viṣaya-viṣayibhāva* is the relation of cognition to its object. According to the latter *viṣayatā* or objectivity consists in the object bearing the result of the cognitive act. From SV, *Śūnyavāda*, vv. 151 and 200 it is clear that *viṣayatā* or objectivity is a unique type of causal relation. Sucaritamiśra[62] says that this subject-object relation is neither conjunction (*saṃyoga*), nor inherence (*samavāya*), but a unique relation. According to NKu, a work of Nyāya, too this relation is *viṣayatā*, but it is held to be *sui generis*

59. Ibid., 12.
60. SV, *Śūnya.*, 259-62.
61. Ibid., 500.
62. KK on Ibid., 64.

or a unique type of relation (*svarūpasambandha*). But the Bhāṭṭa view of *viṣayatā* is that it is a unique type of causal relation. There is some reciprocity between cognition and object. Cognition is a caused phenomenon and in this respect is not different from other occasional phenomena. That which occurs at times must have some cause for its birth. Cognition too has a cause in the form of sense-object contact (*indriyārtha-sannikarṣa*). The object, when it is in contact with a sense-organ, becomes the cause of cognition and again the cognition becomes the cause of the manifestedness (*bhāsana*) of the object. This reciprocal causality is different from the reciprocal causality observed between seed and sprout. The former is not an infinite process while the latter is. In the cognitive situation an object produces a cognition and the same cognition in turn produces cognizedness in the same object, while in the case of seed-sprout relation a seed produces a sprout which in turn produces a seed which though different from the first belongs to the same species and this second seed produces a sprout different from the first but belonging to the same species and so on. Therefore, the causality between cognition and object is held to be of a unique type.

It is easy to see what led the Bhāṭṭa to this conclusion. The Vijñānavādī Buddhist criticised the Sautrāntika vehemently for his causal theory of cognitive relation on the ground that it could not explain the presented character of the object of perception, because causality implies antecedence of the cause to the effect while a perceived object is revealed as belonging to the same time in which the cognition appears. Śabara too in his Bhāṣya recognizes a causal relation between an external object, e.g., a cloth, and the corresponding cognition. Naturally the Vijñānavādī's objection to the Sautrāntika theory applies to Śabara's theory also. Thus to save Śabara from this Buddhist attack and at the same time to explain the presented character of the object of perception the Bhāṭṭa was led to hold the view of a unique relation of reciprocal causality between cognition and object. The object appears to belong to the present time because cognizedness which is produced by cognition in it belongs to the present time. Cognition is produced by an external object. The object is certainly the cause of cognition, but in the process of cognizing this relationship is inverted and the cognition becomes the cause of generating the property of cognizedness in the object.

There is one more factor responsible for the peculiar Bhāṭṭa view. The general tendency of the Indian philosophers has been to maintain that in perception the senses or their modes (*vṛtti*) actively go out to the object and establish contact with it. Naturally there must be some result of this contact accruing to the object, because it is the object that is acted upon. An active force is always seen producing some result in the object which remains passive at the time; but the object which is acted upon is never seen producing a result in the active force. Consequently the Bhāṭṭa thinks that the result inhering in the object must be one which distinguishes that particular object from others which are not cognized and thus it can be nothing but cognizedness which is just like cookedness produced in rice by the act of cooking.

Now, if cognizedness is produced in the object by the act of cognition just as cookedness is produced in rice by the act of cooking, then it must be visible to other persons in the same manner as cookedness is visible. To this Sucaritamiśra answers that the cognizedness is known only to that person in whom the cognition is produced and not to others, just as only that person reaches a distant place who moves and not others who do not move.[63] Again a second objection may be urged: It may be conceived how cognizedness is produced in an object which is present, but how can it be produced in a past or future object by the present act of cognition? To this Pārthasārathi's answer is:

> Just as we comprehend the numerical quality 'tenness' relating to the days that have elapsed, we do admit that manifestedness arises in objects that either existed in the past or will exist in the future though not existing at present and this admission is based on the evidence of common experience.[64]

The same explanation is offered by Cidānanda.[65]

63. यस्यैव तु ज्ञानमुत्पन्नं तस्यासौ ज्ञात इति प्रतीतिसाक्षिकमेव; यथा यस्यैव गमनं तस्यैव देशान्तरप्राप्तिर्भवति । KK, part II, p. 124.
64. SD, p, 57.
65. NTV, p. 135.

2.9. *The Knowledge of Cognition*

Kumārila says that though cognition appears prior to the consciousness of object, yet it is not known at the time of its appearance because of the absence of a suitable means of knowing it; and that cognition is not self-revealing because just as the function of sense-organs is restricted to the manifestation of those objects only which are in contact with them, so the function of cognition is restricted to the manifestation of its object only, so that it is powerless to reveal itself. Cognition cannot turn back upon itself and make itself its own object. Pārthasārathi says that at the time of object-cognition there is no consciousness of cogntion at all so that its immediate knowledge is impossible.[66] It is a psychological fact that we cannot attend to two different things simultaneously. The scope of attention is too narrow to cognize two things at a time. Thus while cognition is busy in manifesting its object it cannot manifest itself; and it cannot be made the object of a second cognition directly, because it, being momentary, is destroyed before the appearance of a second cognition.[67] But how can a cognition reveal its object without revealing itself? Sucaritamiśra says that all existent things do their business by their existence alone, to which their being known is irrelevant and hence cognition by its mere existence fulfills its function of manifesting objects without standing in the need of being known.[68] Thus cognition neither reveals itself nor is revealed directly by a succeeding cognition. Is then there no knowledge of cognition? Kumārila says that there is no apprehension of cognition but its existence is presumed to explain the cognizedness of the object.[69] Pārthasārathi gives the following account of how cognition is presumed in his commentary on SV, *Śūnya.*, 183:

Arthāpatti or presumption is the means of the knowledge of cognition. The presumption takes place from the otherwise inexplicable nature of the cognizedness of an object. Presumption

66. अर्थविभाससमये संविदः प्रतिभास एव नास्ति, नतरामापरोक्ष्यम् । SD, p. 57.
67. NR on SV, *Śūnya.*, 185.
68. मृत्सलिलप्रच्छन्नबीजादिवदविदितस्वरूपसामर्थ्यैव संविद् विषयं व्यवस्थापयति । KK, Part II, p. 20.
69. SV, *Śūnya.*, 182.

does not arise at the time of the appearance of a cognition. Cognition is the cause of the property of cognizedness produced in the object. Hence, as cause and effect do not belong to the same time but to a preceding and a succeeding moment respectively, so some time, however minute, must elapse after which cognizedness is produced. Thus presumption is posterior to cognition. Therefore, it is but reasonable to say that cognition is not cognized first but only after the knowledge of an object.

Here one difficulty arises: Cognizedness of an object is its being the accusative of cognition; it can be known only after cognition is known, and because an unknown cognizedness cannot lead to the presumption of cognition, there will be a sort of mutual dependence—knowledge of cognition depending on the knowledge of cognizedness and again the knowledge of cognizedness depending on the knowledge of cognition. Some people offer the following explanation: The existence of cognition cannot be denied. When an object, e.g., a jar, exists, it is only on certain occasions made the objective of practical activity by someone and not by all. Then it is presumed that there must have arisen some peculiarity in the individual favouring his practical activity and this peculiarity is nothing but cognition. But, though cognition may be presumed in this way, practical activity does not always follow the cognition of an object. Even in the absence of any practical activity everyone remembers his having cognized an object. Without a knowledge of cognition how can one have such remembrance as 'the object was known by me'? The appearance of the knowledge of cognizedness prior to the appearance of practical activity cannot be explained unless the perceptibility of cognition be admitted. The right explanation is this: There is certainly some peculiarity in the object produced by the cognitive act known as cognizedness just as cookedness is produced in rice by the act of cooking, and this peculiarity can be known independently of cognition through perception. Cidānanda[70] and Nārāyaṇa[71] say that it is known through the contact 'identity-with-what-is-in-conjunction' (*saṃyukta-tādātmya*) that is, through the operation of senses which is commonly seen in connection with the perception of qualities. Thus cognition is presumed to

70. NTV, p. 134.
71. MM, p. 255.

have taken place through cognizedness which otherwise remains inexplicable.

Now, granted that when an object is present its cognizedness is known through perception and subsequently cognition is presumed, but what about inferential cognition? In inference the object is not perceived and hence its cognizedness too is not perceived and thus, as an unknown cognizedness cannot lead to the presumption of cognition, it will not be known.

Umbeka says that there are two kinds of results produced by cognition in its object, viz., immediacy (*āparokṣya*) and mediacy (*pārokṣya*), the former in the objects of perception and the latter in the objects of inference.[72] Pārthasārathi makes the same assertion in SD, p. 56. But in NR he seems to have realized the absurdity of conceiving that cognition can produce a result in an absent object. He, according to his revised view, maintains that in such cases the cognitive act produces a relation between the knower and the known and this relation known through mental perception leads to the presumption of cognition whenever there arises a curiosity about the cause of this relation: Even in those cases when someone remembers a previously known object at some later time without having ever presumed the cognition first the knower-known relationship is produced between the self and the object through recollective cognition, then the relationship is mentally perceived and the cognition is presumed on its basis, and lastly, after realizing the impossibility of sense-organs being the cause of this cognition, it is ascertained to be of the nature of recollection, which in turn being impossible unless there was a primary experience, leads to the presumption of the primary cognition.

It may be objected that if cognition is presumed through the inexplicability of cognizedness, then cognition of the cognition too will have to be presumed through the inexplicability of the cognizedness of the cognition and so on without an end, and hence, to avoid this infinite regress, it is proper to maintain that cognition is apprehended simultaneously with the object. This is true, but there is never felt any need of presuming cognitions one after the other in an infinite series. After the knowledge of

72. TT on SV, *Śūnya.*, 183.

an object the corresponding cognition is presumed to explain the cognizedness of the object if there is any curiosity at all. If there is no curiosity and consequently the cognition is not presumed, it does not make any difference in our practical activity for which merely a knowledge of objects is enough. But if afterwards any theoretical necessity or curiosity is felt, we may know the cognition through presumption and this is all. And if there is any further curiosity the cognition of this cognition too may be presumed in a like manner. This process of presumption may go on to any length without causing any logical difficulty. But in actual practice there is none who can go on with this infinite process, because very soon either one becomes tired of it or one's attention is diverted to other more interesting objects of the environment or to other more fruitful activities, and thus the process of presumption is cut short.[73] Thus cognition is not known directly.

In SV, *Śūnya.*, 233, Kumārila refers to a theory according to which cognition is apprehended simultaneously with the object. TT and NR attribute this theory to the Nyāya-Vaiśeṣika. According to later Nyāya a cognition is known directly through a secondary act of mental perception (*anuvyavasāya*) at the time of its appearance. But if cognition is directly perceived, it must be perceived as having a form, because a formless thing cannot be perceived, and thus the postulation of an external object having a form in addition to the cognition becomes logically superfluous. Thus this view and similarly all forms of epistemological dualism logically lead to subjectivism. Therefore, it must be accepted that cognition is not apprehended directly, though its existence is proved afterwards by presumption.

Prabhākara and Śaṅkara hold that cognition is self-revealing.[74] The idealist Buddhist too holds that cognition is self-luminous, but according to his view cognition makes itself its object, while according to Prabhākara and Śaṅkara cognition is never cognized as an object of any cognition. The Bhāṭṭa criticism of the doctrine of self-luminosity of cognition has already been given. The Nyāya-Vaiśeṣika holds that cognition is not self-luminous in the Buddhist sense or in any other sense, but is known directly through a

73. SV, *Śūnya.*, 187-95.

74. बुद्धिः स्वयंप्रकाशेति गुरुशंकरयोर्मतम् । MM, p. 248.

secondary act of cognition of which it is the object. The Naiyāyikas argue that cognition is perceptible because it is a temporary specific quality of the soul, like pleasure etc. All are agreed that pleasure, pain etc., which are the temporary qualities of the soul, are cognized directly through inner perception and cognition too is such a quality. Why, then, should it not be perceived in the like manner? Nārāyaṇa says that this argument is not sound. To be a temporary quality of soul is not a sufficient ground for the inference that cognition is perceptible, because volition, which too is a temporary quality of soul and is the cause of activities like breathing in deep sleep, is not perceived during that state. Therefore, cognition cannot be an object of perception under any logical pressure.[75]

2.10. *The Bhāṭṭa Criticism of Prabhākara's Theory of Triple Perception*

There is apparently some inconsistency in Prabhākara's theory as propounded in his *Bṛhatī* and Śālikanātha's *Ṛjuvimalā*. Prabhākara asserts that *saṃvit*, which is ordinarily supposed to be equivalent to *jñāna*, both meaning cognition, is self-ravealing, while at the same time he supports Śabara's theory that *jñāna* or *buddhi* is known through inference. Śālikanātha says:

> There is no another apprehension of *saṃvit*...*Saṃvit* is nothing but the apprehension of an object and it does not stand in need of a second apprehension, because it is of the nature of apprehension...The *saṃvit* of an object, which is different from the object, being by nature self-illuminating, does not require another illuminator.[76]

Again it is said:

> *Saṃvit* itself is manifestation; there is no manifestation of an object in the absence of *saṃvit* and there can be no manifestation again of this manifestation.[77]

Thus *saṃviṭ* is identified with manifestation of an object and is held to be self-revealing. Therefore, *saṃvit* must be different from *jñāna* which is held to be an object of inference. In many

75. Ibid., p. 251.
76. RV, p. 79.
77. Ibid., p. 80.

passages there are explicit references to their difference, for example, in

> nanu *jñāne* satyapi *saṃvin*nāsti[78]

and

> sā cedarthasya *jñāna*sya vā syāt, tadā nirākārā *saṃvid* apratyakṣā syāt/ tadapratyakṣatve cārtho *jñānaṃ* ceti dvayamasaṃvedyam āpadyate/ *saṃvidi* cedam ākāro niveśitaḥ, apahnute tarhi bhavetām artha*jñāne*/[79]

Now if *jñāna* is different from *saṃvit*, what is its nature? It is said:

> How, then is *jñāna* proved? Because *saṃvit* which is the result is an effect; and an effect cannot take place unless there be some cause; and, because the self cannot be the desired cause, for, it being eternal, its effect too will be eternal, while *saṃvit* is an occasional effect; hence an occasional cause is inferred and this is *jñāna*.[80]

Further *jñāna* is held to be not perceptible on the ground that its specific form is not apprehended,[81] because it is momentary and at the time of the appearance of a second *jñāna* it is absent, while the object of perception is always present.[82] It is said that inference apprehends the mere existence of an object, while perception apprehends the specific form of an object.[83] In a subsequent passage it is stated that the instrumental character of the means of knowledge and the accusative character of the object of knowledge are dependent on the origination of a result, and that while the knowledge of the object is independent of the result, the knowledge of the means, being inferential in character, depends on the result.[84]

It is plain from this that *saṃvit*, according to Prabhākara, is the result of a *pramāṇa* while *jñāna* is the *pramāṇa* or the means of *saṃvit*. Thus *jñāna* is an unconscious inner process intervening

78. Ibid., p. 76.
79. Ibid., p. 78.
80. Ibid., p. 80.
81. स्वरूपाग्रहणाज्ज्ञानमप्रत्यक्षम् । Ibid., p. 84.
82. ज्ञानं तावत्स्वरसभंगुरं, तेन ज्ञानान्तरोदयकाले विनष्टं न प्रत्यक्षं, विद्यमानविषयं च प्रत्यक्षम् । Ibid., p. 84.
83. सन्मात्रग्राह्यनुमानम् । Ibid., p. 81. स्वरूपपरिच्छेदः संवेदनमुच्यते । Ibid., p. 84.
84. प्रमाणप्रमेययोः करणकर्मकारकयोः फलोत्पत्तिनिबन्धना कारकोत्पत्तिः, प्रमितिस्तु प्रमेयस्य प्रत्यक्षतः फलनिरपेक्षा, प्रमाणस्यानुमानिकत्वात्फलायत्तैव प्रमितिरिति । Ibid., p. 88

between an object and its direct consciousness which is termed *saṃvit*, and hence it can be known only indirectly through inference, while consciousness is self-revealing. *Saṃvit* is not revealed in the sense in which an external object is revealed. The object is invariably made the accusative of an act of knowing, but *saṃvit* is never known to be such an accusative. *Saṃvit* is always known as *saṃvit* and never as an object.[85]

Here, let us examine Dr. Jha's interpretation of Prabhākara's view given in his works, *The Prābhākara School of Pūrva-Mīmāṃsā*, and *Pūrva-Mīmāṃsā in its Sources*. Dr. Jha seems to be quite unmindful of the distinction drawn by Prabhākara between '*saṃvit*' and '*jñāna*'. He translates both these terms indiscriminately as 'cognition'. Dr. Randle too neglects the difference. He says: "Prabhākara replies that we are aware of our cognitions as subjective processes but not as object."[86] *Saṃvit* of which we are directly aware, according to Prabhākara, is not a 'subjective process', but the result of a subjective process and this subjective process is called *jñāna* which results in the consciousness of an object and is inferred instead of being directly apprehended. Keith rightly uses the word *consciousness* for '*saṃvit*' but later he too becomes unmindful of the distinction between 'consciousness' and 'cognition.'[87]

Now, if, according to Dr. Jha's interpretation, *saṃvit* and *jñāna* are synonyms, it becomes difficult to reconcile the assertions that '*saṃvit* is self-revealing' and '*jñāna* is inferred'. Dr. Jha says:

> The right conclusion, thus, is that the cognition is self-apprehended and its presence is known by inference.[88]

But it is strange how the same thing, be it *saṃvit* or *jñāna*, can be self-apprehended and inferred at the same time. When cognition is known because of its self-luminosity, it must be known as present, so that the so-called inference of its presence becomes useless. When the sun is directly apprehended by me, why should I take the unnecessary trouble of inferring its presence? Dr. Jha seems to have misunderstood Prabhākara's remark, viz.,

85. संवित्तयैव संवित् संवेद्या, न संवेद्यतया, नास्याः कर्मभावो विद्यते । BR, p. 82.
86. *Indian Logic in Early Schools*, p. 104.
87. *Karma-Mīmāṃsā*, p. 20.
88. *Pūrva-Mīmāṃsā in its Sources*, p. 81.

kiṃ tarhyatrānumānikam? phalameva hi pramāṇam iti pramāṇavido manyante/[89]

Dr. Jha seems to have taken the second sentence as Prabhākara's answer to the question in the first sentence, in which case Prabhākara's view would be that the result, viz., *saṃvit*, which is self-revealing, is inferred. But Dr. Jha has not taken note of Śālikanātha's comment on this sentence. Śālikanātha says:

yadi saṃvit pratyakṣā kim aparam anumeyam? na ca vācyam phalabhūtā saṃvit tatra karaṇam pramāṇarūpaṃ phalajanakam anumeyam iti; phalameva hi yasmāt pramāṇam iti pramāṇavido manyante/[90]

In this passage the idealist Buddhist, apparently under the impression that *jñāna* and *saṃvit* are synonyms, raises the objection that when the Mīmāṃsaka admits the self-luminous character of cognition, why it should at the same time be held to be inferred, and he further points out that because *pramāṇa* and *phala*, i.e., the means and the result of knowing are identical, it is wrong to hold that *pramāṇa* is inferred and *phala* is self-revealed. It should be remembered in this connection that it is the Buddhist alone who holds that *pramāṇa* and *phala* are identical, and this view has been criticised by Kumārila in SV, *Pratyakṣa*, and by Jayanta too in his *Nyāyamañjarī*. Śālikanātha himself is in disagreement with the Buddhist and asserts in the most unambiguous terms that *saṃvit* and *jñāna* are two different things, and that the former is self-revealed while the latter is inferred.

Now, having exposed a serious misinterpretation of Prabhākara's theory, we may give a summary of Prabhākara's theory of knowledge according to KK on SV, *Śūnya.*, 31, which we find quite reliable. We may preface the summary with some remarks on the term *jñāna* used by Prabhākara. By Prabhākara it has been used in the sense of the means of which object-consciousness is the result, and thus *jñāna* becomes identical with the *ātma-manas* contact. Śālikanātha emphatically says:

When the word *pramāṇa* is used in the sense of the means or instrument of knowledge, *jñāna*, which is identical with the

89. BR, p. 83.
90. RV, p. 83.

soul-mind contact, is the *pramāṇa* and its result is *saṃvit*, which is helpful in our practical dealings with the external objects.[91]

Sucaritamiśra says that the words *cetanā*, *buddhi*, *jñāna* and *saṃvit* are used as synonyms in common parlance.[92] From this it is evident that Prabhākara's use of *jñāna* in the sense of soul-mind contact is quite unusual. But why did Prabhākara use this term in such an uncommon sense? It seems that by his personal conviction Prabhākara could not support the theory of the inferability of cognition, which was held by Śabara, and hence instead of criticising him he forced his view on the Bhāṣya passage by using the term *saṃvit* in one sense and the terms *jñāna* and *buddhi* in a different sense. In the following account we will use these words in their common sense, viz., that of cognition and will adopt the words 'soul-mind contact' as equivalent to *jñāna* in Prabhākara's sense.

Prabhākara's theory is as follows: It is a matter of common experience that in every cognition three factors are revealed, viz., the cognizer (*pramātā*), the object (*prameya*) and the cognition itself (*pramiti*). In the cognition 'I know the jar' there is a triple consciousness (*tripuṭī-saṃvit*). Here 'I' refers to the cognizing soul, 'jar' to the object of cognition and 'know' to the fact of cognition. All these three factors are apprehended together, but while the object is apprehended as having a form, the other two are apprehended without a form. The object is always apprehended as the accusative (*karma*), the soul is apprehended as the nominative (*kartā*), and the cognition or awareness as cognition (*kriyā*). The proof for the existence of these three is nothing but direct experience. The self, the object and the cognition are directly revealed in every object-cognition, and, though the first two always stand in need of a revealer, the third is self-revealed. The self and the object are always dependent on cognition for their manifestation. They are not self-luminous, because we see that during sleep they exist yet they are not manifested in consciousness. It cannot be said that they are non-existent

91. PP, p. 64.
92. चेतना बुद्धिः ज्ञानं संविदित्यनर्थान्तरमिति लौकिका बुध्यन्ते । KK, Part II, p. 106.

when they do not appear in consciousness, because on waking they are recognized as the same as they were before. Then, why do they not manifest themselves when they do exist during sleep? This is because they are not self-luminous. Cognition, on the contrary, is self-luminous. There is no time when cognition can exist without manifesting itself. For the manifestation of the self and the object cognition is required, but for its own manifestation there is no need of a second cognition. Cognition is its own manifester, and, though it manifests the self and the object both, yet, unlike the object, the self is never made its accusative. Just as in the act of 'going' the accusative character belongs to 'village' only and not to the 'goer' though the result of 'going', viz., conjunction and disjunction (*saṃyoga-vibhāga*), is related to both, so in the act of cognizing the accusative character belongs to the 'jar' only and not to the cognizer, though the result of the cognitive act, viz., manifestation, is related to both. This is because the accusative character consists in assuming the result of an action inhering in a different thing (*parasamavetakriyā-phalabhāgitā*). In 'going' the action inheres in the body, and, similarly, in 'cognizing' it inheres in the soul, the results being assumed by 'the village' and 'the jar' respectively, which are different from the agents. Thus cognition which is formless, revealing itself by its very nature, reveals the soul and the object also. From cognition its cause, viz., the soul-mind contact is inferred and cognition itself is directly apprehended as cognition. It is not apprehended as its own object as the Buddhist idealist holds. Cognition is self-luminous and illuminates its subject and object just as the light of a lamp being self-luminous illuminates the lamp as well as objects. Just as a second light is not needed to manifest a light, so a second cognition is not required to manifest a cognition. The proof of the existence of all entities depends on their being manifested by cognition, but if cognition itself is not manifested, how can there be the proof?[93]

Prabhākara criticises the Bhāṭṭa view that the self is known in self-consciousness alone which is different from object-consciousness. He says that self-consciousness is not different from object-consciousness. All object-cognitions are at the same time ego-

93. Cp. PP, pp. 56-57.

cognitions. The Bhāṭṭa says that in object-cognition objects are the accusative and in self-cognition the self is the accusative. But Prabhākara maintains that the self is not the accusative of an independent cognition. It cannot be the accusative of any cognition. It is revealed in every cognition as the subject and not as the cognized object. In the so-called self-consciousness 'this I am' (*ahamasmi*) we are not aware of the self 'I' as different from the aggregate of material organs of action called the body. It is the self-luminous cognition which establishes itself as well as the non-luminous self and object. Unless the self be recognized in every object-cognition, no difference between one's own cognition and that belonging to another person, can be ascertained. Therefore, neither the object is manifested without the manifestation of the self, nor the self is manifested without the manifestation of the object. This is why on the cessation of object-cognition the self rests in the state of total unconsciousness like the inert matter. This occurs everyday when one passes into deep slumber. In that state there is absolutely no consciousness of the self and objects. Therefore it is concluded that the self is revealed in every object-cognition.[94]

Criticizing Prabhākara's view Pārthasārathi says that 'this is a jar' and 'I know the jar' are two quite different types of judgements. In the former only the object, 'jar', is manifested, neither the self nor the cognition. In the latter the 'jar' is recollected and the primary cognition of the jar is inferred. Thus the former is a judgment of perception, while the latter is that of inference, and the two do not always go together. The reflective judgment does not always accompany the cognition of an object. It is only when sometimes our curiosity is aroused about the cause of the cognizedness of an object that the reflective judgment follows the primary perceptual judgment. Thus Prabhākara unnecessarily confounds the two when he says that there is a triple consciousness in every cognition.[95]

Sucaritamiśra directs his polemic against the identification by Prabhākara of *jñāna* with self-mind conjunction. *Jñāna* is consciousness (*cetanā*) but the conjunction of soul and mind is not

94. KK on RV, *Śūnya.*, 70; Cp. PP, pp. 152-53.
95. NR on SV, *Śūnya.*, 72.

consciousness, because conjunction is an insentient property as colour etc. are. If conjunction be consciousness, then, the *manas*, being as distinct a term of the relation as the soul is, becomes conscious like the latter, while Prabhākara himself is not prepared to hold such an extraordinary view. Therefore, *jñāna* or *buddhi* can be nothing other than the *saṃvit* which Prabhākara holds to be self-aware, and thus he contradicts Śabara's view which he pretends to support in his commentary.[96]

Again, when Prabhākara says that the self, the object and the cognition are apprehended simultaneously in every cognition though the form that is manifested is only one, then, as in that case there can be no consciousness of their mutual difference, the three become non-distinct from each other, and thus he only contributes to the Buddhist subjectivism. Prabhākara may say that simultaneous apprehension of two things does not necessarily imply their identity: colour and light are apprehended simultaneously, but they are not identical. But this parallel cited by Prabhākara does not help his theory. Colour is sometimes seen in the absence of light as by nocturnal animals whose sight is obstructed by light, and light too is sometimes seen alone. This is why colour and light are held to be distinct, though they are usually apprehended together. But the self, the object and the cognition, according to Prabhākara, are never cognized independently. Therefore they cannot but be identical.[97]

Prabhākara says that the self is revealed in every object-cognition. But what is his reply to the question: "Is I-consciousness different from object-consciousness or not?" If he says that it is not different, then he denies a fact of experience, because experience bears witness to their difference. If he says that there is a difference between the two, then, it may be asked, what is the basis of this difference? In object-cognition an object is apprehended, but what is apprehended in self-consciousness? It is not the body that is apprehended, because the object of self-consciousness is obviously the cognizer, whereas the body which is an aggregate of the insentient material elements is not the

96. KK on SV, *Śūnya.*, 31.
97. Ibid.

cognizer. Sense-organs cannot be the cognizer, because they too are material and unconscious. Cognition itself cannot be the cognizer, because the 'I' in self-consciousness refers to a persistent entity and is recognized as the same through the passing moments of time, while cognition is momentary. Therefore, the object of I-consciousness cannot be anything but the non-material permanent self which is directly established to have a dual form as being a substance qualified by the property of consciousness. Prabhākara's assertion that he does not recognize the self in self-consciousness as distinct from the body, the senses etc. does not prove that the self is not apprehended at all. If water and milk are mixed together and are not seen separately, it is not proved thereby that they are not seen. In a like manner, though the self is indistinctly manifested as mixed with the body in the self-consciousness of ordinary individuals, yet it is distinctly manifested on the practice of abstraction, concentration and the other forms of Yoga, and the more so when all the past *karma*-s are exhausted through enjoyment and there is no fresh accumulation of them. Even Prabhākara, who says that the self is cognized only when objects are cognized, cannot say that it is cognized distinctly. As he too cannot point out the difference of the self from the body, his theory is not an improvement on our theory. As a matter of fact, in object-cognition there is no manifestation of the self at all. In object-cognition nothing except the object is manifested. Even the cognition is not cognized at that time, which is the only basis of all our discriminations among objects. The so-called difficulty pointed out by Prabhākara that if the self is not apprehended in object-cognition there would be no discrimination between one's own cognition and that belonging to another person, is only imaginary. I recognize my cognition as my own, not because my self is revealed in it, but because it is produced in me alone and not in you. How can I know the object whose cognition arises in other selves? In object-cognitions only objects are manifested and not the self. A cognition manifesting X which is its object cannot at the same time manifest Y which is not its object. The assertion that in the absence of object-cognition the self too is not apprehended, is absolutely wrong. If by this Prabhākara's intention be that in the state of release there is no self-consciousness, then such a release is no better than death as it is conceived by the layman.[98]

Again, what is the basis of the differentiation between the nominative character of self and the accusative character of object, which are held by Prabhākara as revealed simultaneously in the same cognition? If both the self and the object are manifested together, then there must be two accusatives and not one as commonly happens. The view that accusativeness (*karmatā*) is the assumption by one thing of the result of an action inhering in a different thing, is mistaken. That which is apprehended on the appearance of cognition is the accusative of the cognitive act, and as the self too is apprehended, according to Prabhākara, it must also be the accusative like the object. Therefore, Prabhākara's assertion that the self is always manifested as the nominative of the cognitive act is self-contradictory.[99]

Prabhākara defines accusativeness or objectivity in the above way to avoid the incompatibility involved in making the same self the nominative as well as the accusative of the same cognitive act (*svātmani kriyāvirodhaḥ*). Pārthasārathi asks as to what this incompatibility is. Prabhākara says that when one is the agent of a particular act that act cannot produce its result in the agent himself. But what is the result of the act of cognition? It is certainly revelation. But does this result not relate to the agent? If Prabhākara says that it does not, then he must point out the manner in which the agent, i.e., the self is revealed in every cognition. When there is no revelation of the self it is not possible to say that it is revealed in every cognition. Therefore when Prabhākara admits that the self is revealed in every object-cognition the objection that the agent cannot bear the result of its own action becomes equally applicable to his theory.[100]

Moreover, what is this action which inheres in the self and imparts its result to the object? If it is the conjunction of the soul and the *manas*, then it inheres in the *mamas* too, and consequently the *manas* also becomes the agent like the self, and thus the same act of cognition will have two nominatives, which is absurd. Therefore, Prabhākara's view that there is a triple

98. KK on SV, *Śūnya.*, 70.
99. KK, Part II, p. 130.
100. SD, p. 122.

consciousness involved in every act of cognition, is absolutely unfounded.[101]

2.11. *A Critical Review of Kumārila's Theory*

We have seen that according to Kumārila cognition in its specific form is essentially an activity of the subject in relation to some object. We have also seen that the act theory of knowledge has certain advantages over the quality theory and the relation theory. A quality characterizes an object without implying its relation to or action upon other objects. It is a static property of a thing. But knowledge necessarily implies an activity of the subject in relation to objects. Knowledge is always knowledge of something. It is a 'self-transcending process' as Reid says. This active reference to an 'other' which is implied in knowledge, is missed by the quality theory. The relation theory takes note of this essential mark of knowledge, but it does not explain knowledge. There is certainly some relation between the subject and the object, but this relation does not constitute knowledge. All relations presuppose some kind of action, and this fact has been emphasized by Kumārila himself. Therefore, knowledge must presuppose some kind of activity belonging to the subject, which consists in attending and actively responding to the influences produced on the subject by the objects in the environment. But an activity is generally conceived as producing some perceptible and tangible results on objects, while in the case of cognition no such results are observed. The mistake of the Bhāṭṭas consists in placing cognition on the same footing as other voluntary activities. They thought that cognition produced cognizedness in objects exactly as cooking produced cookedness in rice. But, while cookedness is a visible and tangible result, cognizedness is not. And there is no ground to suppose that cognizedness is a very subtle and invisible result, because in that case the cognizer himself could not perceive it. Of course, when a man has already known an object, he happens to experience a feeling of familiarity when he is face to face with it on a second occasion. But this feeling does not reside in the object; it resides in the knowing subject.

101. KK, Part II, p. 130.

The Bhāṭṭas were misled by the word 'activity' which in common usage is predicated of 'knowing' as well as of such physical activities as 'cooking' etc. The Nyāya, on the other hand, was led to the quality theory, because it could not conceive 'activity' otherwise than in terms of gross physical movements. In knowing there is a very subtle physiological and neural activity of the sense-argans and the brain, and it cannot be completely detected even by the most sophisticated scientific device. But this does not mean that there is no activity at all; nor does it mean that this activity produces some result on the object which is 'out' there at a distance. The brain does not go out to the object and transform it. It was a common mistake of Indian philosophers to conceive the mind as going out and reaching the object, and the Bhāṭṭa, working out the logical implications of this common conception, exhibits it in a very gross form. The fact is that none of the above theories can explain knowledge. Knowledge is preceded by a subtle and unconscious physiological process, but knowledge itself is not this process; nor it is unconscious. Knowledge is the revelation of objects and is the result of a process, but it cannot be identified with the process. Jayanta is right when, citicizing the Bhāṭṭa theory, he says that cognition is not itself an activity but the result of an activity.[102] A psychologist or a physiologist may discover the details of this unconscious process and this is good so far, but knowledge cannot he identified with this process. It is a fact that we open our eyes, our retina catches the physical energy emitted by an external object and transmits it to the brain which responds in a particular way, but this is not identical with the manifestation of a green tree before us. The differentiation of knowing activity from other physical activities by such phrases as 'an ideal activity' does not throw any light on its essential nature, because the term 'ideal' is unintelligible apart from 'knowledge'. Knowledge is not a 'quality' in the ordinary sense of the term, though it belongs to a knowing subject. Cognizedness, which is said to be a property produced in the object by the cognitive act, cannot explain knowing, because the object has already been known, while cognizedness, as the result of knowing, is produced in

102. न हि क्रियास्वभावं ज्ञानमपितु फलस्वभावमेव । NM, p. 16.

the succeeding moment. So knowledge or consciousness of objects is preceded by a process, but it is not that process; it belongs to a subject, but is not a quality; it implies a relation, but is not itself a relation. Knowledge is a unique phenomenon and cannot be brought under any of the usual categories of substance, quality, relation and action. Knowledge may be knowledge of a substance, of a quality, of a relation, or of an action; but it is neither a substance, nor a quality, nor a relation nor an action. It may, in this respect, be compared to an image reflected in a mirror. The image is not a substance; it is not a quality of the mirror; it is not mere relation of the mirror to the object of which it is the image; nor is it an action of the mirror on the object. It is a unique phenomenon caused by certain forces. It is a spatio-temporal event, but neither it occupies space, nor apparently undergoes temporal changes, though the object, which it represents, occupies a position in space and undergoes temporal changes. Knowledge implies causation, as it is caused by objects, but it cannot be brought under the category of cause and effect. Objects are the stimuli of cognition, but at the same time they are its accusative too. The representative theory of knowledge seems to be nearer the truth. But representationism does not necessarily mean that we are not directly aware of objects. I touch an object with my hand but is does not mean that I touch it indirectly. Similarly, I know an object through a datum, yet I know it directly.

I know an object directly when I perceive it, and I can also be aware of my knowing. The Naiyāyika is right when he says that we are aware of an object and this awareness can be directly known through introspection. Kumārila says that we are aware of objects, but never of the awareness. This can be only partly true. It is a fact that we generally attend to the objects of knowledge and ignore the knowing itself. We usually behave extrovertedly. We are generally interested in the objects of our environment and not in the awareness of them. It is also true that consciousness does not necessarily imply self-consciousness. We cannot suppose that the lower animals are self-conscious. Self-consciousness is a higher stage of mental development. But it does not mean that we can never be conscious of our consciousness of objects. We intimately know that we know external objects. We are not generally attending to our consciousness, but we can do so in a secondary act of introspection. Montague rightly observes:

> The brain state of a given moment is never conscious of itself as object, but it can be conscious not only of extra-organic objects, but also of the brain-state just preceding it.[103]

Kumārila says that consciousness is a momentary thing, which does not stay till the appearance of a second act of consciousness. But this is wrong, and Kumārila's commentators, Sucaritamiśra and Pārthasārathi, too admit that cognition endures for two or three moments. Kumārila seems to have been influenced by the Buddhist doctrine of momentariness. But a moment is not a mathematical point. Consciousness has some duration, however small it may be. Therefore, it is quite reasonable to hold with the Nyāya that a primary awareness is made the object of a secondary awareness. And though we never have an objectless awareness, yet in thought we can distinguish the awareness from the object.

Kumārila is right in asserting that awareness is not possible without a form and form cannot belong to the awareness itself. But this does not imply that we are not directly aware of our awareness. We are conscious of objects; and when we become conscious of our consciousness, we are again conscious of the object; but by a higher intellectual act we can discriminate between consciousness which is formless and the object which has the form. The Buddhist idealist and the Bhāṭṭa realist both are mistaken in ignoring the higher cognitive faculty of the mind, which analyzes and synthesizes the data presented by perceptual activity. Kumārila says that we have sometimes the awareness of cognition immediately after its appearance, but that it is inferential and not direct. But this is wrong. Inference generally presupposes a direct knowledge somewhere and at some time. In those cases in which something is inferred, which has never been perceived, a feeling of unfamiliarity or strangeness accompanies the inference; but in the knowledge of cognition there is no such feeling. We are conscious of consciousness and have a

103 *The New Realism*, p. 290.

feeling of its intimate and immediate presence. We seem to be directly acquainted with cognition. Hence it cannot be said to be inferred. Kumārila wanted to establish the independent existence of external objects against the idealist Buddhist who maintained the identity of objects with cognition or thought on the ground of their simultaneous apprehension, and in his over-zealousness to strike at the very foundation of the Buddhists' argument he preferred to deny a direct knowledge of cognition. Hence, to explain the knowledge of cognition he could have recourse to inference only, and, because inference[104] is not possible without a mark, he supposed the mark to consist in the cognizedness of the object of cognition. Thus, he became successful in saving the independent reality of external objects from the Buddhist who was his main adversary; and his immediate aim having been fulfilled, he did not care to examine the absurdity of his newly invented concept of cognizedness. But the idealist's arguments cannot shake our belief in the reality of external objects. We instinctively believe in the independence and reality of the external world and of our own consciousness, but none of these beliefs has been acquired by inference. Neither objects are inferred as the Sautrāntika holds, nor cognitions are inferred as Kumārila holds. The primary knowledge of objects and cognition is direct. Cognizedness cannot help if we are never directly aware of the fact of cognition. Śrīdhara rightly says that we have no experience of the property of cognizedness in an object as we have of cookedness in rice, and the so-called immediacy (*āparokṣya*) of the object of perception is not a supernatural property generated in it, but is merely its relation to perception. Cognizedness is said to be directly cognized while cognition is said to be inferred. But in that case a new cognizedness will be generated in the first cognizedness and so on leading to an infinite regress. Kumārila says that cognition is presumed as the occasional cause of the effect in the form of cognizedness. But Śrīdhara says that the conjunction of the soul with *manas* and that of the *manas* with the object, which is commonly accepted by all, may as well be presumed to be the desired cause, so that

104. The term 'inference' has been used here in a wider sense including cases of *arthāpatti*.

the presumption of cognition as an intermediary becomes superfluous.[105]

Again, we do not see how the concept of cognizedness can help in explaining the presented character of the object of perception. Kumārila criticizes the Sautrāntika causal theory of knowledge and points out that according to this theory we must always perceive an object as past while actually we perceive it as present, and then he offers his own theory of cognizedness. But this latter theory is equally unable to explain the said character. According to the Sautrāntika an object imparts its own form to cognition, and thus the object being the cause of the form of cognition, must belong to the preceding moment. According to Kumārila cognition produces cognizedness in the object, and thus cognizedness, being the effect of cognition, must belong to the succeeding moment. Hence, if the Sautrāntika cognizes a past object as present, then Kumārila too cognizes a future object as present; and if the Sautrāntika cannot compel the past object which originated the form of the cognition to stay till the appearance of the cognition, then Kumārila too cannot compel cognition to stay till the future moment when cognizedness is supposed to be produced. Again, if the object does persist from the past moment till the future one or even beyond, credit does not go to the Sautrāntika, nor does it go to Kumārila if cognition stays for a few more moments. The fact is that cognition arises in the present moment and whether the corresponding object or fact exists in the present moment or not, whether it will exist in the future moment or not, it must have existed in the previous moment. We are told by astronomers that every night we observe several stars in the sky which existed millions of years ago, but which may be non-existent at the time they are seen. We observe a flash of lightning and hear its thundering sound a few seconds later, while both the phenomena occurred together. Hence to say that an object or fact must be present at the time of its cognition and that a theory of cognition can be true only if it accepts this, otherwise not, is wrong. Actually when we say that 'it is thundering now' we

105. NK, pp. 96-98; Cf. also न चार्थापत्तिरपि ज्ञातृव्यापारकल्पनयैव प्रभवति, इन्द्रियार्थसन्निकर्षवशादेवार्थदृष्टताया घटमानत्वात् । NM, p. 21.

pronounce a judgment based on certain data of knowledge; it is not in itself perception. Sometimes such judgments are found correct on verification and sometimes not. A judgment based on certain data of perception need not always be correct. It is a matter of learning through experience that we acquire the capacity to make correct judgments. Our capacity to judge correctly is as much subject to growth and decay as our other capacities are. Our cognitive faculty too is affected by learning and habit like others. So a judgment of perception is different from the data of perception; and this distinction has been neglected not by Kumārila alone, but by the majority of the Indian philosophers. Despite all this Kumārila has made an origninal approach to epistemological questions and his failure is shared even by the advanced theorists of to-day.

CHAPTER III

VALID AND INVALID KNOWLEDGE

Knowledge* is the revelation of the objective world to a subject. It is a subjective phenomenon representing the world of reality. It is the basis of all our practical activities in relation to objects. Our activities are not blind reactions to objects. A successful activity presupposes a correct knowledge of objects. We proceed to act in a particular way with reference to an object on the belief that our knowledge correctly reveals its nature. But at times we do not find a thing where and how we expect it to be, and thus we are shocked to learn that knowledge is not always a correct representation of reality, and that it frequently misguides us and leads to painful results. Thus we come to distinguish between truth and falsehood.

3.1. *The Bhāṭṭa Definition of Validity*

Knowledge may be true or false, valid or invalid. Now the question arises: What constitutes the validity of knowledge lacking which it becomes invalid? In the Nyāya system valid knowledge is called *pramā* and validity is called *pramātva*. The later Mīmāṃsā writers adopt these terms. But Kumārila and his commentators are not known to have used them. They have used the terms *pramāṇa* and *prāmāṇya* for valid knowledge and validity respectively and *apramāṇa* and *aprāmāṇya* to express the opposite notions. The latter two terms have been invariably taken in the same sense while the former two have been used rather indiscriminately. The term *pramāṇa* sometimes stands for

*We are using the word in a non-specific verbal sense, interchangeably with cognition. The specific sense of 'true belief' in which it is sometimes used by Russell (*Human Knowledge*, p. 170), is not intended here.

a means of right knowledge whose result is termed *pramiti* or *miti*, and *prāmāṇya* then means the capacity of a means to generate a correct knowledge.

Pārthasārathi distinguishes between the terms *satyatva* and *prāmāṇya*. Suppose there are two persons, one asserting "there is Indra" and the other asserting "there is no Indra." These two propositions are contradictory to each other, so that, according to the law of excluded middle, only one of them must be true. Pārthasārathi says that one of them must be *satya*, but, as there is no certitude (*Nirṇāyakatva*) as to which of them is true, there can be no *prāmāṇya*.[1] Thus *satyatva* is not identical with *prāmāṇya*. The latter term implies the former, but the former does not imply the latter. We take the term *truth* as a substitute for *satyatva* and *validity* for *prāmāṇya*. But validity does not here stand for formal consistency in which sense it is used in Logic.

Kumārila defines valid knowledge in the following verse:

> *Tasmāt dṛḍhaṃ yadutpannaṃ nāpi saṃvādamṛcchati* /
> *Jñānāntareṇa vijñānaṃ tatpramāṇaṃ pratīyatāṃ* // SV,2.80.

"Valid knowledge is a firm or assured cognition of objects, which does not stand in need of confirmation by other cognitions." Umbeka says that the word *dṛḍha* excludes doubt from valid knowledge and *na visaṃvādam ṛcchati* (which is not contradicted by other cognitions), which he reads in the place of *nāpi saṃvādamṛcchati*, excludes error or illusion. Sucaritamiśra comments that valid knowledge is not contradicted by a subsequent knowledge in the form 'this is not so' and that it contains some new information (*vijñāna = adhikaviṣayajñāna*) about its object. Valid knowledge, therefore, is a certain, true and informative cognition of something.

Pārthasārathi extracts from Sūtra 1.1.5 of *Pūrva Mīmāṃsā* the definition of valid knowledge as an apprehension of a previously unapprehended object, which is devoid of defects in its source and is not contradicted by subsequent experience.[2] Later on he defines valid knowledge as 'a true cognition which

1. NR on SV, 2.178.
2. कारणदोषबाधकज्ञानरहितमगृहीतग्राहिज्ञानं प्रमाणम् । SD, p. 45.

relates to something previously uncognized.'[3] This definition is practically the same as the former except that in the former one the source from which discrepancy may creep in knowledge, viz., the defects of the sense-organs etc., is mentioned and the possibility of the falsification of a valid knowledge in future is precluded. Pārthasārathi[4] mentions three distinctive features of valid knowledge, viz., (1) its object is not remembered as having been previously known, (2) it conforms to the real nature of its object, and (3) there is a feeling of conviction regarding its conformity or agreement with the real object. Thus novelty, freedom from doubt and truth are the three essential marks of valid knowledge and if anyone of these is absent in a knowledge, it ceases to be valid.

A knowledge which does not add something to our present stock of information, cannot be valid. Validity consists in discovering new objects or new features of known objects for thought. Valid knowledge is an advance on what we already know. The Bhāṭṭa considers knowledge in its relation to our practical needs. There is no use in knowing what we already know. Knowledge cannot be separated from the practical value it has for us. The objects of our environment are always changing and the social conditions never continue in the same form. We have to make fresh adjustment to the changing circumstances, and for this purpose knowledge must reveal the changing aspects of things. The practical side of knowledge cannot be neglected when we consider its epistemological worth. Thus, according to the Bhāṭṭa, a valid knowledge is essentially useful and hence it must reveal something new.

Here a theoretical difficulty arises: Should a continuous perception (*dhārāvāhika jñāna*) of something be treated as valid or not? We have such perceptions very frequently, and what the perception reveals in the subsequent moments does not appear to be different from what it revealed in the first moment. For instance, I have a flower on my table and look at it continuously for some seconds; but I do not find it different in later seconds from what I find it in the first second. The cognitions other than that of the first second do not reveal anything new. Should they

3. Ibid.
4. NRM, p. 35.

then be invalid? The Bhāṭṭa answer is that newness marks every-one of these cognitions, because, though the object of all such cognitions is identically the same, yet it is cognized as existing in a different moment of time in each. The existence of the flower in a subsequent moment cannot be apprehended by its cognition in the preceding moment. If time-moments are symbolized by t_1, t_2, t_3 etc. and the perceived object by O, then the object of the first-moment cognition is Ot_1, that of the second-moment cog-nition is Ot_2 and so on. Thus, because each of the cognitions reveals a new thing, all are valid.

It may be objected that though there is a difference among the successive moments of time, yet it cannot be cognized because it is too subtle. The answer is that such statements as 'I have been seeing this thing since morning till now,' 'I saw the thing just in the preceding moment' and the like become unintelligible if the difference of time is not perceived. In this we have a direct consciousness of time. Time is not imperceptible as the Vaiśeṣikas hold. It is true that time has no shape, but perceptibility has nothing to do with shape. That of which we have a direct con-sciousness is perceptible. Therefore, continuous perception is not excluded when vaild knowledge is defined as the cognition of a previously unknown real object.[5]

The Sāṅkhya and Vedānta systems also define valid knowl-edge along the Bhāṭṭa line. They recognize novelty as a mark of valid knowledge and try to justify the novelty of successive cognitions in a continuous perception similarly. But unlike the Bhāṭṭa they offer an alternative solution of the difficulty. They assert that the continuous perception of an object, for instance a jar, is one cognition and not a series of successive cognitions, because the mental mode (*antaḥkaraṇavṛtti*) that assumes the shape of the jar is one and lasts till another mode arises. Thus, the cognition is one and has one object throughout its duration. The numerical difference among cognitions should be based on that of their objects and not on the moments of time. If I perceive a jar continuously for five seconds, I do not have five cognitions but one. If I perceive a jar continuously for the first three seconds

5. SD, pp. 45-46; KK on SV, 5.11.

and then a flower for the next two seconds, I have two different cognitions and not five.

This seems to be a better solution and it must be accepted by the objector. If the number of cognitions is supposed to depend on the number of time-units merely there is a serious difficulty. A moment or a second is merely a conventional time unit. However small a time-unit may be it can further be divided into still smaller units and thus a perception of one moment's duration may theoretically be resolved into an infinite number of cognitions !

Now, suppose a mental mode is in the shape of a jar for five seconds, then in the shape of a flower and again in the shape of the same jar. Does the later cognition of the jar reveal something different from the first one? In this case the Sāṅkhya and the Vedānta cannot say anything except what the Bhāṭṭa has said. Let us examine the case closely. When I perceive the same jar for a second time, I may judge it merely as 'a jar' or as 'the previously known jar existing now.' The two contents of consciousness differ slightly. In the former consciousness time element is not a part of the content, while in the latter it is a part of the content. It is obvious that the latter cognition reveals a new feature in the already known jar and thus the definition of valid knowledge applies here. But what about the validity of the cognition of the known jar simply as a jar? The Bhāṭṭa is not at all hesitant to call it valid, because its object, the jar, is new in that it is the known jar belonging to a new moment of time.

Now, leaving newness as a mark of valid knowledge aside for the time being a more general question may be asked: Is it proper to go beyond the cotent of consciousness when we examine the epistemological worth of a cognition? We can estimate the worth of the judgment 'this is a jar' in a variety of ways. We can say that it is informative or that it is useful or that it is useless and many more things. But all these are different from the purely epistemological judgment of value 'it is true' in that they have no reference to the correspondence of the content to reality, which is inherent in all cognition. A cognition claims to reveal things as they are. We call a cognition valid or invalid according as we find this claim to be right or wrong. A cognition can claim the truth of only so much as it contains. Therefore, it is not proper to go beyond its content. Epistemologically it is enough if we find the truth-claim of a cognition to be legitimate. Hence the consideration of newness or usefulness is extraneous to the epistemological value of a cognition. 'This is a jar' and 'this jar has a new feature' are independent cognitive judgments and they are separately true if 'a jar' and 'a jar having a new feature' are facts. The latter fact does not affect the truth of the first judgment.

3.2. *The Sāṅkhya View*

The Sāṅkhya defines valid knowledge as the mode of *buddhi* which apprehends an object, undoubted, real and not known before.[6] The definition, like the Bhāṭṭa one, recognizes novelty, absence of doubt and truth as the essential marks of valid knowledge. Both the Sāṅkhya and the Bhāṭṭa are realists. But there is one important difference between the two. According to the Sāṅkhya *buddhi* or cognition assumes the form of the object. Thus the truth of a cognition consists in its being a faithful copy of the object. Valid knowledge has correspondence to its object in the sense in which a true copy has it to its original. But the Bhāṭṭa is opposed to the copy-theory of knowledge. According to him cognition is formless. Knowledge reveals objects, but it does not assume any form. Knowledge is judgmental. It arises in the form of such judgments as 'this is a jar,' 'this is blue' etc., but not in the form of pictures. When I see a rose, I judge it to be a rose, and my seeing is true because the rose is actually there, not because I have a picture in my mind which faithfully copies the rose.

3.3. *The Vedānta View*

The Vedāntic definition of validity has more points of disagreement. Dharmarājādhvarīndra gives two alternative definitions, viz., "valid knowledge is that knowledge which apprehends an object that is not already known and which is not contradicted" and "valid knowledge is an uncontradicted knowledge."[7] The first definition excludes memory from valid

6. SK, 4.
7. VP, p. 6.

knowledge, while the second includes it. Thus the Vedāntin is not necessarily opposed to memory and he does not mention certitude as an essential mark of valid knowledge. However, both the Vedāntin and the Bhāṭṭa mention *abādhitatva* or non-contradiction as a mark of validity. There is a more outstanding difference between the two in that the Vedāntin distinguishes between relative and absolute truth, while for the Bhāṭṭa all truth is absolute and all that is not absolutely true is false. Dharmarājādhvarīndra says : "The term 'not contradicted' (*abādhita*) means not contradicted during the transmigratory state."[8] All empirical cognitions according to the Vedāntin, are true only so long as the ultimate truth, the identity of all existence, is not realized. Even the illusory cognition and dream cognition are true so long as they last. But the Bhāṭṭa is definitely opposed to the truth of illusions and dreams and to the falsehood of empirical cognitions.[9]

3.4. *The Buddhist View*

The Buddhist view of valid knowledge is apparently the same as that of Kumārila. Dharmottara defines valid knowledge as the knowledge of a previously unknown thing (*anadhigata-viṣayaṃ pramāṇam*).[10] The knowledge of an already known thing is not valid because the function of knowledge is to prompt activity in relation to a thing that is presented by it and thus to help in securing it, while if a thing has already been secured there is no use of a further knowledge of it. So memory is not valid knowledge. Similarly, doubt and error too are excluded from valid knowledge. Doubt presents objects indefinitely as existing and not existing at the same time. But there is no object in the world which can exist and not exist simultaneously. Obviously such an object cannot be attained. Error presents an object which does not exist and so one which is incapable of being attained. Again valid knowledge is defined as that which in not contradicted (*avisaṃvādaka*). But here non-contradiction is conceived in a way different from the Bhāṭṭa. If knowledge shows an object and leads to it, it is uncontradicted. Knowledge

8. Ibid. p. 7.
9. SV, *Nirālambana*, 6, 10.
10. NBT, p. 3.

is sought for the sake of successful practical activity by people desirous of an effective dealing with objects. Therefore, valid knowledge is that alone which presents objects capable of fulfilling our pragmatic needs.[11]

The Buddhist conception of truth is pragmatic, while the Bhāṭṭa conception is realistic. According to the Buddhist a knowledge is true if it harmonizes with volitional experience; truth does not consist in its harmony with the real nature of objects, because reality is dynamic, while knowledge represents it as static. If water is perceived and we can go and quench our thirst with it, our perception is true; otherwise it is false. Thus volitional satisfaction constitutes truth; it is not merely a test of truth as the Naiyāyika holds. Correspondence is a meaningless term for the Buddhist, because objects of knowledge are changing from moment to moment, so that correspondence can never be established.

The Buddhist conception of truth has been criticized severely. The Buddhist definition is too wide because it applies to such cases of memory also as possess practical efficiency. It is too narrow because it does not apply to inferential cognitions of past and future objects, which lack practical efficiency.[12] If truth is equated with practical efficiency, the knowledge of such objects as are destroyed instantaneously after their birth, e.g., lightning, will always be false, because they cannot be attained.[13] Again, a cognition showing water to a man who is not thirsty, inspiring no practical activity in him, will be false and the cognition of water in a dream leading to the satisfaction of the dreamer's thirst will be true.[14] The Buddhist wrongly equates truth with practical efficiency. A true knowledge helps us in practical activities. Effective action presupposes a true knowledge of things, but there are other conditions too which are essential. A true cognition presents an object as it actually is, practical efficiency being merely its effect. A cause cannot be identified with its effect. All true knowledge is true independently of the practical value that it may possess.

11. अर्थक्रियासमर्थवस्तुप्रदर्शकं सम्यज्ज्ञानम् । Ibid.
12. MM, p. 1.
13. KK on SV, 2. 76.
14. TT, p. 65.

3.5. *The Nyāya View*

The Nyāya defines valid knowledge as an apprehension of some object (*arthopalabdhi*), which is definite (*asandigdha*) and non-erroneous (*avyabhicāri*).[15] It does not include 'apprehension of the unapprehended' in the definition of validity. Jayanta asserts that the Bhāṭṭa definition is too narrow, because it is not applicable to continuous perception which is definitely the apprehension of the apprehended. Continuous perception of a thing, e.g., the palm, does not reveal any new feature in it even if we observe it for hours.[16] But if newness is not accepted to be a mark of valid knowledge, memory will become valid knowledge. Jayanta says that memory is not valid and that it is excluded from valid knowledge by the insertion of the word *arthopalabdhi* in the definition. What Jayanta means by this word is that valid knowledge is 'an apprehension produced by an object' (*arthajanyopalabdhi*). Memory, then, is invalid on the ground that it is not generated by the object that is remembered, but by its impression left by a former experience on the mind. But if this be correct, the inference of a past object will be invalid. I see that the river in front of me is overflowing its banks today and its water has become muddy while yesterday it was crystal-clear. From this I infer that it must have rained heavily. My knowledge of the past rain is not produced by the rain itself. Is it, then, invalid? Jayanta says that it is valid according to the definition. The rain that is inferred is cognized as a qualification of the river in the form 'the river is one whose past is characterized by the occurrence of rain'; and though this qualification is inferred, the qualified object, the river, is present and produces its cognition directly. The knowledge of future events also is explained similarly. For example, I know that my brother will come tomorrow. Though this event, which will occur tomorrow, cannot be the direct cause of my present cognition, yet 'my brother,' whose qualification is the event, exists now and gives rise to this cognition.

Jayanta's explanation appears to be ridiculously far-fetched. While it is quite obvious that my present cognition of the river

15. NM, p. 12.
16. Ibid., p. 22.

overfilled with muddy water is produced by a present fact, it is quite inconceivable how my present cognition of the past occurrence of rain can be produced by the same fact. In a general sense the perception and the inference both are produced by the river; but in the former the river is the stimulus, while in the latter it is the reason. Thus Jayanta uses the word *arthajanya* in an ambiguous way. Again, how can the rain be an attribute of the river? Jayanta effects the miracle by a grammatical device; but in this way everything can be made an attribute of any present thing. Again, how can a presently existing object, 'my brother,' produce its cognition in my mind when it is not before me? Certainly, Jayanta cannot be supposed to believe in telepathic communication. In the inference of the past rain from the perception of the river the latter does not directly produce the former but indirectly through the memory of the general relation between a swollen river and rain. Now, I see a book and have the memory of its author who was my teacher. Here too in the same manner my memory is produced by the book indirectly through the revival of an impression and so memory also can be valid like the inference of the past rain. Again, there are cognitions which cannot be related to any present object and cannot be said to be produced by an object by any stretch of imagination, e.g., my cognition that Afghanistan was a part of Aśoka's empire or that God is almighty. But are they, then, all invalid? From these considerations we conclude that the difference between memory on the one hand and perception, inference etc. on the other, cannot be maintained on other grounds except that the former is the cognition of something already cognized while the latter are fresh cognitions, and thus, if memory is to be excluded from valid knowledge, it can be done only by inserting 'apprehension of the unapprehended' in the definition of valid knowledge. The later Naiyāyikas, being aware of the difficulties involved in Jayanta's definition, defined valid knowledge as 'true experience' (*yathārthānubhava*) and they opposed experience to memory by asserting that an experience is a cognition different from memory.

Before considering other views of valid knowledge we may briefly examine Jayanta's remark that 'nothing new is seen even if I observe my palm a hundred times'. Modern psychology tells us that we cannot attend to the same thing for more than a few seconds and that in such cases as when we apparently observe the same thing for a long time we are actually discovering new features in the object; and when all the interesting details have been discovered attention moves on to a new object. Thus when I observe my palm I really observe the fingers, the colour, the lines etc. one by one, so that I cannot have identically the same object for all my successive cognitions.

3.6. *The Vaiśeṣika View*

Praśastapāda in his *Bhāṣya* on the *Vaiśeṣika Sūtra* nowhere defines valid knowledge, but he distinguishes between *vidyā* and *avidyā*, the former including perception, inference, *ārṣa* (the intuitions of the seers) and memory, and the latter including doubt, illusion, indefinite cognition (*anadhyavasāya*) and dream. Śrīdhara commenting on the *Bhāṣya* defines *vidyā* as a firm, uncontradicted and definite cognition.[17] It is plain that *vidyā* is valid knowledge and *avidyā* invalid knowledge and that memory is valid knowledge. This definition mentions an additional mark of valid knowledge, viz., *adhyavasāya*. It is meant to exclude *anadhyavasāya* or indefinite cognition such as 'what this may be', which lacks assurance like doubt, but differs from the latter in that the object in it is not conceived in two or more conflicting ways. It is more like absence of cognition. Śrīdhara introduces some inconsistency in the *Bhāṣya* view by distinguishing *vidyā* from *pramāṇa*. He says that memory is *vidyā* or true cognition, but it is not *pramāṇa* or valid cognition, because it reveals an object as past and as already known.[18] In this respect he appears to be influenced by the Nyāya view. But if his view is accepted as a correct interpretation of the *Bhāṣya* of Praśastapāda, it is practically identical with the Bhāṭṭa view of valid knowledge as a definite, true and new cognition.

3.7. *The Jaina View*

The Jaina thinker, Ratnaprabhācārya, a commentator on Vādidevasūri's *Pramāṇanayatattvālokālaṅkāra*, criticizes the

17. निःसन्दिग्धाबाधिताध्यवसायात्मिका प्रतीतिर्विद्या । NK, p. 172.
18. NK, p. 257.

Bhāṭṭa definition of valid knowledge on the ground that it excludes recognition.[19] But this is emphatically denied by Kumārila. Kumārila says:

> That part of perception which has been perceived before cannot be said to be perceived but the present existence is not got at by any previous perception.[20]

In recognition, e.g., 'this is the same man whom I met yesterday', there is an element of memory; still recognition is valid, because it is not a mere repetition of some past experience—it combines the memory-element with the sense-element which reveals a new feature in the remembered object. Vādidevasūri defines valid knowledge as a determinate cognition which apprehends itself and an object.[21] Ratnaprabhācārya explains 'determinate cognition' as that which determines an object in the form in which it really exists. Accordingly, absence of doubt and truth are recognized as the essential marks of valid knowledge, while newness is rejected and thus memory is accepted as a form of valid knowledge.

3.8. *The Prābhākara View*

Śālikanātha, a commentator of Prabhākara, criticizes the Bhāṭṭa definition of valid knowledge as follows:

In a continuous perception the successive cognitions apprehend the same object; so all the cognitions except the first cease to be valid. Kumārila says that they are valid as they apprehend different moments of time. But the difference between two successive moments of time cannot be apprehended, because it is too subtle. Thus the Bhāṭṭa definition is too narrow (*avyāpta*). Again, the word *dṛḍha* in that definition is useless. This word is inserted with a view to exclude doubt from valid knowledeg; but doubt is already excluded when valid knowledge is defined as an apprehension of the previously unapprehended. Doubt is not one cognition. When some tall object is cognized indefinitely as 'a

19. PNT, p. 22.
20. SV, 5. 233, 234.
21. स्वपरव्यवसायिज्ञानं प्रमाणम् । PNT, p. 19.

man or a post', the tallness is perceived which revives the memories of 'man' and 'post' in the mind, and the perceiver doubts whether the tallness belongs to a man or a post. Here the element of perception is valid and the element of recollection is invalid, because it is the apprehension of the apprehended. Therefore, the Bhāṭṭa definition is redundant. It is redundant in one more respect. The word *avisaṃvādi* (unerring) is absolutely unnecessary, because all knowledge which is not memory, is true. Even illusions are true so far as they are of the nature of experience (*anubhūti*) while the element of memory in them is false.[22]

Prabhākara's definition of valid knowledge is the same as that of later Nyāya except that he does not feel the necessity of including the term *yathārthatva* in the definition. Śālikanātha gives the definition of valid knowledge in the following verse :

> *Anubhūtiḥ pramāṇaṃ sā smṛteranyā smṛtiḥ punaḥ/*
> *Pūrvavijñānasaṃskāramātrajaṃ jñānamucyate//* (PP, p. 127)

"Valid knowledge is experience, and it is something different from memory which is the name of that cognition which arises from the impression left by some previous experience." In a continuous perception the later cognitions arising from sense-object intercourse, like the first cognition, are different from memory, and hence they are valid. Recognition too is valid, because it is not produced solely from impression. It is an experience aided by impression. Memory is not valid inasmuch as it depends on a former experience. It does not determine an object independently. Sometimes a past experience reinstates itself and its past character is forgotten and thus it appears to be a new experience instead of a recollection. It also is invalid because it depends solely on impression for its birth.[23]

Prabhākara's definition of valid knowledge as *anubhūti* is vague, for it is difficult to define the term *anubhūti*. From the verse quoted above it is obvious that *anubhūti* is a cognition other than memory and that it is produced sometimes by such causes as the operation of the senses which are different from impressions and sometimes by the cooperation of such causes with impres-

22. PP, pp. 40-42.
23. Ibid., p. 42.

sions as in the case of recognition and inference. So far there is no difficulty. But the difficulty arises when Śālikanātha differentiates *anubhūti* from memory on the ground that the former does not depend on any other cognition while the latter depends on a past cognition. Inference depends on the recollection of a general rule and the perception of some mark, and determinate perception (*savikalpaka pratyakṣa*) too depends on the indeterminate (*nirvikalpaka*) perception. Then, are they not *anubhūti* ? If they are not *anubhūti* they can never be valid according to the definition of valid knowledge.[24] Again, there is a practical difficulty also. We are ordinarily aware, when a cognition arises, of its being a memory if it is memory and thus by the method of exclusion we can easily know whether a cognition is memory or *anubhūti*. But sometimes when memory is obscured a memory-cognition is taken to be *anubhūti* and sometimes an *anubhūti* is taken to be a memory-cognition. Now, as there is no means of knowing the real nature of a cognition except our direct consciousness, we cannot be confident in the above cases as to the correctness of our judgment of validity or invalidity. Prabhākara says that memory is invalid. But he merely says it dogmatically without showing any reason why it should be branded invalid. After all it is also a form of knowledge like *anubhūti*. Kumārila, on the other hand, points out that memory repeats an old experience and does not add anything new to what we already know.[25] The difference between *anubhūti* and memory cannot be other than that the former gives something new while the latter repeats an old experience, and if Prabhākara chooses to appeal to reason rather than be dogmatic, he cannot offer any other ground for the invalidity of memory save its being an apprehension of the apprehended. Hence he cannot but recognize newness as a condition of validity.[26]

Again, Prabhākara's definition is too wide as it applies to doubt and illusion also.[27] He says that doubt and illusion are valid so far as they are *anubhūti*. But this is wrong. The duty of a philosopher is to examine the grounds of the concepts that are

24. SD, p. 45.
25. SV, 5.11.
26. KK on SV, 5.11.
27. MM, p. 6.

universally held and not to destroy them. So Prabhākara cannot go against the verdict of common-sense that doubt and illusion are invalid. He says that doubt and illusion are invalid so far as the element of memory is involved in them. But they are not recognized by people to be invalid on the ground of the memory-element, but on that of their being respectively unassured and false. Therefore, Prabhākara has to accept newness, certitude and truth as the essential characteristics of valid knowledge, and thus all his objections against the Bhāṭṭa definition fall to ground.

Pārthasārathi points out some inconsistencies in Prabhākara's view. According to Prabhākara's definition a dream-cognition, which arises solely from mental impressions, is invalid; but this is not consistent with his view that a dream-cognition is valid so far as the elements of cognition and the cognizer in it are concerned. In all cognitions, whatever their status, the self and the cognition are, according to Prabhākara, necessarily known and validly known, and dream-cognition too is a cognition. If Prabhākara says that a dream-cognition, being memory in respect of its object and *anubhūti* in respect of its form and the cognizer, is partly valid and partly invalid, then recognition too, involving an element of memory and an element of *anubhūti*, must be branded partly valid and partly invalid. But this is against the universally accepted opinion of people. Either a cognition is wholly valid or wholly invalid. Practical activities of life cannot be based on partly valid and partly invalid cognitions. Again, the illusion of a yellow conch will be wholly valid as it does not involve any element of memory and, thus, is purely an *anubhūti*; but none can accept this.[28] Prabhākara's definition is not a definition of valid knowledge at all. When it is said that all knowledge except memory is valid knowledge, Prabhākara must have the generally accepted conception of validity in his mind and after examining all knowledge in the light of that conception he must have arrived at the above conclusion.

3.9. *Forms of Invalid Knowledge*

Valid knowledge is a true and definite knowledge of some new fact. If any knowledge lacks definiteness or certitude or does not

28. SD, p. 45.

convey any new information or does not represent things as they really are, it is invalid. Kumārila says that there are three kinds of invalid knowledge, viz., error or illusion (*mithyājñāna*), non-cognition or ignorance (*ajñāna*) and doubt (*saṃśaya*)[29]. In this statement there is no mention of memory which is definitely invalid according to him. Elsewhere he says that validity consists in knowing something new and that if a knowledge does not give anything new, it is memory.[30] It is strange why he did not mention memory as a form of invalid knowledge together with the other forms. It appears that in the section in which he mentions the three forms of invalid knowledge truth was his only concern, and as memory is not untrue, it was not mentioned by him. Pārthasārathi says:

> Validity does not consist in the truth (*tathātva*) of knowledge alone. However, in the present section (dealing with *svataḥ-prāmāṇya*) this much alone is to be considered whether the truth of a knowledge is ascertained by the knowledge itself or by other considerations extraneous to the knowledge... Newness of a knowledge is not known from the form of the knowledge, but from the non-cognition of what is fit to be cognized (*yogyānupalabdhi*). The cognition of a jar for instance, does not by itself reveal that the jar was previously unknown.[31]

Thus illusion, ignorance and doubt are definitely false, while memory is not false. All knowledge may be classified into that which is valid and that which is invalid. Invalid knowledge, again, may be classified into that which is false and that which is true, and ignorance, doubt and illusion belong to the former class while memory belongs to the latter.

Sucaritamiśra divides invalid knowledge into illusion, doubt, memory and *saṃvāda* which together with valid knowledge make up the five forms of knowledge.[32] In this list there is no mention of ignorance as a form of invalid knowledge. In fact ignorance

29. SV, 2. 54.
30. SV, 5.11.
31. NRM, p. 35.
32. प्रमाणं भ्रमः संशयः स्मरणं संवाद इति पंचधा ज्ञानं विभजामहे । KK on SV, 2.20.

is not invalid knowledge. Validity and invalidity are the properties of knowledge and not of the absence of knowledge. It is true that ignorance or absence of knowledge does not help us in the practical activities of life for which a true knowledge of objects is essential. But the practical disadvantage which is caused by ignorance does not justify our branding it invalid. It is always some knowledge that is judged to be valid or invalid. To call absence of knowledge 'invalid knowledge' is self-contradictory. It is as absurd as to say that a barren mother's son is a disobedient son. Kumārila seems to argue in the following way:

All valid knowledge is knowledge;
No ignorance is knowledge;
∴ No ignorance is valid knowledge.
No invalid knowledge is valid knowledge;
No ignorance is valid knowledge;
∴ All ignorance is invalid knowledge.

In this reasoning the first argument, being the mood *camestres* in the second figure, is correct while the second argument, drawing an affirmative conclusion from two negative premises, is wrong.

3.9.1. *Saṃvāda*

Sucaritamiśra mentions *saṃvāda* as a form of invalid knowledge. Suppose some reliable person tells that there is fire at a distance. Now I go further and see smoke rising skywards and then I infer fire from the smoke. Next I approach the place where smoke was seen and actually perceive the fire. According to Sucaritamiśra the inference and the perception of fire simply restate what I have already learnt from the trustworthy person, and, because they do not add anything new to what I already know, they are invalid while the first cognition is valid. Thus *saṃvāda* is invalid like memory.[33] *Saṃvāda* and memory are alike in that they do not reveal any new truth, but they are different in that the former is presentative while the latter is representative. Next we describe the other more obviously invalid forms of knowledge.

33. KK on SV, 2.74.

3.9.2. *Memory*

Memory is the revival of past experience. It always refers to the past. When some object or event is remembered, it is always known to have existed or occurred in the past. Memory presupposes a direct experience of the remembered object on some past occasion. None can remember a thing which was not experienced by him. The basis of memory is some impression (*saṃskāra*) left on the soul by an experience. Our experiences modify the soul in some way and these modifications are preserved in the soul. These modifications of the soul-substance are called impressions and they are the direct cause of recollection.[34] The impressions are usually dormant and inactive. However active they may be in influencing our conduct, we do not consciously feel their presence. But when they are aroused by certain external or internal causes (*udbodhaka*) and our past experiences reappear in consciousness, we indirectly know their presence.

Some memories require an effort and some are spontaneous.[35] The former are voluntary and are the result of mental concentration (*manaḥpraṇidhāna*). The latter memories crop up automatically in consciousness due to the perception of similar things (*sadṛśadarśanāt*) or to some peculiarities of place and time. External objects help the reappearance of past experiences. Some memories are due to the agency of merit and demerit. Such memories cause pleasure or pain to us and thus they serve a moral purpose.[36]

Not only the experiences of the present life are remembered, but even those of past lives can be remembered by persons advanced in the practice of concentration.

Memory proves the identity and the continuity of soul. It is not possible unless the person who remembers be the same who had the original experience in the past. Memory proves the existence of the inner sense-organ. The external sense-organs cannot explain memory, because we are able to recollect something, e.g., colour of an object, even when the external sense-

34. भावनात्मकस्तु संस्कार आत्मद्रव्यवर्ती विशेषगुणः, पूर्वानुभवोऽस्य कारणं स्मृतिस्तु कार्यम् । MM, p. 254.
35. पारार्थ्येनात्मार्थत्वेन च वशीकृता । NR on SV, *Nirālambana*, 190-93.
36. Ibid.

organs, e.g., the eye, are lost. The inner sense-organ that is operative in causing memory is the *manas*.[37] Memory is different from recognition which is an original experience helped by some impression (*saṃskārasaciva*). Sometimes an old experience is revived without the consciousness of its past character. Dream is an instance of this. A dream occurs as if it were an original experience. But in fact it is nothing but false memory. Dreams appear in the absence of the objects that appear in them. They are caused neither by the activity of the sense-organs which are operative in perception, nor by marks (*liṅga*) which give rise to inference. There can be no other cause of dreams except latent impressions.[38] From the points of view of causation dreams are allied to memory, but from that of appearance they are allied to sensory illusions.

Memory may be true or false according as it reveals a past fact accurately or inaccurately; but it is not a form of valid knowledge, because it does not give a truth hitherto unknown. The ideal knowledge according to the Bhāṭṭa is that which is not only true to reality but also definite and new. Knowledge ought to be a progressive system and not a static one. Memory may be true to reality, but it does not realize the ideal of knowledge completely. Memory is not necessarily false, yet it cannot acquire the status of valid knowledge, because it is not progressive.

We have already referred to the other views of memory and have also shown that the other reasons for rejecting memory as invalid knowledge are ultimately reduced to the reason that memory does not give new knowledge. Here we may again refer to Jayanta's view. He holds that memory is invalid because its object is non-existent at the time of its remembrance.[39] But this does not seem to be a proper reason. It is true that the object of memory is past, but memory does not claim that its object is present. True memory always apprehends a past object as past. Jayanta's statement may be taken to mean that memory is not directly verifiable, because the fact or event that is past

37. मनो हि स्मृत्युत्पत्तौ कारणम् । KK on SV, 4.166.
38. KK on SV, *Śūnya*, 160.
39. तदारूढस्य वस्तुनः तदानीमसत्त्वात् । NM, p. 23.

cannot now be perceived and compared with the content of memory. But this too is not a reasonable ground, because there are cognitions of future objects or events and of invisible things which can never be directly verified and they are not rejected as invalid on this account.

The only reasonable ground for the rejection of memory is the absence of novelty in it and we have already hinted at the inappropriateness of considering novelty in judging the validity of cognitions. Elaborate theories and hypotheses may be examined in the light of Kumārila's ideal of knowledge, but in the case of solitary cognitions it is better not to go beyond their contents. In practice too nobody cares whether a proposition is derived from memory or from some other source of knowledge. If someone asserts that the first atom bomb was dropped in Hiroshima, the epistemological value of the assertion is estimated on the basis of its being a fact. Whether the man asserting the proposition was one of the eye-witnesses now remembering his experience or he learnt it from some reliable source, is irrelevant in considering its validity. Therefore, the whole controversy about the validity of memory seems to be a futile exercise.

3.9.3. *Doubt*

Doubt is an indefinite cognition (*anavadhāraṇātmaka pratyakṣa*), which characterizes an object in mutually conflicting ways. Something is seen, but there does not arise a fixed notion about it whether it is one thing or another. For instance, some tall thing is perceived, but one cannot decide whether it is a man or a post.[40] In a doubtful cognition two or more interpretations of an observed datum are offered, but the mind does not arrive at any fixed decision. Thus doubt is marked by a lack of assurance or belief. It is an unpleasant state of mind in which the mind swings between two or more alternatives without being able to reconcile them. This gives rise to a further exploratory activity of the senses and usually some differentiating mark is found out which ends this unpleasant state. Doubt is not confined to sense-level alone. It is very frequent on the level of higher thought. On the sense-level it occurs under insufficient conditions of sensibility. Sometimes we are confronted by a situation demanding a prompt adjustment which prevents

40. NR on SV, 2.54.

us from making a fuller use of our cognitive faculties and consequently there occurs a doubt.

Kumārila mentions three causes of doubt, viz., the existence of some common quality, the existence of an uncommon quality and the existence of two apparently contradictory qualities. As an example of the first, the existence of the quality of knowability in words leads one to the doubtful notion whether words are eternal or non-eternal, because this quality is found to exist commonly in eternal objects, e.g., the soul, as well as non-eternal objects, e.g., the lightning. A common property leads to no conclusion, because it reminds of two mutually incompatible notions. An uncommon property leads to doubt as follows: Odour is an uncommon property of the earth. It is found neither in eternal things nor in non-eternal things, so that it leads to the negation of both eternality and non-eternality and thus gives rise to a doubt like a common property, because the negation of both eternality and non-eternality is incompatible. The existence of two different properties associated with two contradictory things leads to doubt as follows: Air, for instance, is known to be shapeless and having touch, the former being associated with imperceptibility and the latter with perceptibility. But perceptibility and imperceptibility being contradictory to each other, cannot reside in the same air and consequently there arises a doubt.[41]

Among the three commentators of Kumārila Umbeka accepts these three causes of doubt, while Sucaritamiśra and Pārthasārathi reject uncommon property as one of the causes of doubt. They say that uncommon property is recognized by the Buddhist while Kumārila himself does not recognize it. Sucaritamiśra expresses his view of doubt as follows: Doubt arises from the perception of a common property together with the non-perception of a specific property and the remembrance of objects possessing the common property. For example, from the perception of a vertical height, which is commonly possessed by a man and a post, which are remembered while their differentiating property is not perceived, an indefinite cognition arises in the form 'is it a man or a post'? An uncommon property is not the cause of doubt. Doubt arises when two notions are suggested

41. SV, *Anumāna*, 84-95.

simultaneously, and the mind cannot decide between them. But as an uncommon property, e.g., the odour of the earth, is not concomitant with anything else, it does not suggest anything to the mind, and thus the appearance of doubt is not possible. An uncommon property is merely the cause of curiosity (*jijñāsā-mātrahetuḥ*) and not of doubt. When we observe an uncommon property in something, we simply want to know further details about the thing; it does not suggest conflicting notions to the mind.[42]

Doubt is not valid knowledge, because it lacks belief or firmness which is an essential mark of validity. Doubt neither asserts anything nor denies it positively. It is not a judgment, but a questioning attitude of the mind making no claim to truth.

We have already referred to the Vaiśeṣika view according to which *anadhyavasāya* is a form of *avidyā* or invalid knowledge different from doubt. Sucaritamiśra criticizes this view and says that it is not a form of cognition at all. In cognition something is predicated of something either in a decisive or in an indecisive manner, while in *anadhyavasāya*, as 'what this may be', there is no predication of any form. The so-called *anadhyavasāya* expresses only an attitude of curiosity, the desire to know something about something, and thus it cannot be a form of knowledge at all, so that the question of its validity does not arise.[43]

3.9.4. *Illusion*

Illusion or error represents an object in a form which does not belong to it. It reveals an object differently from what it actually is.[44] We have instances of illusion in dream which reveals objects which are not actually present, in a jaundiced person's cognition of everything as yellow, in the cognition of a double moon and so on. In a dream an object which is really absent is perceived as present, so that it cannot but be false. Dream-objects exist at other times and places and so far they are real. In dreams objects are recalled due to the revival of memory-images and they falsely appear as existing 'here' and 'now'. Actually they have no relation to the particular time and place in which the sleeping person dreams; but due to defects

42. KK on SV, *Anumāna*, 86, 88.
43. Ibid., 88.
44. अन्यथासन्तमाकारमन्यथा गृह्णाति । NR on SV, *Nirālambana*, 118.

caused by sleep they appear to be related to that place and time. It is only when one returns to the normal waking state that the falsehood of dreams is realized. Dreams not only represent objects existing at distant times and places as present 'here' and 'now', but also reveal objects that we cannot remember as having ever existed. In such cases too the objects are not absolutely non-existent; they existed and were cognized during some past life. Sometimes we dream of such impossible events as our own decapitation. In such a case there is a revival of some experience of decapitation relating to some person and is falsely imagined to be related to the dreamer. Dreams distort reality. They falsely combine together the real elements of waking experience.[45]

In the illusion of nacre as silver or of a rope as a snake the eye is actually in contact with a piece of nacre or a rope, but the appearance is of a piece of silver or a snake. The nacre represented by 'this' is real and the silver too is real as existing elsewhere, but their identity is false. The falsity consists in perceiving silver 'here' and 'now', while it actually exists in a distant place. The cause of the illusion is the similarity between nacre and silver and the defective contact of the eye. The similarity suggests 'silver', while the difference between silver and nacre is not observed, and thus the nacre appears in the form of silver. The silver is the form of cognition, which is super-imposed on the perceived 'this',[46] and this superimposition is not detected till one is prompted to pick it up and is disappointed. In the illusion of mirage water is falsely perceived, while the contact of the eye is actually with sand heated by the sun's rays. The illusion is caused by a two-fold defect, viz., the subjective feeling of thirst and the semblance of water due to heat. The sand and the water are real, but their connection is unreal.[47] These are instances of illusion which persist so long as the real character of the object is not recognized. In these as soon as the illusory nature of cognition is detected the object begins to appear in its real form.

There are some illusions which persist even after the revelation of their falsehood, though they cease to delude us afterwards.

45. SD, p. 58.
46. यादृशं हि ज्ञानस्य स्वरूपं तादृशमेवार्थेऽध्यारोपयतीति यावत् । KK on SV, 2.85.
47. KK on SV, *Nirālambana*, 110.

The illusion of a double moon is of this nature. The illusions of this type differ from others in one more respect. They have all the elements of a sensory character, while others have an element of memory. When the eye is pressed slightly with finger the single moon appears to be double. This also occurs in a disease affecting the eyes. This cognition is false and there is no element of memory in it. There is a double error here. First the single moon is perceived in two places and then the doubleness characterizing the places is transferred to the moon which is really one.[48] In the illusion of a white conch as yellow the mind superimposes the percept of the 'yellow' on that of the 'conch,' thereby establishing a relation which is not there. The yellowness caused by bile really belongs to the rays that go out from the eyes to the object which is not yellow. Similarly in the illusion of a red crystal the percept of red and that of crystal are related together due to the nearness of the red japā flower to the crystal.[49] In the illusion of a firebrand circle (*alātacakra*) the cause is the quick circular motion of the firebrand. The firebrand and circularity both are real, but they are falsely related together.[50]

Illusion is a form of invalid knowledge like doubt and memory, but it is different from them. Doubt is invalid not because it is false but because it lacks certitude. It makes neither a definite assertion nor a definite denial. Illusion, on the other hand, makes a definite assertion such as 'this is silver'. There is a feeling of confidence in it as it is there in a valid cognition. The illusory silver is perceived as definitely as the real silver. The difference between the two is discovered only when our attempt to pick up the 'silver' fails. We are as confident of perceiving 'water' in a mirage as of the real water, and it is only on a closer inspection and when there is frustration in the attempt to quench our thirst with it that its illusory character is detected. Unlike memory an illusion is a new experience of some present object. It is invalid because it reveals a present object in the form of a different object. It misrepresents a fact. It distorts the nature of reality and consequently misleads us in practical activity. The object of illusion does not correspond with the real object.

48. SD, p. 59.
49. Ibid.
50. SV, *Nirālambana*, 109.

3.10. *The Bhāṭṭa Theory of Illusion*

The Bhāṭṭa theory of illusion is known as *viparītakhyātivāda*. According to it an illusion manifests a real object in the form of a different object which too is real.[51] In all cases of illusory perception it is only the relation between the subject and predicate elements, e.g., 'this' and 'silver', which is unreal though appearing as real. The relata, however, are always real.[52] Accordingly an illusion is a positive mis-apprehension in which the mistake consists in identifying two unrelated real objects under the influence of some vicious subjective and objective conditions.

This theory is practically the same as the Nyāya theory except that the Bhāṭṭa does not account for illusion through extranormal sense-contact (*alaukika sannikarṣa*). It was pointed out that, excluding dreams, there are two types of illusions, viz., the presentative-representative illusion in which a sensory element and memory element are involved, as in the nacre-silver illusion, and the purely presentative illusions in which only sensory elements are involved, as in the illusion of red crystal. Now the difficulty is: How does the memory element acquire perceptual character in the former illusion ? The Naiyāyika tries to explain it by assuming an extraordinary contact of the eye with the remembered object. Accordingly the eye actually comes in contact with the silver which is elsewhere, e.g., in the shop of the jeweller, through the medium of the idea of silver that is revived in the mind by the perception of characters common to silver and nacre, and this contact is called *jñānalakṣaṇa-sannikarṣa*. Thus in the illusion 'this is silver' both 'this' and 'silver' are perceived, one through normal contact and the other through extra-normal contact with the eye, and the mistake consists in referring 'silver' to the locus of 'this.' This explanation offered by the Naiyāyika does not give any new insight into the perceptual character of the 'silver.' It simply takes for granted that the 'silver' which appears like a percept is actually a percept. Moreover, if both 'this' and 'silver' are perceived, whatever the nature of the

51. तत्र शुक्तिकारजतादिज्ञानं शुक्तिकाख्यं भावं शुक्तिकारूपेण सद्रूपं भावान्तरस्य रजतस्य यत् सद्रूपं रजतरूपं तेन रूपेण गृह्णद् भ्रान्तं भवति । NR on SV, *Nirālambana*, 117.

52. सर्वत्र संसर्गमात्रमसदेवावभासते संसर्गिणस्तु सन्त एव; सेयं विपरीतख्यातिरित्युच्यते मीमांसकैः । SD, p. 58

contacts involved in them may be, the difference between this and the other type of illusion vanishes, because in the latter too both the elements are perceptual. The Bhāṭṭas rightly reject the so-called extra-normal contact. If distant objects could be perceived by an extra-normal contact, everyone would become omniscient.[53]

Modern psychological experiments show that though an image is less vivid in comparison to a percept and consequently the former can be easily distinguished from the latter, yet under imperfect conditions of sensibility, e.g., low illumination, they are apt to be taken for one another. Boring and others in *Psychology* (the chapter on images) describe an experiment in which some subjects were asked to think on a particular theme and look at a thin curtain behind which some objects connected with the theme were moved across slowly by the experimenter under very low illumination. The result was that the subjects 'saw' many forms on the curtain which were not actually shown to them. The conclusion that we draw from this experiment is that there is no essential difference between images and percepts. Thus an image may be taken for a percept when the intensity of real percepts is lowered and also when the intensity of the image is strengthened by a stimulus resembling it, as in the case of nacre-silver illusion. The Gestalt school of modern psychology has drawn our attention to a very important fact of perception, viz., that even in true percepts the details of the perceived object are not actually seen but are supplied by imagination by a process of 'filling up the gaps.' Thus perception is a constructive process guided by some given sense-elements and illusion differs from it in being a misguided constructive process. During sleep the conditions are more favourable for taking images for percepts. We know images as images during waking hours because we compare them with actual percepts which offer a contrast by their superior intensity and because they do not fit in the environment of perceived objects. But during sleep there are no percepts and there is no objective environment so that the images are always taken for percepts. Therefore, for the expla-

53. एवं हि न कश्चिदसर्वज्ञो भवेत्। KK on SV, 5.114.

nation of the perceptual character of illusions there is no need of assuming an extraordinary contact.

According to the theory of *viparītakhyāti* the object of an illusion is real, though its connection with the place and time in which it is seen is unreal. To this the Buddhist objects : How can the absent object, e.g., the 'silver', give rise to its cognition 'here' and 'now'? Sucaritamiśra's answer is as follows: An absent object has the power of producing its cognition though it has no power to inspire other fruitful practical activities in relation to it. In an illusion due to defective sense-functioning an absent object appears to be present through the impression left in the mind by its past experience. A past object, e.g., the 'silver', is not capable of producing its present cognition directly; it is capable of it indirectly through its impression residing in the soul. It could not have the said causal potency if it were absolutely non-existent. The 'silver' that is seen does exist in other places and so there is no absurdity in attributing causal potency to it. In the original experience the object 'silver' was the direct cause of its impression produced in the soul. Thus the cognition producing power of the object was indirectly transferred to the soul, which now gives rise to the cognition of 'silver'.[54]

3.11. *The Theories of Illusion in the Other Schools*

Among the other Indian philosophers the ways of explaining error widely differ. They advocate a theory of illusion suited to their respective metaphysical views. The Bhāṭṭa and the Naiyāyika approach the problem in a purely empirical and psychological way and they are also supported by commonsense. Most of the other philosophers suffer from some metaphysical bias which vitiates their treatment of error. In the works of different writers of the Bhāṭṭa school there are references to Prabhākara's theory of *akhyāti,* the Advaita Vedānta theory of *anirvacanīyakhyāti* and the allied theory of *alaukikakhyāti*, and the Buddhist theories of *asatkhyāti* and *ātmakhyāti*; but there is no reference to Rāmānuja's theory of *satkhyāti.*

3.11.1. *Asatkhyātivāda*

The Mādhyamika 'nihilist', according to all the Indian systems, advocates the voidness (*śūnyatā*) of all existence.

54. KK on SV, *Nirālambana*, 115-18.

He arrives at this conclusion by way of a dialectical examination of all the categories of thought. Accordingly he explains error as the apprehension of non-being (*asat*). Pārthasārathi says that the upholders of *asatkhyātivāda* negate the relata together with the relation, while the upholders of *viparītakhyātivāda* negate the relation only.[55] In the illusion 'this is silver' 'this' is real and 'silver' too is real; but their relation is totally unreal. But, according to the 'nihilist' 'this' and 'silver' are as unreal as their relation. Thus the object of illusion for the 'nihilist' is absolutely unreal, while for the Bhāṭṭa it is real in a different place and time. But how can an absolutely unreal object give rise to its direct apprehension?[56] We know that a sky-flower is absolutely unreal, and however much we try to think of it, it can never be the content of our immediate consciousness. Therefore, the 'silver' that is directly perceived in the nacre-silver illusion, cannot be absolutely unreal like a sky-flower as the 'nihilist' holds.

Here we may refer to Dr. Maitra's interpretation of the *asatkhyātivāda*. He says:

> Now when the cogniser is in error, he cognises, according to the Buddhist nihilist, an absolute nought in one or the other of the above two senses (i.e. the factually non-existent or the logically impossible), for what he cognises is a combination of incompatibles which is without its parallel in experience....He thus perceives what nowhere exists; the snake may exist, but a rope-snake is nowhere found except in cognitions of the false.[57]

This seems to be a wrong interpretation because the 'nihilist' not only negates a rope-snake as absolutely non-existent, but also the rope and the snake. And even if this interpretation be allowed, it goes against experience, because the rope-snake is not at all the content of consciousness in the said illusion. What is perceived in the illusion is the snake alone just as it happens in the perception of a real snake, so that the question of reality or unreality arises only regarding the snake and not the rope-snake;

55. असत्ख्यातिवादिनस्तु संसर्गिणोऽप्यपलपन्तीति विशेषः। SD, p.58.
56. निरुपाख्यानस्यापरोक्षाभासगोचरत्वानुपपत्तेः। SC, p. 50.
57. *Studies in Philosophy and Religion*, p. 212.

and so far as the absolute non-existence of a thing which is a rope and a snake in one is concerned there can be no disagreement among the Indian philosophers.

3.11.2. *Ātmakhyātivāda*

The Yogācāra idealist is dissatisfied with the metaphysical position of the Mādhyamika. He holds that even if everything be accepted to be absolutely non-existent it cannot be proved unless the absolute reality of consciousness apprehending this fact is accepted. Therefore, consciousness, cognition or idea is the only metaphysical reality. The Yogācāra, consistently with his subjective idealism, explains error or illusion as the externalization or objectification of a subjective idea. In the nacre-silver illusion the subjective silver-form of cognition appears as the form of an external object. The 'silver' is not absolutely unreal as the nihilist says. It is real as a form of the internal cognition, but the mistake consists in taking it to be the form of an external object. The 'silver' is a mental fact whereas in the illusion it is taken for an extramental fact. The Yogācāra does not recognize any cognizer other than the momentary idea. So according to him in illusion a momentary idea cognizes itself as 'external'.

But this view cannot explain the consciousness which sublates an illusory cognition. Afrer the cognition 'this is silver' has occurred it is subsequently contradicted in the form 'this is not silver', and thus the former cognition of silver is rejected as false. But if in illusion a cognition wrongly cognizes itself as 'this,' the sublating consciousness, which corrects the mistake, must appear in the form 'I am silver' instead of the form 'this is not silver.'[58] Actually 'this-ness' (*idantā*) is never sublated, which points to the fact that in illusion a real external object appears in the form of another external object. Thus the Yogācāra theory is wrong.

Again, the metaphysical position of the Yogācāra is that the illusory cognition of silver and the so-called right cognition are equally objectless (*nirālambana*). Accordingly he abolishes the universally recognized distinction between a right and a wrong

58. पुरोवर्तित्वेन रजतस्य धाघेऽहं रजतमिति स्यात्। SC, p. 50.

cognition, which is the basis of all practical activities. The Yogācāra tries to justify this distinction by asserting that the objects of cognitions producing practical efficiency (*arthakriyā*) are *saṃvṛtisatya* (empirically real) while the objects of illusion are *mithyā* (absolutely unreal), though both are equally non-existent as external to cognition. But this is only a verbal device to mislead people and not a proper solution, *Satya* and *mithyā* are mutually exclusive terms. If *saṃvṛti* is not *mithyā* it must be *satya* in the same sense in which cognition is taken to be, and if it is not *satya* it must be *mithyā* like an illusion. The existence of an intermediate entity, partly *satya* and partly *mithyā* is logically impossible.[59] Therefore the distinction between a right and a wrong cognition is ultimate and the latter is not an illegitimate projection of the subjective idea, but the appearance of one real thing as another real thing.

3.11.3. *Anirvacanīyakhyātivāda*

Everyone is aware of the difference between a percept and an image. When nacre is cognized as silver or rope as snake, we are not conscious of a mental image but of a percept. What is cognized in the illusion appears to be a given fact and not an imagined one. The Yogācāra cannot explain the presentative character of illusion. The Advaitin offers the explanation that so long as the illusion of a snake or silver lasts there comes into being the corresponding object which is logically indefinable (*anirvacanīya*). The *viparītakhyātivādin* maintains that in the rope-snake illusion the rope is the object of the perception of snake. But this is absurd. The object of a cognition cannot be other than what is revealed in it. So, the object of the cognition of snake cannot be anything but the snake. The Naiyāyika tries to explain the presentative character of the snake by assuming an extraordinary form of sense-contact with the distant snake. But, when the snake is perceived it is known to be 'here' and not in a distant place, e.g., the jungle. Thus the Advaitin arrives at the conclusion that in the rope-snake illusion the snake must actually be present where it is seen, though it enjoys merely a temporary existence so long as the illusion lasts, and because it can be neither absolutely real nor absolutely unreal, nor both together, it must be indefinable. That which is absolutely real, e.g., the

59. SV, *Nirālambana*, 8.

self, can never be sublated and that which is absolutely unreal, e.g., a man's horn, can never be perceived. The illusory snake is perceived for some time and then sublated by a correcting experience. Therefore, it cannot be absolutely unreal or absolutely real. It canot be both simultaneously, because two contradictory predicates can't qualify the same entity. Hence the illusory snake is indefinable. As this snake cannot be the object of our practical activities, it cannot belong to the order of empirical existence to which the real snake belongs. It belongs to a relatively less real order of being called the *prātibhāsika sattā* or illusory reality.

It may be asked: How can an illusory snake be produced in the absence of a cause at the time? The Advaitin's answer is that an illusory object belongs to a different order of being, so it need not be produced by the same cause as produces the empirical object and the desired cause is present in the form of nescience (*avidyā*), impression (*saṃskāra*) and defective sense-organ which combine together to produce the illusory object on the one hand and the corresponding illusion on the other.[60]

The Bhāṭṭa realist sees many reasons to be dissatisfied with this theory. The Advaitin ascribes to the illusory snake an indefinable nature which is different from the absolutely real and the absolutely unreal on the ground of the inexplicability of its being perceived and being sublated. But if his theory be accepted the inexplicability remains as it is. That which is different from the absolutely real, e.g., a man's horn, cannot be perceived and that which is different from the absolutely unreal, e.g., the self, cannot be sublated; hence the illusory snake, which is supposed by the Advaitin to be different from the absolutely real and the absolutely unreal, can neither be perceived nor be sublated, whereas it is actually perceived and sublated. Thus the difficulty is not really solved.

Again, the Advaitin may be asked: If the object of the illusion 'this is silver' be an indefinable silver, what is the object of the correcting cognition 'this is not silver'? The negation of the perceived indefinable silver cannot be the said object; otherwise the relation of the sublated and the sublator subsisting between the two cognitions will be reversed. In the case of the negation of

60. VP, p. 50.

an indefinable silver by the sublating cognition the latter will be equivalent to 'this is not an indefinable silver'; but, because the perceived silver is supposed to be actually an indefinable silver, this sublating cognition will be false.

The Advaitin may say that the sublating cognition is not false, because, though the indefinable silver was actually present formerly it is no more there now, and this fact is revealed by the sublating cognition. But this is wrong. What the sublating cognition reveals is not the subsequent non-existence of the illusory object, but its non-existence at the time when it was perceived to exist. Thus 'this is not silver' does not mean 'this is not an indefinable silver.' Again, it cannot mean 'this is not the usual empirical silver,' because in that case it will confirm the first cognition, which, according to the Advaitin, cognizes an indefinable silver instead of sublating it and thus its sublatory character will become inexplicable.

The Advaitin may say that the sublating cognition means 'the real silver is absent here.' But in this case the first cognition whose object is an indefinable silver and the subsequent cognition whose object is the absence of a real silver, will be as different as the cognition of a jar and that of the absence of a cloth; and so there cannot be the relation of the sublated and the sublator between them. The two cognitions assert two different things so that there cannot be any opposition between them. Thus the Advaita theory is untenable. The fact is that the first cognition wrongly asserts the identity of 'this' and 'silver' and the second one rectifies the mistake by denying the identity; and this is exactly what the theory of *viparītakhyāti* says.[61]

3.11.4. *Akhyātivāda*

Prabhākara as a staunch believer in the Mīmāṃsā doctrine of self-validity of knowledge reduces all error and doubt to simply an absence of knowledge. He asserts that all experience is valid. "It is strange indeed how a cognition can apprehend an object and yet be invalid."[62] Now if all apprehension is valid, whence do we have the distinction of valid and invalid knowledge? Prabhākara says that so far as the element of apprehension is concerned all the so-called invalid cognitions are valid, while the

61. NTV, pp. 108-11.
62. BR, p. 24.

element that is invalid is no apprehension at all. An illusion is not a unitary cognition but a composite of two cognitions whose distinction is not apprehended. Illusion is not a positive misapprehension but a negative non-apprehension. When we fall a victim to illusion and are misguided by it, the error on our part is not an error of commission but an error of omission. The error occurs not because we misapprehend reality but because we fail to apprehend and thus we miss some relevant feature of reality.

Prabhākara's theory of illusion is called *akhyātivāda* because it interprets illusion as the absence of *khyāti* or knowledge. Prabhākara like the Advaitin holds that the object of a cognition is that alone which is manifested by it. In the illusion 'this is silver' what is manifested is the silver; so its object is the silver and not the nacre as the *viparītakhyātivādin* says. Thus the theory that it manifests an object, the nacre, as a different object, the silver, is disproved by experience.

How can a thing appear in the form of another thing? What happens in the illusion of silver is that a piece of nacre is apprehended generically, while its specific features that distinguish it from a piece of silver, are not apprehended due to their suppression, and then the memory image of silver is suggested to the mind by similarity while the character of its being a memory image is forgotten on account of some weakness. Thus the object of recollection, viz., the silver, is not distinguished from the nacre, and consequently the illusion of silver takes place. The silver is represented and the nacre is presented, but they are not discriminated from each other. Thus the illusion is nothing but an absence of discrimination (*vivekāgraha*). This is why Prabhākara's theory is called *vivekākhyāti*. The cause of the non-discrimination is the obscuration of memory (*smṛtipramoṣa*). The object of memory belongs to the past; it is always referred to as 'that' in contrast with the object of perception which is referred to as 'this,' but when it is stripped of 'that-ness' (*pramuṣṭatattāka*) the memory becomes obscured.

But why should it be called memory when it is not recognized as such? Śālikanātha says that the silver is neither perceived nor inferred, because neither there is a contact of the eye with silver nor there is a mark (*liṅga*) of the presence of silver. Thus by the method of elimination it is concluded that the silver is remembered. Due to non-discrimination the illusory cognition of silver appears as similar to the cognition of real silver, and this prompts some practical activity which is similar to that prompted by the real silver. Consequently one bends down to pick up the 'silver' and is disappointed to find merely a piece of nacre. Then it is realized that 'this' is not silver. The part of the illusory experience that is sublated thus by the subsequent volitional experience is the element of memory, the 'silver,' while the presented element 'this' is not sublated.

In a dream the memory images of past experience are revived by some unseen agency (*adṛṣṭakāraṇa*) and they appear like apprehension because the fact that they are recollected is forgotten.

In the illusion of a yellow conch there are really two cognitions, one apprehending the yellowness of the bile residing in the eye without apprehending the substance, the bile, and the other apprehending the substance of the conch without apprehending its whiteness. Then, because a substance and a quality always stand in mutual expectancy (*ākāṅkṣā*), the two apprehensions cannot remain unrelated, and consequently the manifestation appears as similar to the manifestation of a real yellow conch.

In the illusion of the double moon the rays issuing from the two eyes give rise to two different apprehensions of the moon which is one and the illusion persists in spite of the fact that the oneness of the moon is not forgotten. This is not a case of memory-obscuration. Here as in the 'yellow conch' illusion there is a non-discrimination between two apprehensions and not between one apprehension and one memory image as in nacre-silver illusion.

In all these illusions the non-discrimination is caused by defects. Defects simply disturb the normal functioning of a cause; they cannot give rise to a different effect. A defective seed of wheat results either in a deficient growth or in no growth, but it cannot produce a barley-plant. Similarly, the defects of the senses produce either an incomplete cognition of the nacre or no cognition, but they cannot produce the cognition of an entirely different object, viz., the silver, as the *viparītakhyātivādin* supposes.[63]

63. PP, pp. 32-38.

Sucaritamiśra criticizes Prabhākara's view as follows: Prabhākara says that illusion is not one psychosis but a composite psychosis consisting of a perception and a memory, which in their individual capacity are true. But then an illusion ceases to be invalid. Prabhākara disregards the universally accepted view of people that illusion is a single psychosis aad definitely false. Prabhākara's view that error consists in the non-apprehension of difference (*bhedāgraha*) is not supported by Śabara whom he professes to follow. Śabara has declared in the most unambiguous terms that error consists in a positively false cognition and is due to some defects in the source.[64] He has never mentioned non-apprehension as a cause of error. Moreover what is this non-apprehension? Prabhākara cannot say that it is the negation of apprehension, because he does not accept the reality of negation. Memory which does not appear as memory cannot be equivalent to non-apprehension and consequently the cause of illusion, because memory is correct so far as it reveals an object while illusion is not correct but false. Moreover, when I remember something and fail to be conscious of the fact that I am remembering it, the mistake lies in the memory and not in the perception of 'this'. The remembered silver is different from the perceived 'this'. How can a mistake pertaining to one thing falsify a perception of a different thing? The failure of memory cannot convert the perception of one thing, the nacre, into that of a different thing, the silver. Again, in the illusion 'this is silver' 'this' is perceived and 'silver' is remembered according to Prabhākara; but why should a man, however desirous of silver he may be, bend down to pick up 'this'? Unless the man knows 'this' to be silver he cannot be prompted to possess 'this'. If mere non-discrimination can prompt him to pick up, he can be prompted to pick up a lump of clay too. The lapse of the memory of silver is supposed to be the cause of non-discrimination; but the lapse of memory remains the same even if there be a lump of clay in the place of the nacre. So he must pick up the lump of clay as he picks up the nacre. If Prabhākara accepts that the nacre is perceived as silver in order to explain the practical activity

64. यस्य च दुष्टं करणं यत्र च मिथ्येति प्रत्ययः स एवासमीचीनः प्रत्ययः नान्यः।
SB, p. 50-51

consequent upon the illusion, then he accepts *viparītakhyāti*. The similarity of 'this' with silver cannot be the cause of the practical activity. If a man can pick up nacre due to its similarity with silver, then he can also milk a *gavaya*, knowing that it is similar to a cow. The sublating consciousness appears in the form 'this is not silver,' by which silver-ness is denied of 'this'. A denial presupposes an affirmation. But if the silver is independently remembered as Prabhākara says, the subsequent denial becomes meaningless. As a matter of fact in 'this is silver' 'this' is identified with 'silver' and it is a positive experience like the experience of real silver.[65]

Prabhākara's theory is contradicted by experience. We do not perceive any difference between an illusory silver and a real one so long as the illusion persists. The illusion of silver is taken to be as real and valid as the perception of real silver so long as the mistake is not detected. Illusion does not appear to be a negative non-apprehension of difference (*bhedāgraha*) but a positive apprehension of non-difference or identity (*abhedagraha*). It is this positive character of illusion that urges one to act. We are not conscious of two cognitions in illusion, but of numerically one cognition only. If one does not see 'this' and 'silver' as identical, then prior to the appearance of the sublating consciousness he should be able to apprehend their difference. Moreover, if one who covets silver should fetch the silver thinking that he ought to do so when actually he ought not to do so, then it is *viparītakhyāti*, because that which is not to be done appears as that which is to be done. If it does not appear as that which is to be done, then he will not at all try to fetch it.[66]

3.12. *Conclusion*

Comparing the different theories of illusion we find that everyone of them is deficient in one or more respects. The *asatkhyāti* theory, finding that the object that is perceived in illusion is not actually present in the place where it is observed, draws the exaggerated conclusion that it is absolutely non-existent. The *ātmakhyāti* theory asserts that there exists something corresponding to the illusory object, but it is not an objective

65. KK on SV, 5. 19.
66. SD, p. 59.

fact: it is a subjective idea that wrongly appears as an objective fact in illusion. This theory is wrong in holding that the illusory object has no objective basis and that it is purely a creation of mind. It fails to explain the perceptual character of illusion. The *anirvacanīyakhyāti* theory tries to explain the perceptual character of illusion by assuming the temporary production of a real object corresponding to illusion; but it misses the fact that illusion is a false cognition. The *akhyāti* theory offers a good psychological analysis of illusion and it is right in pointing out that in illusion there is some objective fact which is viewed incompletely and there is the memory image revived due to similarity; but it fails to explain how the memory image is synthesized or fused with the given fact. In fact it denies that there is any synthesis at all and it also denies the falsity of illusion, thereby explaining away a fact of experience. The Nyāya theory of *viparītakhyāti* is more satisfactory except that it makes the unintelligible assumption of an extra-normal sense-contact in order to explain the perceptual character of illusion. Like the Vedānta theory it introduces an extraordinary factor in its account of illusion. While, according to the Vedānta, the object of illusion is extraordinary, according to the Nyāya the sense-functioning is extraordinary. The Bhāṭṭa theory is right in rejecting the assumption of an extraordinary factor and in holding that illusion has an objective basis; but it too fails to explain the perceptual character of the illusory object.

CHAPTER IV

TESTS OF TRUTH AND ERROR

It has been observed that the Bhāṭṭa distinguishes between validity and truth. Validity includes truth, novelty and certitude. Truth is the correspondence of a subjective content with an objective fact. Error or falsehood is the absence of correspondence between them. Our cognitions are expressed in the form of judgments. A judgment relates a subject with a predicate. The nature of negative judgment will be discussed in the chapter on negation. An affirmative judgment asserts the identity of a subject with a predicate. If the asserted identity between the subject and predicate elements is real the judgment is true, but if it is unreal it is false. In the previous chapter the Bhāṭṭa definition of validity was discussed and now our concern is the ascertainment of validity. So far as the novelty and certitude of a valid cognition are concerned there is no difficulty in their ascertainment. Certitude is a subjective feeling of the cognizer that may or may not accompany his cognition and it is immediately known whenever it is present. Novelty is always known through *anupalabdhi* or non-apprehension of the apprehensible. There appears a feeling of unfamiliarity or strangeness when some new thing is cognized. It is the truth of a cognition whose ascertainment is more important. How is truth of a cognition known? It is a question whose answer given by different theorists varies widely. How can we know that a cognition is true? What is the test or criterion of truth? Anything which enables us to decide whether a cognition is true or false may be called the test or criterion of truth. Truth is defined as correspondence; but how can we discover this correspondence? We cannot directly know that a cognition corresponds with a fact, because we cannot know a fact otherwise than through cognition. We discover the correspondence between a face and its photograph because we know them independently of each other. But we cannot know a fact independently of cognition. Hence their correspondence can be known only indirectly. With the question of the knowledge (*jñapti*) of truth there is also the question of the genesis (*utpatti*) of truth. Now we have to see what the Bhāṭṭa view about the genesis and ascertainment of truth is and on what grounds the rival theories are rejected.

Mādhavācārya summarizes the various Indian views in the following verse:

> *Pramāṇatvāpramāṇatve svataḥ sāṃkhyāḥ samāśritāḥ |*
> *Naiyāyikāste parataḥ saugatāścaramaṃ svataḥ—||*
> *Prathamaṃ parataḥ prāhuḥ, prāmāṇyaṃ, vedavādinaḥ|*
> *Pramāṇatvaṃ svataḥ prāhuḥ paratascāpramāṇatām||*
> (SDS, Jaimini Darśana, vv. 10-11)

"The Sāṅkhyas hold that both truth and error are intrinsic, the Naiyāyikas that both these are extrinsic; the Bauddhas say that the latter is intrinsic while the former, truth, is extrinsic; the followers of the Veda (i.e. the Mīmāṃsakas) say that truth is intrinsic and error extrinsic."

4.1. *The Sāṅkhya Theory*

The Sāṅkhya theory of intrinsic truth and error is based on the view that an effect pre-exists in its cause (*satkāryavāda*). That which is absolutely non-existent, e.g., the hare's horn, cannot be produced. Therefore, that which is produced must have pre-existence. There is observed a fixed relation between a material cause, e.g., clay, and its effect, e.g., a pot. Whoever wishes to have a pot can have it out of clay alone. A pot cannot be produced from yarns and a cloth cannot be produced from clay. If a pot were absolutely non-existent prior to its production we could bring it about from yarns as well, because in that case there would be no difference between clay and yarns. Hence it must be accepted that a pot exists in a latent form in clay alone and the operation of an agent consists in actualizing or manifesting this form.

What is generally called production (*utpatti*) is a variety of manifestation (*abhivyakti*). When a pot existing in its full form is hidden by darkness, it is said to be manifested by the action of light which removes the veil of darkness. When a pot existing in a potential form is hidden by another form of clay it is said to be produced by the action of an agent who removes that form of clay which veils the form of the pot. There is no essential difference between the two actions, as both remove an obstruction. Therefore, an effect already exists in its material cause and that which does not so exist can never be accomplished. Thus truth and error are inherent in knowledge. They cannot be brought about by any extraneous means. Truth and error depend on the same causes which produce knowledge and not on any additional factor, e.g., merit or demerit, and they are revealed by knowledge itself. We need not go beyond knowledge for the ascertainment of its truth and falsehood.[1]

The Sāṅkhya theory is based on a wrong view of causation. The view that an effect pre-exists in its material cause is contradicted by non-apprehension (*anupalabdhi*). We never perceive a pot in clay prior to its production. The restriction that a pot can be produced from clay alone and not from any other thing is quite explicable on the ground of difference in potency (*śakti-bheda*). The potency of producing a pot exists in clay alone and not in yarns and other things. This potency is subtle and supersensible. It cannot be directly observed through sense-organs. Its existence is known through presumption (*arthāpatti*). The Sāṅkhya says that the form of a pot is veiled by the form of clay and hence, though it is not open to direct observation, it cannot be said to be non-existent on that account. But what does the Sāṅkhya mean by the form of clay that is supposed to veil the form of a pot? If the genus 'clay-ness' (*mṛttvajāti*) is meant, then, as it persists in all the modifications of clay, the pot-form will ever remain veiled or unmanifested. If by clay-form is meant a former arrangement of the parts of a lump of clay (*prācyo mṛtpiṇḍasanniveśaḥ*), then does it not continue when the pot-form is manifested? The Sāṅkhya maintains that nothing can be destroyed just as nothing can be produced. Accordingly the particular arrangement of the parts of a lump of clay can never be destroyed and consequently the pot-form will ever remain veiled. The Sāṅkhya says that there can be no distinction among

1. KK on SV, 2.34.

a material cause, e.g., clay, an efficient cause, e.g., a potter, and a non-inherent (*asamavāyi*) cause, e.g., the colour of clay otherwise than on the supposition that an effect pre-exists in its material cause. But this can be explained on the ground of difference in potency. Not everything indiscriminately can undergo a particular modification. Clay alone possesses the potency of being modified into a pot-form, while the efficient cause, viz., the potter, can assist only by manipulating a lump of clay from outside—he cannot enter, materially into the effect, viz., the pot. Hence a pot cannot exist prior to its production and when it is produced we definitely recognize that it was non-existent formerly. Thus the theory of *satkāryavāda*, being contrary to facts, cannot be the basis of the intrinsicality (*svatastva*) of truth and error.[2]

Truth and error are two mutually contradictory properties. They cannot reside simultaneously in a cognition, just as heat and cold cannot reside simultaneously in water. Water in its natural form is cold and it acquires heat when it has contact with fire. Similarly, a cognition must have only one form naturally belonging to it and the other form must be accidentally produced in it by some extraneous cause; but it can never be supposed to possess two opposite forms, viz., truth and error, inherently belonging to it. The Sāṅkhya can say that some cognition is inherently true and some inherently false and thus he can avoid self-contradiction. But then it becomes difficult to ascertain which cognition is true and which false. None can be sure of the truth or falsehood of a cognition as soon as it is born. Two individual cognitions, one inherently true and another inherently false, possess in common the property of being a cognition and hence their difference cannot be discerned unless some external indicator is noticed to be present in one and absent from the other. If such an indicator is not recognized, there will be suspension of judgment and consequently all practical activity will be arrested. If some external criterion is resorted to in the discrimination of truth from falsehood, then truth and falsehood cease to be inherent and self-evident and thus the Sāṅkhya has to give up his cherished tenet. If truth and falsehood could be known independently of all extraneous considerations, none would suffer from

2. Ibid. 2. 35.

doubt regarding the real character of a cognition. Therefore the Sāṅkhya view is wrong.[3]

4.2. *The Nyāya Theory*

In opposition to the Sāṅkhya the Naiyāyika maintains that truth and falsehood both are extrinsic to knowledge in respect of genesis as well as of ascertainment. The Nyāya theory receives a brief treatment in the *Ślokavārtika* and its commentaries in which the chief rival is the Buddhist. The Nyāya theory coincides partly with the Buddhist (in respect of the extrinsic nature of truth) and partly with the Bhāṭṭa (in respect of the extrinsic nature of falsehood). Hence the Bhāṭṭa arguments against the Buddhist theory of extrinsic truth are applicable to the Nyāya theory too. Below is given Jayanta's account of the Nyāya theory.[4]

Truth and falsehood are specific qualities of cognition. A cognition is the manifestation of some object, which depends on certain causal conditions, e.g., the operation of sense-organs. Now, while object-manifestation is produced by certain general conditions, truth and falsehood, which are specific features of object-manifestation, must be produced by some specific features of the general conditions. The specific features responsible for the production of truth and falsehood are the merits (*guṇa*) and demerits (*doṣa*) of the conditions of knowledge respectively. Merits and demerits are additional features in the cause of cognition, which add the qualities of truth and falsehood respectively in cognition. Hence truth and falsehood are not intrinsic or natural but extrinsic or adventitious.

Merits and demerits are positive features. Merit is not merely an absence of demerit, nor is demerit a mere absence of merit. It is easy to know from the science of medicine what the merits and demerits of sense-organs are. Even a man with healthy sense-organs acquires certain excellences in them by the use of certain medicines and these excellences are their merits. Diseases, e.g., jaundice, are the demerits of sense-organs.

It is said that effects depend on their causes for their birth but they produce their effects independently of their causes, and

3. KK and NR on SV, 2. 35-37; NTV, pp. 30-33.
4. NM, pp. 170-74.

hence a cognition depends for its birth on the operation of the senses but it produces its effect, viz., the manifestation of its object, independently. Kumārila[5] has offered this as a proof of the intrinsicality of truth. But what, it may be asked, is intended by this independence? So far as the conditions of a cognition are concerned their independence in producing the latter is accepted, but it does not prove that truth is independent of any condition and so natural, because it has been shown as depending on the excellences of the senses. And so far as cognition is concerned the question of its dependence or independence in producing its effect does not arise, because it has no effect. Manifestation of object is not an effect of cognition, but is identical with cognition itself. And if activity in relation to the object revealed to the cognizer is supposed to be an effect of his cognition, then it obviously depends on such additional conditions as the desire of the cognizer etc.

The ascertainment of truth depends on some extraneous considerations just as its production depends on some extraneous factors. At the time of the origination of a cognition there is no knowledge of its truth or falsehood. When the cognition of a blue object arises, the object is known to be blue; but the truth of the cognition is not known at that time, and subsequently when it is known it is not known independently because such knowledge depends on fruitful activity (*pravṛttisāmarthya*). Fruitful activity is the test of truth and fruitless activity (*pravṛttivisaṃvāda*) is the test of falsehood.

But how can, it may be asked, any activity ensue on the cognition of an object unless the cognition is already known as true? The upholder of the intrinsicality of truth says that if the knowledge of truth is supposed to depend on the knowledge of successful action there will be mutual dependence (*anyonyāśraya*), as successful action will then depend on the knowledge of truth and the knowledge of truth will depend on successful action, and again the knowledge of truth will become needless because the object of cognition has already been attained.

The Nyāya reply is that there is no mutual dependence, because practical activity with reference to a perceived object

5. SV, 2.48.

takes place in the absence of the knowledge of truth. When a man perceives water and approaches it to quench his thirst, it is not necessary that he must have ascertained the truth of his perception before proceeding towards it. What prompts him to act is his spontaneous or instinctive belief in the reality of the object of his perception. Whether his belief is justified or not is a different question which is decided by ascertaining the truth of the perception. The case of our knowledge of objects which are not directly perceived is different. There practical activity follows from mere doubt, and if it is found successful the corresponding cognition is judged to be true. Our knowledge of such unseen objects as God, heaven etc., cannot be directly verified, yet we can ascertain its truth by the application of such tests as we might have derived from the verification of our knowledge of perceived objects. The ascertainment of the truth of our knowledge of perceived objects by successful activity, though useless in itself, has the value of giving us a knowledge of the means which distinguishes truth from falsehood and which we can avail ourselves of in judging the truth of our knowledge of unseen objects.

The subsequent volitional experience of successful activity is an external evidence which proves the truth of our cognitions. But is the knowledge of successful activity, it may be asked, intrinsically true or does it require verification like the first cognition of an object? If it is intrinsically true, what is its superiority over the first cognition on account of the absence of which the latter is not held to be intrinsically true? If it requires further verification, then the process of verification will never come to an end and consequently no truth of any knowledge will ever be known.

The Naiyāyika answers that verification is not an endless process, because the knowledge of successful activity does not stand in need of further verification. All knowledge is a means to some practical end and hence it needs to be tested in order to attain practical success. The knowledge of the result, on the other hand, ends in itself, not leading to further result, and hence there arises no need to test its truth. When practical success has been achieved one feels no doubt about it, and, because doubt is the motive behind the ascertainment of truth, the ascertainment of the truth of volitional experience becomes motiveless. In the case of the first knowledge of water, for instance, people doubt its truth because such a knowledge is observed to arise even in the absence of water as in the illusion of mirage. So its truth is to be examined and it is known from some extraneous evidence, viz., the knowledge of successful activity. But, as the knowledge of successful activity is never seen to arise in the absence of successful activity, none entertains doubt about it, and consequently there is no motive to examine its truth.

Even when there is a doubt the truth of the experience of successful activity can be ascertained by its harmony (*saṃvāda*) with further experiences of its object. When water is seen we expect that it will quench our thirst and if the expected thing actually happens, i.e., if the cognition leads to a successful action it is proved to be true and there is no reason for doubting the truth of the visual cognition of water. If still there remains some doubt it can be removed by tactual, kinaesthetic and other experiences. A visual perception of water reveals the form of water in a general way and if we notice the special features of water in it by touching, bathing, washing etc. the first visual perception is verified, because such a series of experiences can never be possible unless the perceived water is real. It is true that we sometimes have such a series of experiences in dreams also. But when we have it during waking state we are fully aware that we are not dreaming. In a dream there is no consciousness of the fact that we are dreaming, and so the illusion of volitional satisfaction cannot be avoided in the state. But in the state of wakefulness we are perfectly sure that we are waking and not dreaming and that such a series of experiences cannot arise in the absence of real water. Thus the truth of the experience of successful activity, when it is confirmed by other sensory experiences during waking state, can never be doubted.

The truth of volitional experience can be tested in still another way by examining its antecedent conditions. If even after a vigorous and careful search we do not find any defect in the conditions, we can safely believe that our volitional experience of successful activity is true. The defects of the antecedent conditions that vitiate our knowledge resulting from them are:

rapid movement of objects as in the case of a firebrand in motion, similarity of the objects of knowledge to other objects as in the case of a shell, dimness of light, drowsiness of mind, an acute feeling of hunger, thirst, tiredness etc., the diseases of the sense-organs and so on. If such defects are absent our knowledge of successful activity cannot but be true.

It may be asked: why should we not examine the conditions of the first knowledge of an object in this way instead of examining the conditions of subsequent practical experience? The answer is that we can certainly do so if we choose, but it does not prove the theory of intrinsic truth, nor does it disprove the theory of extrinsic truth. If we ascertain the truth of our first perception of water on the ground of the absence of any vitiating factor in the antecedent conditions, we appeal to an extraneous test, and hence in this case too truth is known extrinsically. But ordinarily people are not interested in the examination of the conditions of their first perceptions. What they are interested in is the attainment of expected results from their first perceptions, and when there is actual attainment of such results the truth of the first perceptions becomes evident. But if there is any doubt the conditions giving rise to subsequent volitional experience are examined by people and not those which give rise to first perceptions. Thus a knowledge of successful activity resulting from a cognition is the test of the truth of that cognition and in the same way a knowledge of disappointment or practical failure (*pravṛttivisaṃvāda*) is the test of falsehood, and both these tests are extraneous to the conditions that give rise to knowledge. Knowledge by itself is neutral, i.e., is not known to be true or false. If it could be possible there would be no disappointment in practical activities. Truth and falsehood are not self-evident; they are always known through inference.

There are some cases of knowledge whose truth appears to be self-evident. The knowledge of familiar objects, e.g., my house, my body etc., is known as true immediately at the time when it arises and we do not feel the need of verifying it by successful activity. Is, then, such knowledge intrinsically true? The Naiyāyika replies that the knowledge of truth in such cases is conditioned by familiarity and that it is not self-evident though it arises quickly. The truth of the knowledge of a new object is ascertained on the ground of practical success to which it leads if it is true. When a new object is cognized repeatedly it becomes familiar and we need not test the truth of its cognition on subsequent occasions in the same way as when it was new. Truth in such cases is known through inference based on familiarity and not on successful activity.

Kumārila and his followers reject the theory of extrinsic truth and falsehood. If truth or falsehood is not natural to knowledge but super-added to it by excellences or deficiencies of the causal conditions, then it would follow that knowledge is characterless (*nissvabhāva*) at the time of its birth. But a knowledge which is neither true nor false is an impossibility. Either truth or falsehood must be natural or inherent in knowledge. Again if the ascertainment of truth and falsehood of knowledge is supposed to depend on inference which takes place at a later time, knowledge will lack certitude prior to the application of the test of truth and hence there will never be any practical activity immediately after knowledge, which is obviously against common experience. No activity is seen to follow from a doubtful knowledge. And if the Naiyāyika maintains that successful activity from a neutral or doubtful knowledge is possible, then he contradicts the very first aphorism of the *Nyāya Sūtra* which says that a study of *pramāṇa*-s is undertaken because it is only through valid knowledge that the useful is attained and the harmful is shunned.[6]

4.3. *The Buddhist Theory*

The Buddhist maintains that falsehood is inherent in all knowledge while truth is extraneous. A mere appearance of knowledge does not guarantee its truth. It is a matter of common experience that the knowledge of an object arises sometimes when the object is not actually present and sometimes when it is actually present. The knowledge of silver, for instance, arises when there is actually silver and sometimes when there is no silver but some other object resembling sliver such as a piece of nacre. Therefore, it is precarious to say that silver is actually present simply on the ground that its knowledge has appeared.

6. KK and NR on SV, 2.35-36.

Hence the truth of knowledge cannot be ascertained by the knowledge itself.

Truth can be ascertained only when it is seen that knowledge leads to successful activity. Successful activity is the result of true knowledge and the truth of the latter is inferred from the former. When a jar is cognized the cognition by itself does not give the assurance that the jar is actually present. But when later on we approach the object and find that we can fetch water in it or cook food, then it is ascertained that the cognition was truly of a jar. Again, even when there is no knowledge of practical success truth can also be ascertained by the subsequent knowledge that the cause of the knowledge possesses excellence (*guṇavatkāraṇajñāna*), or by knowing that the knowledge agrees with another knowledge of the same object (*jñānāntarasaṃvāda*). So the truth of a knowledge is determined by some other knowledge and not by the same knowledge because knowledge by itself is always doubtful, on which account falsehood is inherent in it. All cognitions lack certitude at the time of their origin. Absence of truth is their inherent characteristic.

From the point of view of genesis too falsehood is natural and truth is adventitious. Falsehood is nothing but an absence or negation of truth. Falsehood is a non-entity (*avastu*), and just as a hare's horn, which is a non-entity, cannot be produced by anything, so falsehood too cannot be produced by anything. The Mīmāṃsaka view that falsehood is generated by the defects of the cause of knowledge is wrong, because that which is a non-entity cannot have a cause for its origin. A non-entity has no origin and hence it is causeless. Therefore, falsehood is present in knowledge from the very beginning, while truth, being a positive entity (*vastu*) like a jar, is produced in knowledge extraneously by a cause, viz., the presence of merits in the source, just as a jar is produced by such causes as clay, a potter etc.

By merit or excellence is meant purity (*viśuddhi*) of the sense-organs and other sources of knowledge. When the three *dhātus* residing in the sense-organs are in a state of equilibrium (*sāmya*) the sense-organs are said to be pure and then they generate truth in the knowledge derived from them. If truth were natural to knowledge, who could deny the truth of dream-cognitions? So it is falsehood that is natural and it is not generated by defects.

Even when falsehood is seen to follow from defects of the source, as when the cognition of a yellow conch is seen to arise from jaundice, it is not actually the defects that cause falsehood. What happens in such cases is that defects being present merits disappear; consequently truth cannot be produced and thus falsehood which is inherent persists in cognition. Defects or demerits include those belonging to the cognizer, e.g., jaundice and those belonging to objects, e.g., minuteness, distance etc. Excellences or merits are: healthiness of sense-organs, reliability of a person, nearness of an object and so on. Defects are not active in producing falsehood. Their function is merely to remove merits. Merits alone are the direct cause of truth, and in their absence—which is seen in two ways, viz., when demerits are present, and when either the substratum (*āśraya*) of merits is absent, as in the case of the Vedas which are supposed by the Mīmāṃsaka to be authorless, or it is not functioning as in the case of dreams when sense-organs stop their operations—there is no production of truth. It is an error on the part of the Mīmāṃsakas to suppose that falsehood is caused by demerits. The fact is that demerits merely remove merits. A further proof of the fact that falsehood is not produced by demerits is found in the case of non-cognition (*ajñāna*). The Mīmāṃsaka cites positive and negative concomitance (*anvayavyatireka*) between demerits and falsehood as the proof of the former being the cause of the latter. But this is wrong, because this concomitance, though true in the case of illusion and doubt, fails in the case of non-cognition which is accepted as false and at the same time as not depending on demerits but solely on the absence of the cause of cognition (*jñānakāraṇābhāvamātram*). Therefore, the right conclusion that is forced upon us is that falsehood is uncaused and natural while truth is caused and adventitious.[7]

Criticising the Buddhist view Pārthasārathi says that falsehood is not merely an absence of truth. The Buddhist view that falsehood is a non-entity and hence not produced by any cause is based on a wrong conception of falsehood. Falsehood is not prior negation of certitude (*niścayaprāgabhāva*) as the Buddhist seems to hold. It is true that prior negation of something is uncaused

7. SV, 2. 38-45; KK and NR on ibid.

and the view that falsehood is uncaused might have been true if falsehood were merely prior negation of certitude. In the case of an illusion, e.g., that of silver in shell, which is a form of false knowledge, the perceiver is as confident of the presence of silver as in the case of real silver. False knowledge is positive in character. It represents something as a different thing due to certain vitiating factors (*doṣanimittatvādayathārthatvasya*), and this is known from positive and negative concomitance. The knowledge which is doubtful in its very origin also is known to arise from certain defects. As for non-cognition, it is obviously due to the absence of causes which give rise to cognition. But that which is true in the case of non-cognition need not be true in the case of illusion and doubt. Therefore, falsehood is not uncaused and natural, but is caused by defects or vitiating conditions.[8]

The Buddhist says that truth is caused by excellences and where there are no excellences there is no truth. But if it were true, there could be no iota of truth in the cognition of a white conch as yellow or in that of a shell as silver, which is produced by the visual sense devoid of excellences. In the cognition of a yellow conch the element of conchness is true, though yellowness is false. In the illusion of silver in shell too the cognition is true in respect of such general features as brightness, a triangular shape etc. The elements of truth in the aforesaid cognitions are evidently caused not by excellences, for there are no excellences, but by merely the conditions of knowledge (*jñānakāraṇa-nimittameva*). Moreover, it is the purity of the sense-organs etc., that is meant when the Buddhist talks of excellences. But if this be so, then excellences become equivalent to absence of blemishes (*doṣābhāva*); and the Mīmāṃsaka is not opposed to this view, because it does not interfere with the truth of the Veda. The Veda has no author and so the question of the presence of blemishes in its source does not arise. In fact truth is not caused by the presence of excellences or the absence of blemishes in the generating conditions of knowledge, but it is natural or intrinsic to knowledge. Wherever excellences are seen in the cause of knowledge they are not directly operative in producing truth. They

8. NRM, p. 38.

merely serve as a means of removing blemishes (*doṣanirākaraṇau-pāyikatayā*). The presence of blemishes interferes in the production of true knowledge. But when they are expelled by the presence of excellences they cannot offer any interference. Excellences are not directly the cause of truth.[9]

Thus when it is not established that truth depends on the excellences or soundness of the source of knowledge, the inference of truth from excellences has no justification. The Buddhist contention that all knowledge is known to be false at the time of its origin because falsehood depends on the conditions that give rise to knowledge, cannot be supported. If knowledge is inherently false and immediately known to be false, illusion and disappointment cannot be explained. If a shell is perceived as silver and we immediately know that it is not silver, as we should know according to the Buddhist theory, then our moving and approaching the 'silver' and the subsequent corrective knowledge that it is not silver become inexplicable. On the contrary, even such a false knowledge is accepted to be true at the time of its origin, and this fact shows that knowledge is known to be true intrinsically, while falsehood is a later discovery depending on conditions extraneous to the conditions of knowledge.[10]

The Buddhist may say that knowledge is not known to be positively false at the moment of its origin but that so long as its truth is not ascertained we remain in doubt about its real character and as doubt is a form of invalid knowledge all knowledge must be invalid intrinsically. But this scepticism is quite unfounded and logically it can never be terminated. To say that the knowledge of truth depends on the knowledge of the soundness of its source is beset with difficulties which know no end. If the truth of a cognition is not self-established the truth of the cognition of the soundness of its source is equally non-established by itself. To ascertain the truth of the former we have to ascertain the truth of the latter which again is to be ascertained extraneously in the same way and so on without coming to any

9. NR and KK on SV, 2. 47-48.
10. NTV, p. 35.

end of the process. Thus scepticism about the first cognition will never be removed.[11]

As the knowledge of the soundness of generating conditions cannot establish the truth of a cognition, so the knowledge of successful activity too is incompetent for that purpose. If the cognition of a jar is supposed to be unable to establish its own truth on the ground that such a cognition is seen to arise even in the absence of a jar, then the cognition of successful activity too is unable to establish its own truth on the same ground, i.e., on the ground that it too is seen to arise even when actually there is no successful activity, as in dreams. Consequently, when the knowledge of successful activity itself is not ascertained to be true, how can it prove the truth of the knowledge of a jar? And even if it be granted that the knowledge of successful activity is true by itself, how can it prove the truth of the knowledge of a jar? The knowledge of a jar is as different from the knowledge of successful activity as from the knowledge of a piece of cloth. 'This is a jar' and 'I bring water in a jar' assert quite different things. So how can the latter prove that the former is true? Let this question be left for some later time and let us take up the first again. It will be said that though the knowledge of successful activity does not by itself certify its truth, yet the feeling of pleasure or satisfaction that accompanies successful activity proves its truth. The feeling of pleasure is never known to arise in the absence of pleasure; therefore, the knowledge of pleasure is self-valid. If a knowledge, e.g., of a jar, is true, the activity to which it leads must be successful and if an activity is successful it must result in a feeling of pleasure. As the knowledge of pleasure cannot deceive us it proves the truth of the knowledge of successful activity which in turn proves the truth of the knowledge that prompted the activity. This contention of the Buddhist too is wrong. It is true that the knowledge of pleasure can arise only when pleasure is actually felt and not otherwise and hence it is self-valid. But from the knowledge of pleasure the truth of the knowledge in question cannot be determined, because in dreams, hypnosis etc. it is seen that pleasure may arise from purely imaginary objects.[12]

11. SD, p. 2.
12. NRM, p. 37.

The same reasoning holds in case if agreement with some other knowledge (*jñānāntarasaṃvāda*) is supposed to be the test of truth. The other knowledge with which agreement of a certain knowledge is sought may be either of the same kind or of a different kind; it may be homogeneous (*sajātīya*) or heterogeneous (*vijātīya*). The subsequent visual cognitions of a jar, for instance, arising in the same person or in different persons are all homogeneous with its present visual cognition, while its tactual cognition, inferential cognition and the cognition derived from a reliable person are all heterogeneous to its present visual cognition. Now whatever the knowledge with which agreement is sought may be, the difficulty of infinite regress cannot be avoided by the upholder of the extrinsicality of truth, because none of the subsequent cognitions of the same thing can be supposed to be intrinsically true. When the subsequent cognitions are homogeneous with the first one, they do not differ from the first; hence one possessing no superiority over others, all must be equally true, false or doubtful. Again, heterogeneous cognitions of a thing reveal different aspects of it and consequently there cannot be a real agreement among them. A visual perception of a jar cannot be verified by its auditory, tactual and other heterogeneous cognitions, because they reveal respectively the colour, sound, touch etc., of the jar, which being different cannot corroborate one another. The qualities perceived by the different sense-organs are absolutely different and so there cannot be any agreement among the heterogeneous perceptions of the same thing. If agreement with a heterogeneous cognition is the sole test of truth, then my visual perception of a jar which reveals its colour cannot but be false because the auditory and other perceptions cannot apprehend its colour.[13]

Thus if knowledge is not known to be true intrinsically, no extraneous evidence can prove it. Moreover, the intrinsicality of truth is proved by the very reasoning of the upholder of extrinsicality. It is held that successful activity is the result of true knowledge and the truth of knowledge, though by itself undetermined, is inferred from the knowledge of successful activity, as a cause is inferred from its effect. But such an inference cannot

13. SV, 2. 77-81.

be reliable unless the invariable concomitance between true knowledge and successful activity has been observed repeatedly. We infer the presence of fire from the perception of smoke at a distance on the ground that we have observed smoke and fire together in the past in a large number of instances and have never observed a contrary instance. Accordingly one who infers correctly the truth of a knowledge from successful activity must somehow have known the truth of a knowledge independently of the knowledge of successful activity repeatedly on many occasions, which implies that the truth of knowledge is self-evident.[14]

4.4. *The Bhāṭṭa Theory*

Having examined the views held by others Kumārila concludes that truth is inherent in all cognitions, because, if it were not so, it could not be produced by any extraneous condition.[15] Umbeka[16] distinguishes Kumārila's conception of intrinsicality of truth from the conceptions of the Sāṅkhya, Prabhākara and the Vedānta and also criticises some wrong interpretations of this view. The Sāṅkhya view has already been criticized. Prabhākara's view of intrinsicality is that all apprehension is true and knowledge apprehending reality otherwise than it is, is an impossibility, and thus he closes his eyes to the fact of error. Kumārila, on the other hand, recognizes error and hence his view of intrinsicality is different from Prabhākara's. According to the Advaita Vedānta all empirical knowledge is true so long as the absolute truth, viz., the knowledge of Brahman, is not attained. In the previous chapter it was shown that Kumārila disapproves all these views and hence his view of intrinsicality is different from them.

Some say that the properties of an effect have their origin in the properties of the cause. The sense-organs are the cause of knowledge and they, being of the nature of absence of knowledge (*abodharūpa*), are devoid of cognitive potency (*bodhākhyaśakti*). Hence if there were no cognitive potency inherent in knowledge it could not be produced by the sense-organs. In this view by

14. NRM, p. 37.
15. SV, 2. 47.
16. TT, pp. 48-55.

prāmāṇya is meant the power of revealing objects, which is natural to knowledge and by *aprāmāṇya* is meant the absence of this power, which can be produced by causes not possessing this power. Umbeka says that this interpretation of Kumārila's view is wrong. This view makes truth intrinsic on the ground that it cannot be traced to the cause of knowledge, viz., the senses; truth is intrinsic because it is causeless. But this is wrong. We do not find massiveness belonging to a body in the atoms that are the cause of the body; but this does not imply that massiveness is causeless.

Others say that *prāmāṇya* is the power of producing discernment (*paricchedotpādikā śaktiḥ*) and this belongs to cognition naturally. Cognitions are momentary and if the said power were not inherent in them it could never be produced. It cannot be produced before a cognition comes into being just as a picture cannot be produced before the canvas on which it is painted comes into being. It cannot be produced simultaneously with the origination of a cognition just as a picture cannot be produced simultaneously with the production of the canvas. It cannot be produced after a cognition is produced, because a cognition, being momentary, cannot stay till the said power is produced. Therefore, the power of producing discernment is not an effect at all but a natural possession of cognitions. This interpretation too is wrong because the opposite power of producing non-discernment too will be natural on the same ground, which cannot be Kumārila's view.

Umbeka gives his own interpretation as follows: *Prāmāṇya* consists in the property of a *pramāṇa* or means of knowledge, e.g., perception, by virtue of which it reveals an object as it really exists (*arthāvisaṃvāditva*) and it is produced by the same conditions which give rise to a *pramāṇa*. The natural form (*svarūpa*) of the causes produces truth in knowledge without depending on such additional factors as merits. We do not find any merits in the sense-organs. There is no direct or indirect proof of their existence. They are neither directly perceived nor is there any sign from which they could be inferred. The medicines whose application is supposed to produce merits in the sense-organs do nothing but expel the blemishes that may vitiate them. Falsehood of knowledge, on the other hand, is caused by blemishes or defects which are extraneous to the natural form of sense-organs. Defects, though they are invisible, are presumed to explain falsehood.

It may be objected that falsehood cannot be traced solely to the presence of defects in the generating conditions of knowledge, because where there is presence of defects there is absence of excellences too and hence it is not proper to hold only one of them to be responsible for producing falsehood. The reply is that falsehood is not merely negation of truth but positive in character and hence it must be caused by some positive factor actively producing a misapprehension of things and such a positive factor can be no other than a defect.[17]

Pārthasārathi draws attention to one possible misinterpretation of *svataḥ-prāmāṇya* and *parataḥ-aprāmāṇya*. *Svatastva* or intrinsicality of truth does not imply that all knowledge is born true, and *paratastva* or extrinsicality of falsehood does not imply that knowledge born true is made false by such extraneous conditions as the subsequent appearance of a contradicting knowledge (*bādhakajñāna*) etc. Truth and falsehood are produced in true and false knowledge respectively simultaneously with the production of knowledge. They are properties of knowledge and are present from the very beginning. It is not true to say that truth is born with knowledge and falsehood is added to it subsequently. Falsehood is produced by some vitiating factors, but the vitiating factors are present from the very beginning. When silver is falsely perceived in shell falsehood characterizes the perception from the very moment of its origin, though the consciousness of falsehood does not arise at that time. The true knowledge of shell that arises later on does not produce falsehood in the first perception of it as silver. The falsehood was already there, but it was not known till the appearance of the sublating consciousness.[18] Thus truth is intrinsic in the sense that it is produced by the natural causes of knowledge and falsehood is extrinsic in the sense that it is produced by some additional factor vitiating the natural causes.

17. NRM, p. 38.
18. न हि शुक्तौ रजतज्ञानस्य बाधकादिजन्यमप्रामाण्यं, उत्पत्तावेव तस्याप्रमाणत्वात्। NRM, p. 31.

The next question is: How are truth and falsehood known? Kumārila says:

> *Tasmāt bodhātmakatvena prāptā buddheḥ pramāṇatā/*
> *Arthānyathātvahetūtthadoṣajñānādapodyate //* SV. 2. 53

> The truth, therefore, of knowledge is known through the mere fact of its being of the nature of knowledge and it is set aside (in the form 'this is not so') by the knowledge of the object as being of a different nature or by the recognition of discrepancies in the source.

Knowledge is spontaneously known to be true. All knowledge excluding doubt brings with it the conviction of its truth. As soon as knowledge of something is born it is believed to be true without standing in need of verification. It is this spontaneous belief in the reality of the object revealed by knowledge that prompts us to act in a particular way with reference to it.

It may be said that if the truth of knowledge is known by itself at the time of its birth and no other knowledge is required for that purpose, then a knowledge which is not known to be true by itself at the time may be rejected as false, and thus, just as we need no external criterion for judging truth, so we need none for judging falsehood, the conclusion being that truth and falsehood both are known intrinsically. This objection implies an intuitive knowledge of truth and falsehood and it is rejected on the ground that not only a true knowledge is known to be true by itself, but even a false knowledge, e.g., that of silver in shell, is known as true by itself All cognitions without any discrimination are believed as true by themselves, though some of them may actually be false.[19] The illusion of silver in shell is taken to be true at the time of its origin, but the consciousness that it is an illusion appears only subsequently. A false cognition does not advertise its falsehood and hence at the time it is as good as a true cognition. But when the falsehood of a false cognition is known it is invariably known through a second cognition. "Even a false cognition by itself points out the reality of its object and

19. NRM, p. 34.

it would not cease to do so unless its falsehood were detected by another means".[20] A cognition always appears in the form 'this is P'. But the fact that 'this is not P' (*arthānyathābhāva*), i.e., the falsehood of a cognition, is not revealed by the same cognition, but by another cognition. Therefore, it is said that the truth of knowledge is self-evident (*svataḥ*) while its falsehood is evidenced by other means (*parataḥ*).

Now, what are those other means by which the falsehood of a cognition is detected? They are: (1) a contradicting experience (*bādhakapratyaya*) and (2) the knowledge of defects in the causes of a cognition (*doṣajñāna*). When a cognition, e.g., of silver, appears, we are confident of the real existence of silver. But later in the course of further exploratory activity of the senses or when we manipulate the object, the real character of the perceived object as shell is discovered, the first cognition is directly contradicted in the form 'this is not silver', and thus we become aware of the error. Sometimes, as in the cognition of a yellow conch, the defects of the source are of a more or less permanent nature and not as temporary as in the previous case, and under such circumstances the real character of the perceived object is not directly known. So long as one is not aware of the defect or forgets it for the time being, the cognition is taken to be true; but later when he becomes aware of the defect he rejects that part of the cognition as false which he can reasonably trace to the defect. In the cognition of yellow conch, for instance, he rejects the yellowness as false when he recognizes that his eyes are suffering from jaundice, because he knows that the yellowness actually belongs to the bile present in his eyes while the conch in the state of health was seen as white.

It may be said against this view that when the ascertainment of falsehood is made to depend on another cognition there will be infinite regress as on the theory of extrinsicality of truth. The reply is that mere dependence is not a cause of infinite regress. Infinite regress occurs when one thing is made to depend on another thing of the same kind, for example, when the truth of one cognition is made to depend on the truth of another cognition. Thus if the falsehood of one cognition were known by the

20. SV, 2.85.

falsehood of another cognition the charge of infinite regress might have been true. But actually what happens in the present case is simply that the falsehood of a former cognition is revealed subsequently by the knowledge of contradiction or of defects while this subsequent knowledge is self-valid. When falsehood is thus revealed by a true knowledge there is no need to go on further and hence there is no infinite regress.[21]

It may again be asked: How is it that a later knowledge contradicts a previous one and not vice versa? First there appears the cognition 'this is silver' and then another cognition appears in the form 'this is not silver'. It is said that the second cognition falsifies the first, but it may equally well be supposed that the first falsifies the second. The reply is that the relation of the contradictor and the contradicted (*bādhyabādhakabhāva*) between two cognitions does not depend on a mere wish. When the first cognition 'this is silver' appeared the second 'this is not silver' was non-existent and hence the former could not contradict the latter. But the latter, making its appearance after the former, reveals the object of the former as possessing a contradictory nature and on this account it invalidates the former. The first cognition arises independently of the second, but the very birth of the second presupposes thc first. The cognition 'this is not silver' denies the truth of the cognition 'this is silver' by its mere existence and hence the relation of the contradictor and the contradicted existing between them cannot be reversed.[22]

It has been shown so far that the falsehood of a cognition is known extrinsically through the subsequent consciousness of contradiction or of the presence of defects in the source. But sometimes there follows a third cognition which contradicts the second one and in such cases the truth of the first cognition which was wrongly shown to be mistaken by the second one is restored by the third one. From this it should not be supposed that the truth of the first cognition is known extrinsically, because the first cognition determines its object on account of its own birth and hence it is self-valid. The second cognition of discrepancy contradicted the first only by mistake, but when the

21. NR on SV, 2.57.
22. Ibid.

third one contradicts the second by indicating that there is no real discrepancy, the truth of the first stands unchallenged. The first cognition remains as true as it naturally was. What the third did was just to show that the doubt regarding the first generated by the second was unfounded.

Again seeing that one cognition is contradicted by a subsequent cognition and this too sometimes by still another cognition it is not reasonable to doubt the truth of the third and so on *ad infinitum*. Where discrepancies really exist they are sure to be known sooner or later. We cannot suspect them even where there is no reasonable ground for suspicion. Subjective and objective defects which are the causes of falsehood are found to exist only under special circumstances and not everywhere. When the senses and the mind are in a healthy condition, there is ample illumination, we are in a wakeful state and the object is very near, any doubt regarding the truth of the resultant cognition becomes unnecessary. Thus when there is no occasion for suspecting the presence of discrepancies the fear that a cognition may turn out as false is ruled out. Falsehood may be suspected where there is a possibility of discrepancies. It is not proper to doubt the truth of a cognition merely on the ground that it is a cognition like false cognitions. There are cognitions which arise with the conviction that they are perfectly true. Even when doubt arises due to a greater distance of the object or to other circumstances it is easy to dispel the doubt by approaching the object or by some other recognized method, but universal scepticism is quite uncalled for. If in the third cognition discrepancies are not suspected the matter ends then and there; but if we find a reasonable ground to examine the third decision can be arrived at with the help of a fourth cognition and this is usually enough. When in this way the truth of the first or second cognition is confirmed by the third or fourth one, it, being natural, rests unchallenged, while others are proved to be false.[23]

The Bhāṭṭa view is that truth does not depend on any extraneous factor for its revelation and hence it is self-evident. But how can this view be reconciled with the other view that a cognition does not reveal itself. It is held that a cognition does not

23. NR on SV, 2. 58-61.

reveal itself at the time of its appearance and that if there arises any curiosity it is indirectly known later through another cognition. But if a eognition depends on another cognition for its knowledge, its truth, which is its property, too must depend on another cognition for its knowledge and thus the theory of self-evidence falls to the ground.

In reply to this Pārthasārathi says that the theory of self-evidence does not mean that a cognition apprehends its truth in the form 'I am true'. On the contrary it means that knowledge of truth depends on the knowledge of the cognition itself, and we need not go beyond the cognition for that purpose. When a cognition arises we are not aware of the cognitive act, but the awareness of the object manifested by the cognition definitely occurs and the belief that the object is really as it is manifested remains implicit until reflective consciousness appears. An explicit consciousness of the truth of a cognition appears subsequently and then it depends on the awareness of the cognition itself rather than on any extraneous consideration. When we judge a cognition as true what we judge is that the object revealed by the cognition is actually such as is revealed to us and not different. The sole means of knowing the existence and nature of an object is its cognition and we have to believe what a cognition reveals to us. When I perceive a yellow object the consciousness that the object is actually yellow arises from the perception alone, while the consciousness that the object is actually different in case if the perception be false, arises not from the same perception, but from the knowledge of contradiction or that of defects in the eyes.[24]

4.5. *A Critical Review*

The motive which led the Bhāṭṭa to adopt the theory of intrinsic validity is to seek a theoretical justification for his belief in the intrinsic validity of the Veda. The Mīmāṃsaka does not believe in the divine authorship; he believes that the Veda is eternal and uncreated. He could not base the validity of such Vedic assertions as 'one desirous of heaven should sacrifice' on such extrinsic grounds as the omniscience of God, as is done by

24. NRM, p. 33.

the Naiyāyika, because the hypothesis that there exists a God could not be supported by reason. The supposition that there exists a God is absolutely unverifiable through the available empirical means and to base the validity of the Veda on such a shaky foundation would have been detrimental to the religious feelings of the orthodox Hindus like the Mīmāṃsaka. Under such circumstances the safer course was to prove self-validity in the case of our common beliefs in the objects of sense and then to extend and generalize it to cover the case of Vedic knowledge.

Though the Bhāṭṭa preaches the theory of self-validity on account of his partiality for the Veda and thus his attitude towards the enquiry into the conditions of truth is not expected to be detached and scientific, yet we find that his theory contains much that is true. Our primary attitude towards knowledge seems to be that of belief. The knowledge given by the senses appears with the assurance of its truth. When I see a blue thing I take it to be a real blue thing and act accordingly. Action presupposes belief. Our belief in the truth of our perception appears to be instinctive, while falsebood is a discovery that is made when there is an experience of contradiction and practical disappointment. Montague rightly says:

> It seems probable that the primary condition of consciousness is a condition of acceptance of cerebral implicates or conscious contents at their face value as real and as bases for action. Disbelief and doubt are sophisticated or secondary attitudes which we take towards a content only when it is contradicted by another content or by the system as a whole.[25]

We proceed to act on the implicit belief that what we know is true.

The Buddhist and Naiyāyika contention that mere doubt is a sufficient force to make us act seems to be wrong. Of course, sometimes we do appear to act with reference to an object of cognition of whose existence we are not fully convinced, but in such cases our behaviour is rather tentative, being a part of cognitive activity, and fulfilment of some pragmatic need is not

25. *The New Realism*, p. 294.

our aim. Suppose I see at a distance something like water without being sure of its existence. I approach the object simply to verify this initial cognition with the aim of assuring myself that it is truly water and not of directly quenching my thirst. But if I am sure that it is water that I see, I approach it with the direct aim that I will drink it.

When the upholder of extrinsic validity says that practical activity can be explained by doubt also, he forgets the distinction between real doubt which is a psychological state of oscillating between two or more alternatives and methodic doubt or doubt as a method of enquiry. We may investigate the validity of a judgment by provisionally assuming it as doubtful and then find out the grounds of its validity. Real doubt and methodic doubt are different in that while the former is imposed upon us by the conditions of knowledge, the latter is a matter of choice. That first expedition to the moon will be made within a decade is a matter of real doubt for me, but that the three angles of a triangle are equal to two right angles, though I am sure of it, may be doubted in order to remember the process of reasoning that leads to it.

Thus it is true that some cognitions are really doubtful, but the contention that every cognition is doubtful unless it is verified to be true on external grounds is not true. Our primary attitude towards perceptual cognitions at least is that of belief and it is set aside when they are contradicted by other cognitions. The cognitions derived from the statements made by others too are generally accepted as true if no reason to disbelieve them is found. The Bhāṭṭa theory of intrinsic validity is based on this psychological fact.

But a mere psychological belief cannot be the ground of logical certitude. That I happen to have a cognition is not the proof of its truth. To prove its truth we have to collect evidence that may turn out to be extrinsic to the cognition itself. But the Naiyāyika, though right so far as validity is sometimes proved on extrinsic grounds, is wrong when he asserts that validity is proved invariably by extrinsic evidence. Koffey rightly says: "All extrinsic evidence therefore rests ultimately on intrinsic evidence and cannot itself be the supreme test of truth or the ultimate motive of certitude."[26] The proposition that heaven is attained through sacrifice cannot be proved to be true on intrinsic grounds. We have to seek its proof elsewhere and can give our assent to it if we can find sufficient reason to believe it. The Naiyāyika bases the truth of this proposition on the excellence of its source, viz., God. In the same way the knowledge derived from other persons, e.g., 'snake-bite causes death' is known and proved as true if the person is well-informed and trustworthy or if we actually observe people dying of snake-bite. But for the truth of the propositions 'a well-informed and trustworthy person must be believed' and 'what is perceived in many cases cannot be false', which are the extrinsic grounds of proof in the case of the knowledge that snake-bite causes death, we do not feel the need of proving them, and hence they are self-evident.

> For the truth of these two judgments we must ultimately have adequate intrinsic evidence, i.e, evidence lying in the subject-matter itself of these two judgments; for if we accepted these judgments only on some other authority the same question would arise about the credentials of this latter and thus we should find ourselves involved in an endless regress.[27]

From some cases in which truth is proved on the strength of extrinsic evidence the Naiyāyika concludes that in every case it is so. But this is a mistake. Coherence and pragmatic success which are extraneous tests of truth presuppose a knowledge of truth on intrinsic evidence somewhere and the Bhāṭṭa is quite correct in pointing out this fact. My perception of water through vision is said to be known as true if it coheres with my later experiences of it through touch, taste and other senses. But the different senses reveal different aspects of water and their reports are different which cannot be said to point to the same fact, viz., water, unless on many former occasions water has been experienced through different senses and the different sense-experiences have

26. *Epistemology*, p. 563.
27. Ibid.

been known to be intrinsically true. Let *a*, *b*, *c*, *d* etc. be the different sense-experiences of water. At present I am having the experience *a* and subsequently I have the experiences *b*, *c*, *d* etc. But how can *b*, *c*, *d* etc. confirm *a* otherwise than on the ground of their intrinsic truth? The truth of *a* is known through *b*, *c*, *d* etc. because we already have had all of them together and have known each of them to be independently true. The pragmatic test of successful activity is nothing but verifying an experience by kinaesthetic and emotional experiences. When I believe my visual perception of water to be true when I quench my thirst with it the satisfaction of an organic need gives me an additional emotional experience. But why should this emotional experience prove that what I perceive is really water? There is no *a priori* connection between them. It is because the two experiences, a visual and an emotional one, have been connected in my mind in the past when I had them together and knew them as independently and intrinsically true. Truth is ultimately based on intrinsic evidence. Otherwise the Naiyāyika cannot avoid infinite regress. The Naiyāyika tries to save his position by asserting that we have no motive to examine the truth of our experiences of practical results (*phalajñāna*). But this is merely accepting the theory of self-evidence in the case of the said experiences. We have no motive to examine the truth of our experience of success or failure of our practical activities because we are confident of its truth and there is no scope for doubt, which implies that truth is self-evident in that case.

Another extrinsic test of truth is the knowledge of merits in the source from which a cognition emanates and the ground from which this test derives its legitimacy is the belief that truth is produced by merits and falsehood by demerits of the generating conditions of knowledge. But this involves reasoning in a circle. When the sense-organs are the cause of knowledge we can never be aware of their merits or demerits independently of the knowledge which arises from them. What is the standard by which merits and demerits are judged in sense-organs? It is only when a perception is found to be true or false on other grounds that merits or demerits are presumed in the corresponding sense-organ. Our knowledge of merits and demerits of the senses is primarily based on the knowledge of truth and error and even when we know them they are not a sure guide to the knowledge of truth and falsehood because, firstly, we are never sure that they are known exhaustively and, secondly, a perception may be true in spite of some defect in the sense-organ. For instance, the disease called jaundice is known to be responsible for the illusion of yellowness, but from the knowledge of its presence it cannot be inferred that the perceived yellowness of an object is definitely false and the object is really white, because it may really be yellow. It is true that a white object is seen as yellow through a jaundiced eye, but a yellow object also is seen as yellow through it. In the case when the knowledge whose truth is to be examined is derived from inference, truth and falsehood surely depend on the soundness and defective character respectively of the reasoning process and we can be sure of the truth of the conclusion if there are no logical fallacies in the process. But whence did we know what constitutes soundness and what constitutes fallaciousness? This is primarily known after an independent knowledge of the truth and falsehood of inferences. In the case of knowledge derived from other persons a correct knowledge of things and a faithful statement of what one knows constitute merit; but the merit cannot be ascertained unless the truth of the knowledge is ascertained first. Even when we know a person as possessing the desired qualifications on the ground of our past dealings with him, it is very difficult to ascertain if he knows a particular thing correctly and thus the truth of human assertions cannot be proved through a knowledge of merits. Knowledge of merits has hardly been offered as a test of truth by modern epistemologists. It may be granted that merits produce truth and demerits produce falsehood, but the Nyāya view that in this way truth and falsehood are extrinsic to knowledge is misleading. This view gives the impression that knowledge is first produced as neutral by its causes and subsequently the merits or demerits of the causes add the property of truth or falsehood to it. But this is wrong. The causes and their merits or demerits are simultaneously operative in the production of knowledge. Knowledge is not a product of successive additions of the individual contributions of different elements. Similarly the

Bhāṭṭa view that falsehood is extraneously produced in knowledge by demerits also is misleading, though Pārthasārathi emphatically says that knowledge is true or false from the very origin and that truth and falsehood are not its superadded properties.

The Indian theories of truth start from perception and end in an attempt to explain the validity of knowledge based on authority in the light of the criteria derived from perception. But the Indian philosophers excluding the Buddhists hardly question the truth of our perceptions as much as it has been questioned in recent philosophy. Do we perceive things exactly as they are? In modern philosophy Locke questioned the reality of the secondary qualities of objects, viz., colour, taste etc. He concluded that primary sense-qualities, viz., extension, motion etc. actually belong to objects, but secondary qualities are relative to our sensibility. Kant said that the thing-in-itself ever remains unknown and what we perceive and attribute to things are the effects of things-in-themselves upon our minds. Perhaps due to an inadequate knowledge of physiology Indian philosophers were not troubled by these problems. They seem to accept uncritically what the sense-organs report about the world around us and it is probably right.

Our sense-cognitions are the product of an intercourse between the nervous system and the external world. We have an instinctive belief in the reality of things revealed by the senses. We have other instances also in which things are revealed as they actually are. A mirror reflects images of objects which we find to be more or less exact copies of them. A gramophone reproduces a voice quite faithfully. So why should we doubt that our organism too can faithfully apprehend objects? Perhaps there take place two types of processes in our organism when it is stimulated by external objects. The sense-organs convert the influences produced by external objects into a form of energy and transmit it to the central nervous system in which takes place the reverse process of restoring the original form to this energy. Our perception of objects is undoubtedly relative to our sensibility which is tinged by the peculiarities of the medium through which objects are received; but the central nervous system in the process of restoration counteracts and eliminates these peculiarities and distorting influences. Our organism has been evolved under the pressure of environmental influences and it may reasonably be supposed that it is adapted to reveal objects as they are. We observe instances of adaptation in nature everywhere. Males of a species are adapted to the requirements of the females and vice versa. Our organs are adapted to the peculiarities of the environment. There is no reason why we should not accept that our senses are adapted to reveal objects correctly. Our doubts regarding the truth of our perceptions are useless because perception is the only source of first-hand information about the external world. We are helpless and have to accept things as revealed by perception. Hence our perceptions are intrinsically true.

The Nyāya view that their truth is extrinsic is wrong because there is no test extraneous to perception which is available and is more primary and reliable. The sense-organs are naturally adapted to reveal things in their real form and in this sense the power of producing truth is inherent in them. Falsehood is non-inherent in the sense that it is caused by the distorting influences of the medium which remain uncorrected due to certain defects of the central nervous system. Thus falsehood can be attributed to the agency of abnormal conditions. When the perceptual apparatus is not functioning normally it can be known from the discord among the reports of different sense-organs or among those of different persons or among those of the same person at different times. If many persons perceive the same thing, if we perceive the same thing at different times, if the reports of different senses agree we have no reason to doubt the normal functioning of our senses. Experience teaches us that within certain limits and under certain conditions our perceptions are quite reliable. Beyond these limits our senses may err, but in such cases errors may be detected by different tests suggested by the Naiyāyika and the Buddhist, viz., non-coherence, practical disappointment etc. If an erroneous perception were never contradicted by subsequent experiences of a person or of other persons we could never be aware of its erroneousness. There is no superior and more primary faculty of knowing the real nature of objects than sense-perception and consequently what it reveals must be taken to be real. Intellect or the faculty of reasoning is no doubt superior, but it acquires this superiority owing to its power of comparing, analyzing and synthesizing sense-data which are the result of a direct contact of sense-organs with reality. Thus in the sphere of perceptual knowledge the Bhāṭṭa theory appears quite convincing.

When knowledge is derived from a combined operation of the sense-organs and inference or from inference alone or from verbal testimony, the mere appearance of it is not a proof of its truth. If at night I perceive a light high up in the sky and judge that it is the light of a star, my judgment goes beyond what is given by perception. So far as the perception of light is concerned there is no scope for doubt but the judgement that it belongs to a star may turn out to be false because the light may really belong to an aeroplane. Our judgments based on inference can have a fairly high degree of certitude if the grounds on which they rest are found sufficiently convincing. But their truth is ultimately proved if they are verified by perception. Similarly the truth of human assertions is proved by their correspondence with perception. When the objects of knowledge are not directly open to perception or when they are imperceptible, truth can be tested by coherence. In sciences theories are generally tested through experimentation. In astronomy the implications of a theory are calculated and compared with observations. In history evidences are collected from different sources and compared among themselves. But what we gain from these different tests is only a relatively high or low degree of certainty. Absolute certainty is humanly unattainable. Epistemology cannot provide any hard and fast rule for the discovery of truth. We do have recourse to external evidence for ascertaining truth in the above cases and so far the Nyāya theory of *parataḥ-prāmāṇya* is correct. But the Bhāṭṭa theory of *svataḥ-prāmāṇya* is not thus falsified. It is a fact that the mere appearance of knowledge is not the proof of its truth and this fact is recognized as much by the latter theory as by the former. The difference lies in their respective attitudes towards knowledge. The Naiyāyika first adopts the attitude of neutrality and then delivers his judgment according to available evidence. The Bhāṭṭa first assumes the truth of knowledge and is ready to give due consideration to any evidence that may subsequently crop up and go against it; he is prepared to revise his judgment in the light of fresh evidence. The Naiyāyika is like a judge who sees every man appearing in his court with an unprejudiced eye and the Bhāṭṭa is like one who believes that every man is innocent until his crime is proved. But the attitude of the Buddhist is just the opposite of the Bhāṭṭa attitude. He is like a judge who takes every man to be a criminal until the proof of his innocence is available.

PART II

SOURCES OF VALID KNOWLEDGE

अथातो प्रमाण जिज्ञासा

CHAPTER V

PERCEPTION

In the foregoing chapters we dealt with the Bhāṭṭa views on the most vital problems of epistemology, viz., the nature of knowledge, truth and error. The present chapter and the succeeding ones will be concerned with the *pramāṇa*-s, i.e., the sources of valid knowledge. The different schools of Indian philosophy are not unanimous about the nature and number of the means of valid knowledge. The Bhāṭṭas recognize six *pramāṇa*-s, viz., perception, (syllogistic) inference, verbal testimony, comparison, presumption and non-apprehension. Out of these six *pramāṇa*-s the materialist Cārvāka recognizes perception alone; the Buddhist and the Vaiśeṣika reject all except perception and inference; Bhāsarvajña, the author of *Nyāyasāra*, and the Sāṅkhyas recognize the first three; Udayana and the other Nāiyāyikas recognize the first four; Prabhākara recognizes all except non-apprehension; the followers of Śaṅkara, like the Bhāṭṭas, recognize all the six; and the Paurāṇikas add two more, viz., inclusion (*sambhava*) and tradition (*aitihya*).[1]

In this chapter we deal with perception. Perception as the primary source of valid knowledge is universally recognized, though some have questioned its claim to give valid knowledge. Jayarāśibhaṭṭa, who probably lived in the first half of the seventh century, criticizes the different theories of perception and other *pramāṇa*-s and comes to the conclusion that there are no means of valid knowledge.[2] The *Nyāyasūtra*[3] refers to an objector who is represented as questioning the validity of all the *pramāṇa*-s including perception. Perception must be either prior to or simultaneous with or posterior to its object. It cannot be simultaneous with its object, since, if it were so, there would be

1. MM, p. 8.
2. TPS, cp. the concluding sentence:
   तदेवमुपप्लुतेष्वेव तत्त्वेषु अविचारितरमणीयाः:...
3. NS, 2. 1.8-19.

no succession in our cognitions, as there is none among objects. If it were prior to its object, the object would be revealed as future; and if it were posterior to it, the object would be revealed as belonging to the past, while actually it is revealed as present. Therefore, the objector concludes, perception cannot give valid knowledge. In spite of this objection the validity of perception is defended by the *Nyāyasūtra* and it is said that perception is presupposed by inference which is next to it in primacy.[4]

Perception gives a direct knowledge of reality, because in it we are face to face with reality, whereas the other means give only an indirect knowledge. Prabhākara says that perception apprehends the form of an object,[5] while inference apprehends merely the existence of it.[6] The superiority of perception over other means consists in that it gives a first-hand and detailed information about reality. Explaining '*tatpūrvakatva*' in NS, 1. 1. 4 Vātsyāyana says that inference depends on perception for its premises. The universal major premise of an inference is derived from frequent observations of facts and, again, the sign or middle term is known through perception. Śabara commenting on MS, 1. 1. 4 says that perception is presupposed by inference, comparison and presumption.[7] Kumārila's explanation of Śabara's remark is similar to Vātsyāyana's.[8] Inference depends on perception because the knowledge of the relation of the major and middle terms is given by perception. We infer the presence of fire from smoke on the basis of an invariable connection between smoke and fire, which is known through perception. Even in the case when an inference depends on a previous inference (*anumitānumāna*) the premises are ultimately based on perception. Though the major portion of the stock of information that an individual possesses is derived from verbal testimony of others, yet such testimony ultimately rests on the perception of some person at some time. The Naiyāyikas and others go so far as to maintain that such entities as are imper-

4. तत्पूर्वकत्वात् त्रिविधमनुमानम् । NS, 1.1.4.
5. यत्र हि विषयस्य स्वरूपं परिच्छिद्यते तत्संवेद्यमुच्यते । BR, p. 84.
6. नाप्यनुमानाद्रूपग्रहणं सन्मात्रग्राह्यनुमानं भवति । Ibid., p. 82.
7. प्रत्यक्षपूर्वकत्वाच्चानुमानोपमानार्थापत्तीनामप्यकारणत्वम् ।
8. SV, 2.96.

ceptible to ordinary persons, e.g., atoms, merit and demerit, are perceived by yogins. Comparison and presumption obviously depend on the perception of similarity and apparent inconsistency respectively. The locus, e.g., ground, on which the negation of something, e.g., a jar, is apprehended by non-apprehension is perceived by the eye and so far non-apprehension too depends on perception. Thus perception is the besic *pramāṇa.*

5.1. *The Nature of Perception*

The *sūtra* that forms the basis of Kumārila's theory of perception runs thus:

> That cognition by a person, which appears when there is contact of the sense-organs, is perception, and it is not a means (of knowing *dharma*) as it apprehends only things existing at the present time.[9]

In the preceding *sūtra* Jaimini proposes to examine the means through which *dharma* or duty can be known and in the following *sūtra* he says that *śabda* or scriptural authority is such a means. In the present *sūtra* he rejects perception for the purpose on the obvious ground that it apprehends only those objects which exist at present, while *dharma*, as Śabara says, is 'yet-to-be' (*bhaviṣyat*). In this context Jaimini has not examined the competence of other *pramāṇa*-s, e.g., inference etc. It appears that Jaimini recognized only two *pramāṇa*-s, viz., perception for secular purposes and *śabda* for religious purposes. Dr. Radhakrishnan says: "Jaimini accepts the three *pramāṇa*-s of perception, inference and *śabda*."[10] But it is really odd that such an important *pramāṇa* as *anumāna* has not been mentioned by name by Jaimini. Probably Jaimini belonged to a period when *pramāṇa*-s were not a topic of discussion among scholars and perception was naively taken to be the only *pramāṇa*. Later when the attention of scholars shifted from ritualism to philosophical and epistemological problems, some commentators tried to

9. सत्संप्रयोगे पुरुषस्येन्द्रियाणां बुद्धिजन्म तत्प्रत्क्षमनिमित्तं विद्यमानोपलम्भनात्।
MS, 1.1.4.

10. *Indian Philosophy*, p. 378.

extract a definition of perception from the *sūtra* and again when that definition was criticized by others later commentators asserted that the author of the *Sūtra* had no occasion to define perception and that the present *sūtra* merely stated the ground of rejecting perception as it is commonly known to be for the purpose of knowing *dharma*.

An earlier commentator (Bhavadāsa, according to Pārthasārathi) takes the first part of the *sūtra* to be the definition of perception, viz., 'perception is that cognition which arises on the contact of a person's sense-organs with objects', and the second part as stating the ground of its incompetence for knowing *dharma*. Kumārila says that this cannot be a definition of perception, because any definition does not fit in the context. The author of the *Sūtra* undertakes an investigation of the means of knowing *dharma* and hence a definition of perception would have been beside the point. Moreover, inference etc. which too are means of valid knowledge and are not included in perception should have been defined by Jaimini if he intended to define perception. It cannot be said that the definitions of other *pramāṇa*-s are not given because they are implied in the definition of perception or because they are well-known. The definitions of inference etc. cannot be ascertained from that of perception and the assertion that they are well-known is equally applicable to perception.[11] From this Kumārila concludes that the *sūtra* is meant to state the reason why perception, which is well-known to be a means of valid knowledge, cannot give a knowledge of *dharma*:

> Sense-perception (of yogins) is not the means of knowing *dharma* because it apprehends accomplished entities; it apprehends accomplished entities because it is brought about by a present sense-contact; it is brought about by a present sense-contact because it is perception like the perception of ordinary persons.[12]

The import of the *sūtra* is not that that cognition which arises from a present sense-contact is perception, but it is that that

11. SV, 4. 1-9.
12. NR on SV, 4. 20-21.

which is well-known to be perception possesses the character of being brought about by a present sense-contact.[13] When Śabara in his *Bhāṣya* says *'pratyakṣam animittam evaṃlakṣaṇakaṃ hi tat'* what he means by the term *'evaṃlakṣaṇakaṃ'* is not that such is the definition (*lakṣaṇa*) of perception but that such is the reason (*liṅga*) why perception is not the means of knowing *dharma*.[14]

Bhavadāsa's definition is too wide since it applies to illusion and doubt also. In the illusion of mirage there is a contact of the eyes with heated sand and in the doubtful cognition, e.g., 'is it a man or a post?' the eyes are in contact with something of a determinate character. Bhavadāsa's definition excludes only dream cognitions and hallucinations in which there is nothing objective in contact with eyes. A definition of perception as a means of valid knowledge can be correct only if it covers all cases of true perception and at the same time excludes all cases of false perception. The definition might have been correct if it were stated in the form 'perception is that cognition which arises on the contact of a person's sense-organs with the object that is cognized (*grāhya*).' But as the term *'grāhya'* has not been inserted in the definition the defect of over-extensiveness persists, since, according to the definition, even the cognition of an object from the contact of the eyes with a different object would come to possess the character of being perception.[15]

The author of the *Vṛtti* (admittedly Upavarṣa) rightly saw that the *sūtra* could not give a correct definition of perception and hence be changed the reading of the *sūtra* into *'tatsamprayoge puruṣasya indriyāṇāṃ buddhijanma satpratyakṣam'* meaning 'true perception is that which arises from the contact of a person's sense-organs with that object alone of which it is the perception.' This definition does not cover the cases of illusion and doubt which arise on the contact with a different object. It may be urged that even without changing the reading the definition will not embrace illusion and doubt. In the illusion of silver in shell the object with which there is actual contact is lost sight of

13. SV, 4. 17-18.
14. Ibid., 4.19.
15. Ibid., 4.10-14.

due to some weakness and 'silver' which is revived in mind through association is remembered and thus what is 'perceived' is not in contact with eyes. When without changing the reading perception is defined as that which arises from sense-contact the implication is that it arises directly from sense-contact; otherwise, inference also becomes perception because it too arises mediately from sense-contact. In the inference of fire, for example, there is a contact of the eyes with smoke, which, reviving the memory of fire, leads indirectly to the cognition of fire. Thus illusion, not directly arising from sense-contact, is excluded from perception. Similarly, doubt too is mediated by memory and hence it is excluded. Pārthasārathi, on behalf of the Vṛttikāra, argues that even if it is accepted that 'silver' in shell-silver illusion is remembered it does not cease to be regarded as directly arising from sense-contact because the remembered 'silver' is identified with the perceived 'this' while the eyes continue to be in contact with the latter, so that illusion cannot but be regarded as a case of perception according to the objector's definition. Again, even if we grant that the shell-silver illusion results indirectly from sense-contact over-extensiveness cannot be avoided in the cognition of yellow conch and double moon, because these two arise directly from sense-contact and yet they are cases of illusion. Therefore, the Vṛttikāra's definition is the correct one.[16]

Pārthasārathi appears to have accepted Vṛttikāra's definition of perception. But Kumārila himself neither gives his assent to, nor does he criticize it. The later Bhāṭṭas, Cidānanda and Nārāyaṇa, define perception as the valid knowledge arising from sense-contact.[17] This definition differs from Bhavadāsa's definition in inserting the term *pramāṇa* instead of *buddhi*. *Buddhi* may be true or false but *pramāṇa* is always a true knowledge. This definition does not cover the cases of illusion as they are not *pramāṇa* or true knowledge. Later Nyāya writers, viz., Annaṃbhaṭṭa and Viśvanātha, define perception as the knowledge resulting from sense-object contact.[18] This definition like

16. SD, pp. 49-50.
17. इद्रियार्थसन्निकर्षजं प्रमाणं प्रत्यक्षम् । MM, p. 8 and NTV, p. 57.
18. इन्द्रियार्थसन्निकर्षजं ज्ञानं प्रत्यक्षम् । TS, p. 29 and SM, p. 233.

that of Bhavadāsa is not free from over-extensiveness. The definition offered by the later Bhāṭṭas, though better than the above Nyāya definition, is open to the charge of over-extensiveness in that it applies to inference also because inference too arises from the contact of the senses with some object.

The Vṛttikāra's definition that perception is the knowledge of an object resulting from the contact of the senses with the same object, which is apparently accepted by Pārthasārathi, is more satisfactory, except that it involves the practical difficulty of ascertaining whether the object in contact is the same or a different one. But this difficulty is apparently minimized by the Mīmāṃsā theory of self-validity of knowledge. It is not proper to doubt if the object in contact is the same one that is perceived or different from it unless it is contradicted subsequently or some defect in the senses is discovered. Pārthasārathi suggests that if no sensory defect is found even on a strenuous search and if no sublating consciousness appears, we should believe that the perceived object is actually in contact.[19]

However, Pārthasārathi does not give his assent to the Vṛttikāra's definition in emphatic terms. He appears to waver between different views of perception. At one place he says:

> A direct knowledge of pleasure etc. leads to the inference of some sense-organ as its cause, because in the case of colour etc. direct knowledge is always seen to depend on a sense-organ.[20]

Here he accepts that the essential nature of perception is its immediacy or directness and that its sensuous origin is only a matter of inference. But he does not give the definition of perception in terms of immediacy. A definition must state the essential nature of the thing defined.

A second essential characteristic of perception is referred to when Pārthasārathi gives the definition of sense-organ. He says: "A sense-organ is that which produces knowledge in the form of a distinct and specific consciousness (*viśadāvabhāsaṃ vijñānam*)

19. SD, p. 50.

20. अपरोक्षावभासज्ञानस्येंद्रियाधीनतया रूपादिज्ञानेषु व्याप्तिदर्शनात् सुखादिविषयमपरोक्षज्ञानमिन्द्रियमनुमापयति। SD, p. 36.

when some object is in contact with it."[21] Thus immediacy, distinctness and the character of being specific essentially belong to perception. Again, in his comment on SV,4.254, Pārthasārathi says:

> The immediate knowledge that results from sense-contact and not from any other source is perception and it is commonly known as such without any regard to how philosophers define perception.

Pārthasārathi could have boldly defined perception as a true knowledge which is direct, distinct and specific or which is direct and results from the activity of sense-organs. But perhaps there were certain real difficulties of which we will have some idea in the sequel.

Kumārila and his commentators were undecided as to the definition of perception in spite of the fact that they recognized immediacy of perception and its character of being born of sense-contact. Indian philosophers may be divided in two groups, one group defining perception in terms of immediacy and the other in terms of sense-contact. The latter definition, viz., 'perception is knowledge derived from sense-object contact' appears to be older.

5.1.1. *The Definition of Pratyakṣa in Terms of Sense-contact*

Gotama defines perception as a non-erroneous cognition produced by the intercourse of the sense-organs with objects, which is definite and independent of verbal expression.[22] The term '*avyapadeśyam*' in this definition has been interpreted in diverse ways. Vātsyāyana and Uddyotakara take it to mean 'non-verbal' while Vācaspati interprets it as meaning 'non-inferential'. Jayanta takes '*indriyārthasannikarṣotpannaṃ jñānam avyabhicāri pratyakṣaṃ*' as containing the definition of perception and '*avyapadeśyaṃ vyavasāyātmakam*' as stating the two kinds of perception, viz., indeterminate (*nirvikalpaka*) and determinate

21. Ibid.
22. इन्द्रियार्थसन्निकर्षोत्पन्नं ज्ञानमव्यपदेश्यमव्यभिचारि व्यवसायात्मकं प्रत्यक्षम् । NS. 1.1.4.

(*savikalpaka*) perception. Now, the term '*vyavasāyātmaka*' means definite and if it stands for determinate perception, then indeterminate perception must be indefinite, which implies that it cannot be '*avyabhicāri*' or non-erroneous, because indefinite knowledge, e.g., doubt, is rejected as *apramā* or invalid knowledge. Thus if the *sūtra* is interpreted as containing the definition as well as the kinds of perception, it becomes self-contradictory. Therefore, the whole *sūtra* must be taken as the definition of perception and the term '*avyapadeśyam*' should be interpreted as referring to the fact that words simply express what is perceived but they do not play any vital part in the process of perception, that is, they do not determine the character of the object perceived by way of adding to the content of perception something not given or subtracting from it something given.

Praśastapāda defines perception as the cognition that is dependent on sense-organs.[23] The Sāṅkhya too, according to Vācaspati, defines perception as the cognition dependent on sense-contact.[24]

Kumārila is inclined to define perception in terms of sense-contact. He says:

> The prefix '*sam*' in the word '*samprayoga*' occurring in the *sūtra* is used in the sense of 'right' (*samyak*) and it serves to preclude all faulty '*prayoga*'; and by '*prayoga*' is here meant the functioning (*vyāpāra*) of the senses with reference to their objects. In the case of the cognition of silver in shell the functioning of the eyes is faulty and hence such cognitions become precluded by the prefix '*sam*'. In this way the *sūtra* may be taken as a statement of the definition of perception.[25]

Thus, according to Kumārila's interpretation the *sūtra* gives the definition of perception as the cognition of a person brought about by the correct functioning of his sense-organs, and this is practically the same as that of the Vṛttikāra. Still, Kumārila merely says that this can serve as the definition of perception. He is not sure that this is the required definition. At the close

23. अक्षमक्षं प्रतीत्योत्पद्यते इति प्रत्यक्षम् । PDS, p. 186.
24. अर्थसन्निकृष्टेन्द्रियाश्रितं ज्ञानम् । STK, p. 126.
25. SV, 4.38-39.

of his discussion he says that a cognition which follows from sense-contact is commonly known by people to be perception even without knowing its elaborate definition.[26] The reason why Kumārila could not give his whole-hearted approval to the above definition is that a definition must state the essential nature of the thing defined, while sense-contact merely explains how perception is born. Sucaritamiśra says that those who have tried to define perception in terms of sense-contact simply mention the means or cause of direct consciousness; they do not say that sense-contact is the essential form of perception.[27]

5.1.2. *The Definition in Terms of Immediacy*

Now we have to find out the reason why the definition in terms of immediacy was not accepted. The Jaina, the Bauddha, the followers of Śaṅkara and Prabhākara define perception as the immediate or direct cognition of an object. Māṇikyanandi defines perception as distinct (*viśada*) cognition, which is explained as the knowledge not mediated by another knowledge and as apprehending its object in all its details.[28] Dharmakīrti is well known for his celebrated definition of perception as a cognition free from subjective images and error.[29] This definition provoked much discussion regarding the nature and conditions of valid perception and the role of language in it. But, as Dharmottara tells us, it is merely an explanation (*anuvāda*) of what perception is commonly known to be and the definition of perception presupposed by it is that it is a direct presentation of an object.[30] Freedom from subjective images and non-erroneousness are the qualifications added to ensure the validity of perception. Dharmarājādhvarīndra defines perception as pure consciousness which is direct and immediate.[31] Śālikanātha says that perception is

26. SV, 4.254.

27. अक्षसम्बन्धोऽपि चापरोक्षावभासोपायिकतयैव लक्षणकारैरपि प्रत्यक्षलक्षणत्वेनाश्रीयते न स्वरूपेण। KK on Ibid.

28. PMS, 2. 3-4.

29. प्रत्यक्षं कल्पनापोढमभ्रान्तम्। NB, 1.4.

30. यत्किंचिदर्थस्य साक्षात्कारि ज्ञानं तत् प्रत्यक्षमुच्यते। NBT, 1.3.

31. VP, p. 8.

direct apprehension.[32] The same definition is offered by the Neo-Naiyāyikas in novel terms. Viśvanātha says that perception is that cognition which is not produced through the instrumentality of another cognition, i.e., which is immediate.[33] This definition is offered as an improvement on Gotama's definition which excluded divine knowledge from perception.

The motive behind all the definitions of this class is to bring non-sensuous form of direct knowledge under perception. The knowledge of part, present and future objects attributed to mystics and God, which is supposed to be direct and non-sensuous in origin, is recognized as a form of perception by the philosophers of this group. But, since Kumārila and his followers rejected mystic perception and the existence of God on the ground that their acceptance conflicted with the supreme authority of the Veda so far as the knowledge of *dharma* was concerned, they were unwilling to recognize the validity and perceptual character of non-sensuous direct knowledge. This is why the definition of perception in terms of immediacy was not favoured though immediacy was recognized as a characteristic of perception by the Bhāṭṭas. As we have already pointed out, Pārthasārathi is ready to define perception as immediate cognition if the qualification of being sensuous is added to it.

5.1.3. *The Bhāṭṭa Critcism of Immediacy*

The later Bhāṭṭas reject this definition of perception on the ground that immediacy cannot be defined (*sākṣāttvasyānirūpaṇāt*). Cidānanda examines the term '*sākṣāttva*' thus:[34] What is meant by direct cognition? If it is said that a cognition is direct when the object manifested by it exists at the time, then does it mean that perception apprehends present existence only or that only perception apprehends present existence? If the former alternative is accepted the existence of a jar, for instance, prior and posterior, to the moment of its perception should always be known indirectly; and if the latter alternative is accepted the inferential cognition of external objects too becomes direct. The knowledge of objects existing at present is not always perceptual.

32. PP, p. 51.
33. ज्ञानाकरणकं ज्ञानं प्रत्यक्षम् । SM, pp. 234-37.
34. NTV, pp. 53-55.

It may be said that inference reveals not only present objects but also past and future ones and it is a mere accident that an object of inference may exist at the time of inference. Hence, the upholder of immediacy says, perception is distinguished from inference by the fact that it reveals present existence by its very nature and this is meant by defining it as direct cognition (*svabhāvādhīnañca svakālākalitavastvavabhāsitvaṃ sākṣāttvam*). But how can it be known where present existence is revealed naturally and where not? If it is said that the revelation of present existence is natural when the object itself is the cause of the revelation and it is accidental when the object is not its cause, then the self-revelation of a cognition, which, according to Prabhākara, is direct and non-sensuous, ceases to be perception, because a cognition cannot conceivably be the object as well as the cause of itself. Again, it will be said that a direct cognition is that which reveals an object as qualified by the time of its own occurrence (*svakālaviśiṣṭārthāvabhāsakatvam*). But in that case the self-revelation of a cognition and the cognition of self during the state of indeterminate perception will become non-perceptual. According to Prabhākara the cognizing self is invariably present in a cognition as its subject or nominative. The self is directly apprehended as the subject of every cognition and the element of cognition too apprehends itself directly, so that whatever the nature, perceptual or inferential, of a cognition may be from the point of view of its object, it is always perception from the point of view of the cognizer and the act of cognition. But this is inconsistent with the above meaning of immediacy, because in the state of indeterminate perception the consciousness of the relation of the qualifier and the qualified (*viśeṣaṇaviśeṣyabhāva*) and that of time do not appear. Finally, the upholder of immediacy is supposed to say that direct cognition is the consciousness of an object through a sense-organ in its own form (*akṣāddhi svena rūpeṇa bhānam*) and that inference, presumption etc. are not direct, because in them the consciousness of the object appears in the form of one invariably concomitant with another object and of one which reconciles an apparent inconsistency respectively. In the inference of fire from smoke the fire is cognized as related to the particular visble smoke. In the presumption of Devadatta's presence elsewhere what is cognized is not Devadatta sitting under the shade of a tree but only that if we assume Devadatta's presence elsewhere it will remove the conflict between the observed fact of his absence in the home and the belief that he is alive. Thus, direct cognition is the cognition of an object as it is independently of its relations with other objects, while inference and other *promāṇa*-s cognize objects in their relation to other objects. But, then determinate perception will cease to be direct, since there objects are manifested in their relation to other things, e.g., names. If the phrase 'consciousness of an object in its own form' is interpreted as the cognition of an object not mediated by any cognition of a different object (*svaviṣayānantargatārthāntarajñānāvyavahitatvam*) then, since coninfer ence is mediated by the knowledge of a different object and sequently the knowledge of the cognizing self and the cognition itself is so mediated, the latter ceases to be immediate.

It is clear that the above criticism is directed against Prabhākara's view of immediacy and the conclusion that can be drawn from it is that the various alternative explanations of immediacy are inconsistent mainly with that part of Prabhākara's doctrine according to which the cognizing self is immediately apprehended in every cognition and every cognition immediately apprehends itself.

We have already discussed Prabhākara's doctrine of triple perception (*tripuṭīpratyakṣa*). This doctrine is peculiar to Prabhākara and is the weakest part in his system. If the self can be an object of consciousness at all it should be known through an independent act of consciousness. Prabhākara's view that a cognition knows itself directly can be traced to the influence of the Buddhist who maintains that there is no durable entity like self and that every thought itself is the thinker. Hence the notion of immediacy cannot be rejected with the rejection of Prabhākara's doctrine.

We may not be able to define immediacy in strict logical terms, but we know what an immediate cognition is. The object of immediate consciousness is felt as given and not as imagined or thought. We can say that the object of immediate cognition makes a forced entry into our consciousness and our knowledge of it is conditioned by the presence of the object itself. Hence there should be no objection to defining perception as immediate cognition.

The Neo-Naiyāyika's view of immediate cognition as that which is not produced by the instrumentality of any other cognition is involved in a difficulty if indeterminate consciousness is recognized as a real stage in perception; otherwise there is no flaw in it. But it is recognized by him that perception is of two kinds, viz., indeterminate and determinate, and that the latter is always preceded by and dependent upon the former. Now, if the said view is accepted determinate perception ceases to be perception. The Neo-Naiyāyika tries to evade the difficulty by maintaining that indeterminate perception is real, yet we are not conscious of it.[35] In the light of this view we will have to modify the definition of perception and then say that it is a cognition that is not produced through the conscious instrumentality of any other cognition. But, then, even the cognition which results from an unconscious process of reasoning, that is, which is actually produced through the instrumentality of another cognition but appears to be independent of it, for instance, the idea appearing suddenly in my mind while I am busy in writing that there will occur an earthquake tomorrow, will become perception. It may, however, be remarked here that the distinction between the two kinds of perception observed by the majority of Indian philosophers is really based on different degrees of distinctness of consciousness and not on a real difference of kind. The awareness of first moment is usually vague and it acquires definiteness only gradually with the increase of attention.

Though Kumārila appears to have an attitude of indifference towards the problem of defining perception in a logically satisfactory manner, yet he is emphatic in declaring that perception is always an apprehension of a present thing (*vidyamānopalaṃbhana*), which rules out the possibility of mystic perception.

5.2. *Criticism of Yogic Perception*

All the Indian systems except the Cārvāka and Mīmāṃsā believe in yogic perception. It is held that a yogin or mystic, by

35. ज्ञानं यन्निर्विकल्पाख्यं तदतीन्द्रियमिष्यते । SM, p. 254.

virtue of his power of meditation, can have a direct knowledge not only of present things but also of those that are past, future and distant. Ordinary persons can have a direct knowledge of those objects alone which are present before them, while past, future, distant, hidden and subtle things are beyond the range of their perception. But mystic perception is not subject to these limitations. Dharmottara says that when concentrative contemplation (*bhāvanā*) reaches the point of perfection, mystics have a vivid vision of objects as if they were lying behind a transparent wall of mica. The cognitions of mystics are perceptual in character because they are direct, distinct and devoid of subjective images.[36]

The Jaina view is that souls in their natural condition are omniscient. It is due to the accumulation of karmic matter during transmigratory state that they lose omniscience and consequently they know only so much as is permitted by the sense-organs. But when through the practice of right conduct the veil of karmic matter is destroyed they regain omniscience. Knowledge in this state depends purely on the soul and it is called transcendental perception (*pārmārthika pratyakṣa*). In the initial stage of the annihilation of karmic matter transcendental perception is imperfect (*vikala*) and it is of two kinds, viz., *avadhi* and *manaḥparyaya*. *Avadhi* is the transcendental perception of remote but sensible objects, i.e., objects having colour, taste etc. *Manaḥparyaya* is the transcendental perception of thoughts and feelings of other persons. *Avadhi* is clairvoyance and *manaḥparyaya* is telepathy. When the karmic matter is completely annihilated transcendental perception becomes perfect (*sakala*) and, since it apprehends every object in all its infinite relations, it is called absolute knowledge (*kevalajñāna*).[37]

Kumārila says that mystic perception is impossible. The supposition that yogins an perceive remote and subtle objects is quite illegitimate. Perception is ordinarily seen to be of those objects alone that exist at present. It is impossible to perceive objects that exist no more or that will be born in future. The perception of mystics cannot go beyond the limits of ordinary

36. NBT, 1.11.
37. PNT, pp. 102-120.

perception. It is said that the so-called extraordinary perception results from the perfection of contemplation (*bhāvanāprakarṣa*). But contemplation is nothing except concentration of mind on one object. It consists in having a series of memory-images of an object uninterrupted by the thought of another object (*bhāvanā hi samānaviṣayā vijātīyāvyavahitā smṛtisantatiḥ*). Thus, the so-called mystic perception is really memory. Memory presupposes past perception. In the state of concentration a memory-image appears to be as vivid as perception, because there is no disturbance and on that account it is wrongly taken for a percept. Therefore, mystic perception is essentially hallucinatory and is not at all valid.[38] By the practice of concentration memory alone is improved, but one does not acquire the power of perceiving imperceptible objects. It is impossible that one can ever perceive objects which are beyond the range of sense-organs.[39]

The Vaiśeṣikas too believe in the capacity of yogins to perceive things which ordinary people cannot. Praśastapāda says that yogins, during the state of ecstasy, perceive, through their minds alone which acquire extraordinary excellence resulting from the practice of yoga, the essential forms of their own as well as of other selves, ether, space, time, atoms, air and mind and also the forms of qualities, actions, universals and particulars inhering in them. In the post-ecstatic state, he holds, not only the mind but even the external senses acquire excellence and yogins perceive subtle and remote objects with their help.[40] A similar power of knowing past, present and future supersensuous objects is attributed to the sages who are the authors of the Vedas, though their knowledge is not called perception. The knowledge of sages (*ṛṣis*) is different from perception and inference and is called intuition (*pratibhā*). Praśastapāda says that sometimes ordinary persons too have intuitive knowledge, as when a girl says 'tomorrow my brother will come.'[41]

Kumārila says that the flashes of intuition that we sometimes have are really false inferences resulting from things that bear an appearance of true reason (*liṅgābhāsa*), and, because they cannot

38. SV. 4.26-31 and NR.
39. KK on SV, 4.29.
40. PDS, p. 187.
41. Ibid., p. 258.

determine the true nature of objects independently of perception and other sources of right knowledge, they are not *pramāṇa*. Similarly, the intuitions of sages too are false and unreliable.[42]

That there can be an omniscient person is an unverifiable and absurd hypothesis. Those who say that the Buddha knows everything through his supernatural eye (*divya cakṣu*), must themselves be knowing taste, sound etc. through their eyes! How, otherwise, could they maintain such an absurd position in spite of their knowledge of the law of nature that the eye can apprehend colour only, the tongue can apprehend taste only and so on? We observe that the capacity of the senses is restricted to their own respective spheres and that they cannot transgress their natural limits. We certainly find differences of degrees among the sensory and intellectual powers of different individuals. We find that one can acquire unusual power of observation in the sense that he can see comparatively more distant and more minute things through vision. But we never find if any person has ever improved his vision to such an extent that he could perceive sound through vision. Perception is restricted only to objects existing at present. Hence, through perception alone everything cannot be known. Similarly, inference is possible only when true reason (*liṅga*) can be found out. Therefore, none can be omniscient. At present we do not find any omniscient person and there is no proof that such a person ever existed. There are certain books which claim that their authors were omniscient, but there is no reason why this claim should be accepted. It is argued that this claim should be accepted because it is made by an omniscient person and that the person is omniscient because he makes a true claim. But this argument involves mutual dependence (*anyonyāśraya*) and hence it is false. Moreover, the fact that one person is omniscient, if it be a fact, can truly be known only by another omniscient person, which is impossible. The Jaina view that souls are naturally omniscient and their knowledge is independent of sense-organs, can only be supported by the Jaina scriptures and the validity of the Jaina scriptures depends on the truth of this view, and thus there being a sort of mutual dependence nothing can be ascertained.[43]

42. SV, 4.32.
43. Ibid., 2.112-142.

5.3. *The Sense-organs and Their Functions*

Perception is always of a present object because it always arises from a present contact (*sati samprayoge*) of a sense-organ with an object. Contact is a relation between some sense-organ and some object, and since it is impossible to have a relation between two terms one of which is present and the other absent, perception of absent objects cannot arise. Perception depends on the activity of sense-organs and sense-organs cannot operate upon absent objects. The object on whose contact with a sense-organ perception arises, must be the same object that is perceived. Contact with some object is found in other forms of knowledge too. When the inferential knowledge of past rain arises from observing a river in flood or when future rain is inferred from the observation of dense clouds in the sky, the eyes are in contact with the river and the clouds respectively. In the illusion of silver in shell the shell is present and is in contact with the eyes while silver is absent. In these cases there is sense-contact, yet, the object cognized being different from the object in contact, these are not cases of perception. In perception the object in contact is identical with the object cognized.[44]

5.3.1. *The External Sense-organs*

Pārthasārathi defines a sense-organ as that which generates a vivid and specific cognition of the object with which it comes in contact.[45] Sense-organs are six in number, five external and one internal. The five external sense-organs are those of sight, taste, smell, touch and hearing, and the one internal sense is *manas*. Kumārila does not attempt a detailed description of the nature and number of sense-organs. He seems to have accepted what is commonly known about them and he has nothing to say against the Nyāya view of sense-organs except in the case of the sense of hearing. The later Bhāṭṭas too generally agree with the Nyāya view, but some of them offer different arguments to prove the constitution of sense-organs as it is commonly known to Indian philosophers. The Vaiśeṣika classification of the ultimate constituents of the physical universe into ether, air, fire,

44. KK on SV, 4.21.

45. यत् संप्रयुक्तेऽर्थे विशदावभासं विज्ञानं जनयति तदिन्द्रियमुच्यते । SD, p. 36.

water and earth is generally accepted, and hence the stuff out of which the different sense-organs, which are physical in nature, are made, must be one or more of these elements. According to the Nyāya the visual organ is made of fire (*tejas*) and the gustatory, olfactory, tactual and auditory organs are respectively made of water, earth, air and ether. The basic principle on which this view rests is that like must be apprehended by like. The eye apprehends colour which is supposed to be the specific property of the fire element; therefore, it must be fiery. The tongue apprehends taste which is the specific property of water; therefore, it must be watery. The nose apprehends smell which is the specific property of earth; therefore, it must be earthy. The skin and the ear apprehend touch and sound which are specific properties of air and ether respectively; therefore, the skin must be airy and the ear ethery. Pārthasārathi accepts this reasoning in the case of the visual and olfactory organs, but in that of gustatory and tactual organs he follows a different principle. It is seen that when the tongue is dry there is no sensation of taste but when it is moist gustatory sensation appears. This shows that the water element on the surface of the tongue is the manifester of taste and hence the gustatory organ is watery. Similarly, since we observe that when after plunging in water one comes out and has contact with air he feels the sensation of cold, therefore, skin which is the organ of touch must be airy. In the case of the auditory organ Pārthasārathi does not follow any reasoning but assumes it to be the space (*dik*) enclosed in the ear-cavity on the authority of the scriptures.[46]

Sucaritamiśra gives up completely the Nyāya principle of 'like apprehending like'. His reasoning is based on analogy. The sense-organs are composed of physical elements. They reside in the body and manifest such qualities of objects as colour, taste etc. The external elements too are observed to manifest these qualities. We see that colour is manifested by the light of a lamp which is fiery. Taste is manifested by water element: In dry substances there is taste but it is not manifested unless they are moistened by water. It connot be said that there is no taste in dry substances, because it must be present there as long as the things

46. NR on SV, 4.51.

exist just as colour exists as long as coloured things exist. Therefore, water is the manifester of taste. Some earthy substance is seen to manifest odour, for example, the paste of margosa bark (*nimbatvak*). When the paste of margosa bark is applied to sandal the smell of the latter is manifested more keenly. The cause of such keener manifestation is not the water in the paste but the element of earth in it, because pure water is not seen to possess this property. Therefore, earth is the manifester of odour. Similarly, the external air element is observed to manifest touch. During the cold season the cold touch of the particles of water scattered in the atmosphere is not felt unless air blows. This cold touch does not belong to air because air is neither cold nor hot. Therefore, air is the manifester of touch. Thus when it is seen that external elements (*bhūta*) manifest the different sense-qualities it must be concluded, on the strength of analogy, that sense-organs, which too manifest different sense-qualities, must be composed of the elements. Light and eye both manifest colour; light is of the nature of fire; therefore, eye too is of the nature of fire. The same reasoning is extended to the case of other sense-organs also, the case of the auditory organ being an exception. About the auditory organ Sucaritamiśra says that it is of the nature of ether (*ākāśa*) and he is supported by Cidānanda and Nārāyaṇa. Each of the elements is seen taking part in the composition of body in general and in that of a sense-organ in particular; ether takes part in the composition of body in the form of hollow spaces inside it; therefore, it must take part in the composition of one special sense-organ also. Since the other sense-organs are composed of the other elements, the auditory organ, by elimination, must be of the nature of ether. We arrive at the same result by a different line of reasoning also. In the case of other sense-organs we find that each of them manifests such quality as belongs to the element that it is composed of; sound is not a quality belonging to any of them because it is the quality of ether; therefore, it must be manifested by ether alone, so that the auditory organ must be composed of ether. This assumption is quite legitimate because it accords with what is commonly seen.[47]

47. KK on SV, 4.51.

Cidānanda and Nārāyaṇa differ from Sucaritamiśra in that sound (*śabda*) according to them is not a quality but an eternal substance, and Pārthasārathi differs from them all in that the auditory organ according to him is space (*dik*) itself limited by the cavity of ear. The reason of this divergence of opinion lies in Kumārila's attitude of uncertainty regarding the nature of the auditory organ. He has no positive reason to oppose the Nyāya view that the auditory organ is of the nature of ether. He says:

> If it is absolutely necessary to deny the assertion of the Naiyāyika, then we must seek to establish the fact of space being the sense of audition on the ground of its being laid down in the Veda.[48]

Further, he maintains that this view is as reasonable as that of the Naiyāyika and possesses the additional advantage of being supported by the Veda.[49] All the Bhāṭṭas agree that *śabda* is an eternal substance. *Śabda* is an ambiguous term. It is used in the sense of sound (*dhvani*) as well as word. Word, according to the Bhāṭṭas, is definitely an eternal substance and it is said that audible sound manifests it. But is sound too an eternal substance? Nārāyaṇa answers this question in the affirmative.[50] Sucaritamiśra maintains that it is the specific quality of ether. Pārthasārathi's view is not clear, but Rāmakṛṣṇa in his commentary on SD says that it is a quality of air.[51] Cinnasvāmīśāstrī summarizing the Bhāṭṭa view says that *śabda* has two forms, viz., sound form and letter form and that the former is a non-eternal quality of air because it is produced by an impact of air, while the latter is an eternal substance.[52]

The Bhāṭṭa reasoning to establish the elemental character (*bhautikatva*) of sense-organs appears to be more sound than that of the Naiyāyika. The Naiyāyika's principle of 'like apprehending like' breaks down in the case of *manas* which is supposed to be the inner organ of apprehending pleasure, pain etc. *Manas*

48. SV, *Śabdanityatā*, 149-50
49. Ibid., 153-54.
50. MM, p. 10.
51. SC, p. 137.
52. TSR, p. 44-45.

is a sense-organ like the eye and it apprehends such inner qualities as pleasure, pain etc., but it is not made of the substance of which these are the qualities. These are the qualities of a spiritual substance called soul, but *manas* is not spiritual in nature. Again, this principle cannot explain the perception of sound through ear if, as the Mīmāṃsaka assumes, sound be not a quality of ether but of air or not a quality at all. Moreover, the principle is not supported by facts. Sucaritamiśra seems to adopt it when establishing the etherial nature of the auditory organ, but it is adopted only after he has established the elemental nature of the other sense-organs on a different ground. He does not take it as an *a priori* principle but as a generalization. However, the Bhāṭṭa reasoning is no less fallacious than that of the Naiyāyika and the fallacy is due to an ambiguous use of the term 'manifester' (*abhivyañjaka*). The eye, for instance, is the manifester of colour and so is light, but the two cannot be of an identical nature on this account. Light, is not a manifester in the same way as the eye is. The eye manifests colour while light only helps it by being an accessory (*sahakāri*). If light were of the same nature as the eye is it could not help the latter in colour perception as the eye of another man does not help it.

5.3.2. *The Internal Sense-organ*

The internal sense-organ is called *manas* for which the English word 'mind' has been generally used. This usage, however, is quite misleading. Mind is a conscious principle, whereas *manas* is an unconscious instrument of this conscious principle like the body. As a matter of fact, there is no word in English which can properly express the concept of *manas*.

Kumārila does not try to establish the existence of *manas* by arguments as is done by the Naiyāyikas. He simply says that the cognition of pleasure etc. is perceptual in nature, because it arises when *manas* is in contact with them, and *manas* is a sense-organ.[53] While enumerating the functions of *manas* Kumārila does not mention that it is the cause of the order (*krama*) that we observe among our perceptions. There is usually a contact of sense-organs simultaneously with many things. For example, while I am per-

53. SV, 4.83.

ceiving the words that I write, there is simultaneously an impact of sounds on my ear-drums and a pressure of clothes that I wear on my skin. But I am not aware of the sounds and the pressure simultaneously with the words. There is an order in my awareness of different moments and the Naiyāyika refers to this fact as a proof of the existence of *manas* and its atomic size.[54] It appears that Kumārila did not consider it as the required proof, but, as he does not controvert the Nyāya view, it can also be said that he agreed with it. The assumption of *manas* as a sense-organ is made to explain subjective experiences. Sucaritamiśra, however, assumes it for another reason also. He says that sometimes there is a contact of the soul, a sense-organ and an object, yet no cognition of the object arises, for example, in the state of inattention, though at other times the cognition does appear. There must be some cause for this difference and this cause is the absence of contact with *manas* in the former case and its presence in the latter. Thus *manas* is not only an organ of sense, but of attention too.[55] Sucaritamiśra adds that *manas* is never dissociated from soul, not even in the state of release.[56] But this is not accepted by Pārthasārathi who maintains that in release the soul is dissociated from all knowables (*prameya*) as well as the instruments of knowledge.[57] Cidānanda and Nārāyaṇa, however, agree with Sucaritamiśra on this point. Cidānanda does not feel the necessity of assuming *manas* to explain merely the order of succession in perceptions and he is opposed to the Nyāya view that *manas* is atomic. Below we give Cidānanda's view of *manas*.

Manas exists and it is infinite in size. We have a direct experience of such subjective qualities as pleasure, pain etc. and, since all direct experiences are sensuous in origin while the external sense-organs cannot explain the direct experience of pleasure etc., there must exist an internal sense-organ which is called *manas*. *Manas* is of an infinite size, because, like soul which too is infinite, it is an intangible substance, or because it is a substance without being an effect and a material cause of anything, or because it is

54. NS, 1.1.16.
55. KK on SV, 4.166.
56. Ibid. on SV, *Śūnya*., 70.
57. SD, p. 125.

the substratum of the conjunction which is the non-constituent cause (*asamavāyi kāraṇa*) of cognition.

Others prove the existence and atomic size of *manas* in the following three ways: It is seen that, though there is a contact of the sense-organs simultaneously with many objects, yet their cognitions appear not simultaneously but in succession, and this fact proves the existence of some thing, viz., *manas*, which must intervene between soul and sense-organs before the appearance of a cognition. Now, if *manas* were infinite in size it would naturally be in contact with all the sense-organs simultaneously and thus there would be no order among perceptions. But if *manas* is assumed to be atomic, it can fully explain the order among perceptions on the ground that being atomic it can come in contact with only one sense-organ at a time, and thus the very argument which establishes the existence of *manas* also establishes its atomic size. Secondly, cognition is a transitory and specific quality of an eternal substance, viz., soul, and such a quality of such a substance is seen to originate only by the conjuction of another substance, as is the case of the atoms of earth which acquire the quality of colour by their conjunction with fire. Therefore, the required substance whose conjunction with soul results in cognition is *manas*. This argument also proves the atomic character of *manas*. *Manas* is either infinite, or of a medium size, or atomic. It cannot be infinite, because there can be no conjunction between two substances unless there is movement in one or both of them, and movement is impossible in the case of infinite substances. It cannot be of a medium size, because a thing of medium size is always an effect of some material cause, while *manas* cannot be an effect, for, otherwise, it would not survive death. Therefore, it must be atomic. Thirdly, the existence of *manas* is inferred from the direct cognition of pleasure etc. It is a sense-organ; but if it is assumed to be infinite, it cannot function as a sense-organ unless there be some limiting adjunct (*upādhi*). If some portion of body is supposed to be the limiting adjunct its accidental destruction would lead to the absence of knowledge, as, when the eye is destroyed there is no perception of colour. If the whole body is supposed to be the limiting adjunct, the feeling of pain that originates in the leg only would be felt all over the body. And since there can be no other limiting adjunct, therefore the atomic character of *manas* becomes inevitable.

These arguments are false. The first argument, which is forwarded by the Naiyāyika, does not prove the existence of *manas*. Even if it is proved the simultaneous recollection of all that one has learnt becomes inevitable, because the impressions of all that has been memorized abide in the soul and will be revived simultaneously by the conjunction of *manas* with soul. It cannot be said that all impressions are not revived simultaneously, because through concentration, which is a particular state of *manas* in which sense-organs turn away from their objects, it is quite possible to revive all impressions simultaneously. If it be said that concentration by its very nature revives impressions in an order of succession, or that the revived impressions naturally produce memory in an order of succession, then, for the sake parsimony it is better to assume that soul itself naturally produces cognitions in such an order, and thus we do away with the superfluous assumption of *manas*. It may be said that in that case the process of cognition would be uncaused, for the eye and other sense-organs by themselves are sometimes seen unable to produce cognition and hence they cannot be supposed to be a sufficient cause of cognition. It is true; but then the origination of cognitions in a succession ceases to be the proof of the existence of *manas*. It would then be assumed as the cause of cognitions and then too it would be unnecessary because the body itself could be supposed to be the required cause.

The second argument, which is put forward by Prabhākara, also is not convincing. It is seen that colour is produced in earth by fire alone; but from this the generalization that a transitory quality of every substance is produced by conjunction with another substance, is not legitimate. Thus the major premise of the argument being uncerain the inference of the existence of *manas* becomes fallacious. Or, since fire alone is seen to produce colour in earth by its conjunction, therefore, the substance whose conjunction with soul is needed to produce cognition cannot be different from fire. Or, again, let the body alone be such a substance instead of *manas*. Pārthasārathi also says:

Because the body is the receptacle of food and drink the specific qualities of soul, e.g., pleasure, cognition etc., cannot arise outside the body. Hence, as the conjunction of body alone suffices for their origination the inference of another substance, viz., *manas*, is untenable.[58]

It will be said that conjunction requires movement while soul being infinite cannot move, so that the other required substance must be able to move in order to produce cognition, but body is sometimes seen to be motionless, as in sleep, yet cognition is produced, and hence the required substance must be different from body. This is wrong. What is required must be ever in motion and body too is ever in motion, though its motion may sometimes be very subtle.

The third argument is correct, but is does not prove that *manas* is atomic. Though *manas* is infinite, yet it is able to function as a sense-organ by virtue of the body which is its limiting adjunct. The objection that in that case a pain in the leg will be felt all over the body is not proper, because a similar objection can be raised against the assumption that *manas* is atomic: When pleasure or pain is produced in the whole body by a scented bath or burning, an atomic *manas* could not come in contact simultaneously with the whole of it and then there would be no experience of such a diffused feeling. Therefore, when atomicity and infinite size both are not free from objection, it is wrong to accept atomicity alone. As a matter of fact, this argument proves only the existence of *manas* and not its size. The size is proved by a different argument and it is infinite as has already been shown.

Manas is a substance. But is it one of the other recognized substances or a different one? Pārthasārathi says that whether *manas* be elemental (*bhautika*) or non-elemental in nature, its existence is beyond doubt. Cidānanda says that being different from the external sense-organs which are composed of the elements it cannot be elemental and since it is an instrument it must be different from soul which is the agent. Then, let it be either of the two remaining substances, viz., space and time. No, *manas* is always connected with the object of knowledge either directly as in the cognition of pleasure etc. or indirectly as in

58. SD, p. 36.

external sense-perception. Whatever is perceived is only connected with *manas* in the above way and is not identical with it; space and time too are perceived; therefore, they are not identical with *manas*. So, *manas* must be an altogether different substance and it is eternal, infinite and motionless.

It is maintained that in all forms of knowledge a contact between soul and *manas* is necessary. But the difficulty now arises as to the possibility of any contact between two infinite and motionless substances. Contact between two things is possible when there is activity in one or both of them. But how can there be any activity in motionless things? This difficulty is avoided by asserting that when the motionless substances are infinite in size they are already in contact and thus there is no need of any activity. We directly observe other instances of such a contact, as that between infinite space and infinite sky; otherwise how could we speak of 'eastern sky', 'western sky' etc.?[59]

In the above reasoning the tendency of the Bhāṭṭas to avoid an assumption of the unseen as far as possible is obvious. Others assume *manas* for many reasons and assign many functions to it. But the Bhāṭṭas assume it only to explain our immediate knowledge of subjective qualities and assign other functions to the body. It is true that Cidānanda later admits that *manas* plays a part in external sensc-perception by intervening between soul and external sense-organs, but it is inconsistent with the stand taken by him in the beginning according to which *manas* is unnecessary except for the perception of pleasure etc. This is because Kumārila has emphatically stated that in the perception of colour etc. *manas* functions in cooperation with the visual and other sense-organs.[60] It appears that the Bhāṭṭas were gradually realizing the redundancy of the concept of *manas*. Yet, due to the pressure of scriptural authority and the ignorance of the functions of brain and sensory nerves that give organic sensation, the concept of *manas* could not be abandoned completely.

5.3.3. *Criticism of the Sāṅkhya View*

Sucaritamiśra criticizes the Sāṅkhya view about the constitution of sense-organs. The Sāṅkhya does not believe in the elemental

59. NTV, pp. 61-66.
60. SV, 4.160.

origin of sense-organs. He maintains that the whole universe evolves from *Prakṛti* which is matter in its original unevolved state. The first evolute of *Prakṛti* is *Mahat* or *Buddhi* from which evolves *Ahaṅkāra*. Then the process of evolution proceeds along two different lines, one determined by the preponderance of *Sattva* and the other by that of *Tamas*. The five organs of sense, the five organs of action and *Manas* which partakes the nature of both are the evolutes of *Ahaṅkāra* along the first line and the five physical elements along the second line.[61] Now, the question arises as to what this *Ahaṅkāra* is. In common parlance *Ahaṅkāra* or egoism is understood to be a form of consciousness in which the ego or self is revealed. How then can the sense-organs be of the nature of consciousness? If the Sāṅkhya means by *Ahaṅkāra* something different, then, its existence is not proved by any available means. The Sāṅkhya says that *Ahaṅkāra* is all-pervading. But in that case its evolutes, the senses, too must be all-pervading, and hence in contact with everything. This, however, is inconsistent with the fact that the senses do not come in contact with past, future, remote and subtle things, because we do not have their direct knowledge. Again, the Sāṅkhya says that there are three internal instruments of cognition, viz., *Buddhi*, *Ahaṅkāra* and *Manas*. Thus, when *Ahaṅkāra* itself is an instrument how can other instruments be of its nature? Therefore, sense-organs are not *Āhaṅkārika* but elemental.[62]

5.3.4. *Sense-organs Are Known Indirectly*

The existence of sense-organs is known through positive and negative concomitance (*anvayavyatireka*). They are not directly perceptible. Some philosophers believe that soul is of the nature of pure consciousness and hence knowledge is natural to it, so that there is no necessity of assuming the existence of sense-organs. But this is wrong. If it were true, all persons would have been omniscient. But as none is omniscient and our perception is limited to present and proximate things only, the dependence of perception on some cause is obvious. For the external things we depend on external sense-organs. When the eyes are closed

61. SK, 25.
62. KK on SV, 4.51.

there is no knowledge of colours and when the ears are closed there is no knowledge of sounds. But when they are not closed the knowledge of colours and sounds appears. From this it is inferred that colours are perceived through eyes and sounds through ears. Similarly the existence of other sense-organs is known from positive and negative concomitance. The existence of the internal sense-organ also is inferred from the immediacy of our subjective experiences. If there were no internal sense-organ such immediacy could not be explained. *Manas* is the internal sense-organ and it is different from body as other sense-organs are.[63]

5.3.5. *The Number of Sense-organs*

The number of sense-organs is limited to six, neither more nor less. Some people assert that there is only one sense-organ, viz., the skin, and that others are its different capacities located in different parts. But this view is wrong. One sense-organ cannot explain the variety of perception. To say that one sense-organ can apprehend all sense-qualities is as absurd as to say that the eye can apprehend sound and the ear can apprehend colour. To say that one sense-organ possesses five or more capacities is practically to recognized that there are more sense-organs than one. The skin is of the nature of air and it is but proper that five different capacities should belong to five different substances rather than to air alone.[64]

Some hold that there are innumerable sense-organs corresponding to the innumerable subdivisions of colour, sound and other sensory qualities. Colours are divided into red, blue, green etc. Similarly, sounds, tastes, odours and touches have innumerable subdivisions. Each of these subdivisions, it is said, must be apprehended by one distinct sense-organ. But this assumption of innumerable sense-organs is needless, though it is true that there are innumerable subdivisions of the five main sensory qualities. There are many colours differing in kind and degree, but all are apprehended by the eyes alone. When the eyes are open all the different colours are perceived, but when

63. NR on SV, 4.167.
64. Ibid., 4.163.

they are closed all colours disappear. From this it is plain that all colours are apprehended by the eye. Similarly, all sounds are perceived by the ear, all tastes by the tongue, all odours by the nose and all touches by the skin. Therefore, the number of sense-organs including *manas* is only six.[65]

5.3.6. *The Sense-contact Theory*

Perception is produced by the contact of a sense-organ with an object. In tactual and gustatory perception such contact is quite evident. The particles of air spread over the skin cannot give the knowledge of touch unless the object possessing the quality of touch is brought in contact with the skin. Touch is of three kinds, viz., cold, hot and neither cold nor hot.[66] These are actually kinds of temperature. According to modern psychology we apprehend many qualities through skin such as temperature, pain, roughness, smoothness etc. The reason why temperature sensations alone were enumerated as forms of touch seems to be that the knowledge of pain is attributed to the instrumentality of *manas* and that of softness etc. to that of vision. No difference is observed between the feeling of pain and the sensation of pain.

The particles of water spread over the surface of tongue are said to give the sensation of taste when some substance comes in contact with them. Taste is divided into six kinds, viz., sweet, bitter, sour, astringent, pungent and saline.[67]

These two sense-organs are *prāpyakāri*, i.e., they function by coming in contact with their respective objects. These are not distant senses, because they do not apprehend qualities of objects at a distance. The olfactory organ too is *prāpyakāri*. A particle of earth residing inside the nose comes in contact with the subtle particles of an odorous substance scattered in the atmosphere. Odour belongs to earth alone and it is of three kinds, viz., sweet, noxious and ordinary.[68]

The organs of vision and audition grasp their respective objects from a distance. There is no unanimity about their being

65. SV, 4.169.
66. MM, p. 241.
67. Ibid.
68. Ibid.

prāpyakāri or *aprāpyakāri*. The Buddhists maintain that these are *aprāpyakāri*, i.e., they function without coming in contact with their objects. According to the Jaina only the sense of vision is *aprāpyakāri*. All other Indian philosophers say that both of these are *prāpyakāri* like other sense-organs.

The Buddhist argues that the eye and the ear are peripheral organs and nobody is ever aware of their travelling to a distant object after leaving their abodes in the body. If these organs could come in contact with their objects there would not be any awareness of their being at a distance from us. When an object is seen or a sound is heard we are also aware that the object is at a distance and that the source of sound is far or near. This awareness of distance (*sāntaragrahaṇa*) cannot be explained by *prāpyakāritva*. The organs of taste and touch are *prāpyakāri* and are not seen to give a knowledge of distance. The organs of vision and hearing give a knowledge of distance and hence they cannot be *prāpyakāri*. Again, just as skin and tongue cannot apprehend objects of a size bigger than their own, so the visual organs too could not apprehend trees, mountains etc. which are far bigger than the pupil of the eye, if it were *prāpyakāri* like them. Near and distant objects are seen simultaneously. But if the eye be supposed to reach out to its object in order to come in contact with it, it would take more time to reach a distant object and less time to reach a near object with the result that their perception would not be simultaneous. Therefore, the visual and auditory organs are not *prāpyakāri*.[69]

Kumārila says that even if sense-functioning through contact be disproved by the Buddhist reasoning, it is beyond doubt that perception arises from the activity of sense-organs with reference to their objects. However, the contact theory as held by the Sāṅkhya and others cannot be refuted in its general form. If the visual and auditory organs operated without contact, the Sāṅkhya maintains, everything including that which is remote and hidden would be perceived. The Buddhist says that the eye and the ear are never seen to leave their abodes in the body. The Sāṅkhya asserts that peripheral organs (*golaka*) are not really sense-organs, because these are elemental while the latter

69. SV, 4.41-41.

are *Āhaṅkārika*, i.e., they are made of a subtler stuff than the gross physical elements. The *vṛtti*-s of these organs, which are supersensible, mobile and swift, move out of them and reach the objects located in external space. These *vṛtti*-s assume the forms of objects and thus we are aware of the objects. All the while these *vṛtti*-s are connected with their sites in the body. They extend from their sites to objects without being severed. It may be objected that if the physical eye is not the real sense-organ of vision, how is it that medicines applied to it remove defects and improve vision? The Sāṅkhya replies that this does not go against the view that the real sense-organs are different from the end-organs, because these end-organs contain the real sense-organs and the medicines applied to the former actually benefit the latter. A *vṛtti* issues out just as light issues from a lamp. The perception of a thing bigger in size than the eye is explained by the expansion of the *vṛtti* at the end (*pṛthvagra*). When a *vṛtti* issues out from the eye it goes on expanding and the object-size that is apprehended depends on the magnitude of the stretch of the *vṛtti*. A *vṛtti* can go only to a limited extent and not to an infinite distance so that very distant things remain invisible to us. It may be objected that when a *vṛtti* has once reached its object it must apprehend the object even if the eye is shut or destroyed in the mean time. The answer is that it is not so because with the destruction or shutting of the eye the connection of the *vṛtti* with it is severed like the light of a lamp on its extinction. Or, even if the connection be not severed the object presented by the *vṛtti* is not experienced because then the soul loses its contact with the presented object with the loss of an effort to know. Thus, according to the Sāṅkhya, the visual organ comes in contact with objects through its *vṛtti*-s and similarly the auditory organ too comes in contact with sounds so that both of them are *prāpyakāri*.[70]

The Bhāṭṭas accept that there is sense-contact in visual and auditory perception, but they reject the *vṛtti*-theory. *Ahaṅkāra* is supposed to be all-pervading and so the senses, which are *Āhaṅkārika*, too must be all-pervading; but how can an all-pervading thing move? And what is this *vṛtti*? If it is merely

70. KK on SV, 4.42-51.

the capacity of a sense-organ to apprehend its object, then it is a *śakti* and so immaterial. How can an immaterial thing move? As a matter of fact, the visual organ is made of light (*tejas*) which by its very nature possesses the property of spreading around from its source. So, though the eye does not move away from its place, the light from it goes out and comes in contact with objects.[71]

According to the Naiyāyika the speed of light is so swift that even such extremely distant an object as the planet Saturn can be perceived almost instantaneously with the opening of eyes. But Nārāyaṇa maintains that however speedy light may be, it cannot be so speedy that we could not be able to appreciate the difference between the times that the light of the eye takes to reach an object millions of miles away and another which is at a distance of only a few inches. From the fact that we can see Saturn as soon as we open our eyes it should be concluded that the light of the eye at the moment of coming out becomes one with the all-pervasive external light and so it need not travel to such a long distance. It should not be supposed that, since the external light is all-pervasive, a man living in Kerala could see the river Gaṅgā, because the visual light unites not with the whole of the external light but with only that portion of it which is favoured by the merits and demerits (*dharmādharma*) of the perceiver.[72]

According to modern physics light travels from an external object to the retina of the eye. Nārāyaṇa seems to have struck this truth so far as he maintains that the visual light meets the light coming from external objects; but he stops short of the complete truth because he could not shake off the deeply ingrained belief that the visual organ is made of the fire-element. He is naturally ignorant of the late modern discovery that light travels in the form of rays in a straight line at a tremendous speed.

5.3.7. *The Perception of Sound*

About the nature and perception of sound the Bhāṭṭa had to wage a serious battle against his rivals, since the eternality of

71. Ibid., 4.51.
72. MM, pp. 11-12.

Veda was supposed to depend on the eternality of *śabda*. According to the Bhāṭṭa *śabda* is an eternal and omnipresent substance and the effort of a speaker does not produce it but simply manifests it. The debate regarding the eternality of *śabda* would strike us today as a futile exercise, and hence the following account will be confined to the perception of sound only.

According to the Vaiśeṣika sound is initially produced by conjunction and disjunction, as when one thing strikes upon another and when two closely conjoined things are forcibly separated. This initial sound produces another similar to it, which in turn produces a third similar sound and so on in the manner of a wave giving rise to another wave, till the last one is produced in the ether enclosed within the ear-cavity. It is this last sound in the series that is apprehended by the auditory organ and not the initial one.

This view, according to Kumārila, is not satisfactory as it involves many unverifiable assumptions. We are never aware of a multiplicity of sounds, nor is there any awareness of the heard sound being different from the uttered one. When someone utters some word we believe that we hear the same word and the speaker also believes that the same word that he utters will be heard by others. How can a sound give rise to another sound similar to it? Why is sound heard quickly in the direction of wind and not so quickly in the opposite direction? Why is the supposed series of sounds not produced in all directions and heard by everyone in the world? Why is sound not able to cross such obstacles as a wall etc.? These questions cannot be satisfactorily answered by the Vaiśeṣika, for, according to him, sound is a non-corporeal (*amūrta*) quality of the all-pervading ether (*ākāśa*).[73]

According to the Jaina, *śabda* is substantial in nature. It is composed of very subtle particles of matter (*pudgala*) possessing form and touch and is heard when it travels to and comes in contact with the auditory organ. This view is even more objectionable than the Vaiśeṣika view. The travelling of sound, a material entity, to the ear is not perceived by anyone. The existence of form and touch in sound, the suppression of these

73. SV, *Śabdanityatā*, 88-98.

qualities assumed to explain their imperceptibility, and the existence of subtle parts in sound are simply wild assumptions having no ground. How can the invisible parts of sound be arranged together and how can these arrangements differ among themselves so as to give different words? In the absence of fluidity how can these parts be held together and why should they not be scattered apart by wind before reaching the ear of the hearer? The parts of sound must be extremely light and loosely held together and when they come in contact with such things as a tree etc. in their way they must fall apart like a lump of clay. Moreover, when they enter the ear of one person they must not be heard by others.[74]

According to the Sāṅkhya the *vṛtti* of the auditory organ goes out to the locus of sound. The Sāṅkhya assumes two unverifiable things, viz., the existence of *vṛtti* and its movement. Now, when the *vṛtti* exists at a distance, viz., in the locus of sound to which it moves, how can it affect the auditory organ of the hearer? Certainly the hearing of sound presupposes some modification of the hearing organ; but it is inconceivable how such modification can be produced from a distance. If it be said that the hearing organ is all-pervading, then even a very distant sound should be audible. And, why should a sound obstructed by a wall be not audible? The *vṛtti* of the hearing organ being non-conporeal (*amūrta*) cannot be obstructed by material obstacles. Moreover, the wind blowing in the direction of the sound should not help its perception nor the wind blowing in the opposite direction should hinder it. It is more reasonable to think that the former should hinder and the latter should help hearing because it is the *vṛtti* that is supposed to move, not sound.[75]

The Buddhist says that sound is heard without requiring any contact between the auditory organ and sound. But then near and distant sounds should be equally audible or inaudible, because the absence of contact is common in both the cases. Nor should there be any sequence among heard sounds, and the perception of the same sound as loud by a person who is stand-

74. Ibid., 106-112.
75. Ibid., 113-119.

ing near it and as low by another standing at a greater distance too remains inexplicable.[76]

Having criticized all the above views Kumārila gives his own view as follows: When a person speaks the air inside his body struck by his effort moves out of his mouth and this air is helped by the conjunction and disjunction of his palate, tongue and throat. The extent to which the air goes is determined by its initial velocity which depends on the intensity of the speaker's effort. That is why sound is not heard everywhere. When the air forces its way through the surrounding atmosphere which is calm, its parts have conjunction and disjunction with the latter and so the sound is heard in all directions. When this air reaches the ether of the aural cavity it imparts a certain potency (*śakti*) to the auditory organ, which produces certain modifications (*saṃskāra*) in the latter. Different modifications are caused by different sounds and they are the cause of the differences in sound perception. Sound is not heard when there are obstacles such as a wall etc. because they obstruct the passage of air. When loud sounds are heard some pressure is experienced upon the ear. This is caused by the air-current striking the ear with a great force. The initial velocity of the sound gradually decreases and hence the intensity of sound differs at different points of its passage till it disappears completely. Thus the sequence, loudness, lowness etc. of the heard sounds are fully explained by this theory.[77]

5.3.8. *Forms of Contact*

The objects of which we have a direct knowledge through perception are substances, qualities, actions and universals. The sense-contacts involved in their perception vary according to the object perceived. The older Naiyāyikas enumerate six such contacts (*sannikarṣa*), viz., conjunction (*saṃyoga*), inherence-in-what-is-conjoined (*saṃyukta-samavāya*) inherence-in-what-is-inherent-in-what-is-conjoined (*saṃyukta-saṃaveta-samavāya*), inherence (*samavāya*), inherence-in-what-is-inherent (*samaveta-samavāya*), and the relation of quali-

76. Ibid., 119-121.
77. Ibid., 122-130.

fication and the qualified (*viśeṣaṇaviśeṣyatā*). These are the forms of ordinary contact. The Neo-Naiyāyikas add three forms of extraordinary contact to this list. They are: contact through generality (*sāmānyalakṣaṇa*), contact through association (*jñānalakṣaṇa*), and contact through meditation (*yogaja*).

The knowledge of substances is given through the contact known as *saṃyoga*. The senses are substances and they can directly come in contact with substances alone. They cannot have a direct contact with qualities, actions and universals which inhere in substances. The contact of the senses with these latter is mediated by *samavāya* and hence it is called *saṃyukta-samavāya*. The contact of the senses with universals inhering in qualities and actions is still further mediated by another inherence. Whiteness, for instance, which is the universal of the quality 'white' inheres in a white substance with which the visual organ comes to have conjunction. Hence this form of contact is called *saṃyukta-samaveta-samavāya*. The contact involved in the perception of sound which is a quality of ether, is different from all the above contacts and is called *samavāya*. It is different from *saṃyukta-samavāya* which is involved in the perception of the qualities of colour, taste, touch and smell. The argument advanced by the Naiyāyika for this difference is that sound being a quality of ether inheres in it and the auditory organ itself being a part of ether enclosed within the ear there is no need of its conjunction with any other substance. The colour of a jar inheres in the jar and the eye can apprehend it only after having conjunction with the jar. But, sound, on the other hand, inheres in the organ that apprehends it and hence it is known through *samavāya*. The universal of sound (*śabdatva*) is apprehended through *samaveta-samavāya* because it inheres in sound. The last form of ordinary contact, viz., *viśeṣaṇaviśeṣyabhāva* is assumed to explain the perception of negation (*abhāva*). Negation, i.e., absence of something is supposed by the Naiyāyika to be an object of perception. It cannot be perceived in the manner in which positive entities are perceived, because there is nothing to have a conjunction with sense-organs. Therefore, it is said that negation is perceived as a qualification of some positive locus. In perception of the absence of a jar on the ground there is a union of the eye with the ground and through this the eye comes in contact with the absence of jar as a qualification of the ground. The relation known as *samavāya* which exists between a substance and its qualities, actions or universal, according to the Vaiśeṣika, is imperceptible. According to the Naiyāyika *samavāya* too is an object of perception and the contact which is involved in its perception also is *viśeṣaṇaviśeṣyabhāva*.

Among the various forms of extraordinary contact the first, *sāmānyalakṣaṇa*, is assumed to explain the knowledge of all past, present and future individuals belonging to a class. The Naiyāyika maintains that when the generic character of fire, for instance, is perceived we also perceive all the particular instances of fire at the same time. Through *jñānalakṣaṇa-sannikarṣa*, it is said, we perceive a quality of a substance by a sense-organ which is not ordinarily perceived by that organ. For example, when the eyes are in contact with a sandal tree we are not only aware of its colour but also of its sweet smell. The tree is at such a great distance that the olfactory organ cannot come in contact with its smell and hence it cannot be a case of olfactory perception. It is a case of visual perception and yet smell is not ordinarily an object of visual perception. What happens is that on a direct contact of the eye with the colour and shape of the tree the olfactory image of the sweet smell is revived through association. But it cannot be said to be a case of memory for this reason, because the cognition of sweet smell of sandal-wood is an extraordinary form of perception. The cognition of the heat of fire at a distance is another instance of such perception. The *yogajasannikarṣa* is involved in the perception of *yogins*. Through the power of meditation their sense-organs can come in contact with all past, future, minute and remote objects.[78]

The three forms of extraordinary contact are ruled out by the Bhāṭṭa rejection of the possibility and validity of extraordinary perception. The Bhāṭṭa criticism of *yogaja* perception has already been given. Perception dependent on the contact known as *sāmānyalakṣaṇa* was assumed by the later Naiyāyikas to

78. Bodas: TS, pp. 221-27; See also Sinha, *Indian Psychology: Perception*, pp. 75-76.

safeguard the validity of the universal major premise (*vyāpti*) on which the validity of an inference depends. But, since the Bhāṭṭas do not recognize this sort of perception as the source of our knowledge of *vyāpti*, *sāmānyalakṣaṇa* is rejected. This point will be explained in the chapter on inference. Perception based on *jñānalakṣaṇa-sannikarṣa* is not perception at all. It is really inferential in nature and to call it perception is wrong. To say that smell can be apprehended by vision is absurd. The visual organ has the capacity of responding to colours alone. The strongest proof of the fact that the said cognition is not visual perception is that a person who is not acquainted with the smell of sandal does not perceive it when the sandal tree is at a distance, though he perceives the form and colour of the latter like one who is acquainted with its smell. Only the olfactory organ responds to odours, but at the time, due to the distance, the odour of sandal does not fall within the range of the activity of this organ. Hence it cannot be perceived at the time. It is only a person already aware of the association between sandal and sweet smell who cognizes sweet smell on recognizing a sandal tree through vision, and for this reason this cognition is inferential in nature. Similarly the cognition of the warmth of fire from a distance is inferential.[79]

The Bhāṭṭa recognizes only two forms of contact, viz., conjunction (*saṃyoga*) and identity-with-what-is-conjoined (*saṃyukta-tādātmya*). The various substances are perceived through the conjunction of sense-organs with them. The contact known as *samavāya* is rejected, because sound which is said to be perceived through this contact is not a quality but an eternal substance and hence it is apprehended through conjunction with the auditory organ like other substances.

Leaving aside the controversy whether sound is a substance or a quality we can say that the Naiyāyika's view of auditory perception does not seem to be consistent with his realistic position. The Naiyāyika maintains that sound is produced in the ether of the aural cavity, which implies that our awareness of sound as produced by an external object and coming from a distance is an illusion. In other words, sound thus becomes a subjective appear-

79. NR on SV, 4. 252-53.

ance and loses its objectivity. The Naiyāyikas were not aware of the functions of the cortex. But following the line of their reasoning it can be said that sound is not the quality of the aural ether even, but a specific response of the cortex to some objective fact whose real nature we do not know. Extending the reasoning to other forms of perception we can conclude that our perceptions are only subjective appearances of some objective reality whose actual character we can never know and thus we land on the Kantian phenomenalism which is but a step towards Berkeleyan subjectivism. It is true that according to the Naiyāyika sound is produced in the external space and what is perceived is the sound produced in the aural cavity which is the last in the series of sounds initiated by the first external sound. But this amounts to saying that what is actually perceived is subjective while its objective character is a matter of belief, rational or irrational. In the same way we can also say that the perceived colour, touch, taste and smell actually belong to the fire, air, water and earth residing in the eye, skin, tongue and nose respectively, while their objectivity is a matter of belief which may or may not be true. The Nyāya view of auditory perception is wrong for one more reason. If the perceived sound is the quality of the aural ether which, again, constitutes the auditory sense, then it apprehends its own quality. But this goes against the generally accepted view that a sense-organ cannot apprehend itself or its own quality. The sense-organs and their qualities are rightly held to be supersensible and knowable through inference alone.

Returning to the Bhāṭṭa view of contacts, when *samavāya* as a form of contact is rejected *samavetasamavāya* is automatically rejected. *Viśeṣaṇatā* is rejected because negation according to the Bhāṭṭas is not an object of perception but of a different means of knowledge known as *anupalabdhi* or non-apprehension. Out of the remaining two forms of contact, viz., *saṃyuktasamavāya* and *saṃyuktasamavetasamavāya*, the first is accepted but only under the changed name *saṃyuktatādātmya*, where *tādātmya* is substituted for *samavāya*. The reason is that *samavāya* or inherence as a form of relation subsisting between two naturally inseparable things is rejected by Kumārila, and *tādātmya* or identity is accepted in its place. Thus qualities, actions and universals of substances are perceived through the contact *identity-*

with-what-is-in-conjunction. The universals subsisting in qualities and actions also are perceived through this form of contact because indirectly they too have identity with the substances in conjunction with sense-organs. Or, for their perception a third form of contact *saṃyuktatadātmatādātmya* corresponding to *saṃyuktasamavetasamavāya* may be assumed in which case the number of contacts will be three only.[80]

The different forms of contact are not facts of experience. They are assumed to explain the functioning of the sense-organs. Modern science does not favour the view that there is a mechanical conjunction between the senses and their objects. It explains sense-functioning in terms of certain chemical and electrical changes produced in sense-organs by certain energies coming from the environment. Kumārila personally does not make any dogmatic assertion about contact. But he emphasizes that there is an activity of sense-organs in perception. Since activity from a distance is not generally seen to take place, it is more probable, according to him, that there is some form of contact between sense-organs and objects. The second point that he emphasizes is that a sense-organ is naturally adapted to respond to only a certain class of stimuli. This is why the visual organ, though indirectly in contact with all the qualities inhering in a visible object, does not give the knowledge of such qualities as smell, taste, touch etc. except that of colour and form. Thus contact determined by the natural capacity of a sense-organ is the cause of perception.[81]

5.4. *Indeterminate and Determinate Perception*

Two forms or rather stages of perception have been generally recognized in Indian philosophy. They are: *nirvikalpaka* or indeterminate and *savikalpaka* or determinate perception. The former precedes the latter and the latter is more advanced than the former. Perception that arises immediately after the contact of a sense-organ with some object is *nirvikalpaka,* i e., devoid of *vikalpas* or determinations; but the next moment while the sense-object contact still continues the object is determined as belonging

80. MM, pp. 12-17.

81. योग्यतासहिता प्राप्तिः । NR on SV, 4.63-64.

to a particular class or as possessing some qualities etc., and then the perception becomes *savikalpaka* or determinate. Indeterminate perception is also called simple apprehension (*ālocana-jñāna*).

The word *kalpanā* which is similar in form (derived from the root *kalp*) and identical in meaning with the word *vikalpa* was first used in philosophical literature probably by Diṅnāga, a Buddhist logician, in his *Pramāṇasamuccaya* where perception is defined as knowledge free from imagination and unconnected with name, genus etc.[82] The earliest use of the word *ālocana* is seen in Praśastapāda's *Bhāṣya*. From this it appears that earlier philosophers were aware of the two forms of perception, though a clearer and detailed description of them was attempted for the first time by Kumārila. Kumārila maintains the distinction against rival theories which, according to the commentators, are held by the Buddhist, the Advaitin and the Grammarians. The Buddhist holds that there can be no determinate perception; the Advaitin says that determinate perception does not give a knowledge of reality; and the Grammarian says that indeterminate perception is impossible.

5.4.1. *Dharmakīrti's View*

According to Dharmakīrti, another Buddhist logician, a contemporary of Kumārila, perception is devoid of determinations and non-erroneous (*kalpanāpoḍhamabhrāntam*). Non-erroneousness is a general condition of all forms of valid knowledge. The word *kalpanā* is explained as meaning a cognition capable of being associated with a name (*abhilāpasaṃsargayogyapratibhāsa-pratītiḥ*). When a man knowing the relation between a name and the named determines an object as jar his cognition is mixed with the word 'jar'. In the case of one who has not yet learnt the relation between a name and the named, e.g., a child, the cognition is not actually mixed with a name, still it is capable of being expressed by a name. Both of these cognitions are excluded from perception.

But, how, it may be asked, can a cognition which is not actually mixed with a name be ascertained to be capable of

82. प्रत्यक्षं कल्पनापोढं नामजात्याद्यसंयुतम् ।

being so? Dharmottara says that when a cognition is independent of or unconditioned by the object cognized it is ascertained to be capable of being associated with a name. Perception is that cognition whose content is determined exclusively by an objective fact; but *kalpanā* is purely a subjective idea having no regard for an objective fact. Perception depends on the immediate presence of the object perceived while *kalpanā* is independent of its object. Though a child does not know the use of words, yet his cognition of the mother's breasts is *kalpanā* and not perception. Unless the child recognizes the mother's breasts as the things which satisfied his hunger in the past he does not suck them. The child definitely identifies what he sees now with what he saw in the past, and, as what is past and gone cannot be the object of present perception, the child's present cognition is mixed with an element of *kalpanā*. The child does not know the use of names, yet his cognition is *savikalpaka*, and hence not perception.

Perception in the true sense is produced purely by the object perceived and is free from verbal expression and all other subjective contributions. In auditory perception, though words are heard, yet there is not necessarily a recollection that they signify objects, and so far it is free from *kalpanā*. The object of perception is the unique individuality of something (*svalakṣaṇa*). Things have a twofold nature. In some respects they are unique and in others they are alike. A thing possesses a unique individuality of its own and also features that it shares with other things. The moments of an object-series possess their own unique individuality and at the same time they all possess the common feature of belonging to the same series. The latter aspect of them, as distinguished from the former is called *sāmānyalakṣaṇa*, and it cannot be an object of perception. *Svalakṣaṇa*, which is the real object of perception, is that which makes a difference between cognitions arising out of a close and a remote observation of a thing. When an object is observed from a distance the resulting cognition is indistinct. But when it is observed closely the cognition is distinct. That which is cognized distinctly on a closer approach and indistinctly from a distance is *svalakṣaṇa* and it is the 'real' (*paramārthasat*) because it is free from conceptual impositions (*anāropitaṃ rūpam*) or thought-determinations.

Sāmānyalakṣaṇa or the form of an object which is common to other objects, e.g., 'cowness' does not really belong to the object, but is imposed upon it by the knower, and hence it does not make any difference in cognition, whether an object is observed closely or from a distance. Therefore, it is not an object of perception. *Sāmānyalakṣaṇa* is a mode of thought and not a mode of existence. Our modes of thinking or categories of thought are external to things-in-themselves; they cannot touch reality.[83]

5.4.2. *Advaita View*

According to the Advaitin the sole object of perception is pure being (*sanmātra*). Perception apprehends neither unique particulars, such as *svalakṣaṇa*-s, nor particulars of a relative generality, such as cowness. *Svalakṣaṇa*-s are exclusive characters of things while cowness etc. are inclusive. Both are the products of discursive thought, because they presuppose the relational activity of mind. Reality by itself is neither exclusive nor inclusive. The determination of objects as possessing exclusive or uncommon features and inclusive or common features is alien to their real nature, because exclusiveness and inclusiveness are not given in perception, but imported by the relational intellect. Indeterminate perception is the only form of perception. It reveals reality in its true form. In it there is no differentiation between a cow and a horse.

Particulars such as 'this is a cow', 'this is a horse' etc. are not given by perception. The knowledge of particulars depends on the knowledge of difference which is of the nature of mutual negation (*anyonyābhāva*). Consciousness in the form 'this is a cow', for instance, depends on the consciousness that 'this' is different from a horse etc. The difference of a cow from a horse is nothing but the absence of horseness in it and the absence of cowness in a horse. This mutual absence being a form of negation cannot be the object of perception which apprehends only positive entities. It is the object of an independent means of cognition known as *anupalabdhi*. The perception of particulars is impossible for another reason also. A particular A cannot be

83. NBT, pp. 6-14.

cognized unless it is preceded by the cognition of its difference from B, C etc. But in order to cognize A's difference from B, A and B should first be individually cognized. The difference is a property of A. How can a property be cognized unless the object of which it is the property is cognized? The cognition of the difference of A presupposes the cognition of B also, because unless it is so how can it be known that A is different from B? A is the substratum (*āśraya*) of difference and B its counter-correlate (*pratiyogin*). Thus the cognition of a particular depends on the cognition of its difference from other particulars and the cognition of the difference again depends on the cognition of the particular which is the substratum of the difference and the particular which is its counter-correlate. The whole process involves mutual dependence (*anyonyāśraya*). Therefore, the cognition of particulars is impossible.

Metaphysically particulars and difference both are unreal, because they are self-contradictory, while reality being a harmonious whole cannot allow any contradiction in itself. Particulars are merely creations of imagination under the influence of *avidyā* which is beginningless. One and secondless being is the only reality and particulars belong to the realm of appearance. The distinction of universal and particular is illusory and what is apprehended by indeterminate perception is neither universal nor particular but pure being.[84]

5.4.3. *Bhartṛhari's View*

The Buddhist and the Advaitin recognize only indeterminate perception as valid perception. Bhartṛhari, the grammarian, on the other hand, recognizes only determinate perception. Not only perception but all forms of cognition are determinate as all of them are verbalized. "There in no cognition in the world which is not accompanied by words; all cognitions are, as it were, interpenetrated by words."[85] Thought and language are inseparable. Knowledge is not an end in itself. It is only a means to successful practical behaviour which depends on a

84. SV,4.114-16; See also NR and KK.

85. न सोऽस्ति प्रत्ययो लोके यः शब्दानुगमादृते।
अनुविद्धमिव ज्ञानं सर्वं शब्देन गृह्यते ॥ Va.

proper discrimination between things. The differences among things cannot be ascertained properly unless knowledge is determinate. Even the behaviour of children and animals presupposes a determinate knowledge of things. Bhartṛhari identifies determinate knowledge with verbalized knowledge. The behaviourist says that thinking in human beings is nothing but subtle speech. Bhartṛhari goes even further and says that thought and perceptions of even small children and animals are accompanied by subtle speech (*sūkṣmavāk*). Children learn speech and the relation between words and things later and hence it is absurd to say that their cognitions are accompanied by words even before they learn the use of words. But Bhartṛhari explains the presence of subtle speech before learning by assuming impressions (*saṃskāra*) of previous births, which, he says, are now aroused by some unseen power. Thus perception in his view cannot be indeterminate.[86]

5.4.4. *Kumārila's View*

Against the grammarian's view Kumārila asserts that the denial of indeterminate perception is the denial of a well-established fact. Experience proves that on the contact of a sense-organ with an object the cognition that arises in the first moment is indeterminate. It is a simple apprehension or a bare awareness of an object and is the basis of the predicative consciousness that arises in the next moment. The consciousness of the first moment is characterless (*nirviśeṣa*) and it is presupposed by and develops into the consciousness of the object as possessing distinct features. It resembles the perception of infants, dumb persons and animals and is produced purely by the object (*bālamūkādivijñānasadṛśaṃ śuddhavastujam*) because it is not mixed with anything contributed by the knower's mind. In the absence of indeterminate perception determinate perception too is not possible.

In the determinate stage the object is conceived as belonging to a class and possessing a certain name. The class-concept and the name are given by memory. But memory cannot arise all of a sudden without some cause. As a matter of fact, what is per-

86. KK on SV, 4.112.

ceived in the indeterminate stage arouses latent impressions and then alone can the object be determined as possessing a class-character and a name. The grammarian's view that indeterminate perception cannot initiate practical activity is wrong, because certain practical activities (e.g., what are known as *reflex actions* in modern psychology) are seen to follow indeterminate perception. When the sensation of burning is felt a person immediately moves away from the object that causes it before discovering the specific nature of burning. The activity is complete before determinate cognition appears. Moreover, it is not proper to deny indeterminate perception merely on the ground that it has no pragmatic value. Value is not a proof of reality. The behaviour of children and animals is based on indeterminate perception alone. It is strange how infants could be in possession of subtle speech even before they learnt the use of language. If the impressions of a former birth when language was learnt are supposed to be present in the infant, what is the use of taking pains to teach him language? Why should the infant not remember the language learnt in a former birth later on? It cannot be said that the impressions are destroyed when the infant grows up. When the agonies of death and rebirth are not able to destroy the impressions, why should they be destroyed in the process of growth? Hence it is certain that the perception of infants and animals is indeterminate and similar in nature is the perception of adults at the first moment of sense-contact.[87]

5.4.5. *The Object of Indeterminate Perception*

The object of perception in indeterminate stage is neither a universal nor a particular, but the individual (*vyakti*) which is the unity of universal and particulars. A universal or class-character resides in many individuals in common and a particular resides exclusively in one individual. In indeterminate perception there is no consciousness of these, because there is no assimilation and discrimination at the time. Through the process of assimilation an object is cognized as having some common properties and through the process of discrimination

87. NR and KK on SV, 4.112.

it is differentiated from other objects. Both of these processes involve a memory of other objects and a comparison of the perceived object with them. Unless there is a comparison with other objects the perceived object cannot be determined as having some common properties and some specific ones. Before the appearance of memory and comparison the object is perceived as an individual whole in which the generic and specific characters are fused together. Indeterminate perception is non-conceptual and non-relational, because it is not the result of the analytic activity of thought.[88]

The Advaitin's assertion that indeterminate perception apprehends pure being and that the perceptions of a cow and a horse are identical in this stage is wrong. Is it that there is no consciousness of difference (*bhedabuddhi*) between blue and yellow, sweet and bitter, cold and hot, cow and horse, when their cognition arises immediately after sense-contact? If the Advaitin answers this in the affirmative he must be too bold to ignore or rather contradict the testimony of direct experience. If the consciousness of difference at the time is absent, how can its appearance in subsequent moments be explained? It is true that in the indeterminate stage difference is not apprehended in an explicit form like 'this is different from that'. But it is also true that the indeterminate consciousness of a blue object is different from that of a yellow one. We are not able to express the difference of a blue object from a yellow one in words, but from this inability it is not proper to deny the difference. Difference is an objective fact and it reveals itself in perception, though in the initial stage of perception it is not known distinctly that things differ from one another in this or that particular respect. Objects are perceived in their individual forms and then their mutual exclusiveness is discovered. Things have their own positive character which differs in each individual case and is the basis of their mutual exclusiveness. A is A not because it is not B or C, but because it has a positive nature of its own on whose account it is not B or C. The form of blue is different from the form of yellow and it is apprehended by indeterminate perception in its own form, not in the form of its

88. Ibid., 113.

difference from other things. Therefore, the different forms having been apprehended first, there is no incongruity in the manifestation of mutual negation which appears subsequently. Otherwise, determinate cognition of difference itself remains unexplained. Even *Avidyā* cannot make it intelligible. If the alleged difficulty of mutual dependence (*anyonyāśraya*) between the apprehension of particularity and that of difference be real, how can *Avidyā* resolve it? The seed-sprout process cannot be of any avail. It cannot be said that the apprehension of difference and that of particularity give rise to each other in a beginningless series like the seed-sprout series. Will one who has just got up from deep sleep, during which state, according to the Advaitin, we have a vision of the absolute reality, first apprehend difference or particularity ? If the two are mutually dependent no cognition will arise. If it is said that the apprehension of particularity will arise first due to *Avidyā* alone even without the apprehension of difference, then let it be due to the sense-organs alone. What need is there of postulating *Avidyā*? The Advaitin's view of perception is vitiated by the metaphysical dogma that the diversities and differences of things are unreal and this dogma is supported by the apparently self-contradictory nature of the concept of difference. But difference and diversity are real facts of experience. It is wrong to negate an observed fact not favouring a preconceived theory. The business of a philosopher consists in explaining and systematizing facts of experience into a self-consistent whole and not in explaining them away. Therefore, pure being is not the object of indeterminate perception.[89]

Is, then, particularity alone the object of indeterminate perception? No. It has been shown that pure individual is apprehended by indeterminate perception and it has a twofold character. It has a generic and a specific aspect (*sāmānyaviśeṣātmaka*). Both these aspects manifest themselves in the indeterminate stage. Otherwise how could they be apprehended by determinate perception? Generality and particularity are not introduced by subjective thought into the being of an individual. They are not imaginary impositions but objective characteristics of things.

89. SD, pp. 40-41.

Even when an individual object is apprehended without being related to other objects it is presumed that they too are apprehended, because they constitute the very being of an individual object. In the determinate stage they are recognized to qualify the individual, and, since recognition of an unperceived thing is not possible, it is but reasonable to suppose that they are apprehended in the indeterminate stage also. The only difference lies in that in the indeterminate stage they are not discriminated from each other. Though the object of indeterminate perception is of a manifold form, its various aspects are fused together and we are not fully conscious of them. In that state there is no memory of other objects similar and dissimilar to the object in front. In the absence of memory there is no consciousness of the object as having a nature possessed by other objects of the same class (*anuvṛtti*) and as having a character not shared by others but exclusive to it (*vyāvṛtti*). Therefore, in indeterminate perception generality is apprehended but not as common to many objects and particularity also is apprehended but not as peculiar to the object. They are apprehended in their own forms. An individual object is the unity of its generic and specific characteristics. The characteristics can be discriminated from each other only by the analytic activity of mind. In indeterminate perception there is no analysis and hence they are not recognized distinctly. From this account of indeterminate perception it is clear that it is an unverbalized judgment. That is, it cannot be expressed in linguistic terms. Words help in analysing a datum of perception into a subject and a predicate. Before they come to our help the perceived something remains an unanalysed mass, incommunicable to others. Therefore, indeterminate perception is non-relational and non-predicative and forms the basis of subsequent determinations.[90]

5.4.6. *An Analysis of Determinate Perception*

Indeterminate perception is followed by determinate perception which analyses the unity of sense-datum into a diversity of attributes in the form of generality, particularity etc. All that was implicit in indeterminate perception is made explicit with

90. NR & KK on SV, 4. 118-19.

the help of the processes of recollection, analysis and synthesis in determinate perception. The datum is analysed into its component elements and is interpreted in the light of previous experience and then we have such consciousness as 'this is a cow', 'this is white', 'this is moving' etc. This relational consciousness is effected by the processes of analysis and synthesis. The given '*this*' is analysed into its attributes and then they are synthesised with the '*this*' in the form of a subject-predicate relationship. The datum is a whole which is dissected by the intellect into artificial bits as it were, but as a compensatory measure unity is restored to it again in the form of a proposition. In the process of determination nothing is attributed to the thing which was not already there. The various forms in which a thing is determined belong to the thing and not to the mind of the cognizer. Though recollection is involved in the process of determination, generic and specific properties do not cease to be objective on that account, because they are not imagined but discovered and what is remembered is that such properties have been observed or not observed in other things in the past. The cognition arising in this way is perceptual in character just as indeterminate cognition is, because in the course of determination there is no loss of contact between sense-organs and object. When the object in front is determined to be a cow and white in colour, the eyes are throughout open and active. It does not cease to be perception merely because it is mediated by the memory of the words 'cow' and 'white'. Though memory steps in before apprehending the object as 'cow', yet the apprehension depends on sense-object contact and hence it is perception. It cannot be said that determinate cognition is not perception because perception depends exclusively on the operation of sense-organs while determinate cognition depends on memory also. That which is independent of sense-object contact cannot be called perception. But perception does not depend solely on sense-object contact. Even indeterminate perception is not solely due to such contact, because the contact of *manas* and soul with the senses also is needed for its birth. In determinate perception also the activity of *manas* and soul is necessary in addition to the activity of the senses and recollection which is involved in it is their joint product. Soul and *manas* are operative in all forms of cognition. Perception is called perception not because there is no operation involved other than that of the senses but because the operation of senses is peculiar to it. Recollection which is involved in determinate perception, though not a function of sense-organs but of mind, does not exclude it from being perception. The operation of sense-organs which is a necessary condition of perception is present in determinate perception also. If someone were to determine an object of simple apprehension as 'cow' or 'white' after closing his eyes it would be wrong to call it perception, because in that case the cognition would not be the result of sense-object contact. In the present case, however, sense-object contact continues throughout.

It may be objected that sense-object contact is not the cause of determinate perception, because, if it were the cause determinations would arise immediately in the first moment of contact and not subsequently. This is not right. When a person enters a dark room the inside objects do not immediately manifest themselves to him. It is only after some time that they become visible. But this does not lead to the conclusion that the objects are not perceived. Just as the person at first has a faint consciousness of the objects and then perceives them distinctly, so generic and other properties of an object are perceived indistinctly in the first moment of sense-object contact and then they are perceived distinctly in the determinate stage. The determination of an object in contact with the senses in terms of generic and specific properties, action and name is not a case of inference because there is no middle term from which they might be inferred. Inference presupposes frequent past observation of a 'sign' and the object that is inferred from it. It is not memory because it is not the revival of a past experience but a fresh experience. Therefore, by elimination it is proved to be perception. Nor is it false. It is said that the properties which are apprehended to belong to an object by determinate perception are really different from the object because, if they were identical with it the relation of qualification and the qualified subsisting between them would be meaningless, and hence determinate perception superimposing a different thing on a different thing is erroneous like the illusion of a yellow conch. This is wrong. The properties that are attributed to a thing are not different from the thing, nor are they absolutely identical with it. If a qualification were different from the qualified, how could it be possible to cognize the latter in the form of the former? An individual cow is always perceived as cow. This could not be possible if the universal cow were different from the individual cow. An individual cow is never seen without its class-character while a conch on which the form of yellowness is imposed in illusion is normally perceived without yellowness. So the former cannot be illusory like the latter. An illusion is detected only when it is contradicted; otherwise, who could ever doubt its truth? But the attribution of cowness and other properties to an individual cow is never contradicted. Hence it must be true.[91]

The Buddhist denies determinate perception on the ground that the determination of an object as having a name and a class-character is not conditioned by the object itself but is purely a subjective construct imposed upon it by the cognizer. The real is unique and changes from moment to moment. The real of the previous moment is absolutely different from the reals of the present and succeeding moments. Therefore, there can be nothing common to the reals of different moments. The cognition of common character is not conditioned by the real object because it makes no difference whether the object is perceived from a distance or from vicinity. The apparent distinctness of the class-character of a thing, for example, cowness when a cow is observed closely is due to its association with the *svalakṣaṇa* or the unique character of the cow, which is given in indeterminate perception.

There is no proof of this theory. Consciousness itself does not support it, because when a person with his eyes wide open determines the object in front of him in the form 'this is a cow' it appears to be directly cognized. There is no evidence that the distinctness of such a determination is caused by anything except the immediacy of cowness. Class-character, though fit to be expressed in words, is cognized distinctly through sense-organs and indistinctly through inference. The division of cognitions into distinct and indistinct, immediate and mediate, is not based on the nature of objects as the Buddhist seems to assume. The

91. SV, 4. 120-45.

same object can be apprehended mediately or immediately, distinctly or indistinctly on different occasions. If mediacy and immediacy, distinctness and indistinctness depended on the nature of objects, the cognition of some would always be of one kind and that of others of another kind. In that case the cognition of universal would always be mediate and indistinct and that of *svalakṣaṇa* always immediate and distinct. As a matter of fact, the cognition of universal is sometimes immediate and sometimes mediate. When a person sees a patch of white colour at a distance he is not sure whether it is the colour of a cow or of a horse. If at the same time he happens to hear the sound of neighing he decides that it is the colour of a horse. Here horseness is known through inference. Now when he approaches the object he clearly apprehends that it is a horse. In the observation from a distance his immediate cognition was merely of a bare particular and horseness was cognized mediately. But later horseness also was cognized immediately. In fact the man himself may be heard saying: "Though this is a horse, yet it is not revealed to the eye as such". Approaching the object he says: "At first horseness was not visible but now I see it with my own eyes". So far as the *svalakṣaṇa*, the patch of white colour, is concerned it was immediately and distinctly cognized even before. The difference between the preceding and succeeding cognitions was caused not by the *svalakṣaṇa* but the class-character 'horseness'. The cognition of horseness was distinct or indistinct according as the object was near or far. Thus a class-character also is an object of perception and hence determinate cognition also is perceptual in character.[92]

The Buddhist view of perception that it is devoid of *kalpanā* is correct so far as *kalpanā* means the attribution to an object of something not possessed by it. But this does not exclude determinate cognition from perception because this latter does not make any false attribution. Universal is as real as particular. The Buddhist rejects it as unreal because of his metaphysical prejudice.

5.5. *Perception and Language*

Determinate perception specifies its object in diverse ways as

92. SD, pp. 38-39.

being a thing, belonging to a class, possessing certain common and uncommon properties, related to other objects in certain ways, having certain actions, and called by a name. And it is not invalid, since the forms in which an object is determined are not the forms of the perceiving mind but of the object itself. Determinations appear in linguistic terms such as 'this is a cow', 'this is a white' etc. Perception thus becomes verbalized. For almost every object and concept there are ready-made words in language and the association between things and their names is so deeply rooted in our minds that names readily make their appearance as soon as the corresponding things are perceived. Consequently all our determinate perceptions automatically assume propositional forms.

Misled by this as well as by the fact that we cannot communicate what we perceive to others otherwise than through words some thinkers have developed a curious view about determinate perception. From the verbal images that frequently accompany determinate perception they conclude that perception is false because in it word-forms are imposed on object-forms. They think like modern nominalists that universals etc. are nothing but word-forms while an object is different from words. An individual cow never appears in the form of the universal 'cow' unless the cognizer has a prior knowledge of the relation subsisting between the word 'cow' and the object denoted by it. If cowness were the form of that individual animal, even one who does not know the word 'cow' would recognize that the perceived animal belongs to the class 'cow'. Therefore, the genus 'cow' is identical with the word 'cow' and the perception 'this is a cow' identifying, as it does, an object with a form which is not its own, is false.

This word-imposition (*śabdādhyāsa*) theory is wrong. There is no identification of words with objects. What is apprehended before the appearance of words exactly the same is apprehended even afterwards. Just as colour, taste etc. reveal themselves in indeterminate perception without words, so universal, action etc. also are revealed in their own forms in perception without being tinged with word-forms. But one who knows language simply remembers the corresponding names and the only additional knowledge he can have at the time of perceiving an object is that the object is called by such a name. The remembrance of a name does not make any difference in actual perception. To say that one who does not know the word 'cow' cannot perceive a particular object as cow is wrong, because even one who does not know the word does have such perception. The knower of the word-object relation too does not identify word and object. The object 'cow' is perceived through the eye while the word 'cow' is perceived through the ear and hence the cognizer well aware of the difference between a visual image and an auditory one cannot identify the one with the other. Word is only a means of singling out one of the infinite properties of an object. It cannot be the cause of imposing its own form on the object. Just as other accessories of cognition, e.g., light, a sense-organ etc. do not impose their own forms on the object cognized through them, so word too cannot. It is an illusion if the hearer identifies words with objects and the cause of this illusion is that an object, its cognition and its name, all the three are expressed by the same word. Whenever a speaker wants to speak about the animal cow, the corresponding cognition, or the name, he uses the same word 'cow', and consequently the hearer may wrongly think that all the three are identical. The mistake of the hearer is like the mistake of the subjective idealist who wrongly identifies things with cognitions. As a matter of fact, there can be no identification of the form of the word 'cow' with the animal cow, because the form of the former consists of the letters c, o, and w while that of the latter consists of the dewlap and other parts.[93]

The function of a word is merely to remind one of the form of an object that was perceived when the relation between it and the object was first learnt or even prior to such learning. A word denoting a class serves as a means of remembering the corresponding class-character which then is identified with the perceived individual object. When an object is specified in the form 'this is a cow', it does not mean that the object 'this' is the word 'cow'. It only means that the object possesses a class-character that is signified by the word 'cow' and is possessed by other individual objects also commonly with the present one,

93. SV, 4. 171-85.

which were perceived in the past. Similarly words signifying a quality, an action and a name too serve as the reminders of corresponding objective facts known in the past and thus they assist in specifying the object in front as identical with such facts and not with words. When an individual is determined as 'Ḍittha', we do not mean that the individual is the word 'Ḍittha'. By the assertion 'this is Ḍittha' we simply recognize a particular individual as the same that we met in a particular place at a particular time and who is called by the name 'Ḍittha'. In all these cases word-form is not taken to be the qualification of the object of sense. The function of words ceases with the recollection of the things of past experience and what is predicated of an object is some fact other than a word. Therefore, there is no imposition of word-form on object-form.[94]

Though a cognition arising in a cognizer after recollecting the relation between a name and the named is mixed with memory, yet it does not cease to be a valid perception, because the object continues to be in contact with sense-organs. There is no confusion between what is perceived and what is remembered, because they are distinctly discriminated from each other. A word is remembered as signifying an object, but the cognition of the object does not lose its perceptual character on that account. The genus 'cow' was apprehended in the past and now its memory is brought about by the word 'cow', still the present perception apprehends something not contained in the memory. The present cognition apprehends a new instance of the genus 'cow' or a formerly cognized instance existing in a new place or a new moment of time, which was not apprehended by the previous cognition. It is not a rule that the name perception should be restricted only to that cognition which arises before the appearance of memory. Nor is the operation of senses precluded after memory. Therefore, all cognitions arising from sense-contact are perception and it does not affect their perceptual character if they are preceded or succeeded by memory. Memory of words is a means of discrimination (*vivekopāya*). Just as one endowed with sense-organs is able to discriminate between colour, taste etc. with their help and one not endowed with a

94. NR on SV, 4. 226.

particular sense-organ, e.g. eye, is unable to distinguish colours or other qualities, so one having a knowledge of words discriminates properly between genus, action etc. and one devoid of such knowledge has only an undefined perception of these. With the help of words we distinguish among different aspects of a thing and have their determinate perception; but those who have no knowledge of words cognize a thing as a mass of sensations and consequently their perception is indeterminate. Indeterminate perception arising in the absence of a means of discrimination, viz., words, is like the perception of a layman in music who cannot distinguish the different sounds in a piece of music. The connoisseur, however, is able to distinguish them properly, because he is equipped with the proper means and, similarly, one equipped with the knowledge of words can clearly distinguish between various aspects of a thing. Just as the consciousness of the connoisseur is not illusory, so, that of the latter too is not. With the help of words an object is determined in its own character and hence the resulting perception is not invalid. A perception is invalid only when an object is determined in the form of a different object, but not when it is determined in its own form.[95]

95. SV, 4.229-47.

CHAPTER VI

INFERENCE

6.1. *The Nature of Inference*

Śabara's definition of inference is contained in the statement: "*anumānaṃ jñātasambandhasyaikadeśadarśanād ekadeśāntare'sannikṛṣṭe'rthe buddhiḥ.*"[1] This is the basis of both Kumārila's and Prabhākara's theories of inference. The compound '*jñātasambandhasya*, is interpreted by Kumārila in four alternative ways. According to Prabhākara it qualifies the word '*ekadeśa*' in the compound '*ekadeśadarśanāt*', meaning 'one whose invariable concomitance with another is known.'[2] As we shall see presently, the various interpretations of the compound do not make much difference in the definition of inference. The word '*asannikṛṣṭe*' is explained differently by Kumārila and Prabhākara. According to Kumārila it refers to two things, viz., (1) that the object of inference should not be known beforehand through a stronger *pramāṇa* as possessing the character sought to be proved by the inference, and (2) that it should not be known beforehand as possessing a character contrary to what is sought to be proved.[3] Prabhākara explains it as meaning that the object of inference should not be one that is remembered (*smaraṇābhimānaśūnyasya*).[4] What Prabhākara emphasises thus is that inference is apprehension (*anubhūti*) rather than memory. Śālikanātha, however, interpets the word '*asannikṛṣṭe*' to mean that the object of inference should not be contradicted by a stronger means of right knowledge.[5] It is plain that all these are forced interpretations. What Śabara intends by the word is quite simple. The word '*sanni-*

1. SB, 1.1.5.
2. PP, p. 64.
3. ताद्रूप्येण गृहीतत्वं तद्विपर्ययतोऽपि वा । SV, *Anumāna*, 56.
4. BR, p. 103.
5. PP, p. 64.

karṣa' has been used in NS, 1.1.4 in the sense of sense-contact. Though Jaimini uses the word '*samprayoga*' instead of '*sannikarṣa*' in the definition of perception, yet its use in later philosophical literature is rare and that of the word '*sannikarṣa*' is very common. Thus the word '*sannikṛṣṭa*' means an object in contact with the senses and the word '*asannikṛṣṭa*' then means an object not in contact with the senses. Accordingly, Śabara's definition of inference should be formulated thus:

> When the perception of one term of a well-known relationship leads to the cognition of the other term of that relationship, which latter is not in contact with the person's sense-organs, this second cognition is called inference.

Kumārila gives four alternative explanations of the compound '*jñātasambandhasya*'. First, it may be explained as referring to the person who knows well the relationship, i.e., the invariable concomitance between two things, e.g., smoke and fire. A person knows from his past experience that smoke is always accompanied by fire. When that person, later on, sees smoke rising upwards from a hill, he immediately after remembering the constant relationship between smoke and fire becomes aware of the presence of fire on the hill. This cognition of fire on the part of the person is inference. It is not perception, because, though the smoke is perceived, fire is not perceived.

Secondly, the compound may be explained as referring to the substratum (*ekadeśin*) where the relationship of smoke and fire is apprehended. There are innumerable places where smoke and fire are seen together. The commonest place where none misses to see them together is the hearth. The hearth is one of the substrata of smoke and fire. The hill where smoke is observed now and fire is inferred is another substratum. This latter substratum is called '*pakṣa*' or the minor term of the inference and the hearth and other places where smoke and fire were actually observed in the past are called '*sapakṣa*', i.e., instances which resemble the *pakṣa* in having smoke and fire together. The *pakṣa* and the *sapakṣa* both are *ekadeśins* and smoke and fire are *ekadeśas*, the former being the container and the latter the contained. Now the *ekadeśin* which is referred to in the compound is one where the smoke-fire relationship is known and hence it cannot but be a *sapakṣa-ekadeśin*, i.e., a known instance. Accordingly, Pārthasārathi states the definition of inference thus: When an *ekadeśa*, e.g., smoke, of a *sapakṣaikadeśin*, e.g., hearth, where the invariable concomitance of smoke and fire has already been recognized, is perceived in the *pakṣaikadeśin*, e.g., hill, and there arises the cognition of the second *ekadeśa*, e.g., fire, this latter cognition is inference.

Sucaritamiśra, on the other hand, holds that the *ekadeśin* referred to is the *pakṣaikadeśin*, i.e., the hill. But this view is beset with one difficulty. The relationship of smoke and fire on the hill is known only through the inference, because one of the members of the relationship is not directly observed. So, how can it be said before the appearance of inference that the smoke-fire relationship is known on the hill? Sucaritamiśra tries to avoid the difficulty by asserting that the smoke-fire relationship is a generalized relationship which is not restricted to particular observed places only, so that when it is known in the hearth the case of the hill is not excluded. The probable existence of smoke and fire on the hill is already known when the relationship is apprehended and so far it can be said that the relationship on the hill is known. The difference between this knowledge and the present inference is merely that the former is a knowledge of probability while the latter is a knowledge of actuality.

Thirdly, the compound may mean simply a known relationship and the word '*ekadeśa*' will then mean a member of this relationship. When it is said that smoke is always accompanied by fire, it is the statement of a known relationship and smoke and fire are the two members or terms of this relationship. According to this explanation inference is the cognition of the second member, e.g., fire, of a known relationship resulting from the perception of the first member, e.g., smoke. Inference is possible only when the constant relationship between two terms is already known. There are innumerable relationships between things, but their mere existence cannot be a ground of inference. It is the knowledge—a correct knowledge of the relationship existing between two terms, which justifies the inference of one term from the perception of the other term.

Fourthly, the compound may be explained as referring to both the *liṅga* and the *liṅgin* taken together, whose relationship is known. The *liṅga* is that which indicates the presence of another thing and the *liṅgin* is that whose presence is indicated by the *liṅga*. Smoke always points to the presence of fire. Smoke is the indicator or sign and fire is the thing indicated or signified by it. Smoke and fire are parts (*ekadeśas*) of a logical whole. Accordingly, the definition of inference will be stated as follows: When on the perception of one part of a logical whole the cognition of the second part arises, a known relationship of invariable concomitance between the two parts being the ground, then this cognition is inference.[6]

Let us now compare the Mīmāṃsā definition of inference with the definitions offered by other schools. Gautama does not give any definition. He simply states that inference presupposes perception and is of three kinds.[7] Vātsyāyana gives an etymological definition of inference as that cognition of *liṅgin* which arises after the cognition of *liṅga*.[8] This definition misses the most essential factor of inference, viz., the knowledge of *vyāpti* or invariable concomitance of the *liṅga* with the *liṅgin*.

Jayanta says that the cognition of the *liṅgin* which is not perceived, after the apprehension of the *liṅga* which is of a fivefold nature, combined with the recollection of the law of invariable concomitance, is inference.[9] The fivefold nature of *liṅga* is explained as follows: The *liṅga* is that which resides in the *pakṣa* (*pakṣe sattvam*) and those which agree with the *pakṣa* in possessing the *liṅgin* (*sapakṣe sattvam*), which does not reside in those in which the *liṅgin* does not reside (*vipakṣād vyāvṛttiḥ*), which is not related with the contradictory of the *liṅgin* (*abādhitaviṣayatva*) and which is not counter-balanced by another *liṅga* associated with the contradictory of the *liṅgin* (*asatpratipakṣatva*). To illustrate, smoke is the *liṅga* or sign of fire, because it resides on the hill and also in such other places as possess fire, e.g., the hearth; it does not reside in the lake and other places where fire is not found; it is not associated with a contradictory *liṅgin*, i.e., the

6. SV, *Anu.*, 2-3 and NR and KK on ibid.
7. NS, 1.1.5.
8. मितेन लिंगेनार्थस्य पश्चात्मानमनुमानम् । VB on NS, 1.1.3.
9. NM, p. 109.

absence of fire; and, finally, it is not counter-balanced by any *liṅga* leading to the cognition of the absence of fire.

This definition of inference presupposes a complete understanding of the theory of inference and hence it is useless for the beginner. A definition must state the essential nature of the thing defined in simpler and more intelligible terms than the term defined. Jayanta's definition involves the use of a term which the beginner cannot easily understand. To understand inference one has to understand what is meant by the fivefold nature of *liṅga*. Instead of stating the essential form of inference it states the conditions of its validity. The Mīmāṃsā definition, on the other hand, is free from these flaws. When two terms are known to have an invariable relation and subsequently only one of them is apprehended, the other too is apprehended. This is the nature of inference. This definition does not omit anything essential nor does it add anything inessential and at the same time it is perfectly intelligible.

The later Nyāya definitions are more technical. Viśvanātha distinguishes between *anumāna* and *anumiti*, the former standing for the process of inference, i.e., the syllogism and the latter for the result of the process, i.e., the conclusion of the syllogism. He defines *anumiti* as the knowledge derived from *parāmarśa*.[10] Annaṃbhaṭṭa explains the term *parāmarśa* as meaning the knowledge of *liṅga* residing in *pakṣa*, e.g., 'the hill has smoke', qualified by the knowledge of *vyāpti*, e.g., 'wherever there is smoke there is fire'.[11] Viśvanātha alternatively defines inference as the knowledge of something derived through the instrumentality of the knowledge of *vyāpti*[12]. This definition is incomplete as it does not make an explicit statement of the apprehension of *liṅga* which is as essential as the knowledge of *vyāpti*. A good definition must make an explicit statement of the connotation of the term defined. It must not leave anything essential implied. Thus the Mīmāṃsā definition is superior to the Nyāya definitions insofar as it is explicit, simpler and more intelligible.

Praśastapāda defines inference as the knowledge which results

10. SM, p. 238.

11. व्याप्तिविशिष्टपक्षधर्मताज्ञानम् ।'TS, p. 34.

12. व्याप्तिज्ञानकरणकं ज्ञानम् । SM, p. 238.

from the apprehension of a sign.[13] The term 'sign' (*liṅga*) is further explained as that which is related with that which is inferred and is well-known to have co-presence and co-absence with the latter. This definition does not explicitly mention the knowledge of *vyāpti*. It is, however, superior to the Mīmāṃsā definition in one respect. Śrīdhara says that the word '*darśana*' in Praśastapāda's definition does not necessarily mean the perception of sign but that it means a definite knowledge of sign through any means whatever.[14] From the perception of smoke on the hill we infer the presence of fire there and, again, we infer that there is heat. This is an inference based on another inference (*anumitānumāna*). The latter inference has the inferred fire as its *liṅga*, which is not perceived. If perception of *liṅga* is made an essential condition of inference, then such an inference cannot legitimately be called inference. So, it is not necessary that the *liṅga* should be perceived. What is necessary is that there should be a conviction in the reality of the *liṅga*. The word '*darśana*' literally means visual perception. If this literal meaning is retained the Mīmāṃsā definition ceases to apply to *anumitānumāna* which is recognized by Kumārila also.[15] But neither Kumārila nor his commentators try to set aside the misunderstanding caused by the use of the word '*darśana*' whose literal meaning restricts the application of the word 'inference' to that inference alone in which the *liṅga* is directly perceived. Even in later treatises on the Bhāṭṭa system the word '*darśana*' is retained. In NTV (p. 137) and MM (p. 25) inference is defined in the words "*vyāpyadarśanajanmāsannikṛṣṭārthaviṣayaṃ jñānamanumānam*", i.e., inference is the knowledge that results from the perception of *vyāpya* or the 'pervaded' and whose object is not directly perceived. The use of the word '*grahaṇa*' or '*upalabdhi*' would have been more appropriate in the place of the word '*darśana*'.

Dharmakīrti defines inference thus: Inference is the cognition of the inferrable from the sign having a three-fold character.[16] The three characteristics of a sign are: (1) its presence in the *pakṣa*, (2) presence in the *sapakṣa*, and (3) absence from the

13. लिंगदर्शनात् सञ्जायमानं लैंगिकम् । PDS, p. 200.
14. NK on ibid.
15. SV, *Anu.*, 170.
16. त्रिरूपाल्लिगाद् यदनुमेये ज्ञानं तदनुमानम् । NB, 2.3.

vipakṣa. Like Jayanta's definition it enumerates the conditions of validity rather than state the essential nature of inference. The inclusion of the word 'inferrable' in the definition makes it open to the charge of circularity. There is no mention of *vyāpti*. Another defect is that instead of stating that inference is a cognition resulting from the cognition of a sign it merely states that inference is a cognition from a sign. From a mere sign, e.g., smoke, nothing can be cognized unless it is known to be the sign of something, e.g., fire. Sucaritamiśra rightly says that nothing can be cognized from the mere existence of something.[17] Anything can be a sign of anything, but it can be the ground of inference only when it is known to be so. Dharmakīrti is quite aware of this and makes the necessary amendment in the next *sūtra*, but in the actual definition he misses it. The other schools adopt one or the other definition criticized above and hence it is useless to repeat what has already been said.

6.2. *The Constituents of Inference*

From the definition of inference it follows that there cannot be less than three terms and three propositions in it. The three terms of inference are: the *pakṣa*, the *vyāpya* and the *vyāpaka*. These correspond respectively to the minor, middle and major terms of syllogism. The *pakṣa* is the substratum possessing the *vyāpya* and the *vyāpaka*, the former being a thing already known and the latter one which is yet to be known. The hill, for instance, in which smoke is perceived and fire is inferred is the *pakṣa*. The word '*ekadeśin*' implied in the definition of inference refers to the *pakṣa*. The *vyāpya* is also called '*gamaka*', '*liṅga*', '*hetu*' and '*sādhana*' and the Mīmāṃsaka adds one more synonym to the list, viz., '*niyamya*'. In the common example of inference smoke is the *vyāpya*. It is called *gamaka* because it leads to the knowledge of something not directly perceived. It leads to the knowledge of something because it is the sign or indicator of that thing and hence it is called *liṅga*. Smoke is the sign of the presence of fire so that whenever we observe smoke we know the presence of fire. Smoke is the *ratio cognoscendi*, i.e., the reason

17. नैकदेशः सत्तामात्रेण लिंगं, किन्तु स्वप्रतिपत्तौ ज्ञातः परप्रतिपादने च ज्ञापितः।
KK on SV, *Anu.*, 75.

of our knowledge of fire. Therefore, it is called '*hetu*' or reason. Smoke is not the *ratio ascendi* or the cause of the existence of fire, because actually fire is the cause of the existence of smoke. The middle term is called '*sādhana*' because it is the means of proving the major term.

The major term is called '*vyāpaka*', '*gamya*', '*liṅgin*', '*sādhya*' and '*niyāmaka*'. It is called '*gamya*' because it is known with the help of the middle term which is its *gamaka*. It is *liṅgin* or the possessor of the *liṅga* or sign. It is *sādhya* because it is sought to be proved by means of the *sādhana*. The words '*sādhana*' and '*sādhya*' are generally translated as '*probans*' and '*probandum*'.

The names '*vyāpya*' and '*vyāpaka*' are yet to be explained. Smoke and fire, which are respectively the probans and the probandum in the given example, vary in their extension or denotation. Smoke is a term of narrower denotation while fire is a term of wider denotation. The particulars denoted by the former are less in number than the particulars denoted by the latter. Whenever and wherever smoke is present fire also is present, but sometimes fire is present though smoke is not present, for example, in the case of a red-hot iron ball which does not emit smoke. When we say 'all men are bipeds' the term 'man' has a narrower extension than the term 'biped', because no man is non-biped while there are bipeds other than men. If the extension of the two terms is represented by two circles the cirle representing the term 'men' will be included in the circle representing the term 'biped'. The former circle is 'pervaded' by the latter. The middle term is called '*vyāpya*' or the pervaded and the major term '*vyāpaka*' or the pervader, because the extension of the former is always included in and never exceeds the extension of the latter. The middle term cannot be of a wider extension than the major term, because if it is the inference cannot be valid. From a term of narrower denotation we can validly infer a term of wider denotation, but not *vice versa*. From the character of being a cow we can validly infer the character of having horns, because the latter pervades the former, but we cannot infer the former from the latter, because hornedness is possessed not only by cows but also by baffalos etc.

The middle and major terms can, however, be of an equal extension; for example, in the case of the inference of non-eternality from the property of being a product, the two terms are co-extensive. Whatever is a product is non-eternal and whatever is non-eternal is a product. In such cases each of the terms can serve as the probans of the other. When the middle and major terms are of an unequal extension the relation of probans and probandum between them cannot be reversed, but when they are co-extensive we can safely do so.[18]

The terms '*niyamya*' and '*niyāmaka*' derive their significance from the relation of the middle and major terms, which is called '*niyama*' in Mīmāṃsā. The relation between smoke and fire is *niyama* or rule of their invariable association. Smoke is the ruled (*niyamya*) and fire is the ruler (*niyāmaka*). The being of the former is ruled or restricted by the being of the latter.

The word '*sādhana*' has one more meaning according to which it stands for the whole syllogism instead of a part of it. That statement is termed '*sādhana*' or the instrument of proof by which the knowledge of inference arises in a person other than the one making it.[19] There are three propositions in inference. This is evident from the definition of inference according to which a relation between two terms is known, one of the terms is also known and the other term is inferred. The relation of the probans and the probandum is called '*vyāpti*' or '*niyama*' and is expressed in the form of a proposition corresponding to the universal major premise of a syllogism. 'Where there is smoke there is fire'. This is the *vyāpi* or the relation of pervasion between smoke and fire. The second proposition states the knowledge that the probans is present in the *pakṣa*, e.g., 'the hill has smoke', and is called '*pakṣadharmatā*', '*hetu-vākya*' or simply '*hetu*'. *Pakṣadharmatā* is the assertion of the fact that the probans characterizes the *pakṣa*. These two propositions are the basis of inference. The conclusion that follows from them is called '*nigamana*'. It states that the presence of the probandum in the *pakṣa* is established. It is also called '*pratijñā*'. There are two alternative ways of stating the conclusion. It may be stated in the beginning followed by the premises that prove it, or, it may by stated in the end preceded by the

18. SV, *Anu.*, 5-9.
19. येन वाक्येन यस्यानुमानबुद्धिरुत्पद्यते तत् साधनमित्युच्यते । SD, p. 64.

premises. In the former case it is called '*pratijñā*' or the thesis to be proved and in the latter case it is called '*nigamana*' or the conclusion that follows from the premises. Thus a *sādhana* has the following alternative forms:

Whatever has smoke, has fire (*vyāpti*);
The hill has smoke (*pakṣadharmatā* or *hetu*);
∴ The hill has fire (*nigamana*);

Or, The hill has fire (*pratijñā*);
∵ It has smoke (*hetu*);
And, whatever has smoke has fire (*vyāpti*).

According to the Nyāya-Vaiśeṣika in inference there are five propositions instead of three:

The hill has fire (*pratijñā*);
Since, it has smoke (*hetu*);
Whatever has smoke has fire, e.g., the hearth (*udāharaṇa*);
The hill has smoke (*upanaya*);
∴ The hill has fire (*nigamana*).

Here we see that there is no difference between *prātijñā* and *nigamana* and also between *hetu* and *upanaya*. The proposition 'the hill has fire' occurs twice—once in the beginning in the form of what is to be proved and again in the end in the form of that what has been proved. The proposition 'the hill has smoke' also occurs twice—once before *udāharaṇa* and again after it. Now, what is the necessity of re-stating it after *udāharaṇa*? *Udāharaṇa* is the statement of *vyāpti* together with an example. It is a memory judgment. We already know from past experience that smoke is always accompanied by fire and it is remembered at the time of inferring fire. Now, if the conclusion is stated immediately after *udāharaṇa* it would mean that it is derived from memory, i.e., that memory is the instrument (*karaṇa*) of inference. But, since memory is not apprehension (*anubhava*), it is held to be invalid knowledge in which case the conclusion 'the hill has fire' too would be invalid, because no valid knowledge can be derived from invalid knowledge. This is probably the reason why the Naiyāyika feels the necessity of restating the proposition 'the hill has smoke' after *udāharaṇa*.

The Mīmāṃsaka rejects the Naiyāyika's five-membered inference on the ground that it involves unnecessary repetition. Restatement is a fault. To state too much is as much a fault as to state too little. In an inference only three propositions are needed, neither more nor less. That the five-membered inference is unnecessary is admitted by the Naiyāyikas also who have stated their arguments in the form of a three-membered inference. The conclusion is the result of *vyāpti* and *hetu* combined together. It does not follow from *vyāpti* alone. It is a product of memory and apprehension. Memory too is not invalid in the sense of being false as the illusion of silver in shell is. It is true if it reproduces the original experience faithfully, though it does not have the status of *pramāṇa*, because it does not give new knowledge. The conclusion of an inference is true because the premises, though one of them is of the nature of memory, are true, and it is a new knowledge, because one of the premises is of the nature of apprehension. Therefore, only three propositions should be stated in an inference.

The Buddhists maintain that *pratijñā* is unnecessary and that only two propositions should be stated. For instance, when someone wants to prove the non-eternality of sound he should simply say that whatever is produced is non-eternal, like a jar (*udāharaṇa*) and sound is produced (*hetu*). They hold that the hearer will automatically come to realize that sound is non-eternal after hearing the premises, so that the statement of it becomes superfluous. What is essential in an argument is the reason or ground of inference, not the conclusion which follows from the premises.

This, according to the Mīmāṃsaka, is stating too little. When someone says "what is produced is non-eternal and sound is produced" the hearer remains in a state of expectancy (*sākāṅkṣa*). Therefore, the conclusion also must be stated. Though the conclusion follows from the premises, yet it requires some intelligence to extract the correct conclusion from them. If the conclusion is not stated in clear terms and the hearer does not possess the required degree of intelligence he may suspect that the speaker is speaking irrelevant things, or that what he is speaking is too obvious to be stated, or he may draw a wrong conclusion not intended by the speaker, e.g., that all produced things are non-eternal and of the nature of sound or that all non-eternal things are sound. Therefore, it is undesirable to reduce the three-membered inference to a two-membered one.[20]

6.3. *The Probandum*

Kumārila emphasizes that the probandum or object of inference is neither the *liṅgin* alone nor the *pakṣa* alone, but the *pakṣa* qualified by the *liṅgin*. What is inferred is neither the hill nor fire, but the hill possessing fire, i.e., the fiery hill. Fire is already known at the time of apprehending the *vyāpti* between smoke and fire and the hill is known through perception. These by themselves do not stand in need of a fresh *pramāṇa*, because they are already known. The fiery hill, on the other hand, was not previously known, but is known now through inference. The ground of inference, likewise, is not the middle term by itself, but the minor term qualified by the middle. We infer the fiery hill from the smoky hill. The minor term has two forms and is the *gamaka* in one form and the *gamya* in the other. It is the *gamaka* insofar as it is the possessor of a known property and it is the *gamya* insofar as it is the possessor of a previously unknown property.

There are two optional ways of stating the object of inference in a syllogism. The major term may be stated as related to the minor by way of identity or difference. For example, in the inference of fire we may put the conclusion in the form 'the hill is fiery' or in 'there is fire on the hill'. In the inference of non-eternality of sound the conclusion will be put either in the form 'sound is non-eternal' or in 'non-eternality exists in sound'.

The object of inference is neither the major term independently of the minor, nor the minor term independently of the major, nor the two together, nor the relation between them. The major and minor terms in their respective independent forms are already known. If the existence of non-eternality by itself is to be inferred, then the conclusion will be 'non-eternality exists'. But then, there will be no ground for such a conclusion since the character of being a product not being a property of non-eternality, cannot serve as the middle term. The minor premise is

20. SD, p. 64 and KK on SV, *Anu.*, 54.

'sound is a product', while for the conclusion 'non-eternality exists' the minor premise must be 'non-eternality is the character of being a product' which is false. Similarly the existence of sound by itself cannot be inferred, because we cannot point out any instance of its relation with the character of being a product in the form 'what is a product is sound'. The relation perceived in a jar is between the character of being a product and non-eternality, not between the character of being a product and sound. Likewise, we cannot argue that 'fieriness exists, because it is smoky and whatever is smoky is fiery' or that 'the hill exists, because it is smoky and whatever is smoky is hill'. The aggregate of the minor and major terms cannot be the object of inference. For example, we cannot prove that sound and non-eternality exist or that hill and fieriness exist, because the character of being a product, the middle term, is not a property of both but of sound alone, and smokiness is not a property of both the hill and fieriness but of the hill alone. Lastly, the relation of the minor and major terms is not the object of inference, because such a relation is neither asserted by name, e.g., 'the relation between the hill and fire exists', nor by the word 'of', e.g., 'there exists fire of the hill'. The common mode of assertion is 'the hill is fiery' or 'there is fire on the hill'. Moreover, we do not have a *vyāpti* in the form 'wherever there is smoke, there is hill-fire relation', because in the hearth and other instances the *vyāpti* is observed between smoke and fire only. There is no doubt that the relation between hill and fire exists, because in the absence of any relation we cannot assert that the hill is fiery. When it is said that the hill-fire relation is not the object of inference, what is intended is only that it has no place in the logical form of the syllogism, though it is implied in the assertion 'the hill is fiery'. Thus the direct object of the inference is the fiery hill, not the relation between the hill and fire, just as the direct meaning of the word '*daṇḍin*' is a person characterized by a stick instead of the relation between the person and the stick. Therefore, the minor term qualified by the major (*dharmaviśiṣṭo dharmī*) is the probandum in inference.

Though it is certain that in inference a property (*dharma*) of some property-possessor (*dharmin*) is known through another property of it, yet some people assert that there is no restriction as to which of them is to be made the qualification and which the qualified (*viśeṣaṇaviśeṣyatva*). They hold that the property may be made the qualified thing and the property-possessor the qualification or the property-possessor may be made the qualified thing and the property the qualification. According to them both the modes of statement, e.g., 'non-eternality exists in sound' and 'sound is non-eternal' are correct. But this is wrong. The former mode of statement involves an unnecessary complication. If the conclusion were of the form 'non-eternality exists in sound' then sound would be a secondary element and as such its connection with the middle term, 'the character of being a product' would not be clear, so that in order to make it clear the simple minor premise 'because it is a product' would have to be changed into the form 'because the character of being a product belongs to sound'. Therefore, the major term cannot be the qualified thing. Another reason for it is the following: When the major term, e.g., fire is made the qualified thing the possible alternatives are, (1) fire in general is in space in general, (2) the fire that was seen is wherever it has been seen, (3) the previously perceived fire is in space in general, (4) fire is in this place, (5) the fire that was previously seen is in this place, (6) this fire is in space in general, (7) this fire is in the previously seen place, and (8) this fire is in this place. Now, the first two alternatives state what is already known and the other alternatives involve self-contradiction. To take the third alternative, how can the previously perceived fire, e.g., the fire in the hearth, be in all places? The fourth alternative states that all fires are in this place and the sixth that this fire is in all places, which are obviously wrong statements. The fifth and the seventh too are wrong, because neither the previously experienced fire can be in this place, nor the present fire can be in the previously experienced place. Lastly, to say that this fire is in this place is a mere tautology, since the fire cannot be designated by the word 'this' unless it is known that it exists in this place, so that the statement 'this fire is in this place' is equivalent to the statement 'the fire that exists in this place is qualified by this place.' Thus the only valid mode of stating the conclusion is 'the hill is fiery' or 'the hill has fire' in which an unknown property, the major term, is made the qualification of the property-possessor, i.e., the minor term.

It is established that the minor term qualified by the major is the object of inference. But there are some who hold that in the inference of fire from smoke the object of the inference is the smoke qualified by fire, i.e., the middle term qualified by the major.

Pārthasārathi attributes this view to the Naiyāyikas. Vātsyāyana is not known to hold this view. He holds the view criticized in the preceding paragraph as is evident from his assertion that in the inference of the non-eternality of sound the object of the inference is either sound qualified by non-eternality or non-eternality qualified by sound.[21] The view in question is of Uddyotakara who does not oppose the general rule that the object of inference is the major term and the minor, anyone of the two being the qualification of the other, but simply points out an exception, viz., the case when the locus of fire is not definitely seen. When the hill or any other place in which smoke exists is not visible due to distance or a large volume of smoke, the inference that arises has this form: All smokes are accompanied by fire; this is smoke; therefore, this is accompanied by fire. Here fire is predicated of a particular visible smoke, not of the hill or any other place.[22]

Sucaritamiśra commenting on SV, Anu., 48, says that this view also is correct (*tadapi sādhveva*). Kumārila anticipates an objection against this view: If smoke qualified by fire be the object of inference, then there will be only two terms in the inference instead of three, viz., the middle and the major. The reply given by Kumārila is that the number of the terms is still three—the minor term is the particular visible smoke, the middle term is general smoke and the major term is fire. From the syllogism, however, it is obvious that the minor term is not smoke, particular or general, but 'this', though it does not refer to a place like the hill. Thus in this case too the object of inference is not the middle term qualified by the major as is held by Uddyotakara, but it is the minor term qualified by the major, which is in perfect agreement with Kumārila's view. Diṅnāga also says in NP that the minor term qualified by the major is the object of

21. VB, 1.1.36.
22. Cp. A. B. Dhruva's Introduction to NP, pp. XXII-XXIII.

inference. It appears that Uddyotakara, due to his hatred for the Buddhist view, wanted to refute Diṅnāga's view by pointing out an exception, but, as we have just seen, the said case is not really an exception.[23]

6.4. *The Ground of Inference: Vyāpti*

Vyāpti and *pakṣadharmatā* are the grounds of inference. *Pakṣadharmatā* is usually a judgment of perception. Smoke is perceived on the hill and fire is inferred. But the inference takes place only when the universal relation between smoke and fire is already known. This relation called '*vyāpti*', between the middle and major terms is a more important ground of inference, though the conclusion that is drawn does not follow exclusively from *vyāpti* but from *vyāpti* and *pakṣadharmatā* jointly. Kumārila says that *vyāpti* is not a simple assertoric judgment but that it is a necessary judgment. 'Smoke is accompanied by fire' is an assertoric judgment while 'smoke must be accompanied by fire' is a necessary judgment. *Vyāpti* is a necessary relation having the form 'this happening that must happen'.[24] The conclusion that is drawn cannot be certain unless the relation between the middle and major terms is necessary.[25]

The problem of ascertaining the necessity of a relation is the problem of induction. How is *vyāpti* known? Kumārila says that *vyāpti* is known through repeated observation (*bhūyodarśana*). When we experience smoke and fire together in a number of cases, we connect smoke in general with fire in general (*sāmānyadharmayoḥ*) after eliminating their non-recurrent features (*bhedahānena*) such as a particular shade of colour, a particular shape or size etc. *Vyāpti* is a necessary relation generally between two universals, but sometimes between two particulars also, e.g., between *Kṛttikā* and *Rohiṇī*.[26] A frequent observation of two things together is not the only means of knowing *vyāpti*. When two things are known to be associated together in some places (*anvaya*) and there is no experience of their dissociation (*vyatireka*),

23. SV, *Anu.*, 24-51 & NR & KK on Ibid.
24. अस्मिन् सत्यमुना भाव्यमिति शक्त्या निरूप्यते । SV, *Anu.*, 14.
25. तैर्दृष्टैरपि नैवेष्टा व्यापकांशावधारणा । Ibid., 15.
26. Ibid., 12.

vyāpti is established.[27] Smoke and fire were observed together in the past and smoke was never observed without fire. From this it is ascertained that there is *vyāpti* between smoke and fire. Thus *vyāpti*, the universal major premise of inference, is known from *anvayavyatireka* or the joint method of agreement and difference. *Vyāpti*, according to Kumārila, is induction per simple enumeration. It is extracted from a limited number of observed cases (*mitadeśa*). In the past we perceived some positive instances of smoke and fire and did not perceive any instance in which smoke was present and fire absent. On the basis of such a limited number of perceptions and non-perceptions we came to know that smoke is invariably concomitant with fire. Kumārila does not explain how a necessary relation can be derived from a limited number of experiences. This, as a matter of fact, is a perpetual problem of induction.

Pārthasārathi, commenting on SV, Anu., 12, raises the problem and gives his own solution thus:

> Well, from a limited number of (perceptions and) non-perceptions it cannot be proved that (in all instances of the presence of smoke fire is present and) in all instances of absence of fire smoke is absent. But who says that it is proved? We simply say that only so much is proved as is experienced. From the concomitance of smoke with fire in some observed places and times together with its non-concomitance with non-fire in as many instances as we have actually observed the law of smoke-fire relationship is known, and this is enough for the inference of fire from smoke. As regards, the cognition 'where there is smoke there is fire', we say that it is inferential in nature, since it is not a direct cognition and hence no perception.

From this it is evident that, according to Pārthasārathi, the ground of the inference of fire from smoke is the premise 'all observed cases of smoke are cases of fire' instead of the premise 'all the observed and non-observed cases of smoke are cases of fire'. In other words, in inference we reason from particular to particular rather than from universal to particular.

27. SV, *Arthāpatti*, 42.

We reserve a fuller criticism of Pārthasārathi's view for a later occasion. Here we may say only that what Pārthasārathi says cannot be Kumārila's view. Kumārila admits that *vyāpti* which is the ground of inference is a necessary proposition. The necessary relation of smoke with fire implies that not only the observed cases of smoke are cases of fire, but that all the past, present and future cases of smoke are cases of fire. Kumārila, no doubt, says that *vyāpti* is known from some cases of concomitance, but this is what everyone would say, because the observation of all the past, present and future cases is humanly impossible. Now we give in detail the various views about the nature and method of *vyāpti* and their criticism from the Bhāṭṭa point of view.

6.4.1. *The Nature of Vyāpti*

According to the Vaiśeṣika *vyāpti* is a relation between a cause and its effect, between an effect and its cause, between two things one of which is either conjoined to the other or inherent in it, between two things inhering in the same thing or between two things one of which is opposed to the other.[28]

The Bhāṭṭa has reasons to disagree with this list of terms between which the relation of *vyāpti* can hold. The first reason is that this list is not exhaustive. The astronomers infer the rise of *Rohiṇī* following the rise of *Kṛttikā.* This cannot be possible unless the *vyāpti* between *Kṛttikā* and *Rohiṇī* is recognized. The relation, however, between them is none of those mentioned in the Vaiśeṣika list. It cannot be said that this sort of relation is covered by the word '*sambandhi*' because only two *sambandha*-s are recognized by the Vaiśeṣika, viz., conjunction and inherence, while the relation in the case in question is neither of them. If the word '*sambandhi*' is intended to cover all sorts of relations, then it is useless to mention causality etc. separately. The second reason is that the *sūtra* justifies the inference of smoke from fire, because the former is the effect of the latter, and also of the character of being a *śiṃśapā* from the character of being a tree, because the two characters inhere in the same substance. But this is wrong. From fire smoke cannot be inferred, because a red-hot iron ball has fire but no smoke. Similarly, we cannot say that a

28. अस्येदं कारणं कार्यं सम्बन्ध्येकार्थसमवायि विरोधि चेति लैंगिकम् । VS, 9.2.1.

particular tree is *śiṃśapā* from its being a tree, because it may as well be a mango tree. The Vaiśeṣika may say that the reason why these inferences are false is that the relation between fire and smoke on the one hand and between tree-ness and *śiṃśapā*-ness on the other is not invariable (*niyata*). This is true; but then the Vaiśeṣika should simply say that *vyāpti* is an invariable relation between two things instead of enumerating the types of relations. That which is essential for *vyāpti* is its invariability alone.[29]

According to the Buddhist *vyāpti* is an inseparable relation (*avinābhāva*) between two things and is of two forms, viz., the concomitance (*anvaya*) of the middle term with the major and the non-concomitance (*vyatireka*) of the middle with the negation of the major. It is further said that such a relation can hold between those things only which are related by way of causality or of identity (*tatsvabhāvatadutpattī*). Smoke and fire are related by way of effect and cause. An effect cannot be separated from its cause. It cannot exist without a cause. If an effect were independent of its cause it would either exist eternally or would not exist at all. Contrarily an effect is neither eternally existent nor non-existent, but has an occasional existence. Hence it stands in need of a cause.[30] Thus the relation between smoke and fire is inseparable, because the former is the effect of the latter. Similarly the relation of identity also is inseparable. *Śiṃśapā* is a tree. Tree-ness is the essential nature of *śiṃśapā*, because a *śiṃśapā* cannot exist without being a tree, just as fire cannot exist without being hot. *Śiṃśapā*-ness is identical with tree-ness. The relation of causality is one of succession and the relation of identity is one of co-existence. There can be no other inseparable relation, and hence the ground of inference must be a relation either of causality or of identity.

Against this Buddhist view the Bhāṭṭa objection is that the inference of the rise of *Rohiṇī* after that of *Kṛttikā* would be invalid because the former is neither the effect nor the essential nature of the latter. Again, a man when it is dark could not validly infer the green colour of a mango from its sour taste, if

29. NRM, p. 56.

30. Cf. नित्यं सत्त्वमसत्त्वं वा हेतोरन्यानपेक्षणात् ।
अपेक्षातो हि भावानां कादाचित्कत्वसम्भवः ॥

the Buddhist view is accepted. The Buddhist says that in this case we first infer from the sour taste its material cause which is also the material cause of the green colour and then we infer from the material cause of the green colour the colour itself. But this is wrong for two reasons. People infer the green colour directly from the sour taste, so that there is only one inference instead of two. Secondly, the inference of a material cause from its effect, viz., sour taste is valid, but the inference of an effect, viz., green colour from its material cause, according to the Buddhist, is invalid. If it be accepted that an effect can be validly inferred from its cause, then smoke too can be inferred from fire. But this latter inference is really invalid. As regards identity, it may be said that there remains nothing to be known (*meyābhāva*) when a *śiṃśapā*, for instance, has already been known. Tree-ness is the *svabhāva* of *śiṃśapā*. But when we perceive a particular *śiṃśapā* tree we also perceive its character of being a tree, so that there remains no scope for inference.[31]

Pārthasārathi suggests some terminological reforms also. The Buddhist terms the positive relation of smoke with fire as '*anvaya*' which literally means the action of following. But smoke which rises upwards is not seen to follow fire which is on the ground. We infer the position of the sun in the sky from the length of the shadow cast by a stick; but the latter does not follow the former. So '*anvaya*' is a misleading term. Similarly, the term '*vyāpti*' generally used by the Naiyāyikas is misleading. It literally means pervasion. But the fire on the ground does not pervade the smoke in the sky. The right term for the invariable relation of the middle term with the major suggested by the Mīmāṃsaka is '*niyama*'[32]. It was pointed out that the term *vyāpti* derives its significance from the fact that the denotation of middle term is included in the denotation of major term. From this point of view the term *vyāpti* is not objectionable. However, the term '*niyama*' (law or rule) is preferable, because the term *vyāpti* gives undue importance to the denotative meaning of terms.

Niyama is the empirical law of invariable association of two things on the basis of which the knowledge of one of the things

31. NRM, pp. 56-57 & KK on SV, *Anu.*, 4.
32. Ibid.

leads to the knowledge of the other. This empirical law may imply any kind of relation between two things and the inference based on it is strictly in accordance with the past experience of the relation. When in several instances a particular something having a particular nature and particular spatio-temporal references has been ascertained directly or indirectly to possess a specific invariable relation, say, *saṃyoga*, *samavāya*, etc. with a second something having a different but equally particular nature and spatio-temporal references, then, whenever the first is seen subsequently in some new instance not previously examined, it leads to the inference of the second as related to the first in exactly the previously known way. Thus smoke rising skywards is known to be related invariably with fire not very far away from the place of smoke. The rise of the moon is known to be related invariably with the rise of sea water almost simultaneously and having a measure corresponding to the height of the moon in the sky. *Niyama*, according to Pārthasārathi, is a rule or principle derived from observed facts and inference is an attempt to extend its application to unobserved cases.[33]

Nārāyaṇa defines *vyāpti* as a natural relation. By 'natural' he means that which is not dependent on eliminable conditions (*upādhi*). The relation between smoke and fire is natural, i.e., devoid of any *upādhi*. '*Upādhi*' is defined as that which is coextensive with the *sādhya* but less extensive than the *sādhana* (*sādhanāvyāpakatve sati sādhyasamavyāptaḥ*). When it is said that fire is always accompanied by smoke the relation of fire with smoke is not *vyāptī* because it depends on an *upādhi* or extraneous condition, viz., the presence of wet fuel which always accompanies smoke, the *sādhya*, but does not always accompany fire, the *sādhana*. Similarly, there is no *vyāpti* between *hiṃsātva* (killing) and *adharmatva* (sin), because *adharmatva* depends not necessarily upon *hiṃsātva* but on an *upādhi*, viz., *niṣiddhatva*. The Mīmāṃsaka believes that only that act can be called sinful which is prohibited in the scriptures and hence killing as such cannot be sinful, because only that form of killing is prohibited which is committed for a purpose other than religious.[34]

33. Ibid.
34. MM, pp. 26-27.

Upādhi literally means an extraneous condition. An extraneous condition is always an unnecessary condition. We observe many circumstances which precede the rise of smoke in a washerman's house, but all the observed circumstances are not necessary for the rise of smoke. There are some circumstances which are irrelevant. For example, the washerman's ass is irrelevant for the rise of smoke. Such irrelevant circumstances are *upādhis*.

Now, is the presence of wet fuel or *niṣiddhatva* an *upādhi* in this usual sense of the term? Certainly not. Wet fuel is the most relevant circumstance for the production of smoke and *niṣiddhatva* is the most relevant circumstance for *adharmatva*. From this it will be clear that Nārāyaṇa's use of the term *upādhi* in the present context is misleading. The statement 'wherever there is fire there is smoke' is wrong, not because wet fuel is an eliminable circumstance but because an essential circumstance has been left out in the statement. Similarly, the statement that killing is a sin is wrong only because an essential qualification of 'killing' has been left out. These statements are wrong because they are incomplete. Contrarily, the statements 'where there is fire feeding on wet fuel there is smoke' and 'all killing prohibited by the scriptures is sinful' are correct, not because an *upādhi* has been eliminated but because an essential qualification which was left out has been mentioned. *Vyāpti* is a *nirupādhika* or unconditional relation and a relation which is *au ādhika* or conditional, i.e., which depends on an accidental condition, is not *vyāpti*. But the examples of an *aupādhika* relation given above are wrong. 'Where there is white smoke there is fire'. This is a true example, because the white colour of smoke is an eliminable condition or *upādhi*. It is true that there is no *vyāpti* between fire and smoke, but it is not because of the presence of an eliminable condition, but because of the non-inclusion of an uneliminable antecedent of smoke.

Vyāpti is a necessary relation according to Kumārila and his followers. But *vyāpti* as viewed by Pārthasārathi cannot be a necessary relation. The *vyāpti*, according to him, between smoke and fire amounts to the statement that all the observed cases of smoke are cases of fire. It expresses a regular sequence between observed smokes and observed fires. But how can this be a necessary relation so long as it restricts the relation to only such places and times as have been actually observed in the past? A necessary relation is not subject to spatio-temporal limitations. If I saw many instances in which smoke and fire were found together, I cannot say that smoke must be accompanied by fire on merely this ground. And if there be any necessity in this relation it can at most be only a psychological or subjective necessity, in which case the person inferring fire in an unobserved instance would be no better than Pavlov's dog secreting saliva on hearing a bell after it has been conditioned to the bell-food sequence. The psychologists of the associationist school, Hume, Mill etc., also reduce the necessity involved in inference to a mere psychological necessity. The necessity of the smoke-fire relation is, accordingly, explained in terms of neural connections in the brain. By the repeated experience of smoke and fire a bond of association is created in the mind and a corresponding bond is created in the nervous system, so that whenever in future smoke is perceived the idea of fire is revived. Thus inference, according to the associationists, is merely a conditioned response and the mental state during inference is that of expecting a correlate. But if this is the whole account of inference, we have no logical justification for inferring fire from smoke and also for imposing our own conclusion on others. Why there must be fire where smoke is visible, cannot be explained unless there be a logical necessity in the smoke-fire relationship. If there is no logical necessity the inference will be no better than an argument from analogy and then the conclusion will be merely a probable one.

The logical necessity involved in *vyāpti* is well accounted for by the Buddhist who says that a *vyāpti* is based either on causality or on identity. If two things are known to be related by way of cause and effect or if one of them is an essential nature of the other, the relation between them cannot but be a necessary one. If one thing is the effect of another thing then the former cannot come to be independently of the latter. If something is the nature of some other thing, how can the latter be without the former? Suppose A is the effect of B and C is its nature. To say that A can be without B involves self-contradiction, because it is equivalent to saying that B is the cause of A and B is not the cause of A. Similarly, to say that A can be without C involves self-contradiction, because it is equivalent to saying that A is A as well as non-A.

Theoretically this explanation of logical necessity is quite satisfactory. But practically it is very difficult to ascertain what is the cause of what and what is the essential nature of what. When the relation of cause and effect between two things is known with perfect accuracy each of them can serve as the *liṅga* of the other, because strictly speaking, there can be only one cause of one effect and one effect of one cause. In the absence of exact knowledge of cause and effect it is not quite safe to infer a cause from an effect or an effect from a cause, because there is such a thing as plurality of causes and plurality of effects, though this conception of plurality is contradictory to the conception of causality. Sucaritamiśra says that if one thing is known to be a *śiṃśapā* it is useless to infer that it is a tree. This criticism of the Buddhist is justified so far as the given example is concerned. It is an instance of the fallacy called *petitio principii.* When it is argued that 'all *śiṃśapā*-s are trees and this is a *śiṃśapā*, therefore this is a tree', the conclusion is already known through the minor premise, because to know a thing as *śiṃśapā* is to know it as a tree. In the words of Locke tree-ness is the 'nominal essence' of *śiṃśapā.* Similarly the nominal essence of triangle is its character of being a three-sided rectilinear figure, so that when we call a figure 'triangle' what we mean is that it possesses this character, and then the inference of this character becomes superfluous because it gives no new information. The inference of essential nature, however, does not always involve *petitio principii.* When the ascertainment of essential nature is based on experience the inference is necessary as well as new. We know that the character of having its three angles equal to two right angles is the essential nature of a triangle, not its nominal essence, i.e. not a character on the ground of which we agree to call it by the name triangle. Then, on knowing that a particular figure is a triangle we immediately infer with logical necessity that its three angles are equal to two right angles without committing the fallacy of *petitio principii.* In conclusion we may say that the Buddhist view regarding the nature of *vyāpti* is most satisfactory and it is to be regretted that other Indian philosophers due to their prejudice against Buddhism, could not develop this fruitful line of thought.

6.4.2. *The Ascertainment of Vyāpti*

What is the means or method (*pramāṇa*) of knowing *vyāpti*?

6.4.2.1. *The Buddhist view*

The Buddhist answer to this question is given in the following verse:

> *kāryakāraṇabhāvādvā svabhāvādvā niyāmakāt |*
> *avinābhāvaniyamo'darśanānna na darśanāt ||*

Vyāpti is established neither by non-observation nor by observation. The mere observation of some positive instances of a relation, e.g., between smoke and fire, is not enough to prove that smoke and fire are invariably connected, because what is observed proves only that they have been connected together in the past, but this does not guarantee a universal and necessary connection between the two. The mere non-observation of fire and smoke together in a limited number of negative instances too cannot ensure that there will be no instance in future of the presence of smoke in the absence of fire. Therefore, *vyāpti* is proved neither by perception, nor by non-perception, but by the knowledge of causality or identity. When it is known that smoke is produced when fire is produced and it is not produced when fire is not produced, we conclude that smoke depends for its existence on fire, i.e., it is the effect of the latter, and then, since the relation of cause and effect is necessary, we know that smoke is invariably concomitant with fire. Similarly, when it is known that a thing A possesses a nature B the invariable connection between A and B is proved, because it is inconceivable that a thing can ever exist without its nature.

The Buddhist view is rejected by the Bhāṭṭa on the ground that causality is nothing but a law of regular sequence and *vyāpti* also is a law, so that if a law is made the *pramāṇa* of another law there will be the fault of self-dependence (*ātmāśraya*). What is the proof of the *vyāpti* that A is invariably connected with B? The Buddhist says that the proof lies in their being related by way of causality. But causality between A and B is nothing except the *vyāpti* that A is invariably succeeded by B. And, then the question arises as to how it is known that A will be always succeeded by B in future also as in the past. There is no extra-empirical means of knowing that A is the cause of B, and experience reveals nothing except that one has been observed to succeed the other. Therefore, causality cannot be the basis of the knowledge of *vyāpti*.

The law of identity also is equally without a proof. It is true that *śiṃśapā* is a tree. But *śiṃśapā*-ness and tree-ness cannot be bound together for ever. That which is the nature of one thing inheres in that thing alone. But tree-ness does not inhere in *śiṃśapā* alone, because there are trees other than a *śiṃśapā* tree. It is true that tree-ness has never been found to inhere in non-trees. But though it has not been found, yet the possibility that it may be found in some other place or time cannot be excluded altogether. To give another example, gold is found to be yellow. But merely on this basis it cannot be asserted with certainty that yellowness is the nature of gold, because there is no means of ruling out the possibility of a piece of gold to be found in future turning out to be black. Experience reveals merely that goldness and yellowness coexist and that fire is succeeded by smoke. But it does not reveal that the latter is the nature or effect of the former. Therefore, causality and identity cannot be the *pramāṇa* of *vyāpti*.[35]

6.4.2.2. *Mānasa-pratyakṣa Theory*

Some people say that *vyāpti* is known through mental perception (*mānasapratyakṣa*). This view is rejected on the ground that the object of mental perception is the self and its qualities, e.g., pleasure, pain etc., *Vyāpti* is not a quality of the self, but a relation between external things. If *vyāpti* can be known through perception at all it can be only external perception which is the source of knowing external things and their qualities and relations. *Manas* cannot function independently of the external sense-organs in the case of external things. *Manas* is inside the body while objects are outside. So, it cannot establish a direct

35. NRM, p. 58.

contact with external objects. It may be urged that *manas* can function in cooperation with repeated observation and then give the knowledge of *vyāpti*. But this is wrong. In observation eyes and other sense-organs as well as *manas* are involved. Eyes come in contact with an external object on the one hand and with *manas* on the other. But the contact of eyes with *vyāpti* is not possible, because *vyāpti* is not a thing found in one particular place or time like a tree. Repeated observation reveals only that smoke is connected with fire, but this is not *vyāpti*. *Vyāpti* is a universal connection and it implies a knowledge not only of the present time and place, but also of past and future times and places. Eyes, however, cannot come in contact with the past and future times and places and *manas*, whose functioning is dependent on that of eyes and other senses, cannot come in contact with them independently. Even those who hold that *manas* is all-pervasive cannot say that it can function independently of eyes etc., because then all persons would be omniscient. The operations of *manas* are restricted to 'here and now' in perception, so that it is impossible for it to give the knowledge of a universal relation. Even if it be accepted that observation can give the knowledge of *vyāpti*, it cannot be said that *manas* is the source of such knowledge simply on the ground that it is involved in it. *Manas* is involved not only in perception but also in inference and other *pramāṇa*-s. If by the mere presence of mental functioning a *pramāṇa* can be called mental perception, then the distinction of perception, inference etc. will vanish and there will be only one *pramāṇa*. When *manas* functions with the help of external sense-organs the *pramāṇa* is called perception, when it functions with the help of *liṅgajñāna* the *pramāṇa* is called inference, and when it functions exclusively by itself as in the case of pleasure etc. the *pramāṇa* is called mental perception. In the case of *vyāptijñāna manas* cannot function with the help of external senses, nor with the help of *liṅgajñāna*, nor exclusively by itself. Therefore, the *pramāṇa* of *vyāpti* is neither perception, nor inference, nor mental perception, but different from them.[36]

6.4.2.3. *The Prābhākara View*

Prabhākara maintains that the knowledge of *vyāpti* is obtained

36. NRM, pp. 58-60.

by a single act of sense-perception. The *vyāpti* between smoke and fire is apprehended in the very first observation of the two together and what subsequent observations do is merely to remove extraneous conditions (*upādhi*), if any, and thus to confirm the *vyāpti* apprehended in the first observation. The *vyāpti* of smoke with fire, which means a relation of the two free from all spatio-temporal limitations (*deśakālānavacchinna*) is cognized through perception. *Agnimattā*, i.e., the property of being conjoined with fire, belongs to smoke, and it is perceived just as the other properties, e.g., grey colour of smoke, are perceived. *Agnimattā* is as natural a property of smoke as its grey colour is. It may be objected that the object of sense-perception is something existing at the present time and place (*sannihitadeśakālaviṣayatva*) while the *vyāpti* between smoke and fire expresses their conjunction in all times and places, so that it is beyond the comprehension of perception. The answer is that existence at the present time and place is indicated by the use of the word 'this' (*idantā*), which applies to substances only, not to their conjunction. The perceptual consciousness arises in the form 'this is smoke', not in the form 'this is the conjunction of smoke and fire'. We always say 'smoke and fire are conjoined', but never say 'this is the conjunction of smoke and fire'. Thus experience itself reveals that spatio-temporal limitations are imposed on substances alone, while conjunction is free from these. Therefore, the conjunction with fire that is independent of space and time is ascertained by perception as belonging to smoke, and then what is required to be known in other places and times is the existence of smoke alone, not its conjunction with fire which is already known. It may be remembered here that inference, according to Prabhākara, is the apprehension of the apprehended (*gṛhītagrāhi*), though it is not of the nature of memory. Now, if the conjunction of smoke with fire, which is revealed by the first perception, can acquire the status of *vyāpti*, why should the conjunction of fire with smoke, which too is similarly revealed, not acquire the same status? Prabhākara answers that the conjunction of fire with smoke, though revealed by the first perception, is known through subsequent perceptions as depending on an extraneous condition, viz., wet fuel, and on this ground *dhūmavattā* of fire is determined not to be natural to fire, while *agnimattā* of smoke is determined to be natural to smoke, for, no extraneous condition is observed in the latter case. Though both the conjunctions, viz., that of smoke with fire and that of fire with smoke are given by the first perception, yet the former attains the status of *vyāpti* because it is never contradicted, while the latter loses it because it is found to be contradicted when subsequently fire is seen without smoke.[37]

Prabhākara's view is rejected on the following grounds[38]:

The view that substances are limited by space and time while their conjunction is not, is not supported by experience. Such common expressions as 'these were conjoined', 'these are conjoined' and 'these will be conjoined' clearly point out that it is the conjunction that is determined by past, present and future times. Time does not determine an agent (*kāraka*) but the action of an agent (*kārakavyāpāra*). When smoke is perceived to be conjoined with fire it is the action of its being conjoined that is determined by the time when the perception takes place. Thus the conjunction of smoke with fire cannot be proved to be permanent by a single act of perception. Moreover, the view that time is indicated by the word 'this' (*idam*) is wrong, because it is better indicated by different verbal forms called tenses, such as 'is', 'was' 'will be' etc. These verbal forms indicate the time-relations of actions, not of substance. Time determines a substance not independently of its qualities and actions but with all the qualities and actions inhering in it. When smoke is perceived now it is impossible that it should be apprehended as existing at the present time while its qualities and actions such as colour, conjunction etc. should be apprehended as existing at all times.

Let us even accept that conjunction is not apprehended as having any spatio-temporal limitations. However, there is no proof of its naturalness (*svābhāvikatva*). Non-apprehension by itself cannot prove that conjunction is not determined by place and time, because there may be temporal and spatial determination though it is not apprehended. So long as this possibility is not ruled out naturalness cannot be proved. Or, if the conjunc-

37. NRM, p. 60; Cf. PP, pp. 70-71.
38. NRM, pp. 60-63.

tion of smoke with fire is proved to be natural, then its character of belonging to the present time (*vartamānakālatā*) also is equally well proved to be natural to smoke. If on the strength of perception it is said that the conjunction with fire is natural to smoke, then it can also be said that the present time also is natural to smoke. Time is as much an attribute of the substance of smoke as its conjunction with fire. Just as smoke cannot exist apart from its conjunction with fire, so it cannot exist apart from the present moment, which amounts to saying that smoke is momentary. Thus instead of proving his own theory Prabhākara proves an alien theory, viz., the Buddhist theory of momentariness. If in order to avoid this conclusion the relation of smoke to the present moment is not admitted to be natural, then there is no reason why its conjunction with fire should be admitted to be natural. If smoke can exist without its relation to the present moment that is known to be natural on the evidence of perception (according to Prabhākara's reasoning), then its existence without conjunction with fire can also be possible. The result is that the *vyāpti* between smoke and fire cannot be established by perception. It may be said that subsequent recognition of smoke proves that it is not momentary but exists even after the present moment is gone, while the existence of smoke without fire is never observed. Prabhākara may, then, be asked whether he holds the view that momentariness is apprehended by perception and is subsequently contradicted by recognition. Certainly such a view is not accepted by him. Even if it be accepted that previously perceived momentariness of smoke is contradicted by the perception of its existence at another time, it cannot be explained how the previously perceived momentariness of fire is contradicted when it is not actually perceived but smoke alone is perceived and consequently how we can infer the existence of fire having relation to another time-moment. During the first observation smoke and fire were perceived to have a momentary character. Now we perceive smoke alone and recognize that it is not momentary. But we do not perceive fire. So, how can we know that it is not momentary? If it be urged that the momentariness of fire is contradicted by inference which proves its relation to a moment different from the first then the view that inference apprehends the apprehended is to be given up, for the new moment was not apprehended by perception.

Again, when it is seen that the previously apprehended relation of smoke to the moment of perception is subsequently contradicted by recognition, then the possibility of the contradiction of its conjunction with fire can never be ruled out. It is true that its conjunction with fire has not been contradicted even after a deliberate search; but who can dispel the suspicion that it may be contradicted in future? Perception is not competent to do so, because its function is confined to the present time and place. Inference also is powerless. Inference depends on the ascertainment of *vyāpti*, but the point at issue is how to ascertain *vyāpti*, and the *pramāṇatva* of inference depends on the settlement of this issue. It may be urged that what is natural cannot be contradicted. It is true. But what is the proof that conjunction with fire is natural to smoke? That which is natural does not depend on any extraneous conditions. But what is the evidence to prove that the conjunction of smoke with fire does not depend on any extraneous condition? There may be some hidden extraneous condition without revealing itself to the observer. It is not true to say that that which exists must necessarily be open to observation. There are many things which are real but are never observed. In spite of the fact that fire is seen to have conjunction with smoke and smoke is seen to have conjunction with fire, the former conjunction is later seen to be inconstant. How can, then, it be guaranteed that the latter conjunction will never be found to be inconstant like the former?

The smoke and the fire whose conjunction was apprehended by the first perception in the hearth are different from smokes and fires existing at other times and places. How can, then the smoke on the hill, which is perceived now and was not perceived before, be the *liṅga* of fire? It will be said that the universal of smoke (*dhūmatva*) is the *liṅga* in the inference, not a particular smoke. But, then, there can be no inference unless the relation of the universal of smoke with the universal of fire is perceived. Place, time, relation and universal all qualify substance. There is no direct relation between two universals. Such a relation is possible only indirectly through the substances of smoke and fire. But the smoke perceived on the hill now and the smoke perceived in the hearth do not possess an identical substance. When the substance has changed, how can the relation mediated by it be the same? Thus the previously observed conjunction cannot be the ground of the inference of fire on the hill. The relation between two universals cannot be ascertained by one single observation, because it depends on the elimination of non-recurrent particulars, for which repeated observation is needed, and it is yet to be seen whether repeated observation can conclusively prove a *vyāpti*.

6.4.2.4. *Sucaritamiśra's View*

The next view criticized by Pārthasārathi is advocated by Sucaritamiśra. Though Pārthasārathi has not named him, yet there is a complete agreement between the view he citicizes and that defended by Sucaritamiśra in his commentary on SV, Anu., 12. Sucaritamiśra says that by the first perception we cannot acquire the knowledge of *vyāpti*. The knowledge of *vyāpti* arises after several observations of two things together. We know the invariable relation of smoke and fire in one perception, but not in the first perception as Prabhākara maintains. Before the knowledge of the *vyāpti* arises in the mind there must have been a series of experiences of smoke together with fire. On the final experience helped by the revival of the memory-impressions of previous experiences a person comes to know that smoke possesses the nature of being invariably accompanied by fire.[39] When a person has had several experiences of smoke-fire relationship, these experiences are retained in the mind in the form of latent impressions and on the final experience they are synthesized and give rise to a single judgment such as 'all smoky things are fiery'. After a uniform experience of two things together occurring simultaneously or in succession on several occasions the knowledge of *vyāpti* between them arises in the mind like a flash of light just as the knowledge of the true character of a jewel, though not obvious at first sight, arises after it has been examined several times. This is the first stage in the knowledge of *vyāpti*. In this stage a *vyāpti* is merely suggested by a uniform positive experience.

39. प्राचीनानेकदर्शनजनितसंस्कारसहाये चरमे दर्शने चेतसि चकास्ति धूमस्य वह्निनियतस्वभावत्वम् । KK on SV, *Anu.*, 12.

In the second stage the *vyāpti* is confirmed by a uniform negative experience. We not only perceive that smoke is accompanied by fire but also that there is no smoke when there is no fire. In the third stage there is a process of reasoning. When a person has uniformly observed smoke with fire and has not observed smoke without fire, he thinks that there must be an invariable concomitance of smoke with fire, since the fact that smoke follows fire without any regard to the difference of places, times, fuel and other conditions and that it is totally absent in the absence of fire, cannot be explained otherwise than on the basis of an essential or natural relation between smoke and fire. Thus a firm conviction arises in the mind of the observer and is supported by the evidences offered by other observers. Then, if in spite of there being no evidence to the contrary he entertains any doubt it has no foundation. It does happen sometimes that our firm beliefs are shaken by fresh evidence. For instance, a person having once acquired the belief that snake-bite is fatal is rather shocked to learn that a person bitten by snake did not die. However, in such a case the *vyāpti* between snake-bite and death is not actually disproved but is restricted in scope, for the fresh evidence only shows that a particular species of snake is poisonless. Thus *vyāpti* is known through perception and is confirmed by the non-perception of any exception.

It may be objected that perception is confined to the present time and place only, while a *vyāpti* implies the knowledge of future times and places also, so that if *vyāpti* is held to be an object of perception it would amount to saying that perception can apprehend remote times and places, which is absurd. But Sucaritamiśra denies any such absurdity. Perception apprehends such object-forms as are in contact with the senses. Conjunction with fire is a form of smoke and hence it is perceptible. When we say that there is a *vyāpti* between smoke and fire what we mean is that the conjunction of smoke with fire is not transitory but permanent. We perceive both the transitory and permanent forms of things. When we perceive a solid wall we also perceive that its form is stable or permanent and when we perceive the form of lightning we also perceive its transitoriness. If a permanent form were not an object of perception there would be no contradiction of such an experience as 'this is silver' subsequently by such an experience as 'this is not silver', because the objects of the two experiences would then be as different as those of 'this is silver' and 'this is mango.' If the 'silver' were perceived as transitory its form would not last till the appearance of the consciousness 'this is not silver', and then there would be no sublation (*bādha*) of the former consciousness of 'silver' by the latter. But actually we do perceive the form of 'silver' to be a lasting one so that the perception of 'silver' has co-objectivity with the non-perception of silver subsequently and thus the sublation of the first by the second becomes perfectly intelligible. Thus the *vyāpti* of smoke with fire is a permanent form of smoke and it is an object of perception like the permanent form of a wall.

Pārthasārathi criticizes this view as follows[40]:

Vyāpti cannot be an object of perception, because it implies a knowledge of remote times and places, which cannot come in contact with the senses. It may be granted that the *vyāpti* of smoke with fire is a form (*rūpa*) of smoke; but even then there can be no denial of the fact that it is a form which is never discrepant (*avyabhicārātmaka*), i.e., is inseparable from smoke. This inseparability or non-discrepancy is nothing other than that in whatever place and time smoke exists its association with fire always continues. If this is supposed to be an object of perception the absurdity of sense-contact with remote places and times becomes inevitable. If the *vyāpti* between smoke and fire is supposed to be a form of smoke, different from a universal relation of smoke with fire, and similar to such other forms of smoke as its grey colour etc., then let it be an object of perception, but that will not help a person who wishes to know that smoke is accompanied by fire in all places and times. Actually the invariable relation of smoke with fire is totally different from the grey colour and other visible forms of smoke. The former is not apprehended like the latter, and one who wants to infer fire from smoke stands in need of the former instead of the latter. Even if the *vyāpti* were a perceptible form of smoke, by perception it would be apprehended as confined to the present time and

40. NRM, pp. 64-67.

place alone and as such it would be irrelevant for the purpose at hand.

It has been said that just as we perceive a wall as having stability (*sthiratva*), so we perceive the association of smoke with fire as having stability or permanence and that this permanence of association is what is meant by the *vyāpti* between smoke and fire. Now, it is true that the *vyāpti* of smoke with fire means the permanence of their association, but that the permanence is an object of perception is false. When a wall is perceived its stability cannot be perceived, because stability means existence extending over several moments of time, while perception apprehends only existence at the present moment. If perception could reveal the existence of a thing in a future moment of time recognition would cease to have any use. A man was perceived yesterday and again today when we recognize him to be the same man. By recognition we apprehend his persistence during the interval, but the perception of yesterday alone could not have revealed that the man would exist today also. The stability of a thing can be apprehended only by the continued perception of it over a long time. But when I perceive a wall at this moment and apprehend its stability without actually perceiving it over a long time my apprehension is really inferential. I think at the moment of perception that this wall is solid and cannot easily be pierced by strong weapons and then I infer that it will continue to exist for more than one moment. Thus the stability of the wall is inferred from the strength of its structure. The sublation of the consciousness 'this is silver' by the subsequent consciousness 'this is not silver' can be explained thus: When 'silver' is perceived it is inferred that, because an existing thing cannot disappear all of a sudden without any cause or because a thing of one form cannot suddenly change into a thing of a different form, the 'silver' will persist at least for some more time. Then, when later on no silver is perceived in that place it is inferred that it was not actually present, because if it were present its sudden disappearance would be inexplicable, and thus we conclude that the former perception of its presence was illusory. When, however, there is a long gap between the earlier perception of silver and the later non-perception of it and the observer has moved elsewhere during the gap, he cannot be sure that his earlier perception was illusory even though it may be really so, because there is every possibility of the real silver having been removed by someone. Thus persistence or permanence is not an object of perception, and consequently, *vyāpti*, which is a permanent relation between two things, cannot be an object of perception.

6.4.2.5. *Umbeka's View*

Umbeka, another commentator of Kumārila, holds the view that *vyāpti* is known through *arthāpatti*.[41] *Arthāpatti* is the presumption of something to explain a known fact which remains otherwise unexplained. When we observe smoke with fire a hundred times and never observe it without fire, we cannot explain this fact otherwise than by presuming that smoke must be invariably concomitant with fire. If there were no such invariable concomitance we could have observed smoke without fire at some time or some place. But, since we have never observed such a thing we are led to believe that there is a *vyāpti* between smoke and fire.

Pārthasārathi rejects this view. What, he asks, is that remains inexplicable without presuming a *vyāpti* between smoke and fire? The fact of non-observation of smoke without fire is quite explicable by the non-existence of smoke and the non-existence of fire. By non-observation alone it is not proved that future cases of the non-existence of fire will also be cases of the non-existence of smoke. The fact of a hundred observations of smoke and fire is explained by the existence of smoke and fire together in a hundred instances. But this does not prove that smoke and fire will exist together in future also. Thus *arthāpatti* cannot prove *vyāpti*.[42]

6.4.2.6. *Pārthasārathi's View*

Pārthasārathi's own view is as follows[43]: *Vyāpti* is known from frequent experience (*bhūyodarśana*). The *pramāṇa* through which we have a frequent experience of the relation of smoke and fire cannot be specified. It may be any of the recognized

41. TT on SV, *Anu.*, 12.
42. NRM, p. 67.
43. Ibid., pp. 67-70.

pramāṇa-s. Whatever the *pramāṇa* may be it always works in cooperation with the non-apprehension of contrary instances. It is true that frequent experience proves the *liṅga-liṅgin* relationship only in a limited number of cases, not in all cases, and non-observation of contrary instances proves the relationship between the absence of *liṅgin* and the absence of *liṅga* only to the extent to which non-observation has actually gone. It is also true that one who wishes to establish on the basis of experience a universal relation between *liṅga* and *liṅgin*, say, smoke and fire, can do so only after he has had an experience of an infinite number of positive instances and an equally infinite number of negative instances, which is not possible during the life-span of a person. But this presents an insurmountable difficulty only to those who maintain that the ground of inference is such a proposition as 'all cases of smoke are cases of fire.' For those, on the other hand, who maintain that we can validly infer the presence of fire from the proposition 'all observed cases of smoke are cases of fire,' there is really no difficulty. People are seen to infer fire correctly after this much alone that in all the past observed cases smoke has been found to be accompanied by fire and that no exception has ever been observed in which smoke was present without fire. Thus the proposition which is actually made the basis of inference is easily secured through repeated experience and it does not stand in need of the knowledge of an infinite number of instances.

Pârthasārathi makes an observed rule the ground of inference. Now, the question may be asked as to how he can explain such a cognition as 'all cases of smoke are cases of fire.' It cannot be said that this cognition does not arise or that it is doubtful or wrong, because people are seen to have such a cognition and are sure of its truth. What kind of *pramāṇa*, then, is the basis of this cognition? Pārthasārathi answers that this cognition is inferential in nature, because it is derived as a conclusion from an observed concomitance of smoke with fire. To say that it is perceptual in nature is wrong. It cannot be sensuous in origin, because it is not immediate or direct. The inference which is the source of this cognition may be stated thus:

All the past, future and remote cases of smoke are cases of fire, because they are cases of smoke like the cases which have been actually observed, e.g., that of the smoke in the hearth.

6.4.2.7. *The Later Bhāṭṭa View*

Pārthasārathi's view that the major premise of syllogism is a particular proposition and that which is called *vyāpti* by others is really inferential in nature is not accepted by other Indian philosophers, not even by the later Bhāṭṭas. The contribution of the later Bhāṭṭas to the theory of *vyāpti* is not substantial. They follow the Neo-Naiyāyikas and recommend that a more vigorous search should be carried on to ascertain the *vyāpti* between the middle and major terms in order that its unconditionality and the consequent validity of the conclusion may be ensured. Over and above the method of agreement and difference they add one more, viz., the method of *tarka*. The aim of this method is a complete elimination of extraneous conditions and the attainment of the unconditionality of a relation beyond a reasonable degree of doubt. The joint method of agreement and difference can eliminate visible extraneous conditions only while *tarka* eliminates the suspicion of invisible extraneous conditions.[44] It is assumed that where extraneous conditions are not visible their suspicion is illegitimate. The method of *tarka* is illustrated thus: If someone doubts the validity of the invariable concomitance between smoke and fire the doubt may be removed by the following process of reasoning: If there were no fire there would be no smoke, because, if there were smoke in the absence of fire, then an effect would be produced even when its cause is absent. Therefore, to avoid this absurdity it must be accepted that smoke is invariably related with fire. From this example it is clear that *tarka* is *reductio ad absurdum*.

Tarka is defined as a method of removing doubt regarding the validity of a proposition by first assuming the truth of its contradictory and then showing that such an assumption leads to an absurd conclusion.[45] In the given illustration the assump-

44. भूयोदर्शनतो शक्या दृश्योपाधिनिराक्रिया।
अदृश्योपाधिशंका तु तर्केरेव निरस्यते ॥ MM, p. 47.

45. प्रमाणेन साध्यमानस्यार्थस्यान्यथात्वशंकायां तन्निरासार्थमन्यथात्व दोषकथनं तर्कः। Ibid., p. 35.

tion is made that there may be smoke in the absence of fire. This is an O proposition ('some cases of smoke are not cases of fire') and is the contradictory of the *vyāpti* 'all cases of smoke are cases of fire' (an A proposition). The absurdity pointed out in this assumption consists in its being contradictory to the law of causation and thus the *vyāpti* is indirectly confirmed. The reasoning, however, is fallacious, because it assumes the law of causation. Sucaritamiśra and Pārthasārathi hold that the law of causation is an empirical law of regular sequence. But if this is true then to prove the *vyāpti* between smoke and fire we have to prove the law of causation, a task much more difficult than the first. Even if the law of causation be an *a priori* law, though the Bhāṭṭa who is an empiricist cannot believe in any *a priori* law, the reasoning is vitiated by the defect of assuming what is to be proved, because it assumes that there is a relation of cause and effect between fire and smoke which is the very thing to be proved. The Bhāṭṭas, equally with other philosophers, have criticized the Buddhist view that *vyāpti* is based on the laws of causation and identity and again they assume it in their method of *tarka*. This is merely smuggling through the back door what has been refused through the front door.

The real problem of induction is that of ascertaining specific causal relations among observed phenomena and the method of *tarka* does not make any real advance towards the solution of the problem. A complete elimination of extraneous conditions cannot be achieved by arguments in a debate. The only method is isolating the observed antecedents of a phenomenon and experimenting with them one by one. The joint method of agreement and difference is a method of observation recognized by all Indian philosophers. Kumārila suggests the method of concomitant variation also. He illustrates it as follows: When dust is seen the question arises as to what its cause may be. Is it produced by the movement of cows and other hard-bodied animals or by the movement of ants? The latter alternative is rejected because we observe that when the number of cattles is greater there is a correspondingly larger quantity of the dust thrown above, while no such correspondence is observed between the number of ants in motion and the quantity of dust.[46]

46. SV, *Vākya*, 165-66.

6.4.2.8. *The Nyāya View*

The Nyāya method of ascertaining *vyāpti* consists of four steps, viz., *anvaya*, *vyatireka*, *vyabhicārāgraha* and *tarka*. *Anvaya* is a uniform experience of two things together, i.e., their co-presence. *Vyatireka* is the uniform experience of their co-absence. *Vyabhicārāgraha* is the non-observation of any contradictory instance. We always observe that whenever smoke is present fire is also present and also that whenever fire is absent smoke also is absent. We never observe a case in which there may be smoke without fire. From the observed double agreement of smoke and fire in their presence and absence together with the non-observation of any exception the *vyāpti* between smoke and fire is known. In this process such irrelevant circumstances as may vitiate the *vyāpti* are eliminated, because when smoke and fire are observed repeatedly under varying circumstances the conditions which are inessential and hence non-recurrent are gradually detected and left out. If even after this there remains any doubt regarding the unconditionality of the *vyāpti* it is removed by *tarka* as shown above.[47]

From this it is obvious that the view of the later Bhāṭṭas about the method of ascertaining *vyāpti* closely follows that of the Naiyāyikas, particularly of Gaṅgeśa and other Neo-Naiyāyikas. There is, however, one difference between the two views. The Naiyāyikas are aware of the fact that the above method is not the proof of the absolute validity of a *vyāpti*, because in spite of the most careful search of irrelevant conditions the possibility of a contradictory instance making its appearance at some future time cannot be completely ruled out. So, the Naiyāyikas assume a kind of perception called *sāmānyalakṣaṇa* in which, it is said, we directly become aware of all the past, future and present instances of a class through its universal. When we perceive fire and smoke we also perceive the universals 'fireness' and 'smokeness', and through this latter perception we perceive all the actual and possible instances of fire and smoke. Thus we have a direct knowledge of the *vyāpti* between them in the form 'all cases of smoke are cases of fire'. The Bhāṭṭas do not accept this method

47. Cp. SM, 137.

of guaranteeing the absolute validity of *vyāpti* and quite reasonably so. The *sāmānyalakṣaṇa* form of perception is not a fact of experience, but only an hypothesis, as is clear from the words of Viśvanātha:

> How otherwise could we know all the instances of smoke and fire than through the generality of smoke and the generality of fire? Therefore, the *sāmānyalakṣaṇa* form of perception is accepted by us.[48]

This clearly shows that the Naiyāyika takes the absolute validity of *vyāpti* as a fact and in order to explain this 'fact' he proposes the hypothesis of *sāmānyalakṣaṇa pratyakṣa.* But actually what the Naiyāyika takes for granted as a fact is not a fact, but is the very problem of induction. The problem of induction is: how to secure an absolutely valid universal premise so that the conclusion based on it may be true. The absolute validity of the proposition 'where there is smoke there is fire' is to be proved. But the Naiyāyika, by assuming *sāmānyalakṣaṇa*, takes that which is to be proved as the proof of what is not borne out by facts. Hence, the Bhāṭṭa does not agree with the Naiyāyika in this respect and instead of trying to secure the absolute validity of *vyāpti* he is satisfied with its mere empirical validity.

6.4.2.9. *Criticism of the Different Views*

We shall conclude this discussion with some critical remarks. Pārthasārathi's view of *vyāpti* is an exact parallel of Mill's.

> He (Mill) held that the evidence for the conclusion is the same as the evidence for the major premise, so that either could be drawn immediately from the same data.[49]

Pārthasārathi also holds that from the uniform experience of invariable concomitance between the observed cases of smoke and the observed cases of fire you can draw the conclusion that there is fire on the hill or that all the unobserved cases of smoke are cases of fire. This view, however, is wrong. The evidence on which an induction rests and that on which a deduction rests

48. सामान्यलक्षणेन विना धूमत्वेन सकलधूमानां वह्नित्वेन सकलवह्नीनां च भानं कथं भवेत् तदर्थं सामान्यलक्षणा स्वीक्रियते। SM, 65.
49. Stebbing, *A Modern Introduction to Logic*, p. 219.

must be different. A uniform and uncontradicted experience by itself is not the ground of induction. It is merely the material ground of induction, while the laws of causation and uniformity of nature are its formal grounds. From a mere observation of uniform relation between particular smokes and particular fires we are not justified in generalizing that smoke as such is related with fire as such, unless we believe that the former is the effect and the latter is the cause and that the course of nature is uniform, i.e., that the same phenomenon will recur in future when exactly the same antecedent conditions are repeated. Similarly, the ground of deduction is not a mere uniform experience. We cannot validly infer the presence of fire in a place where smoke alone is perceived unless we know that smoke must be accompanied by fire. The ground of deduction is a true universal proposition which is an assertion about all the known and unknown instances of the middle term. It is not a mere summation of past observations, because logically we have no right to expect a thing to happen now in a way it was found to happen in the past.

Pārthasārathi is, however, right insofar as he holds that the induction 'all cases of smoke are cases of fire' is not directly given and hence is non-perceptual. Now, the question arises regarding the *pramāṇa* or means of cognition from which it is derived. In modern logic all indirect knowledge other than the knowledge from the statements of others is called inference. Induction thus is the inference of the general from the particular and is different from deduction which is the inference of the particular from the general. In Indian logic the name inference is restricted to the subsumption of a particular case under a general rule, so that inference cannot be the *pramāṇa* of *vyāpti* or induction. Those Indian philosophers who believe in only two or three *pramāṇa*-s, viz., perception, inference and verbal testimony, have no alternative other than to say that *vyāpti* is known through perception. The Naiyāyika too, who accepts a fourth *pramāṇa*, viz., *upamāna*, had to invent the absurd hypothesis of *sāmānyalakṣaṇa pratyakṣa* in order to defend the perceptual character of *vyāpti*, because *upamāna*, which gives a knowledge of similarity, is obviously of no help. Prabhākara who recognizes a fifth *pramāṇa*, *arthāpatti*, could not take its help, because *arthāpatti* according to him, depends on the knowledge of *vyāpti* like inference.[50] The sixth *pramāṇa*, *anupalabdhi*, recognized by Kumārila also is of no avail. The Bhāṭṭa view of *arthāpatti*, however, is different from Prabhākara's view. Thus there are only three alternatives open to the Bhāṭṭa. Either a seventh *pramāṇa* should be recognized, or the definition of inference should be amended, or the knowledge of *vyāpti* should be included in *arthāpatti*. Umbeka accepts the third alternative. This view may be defended as follows: We have uniformly observed in the past the copresence of smoke and fire and we have never had a contradictory experience. From this we come to think that probably there is a necessary relation between smoke and fire. Now we perceive smoke alone from a distance and in accordance with our past experience we think that if there be a necessary relation between smoke and fire there should be fire in the place where smoke is seen. Next we go nearer and actually perceive fire. Thus a mere guess is verified by perception. This cannot be called inference, because before actual perception we were not confident of the presence of fire. Our thinking so far is of the nature of trial-and-error. Next we think that if the relation of smoke with fire be a mere accidental one, why should our suspicion about the presence of fire when only smoke is perceived, turn out to be true? This conflict is resolved by presuming that smoke is necesarily related with fire. Thus the *vyāpti* between smoke and fire is known through *arthāpatti*, and then whenever we infer fire from smoke in future our inference follows logically from the universal proposition 'all cases of smoke are cases of fire.' As for the proposition 'all cases of fire are cases of smoke,' our guess about the presence of smoke on the perception of fire is on many occasions not confirmed, and so we conclude that the concomitance of fire with smoke is not necessary.

6.5. *The Charge of Petitio Principii in Inference*

Mill adopted the view that inferential reasoning proceeds from particular to particular, because he wanted to save inference from the charge of *petitio principii*. It is said that when

50. अर्थापत्तिरपि सम्बन्धनियमसापेक्षाऽनवस्थाप्रसंगादेव नानुमानवत् प्रमाणम्। PP, p. 62.

we argue from the mortality of all men to the mortality of Socrates, the truth of the conclusion is already assumed in the major premise, so that what is proved is not a real advance from the known to the unknown. The Cārvāka has levelled a similar charge against inference. He says:

> If the inference is of the particular, viz., hill-fire, then the awareness of the relation of concomitance (which could be the basis) is absent, because the known relation refers to the universal; if the universal alone is to be inferred, then the inference proves the proved.

Like Mill, Pārthasārathi tries to save inference from the charge of *siddhasādhyatā* (*petitio principii*) by asserting that the major premise from which the conclusion is drawn is not a universal proposition like 'all that has smoke, has fire', but that it is a particular proposition like 'all that has been observed to have smoke has been observed to have fire.'

> If it be that in all cases where the pervaded exists, the existence of the pervader is also known, then the doubt might justly arise that inference gives what is already known. But the fact is not so. It is only in such familiar examples as the hearth etc. that the coexistence of smoke with fire is observed before the rise of the inferential knowledge but not everywhere.[51]

This answer, however, does not really set aside the charge of *petitio principii*, because, as we have seen, the view that the major premise is a particular proposition is mistaken. Fortunately, Pārthasārathi has met the charge from the view-point of those also who maintain that the major premise is a real universal proposition. The charge of *petitio principii* would have been true if the knowledge of the universal major premise were dependent on the knowledge of the conclusion, i.e., if the universal major premise depended 'epistemically' on the conclusion. But such is not really the case. At the time when the *vyāpti* between smoke and fire was apprehended we were not at all aware of the existence of the hill. And when the hill itself was not known, how could we have known the fiery hill?[52] It is impossible that we could have known that all men are mortal after an

51. SD. p. 61.
52. Ibid., p. 62.

examination of the whole class of human beings including even those who are still living and those who are not as yet born. Therefore, to say that the universal major premise is epistemically dependent on the conclusion is absurd. The universal major premise is based not on perfect enumeration but on simple enumeration. Therefore, there is no apprehension of the apprehended in inference. Those who say that the existence of fire on the hill is already known when the major premise 'all that has smoke has fire' was known, forget the function of the minor premise, 'the hill has smoke.' If the presence of fire on the hill is a previously known fact the minor premise becomes superfluous. In inference the conclusion is drawn from two premises. It is the joint result of two premises. The minor premise is not superfluous. If it were superfluous, one who wanted fire would go to the hill without caring to know whether the hill possessed smoke which is the mark of the presence of fire.

Prabhākara, on the other hand, accepts the charge of *petitio principii*, but at the same time he denies that inference is invalid. He says that the existence of fire is already known when the invariable concomitance of smoke with fire is known, so that what we require to know later on is merely the existence of smoke at a particular place and time. But, though inference gives a knowledge of the known, it cannot be rejected as invalid on that account, because the mark of validity is not novelty but experience (*anubhūti*) which excludes memory. Only memory is invalid, because it arises solely from latent impressions. The cause of inference is not purely the revival of latent impression, because inference arises from the memory of the *vyāpti* together with the perception of the mark, e.g., smoke. And it is not obscured memory (*smṛtipramoṣa*) like the illusion of silver in shell, because in it the memory-element, viz., the *vyāpti* and the element of experience, viz., smoke, are clearly distinguished, while in the said illusion the remembered silver is confused with the experienced 'this'.

Prabhākara's view is wrong. If the existence of fire on the hill is already known, then the existence of smoke on the hill too must be already known, because the former cannot be known to one who is ignorant of the latter. If it be said that smoke is certainly known but not as a qualification of the hill, then, as fire too is known but not as a qualification of the hill, there ceases to be any difference between the middle and major terms in this respect, and thus Prabhākara's assertion that in the inference of fire the existence of smoke alone requires to be known in a new place and not fire, becomes a vain cry. Again, just as by the knowledge of the *vyāpti* between smoke and fire the latter is said to be an already known fact, so by the knowledge of the *vyāpti* between fire feeding on wet fuel and smoke the latter too becomes a known fact, so that both fire and smoke being past cognitions, there remains nothing to be gained by the perception of smoke on the hill.[53]

6 6. *Kinds of Inference*

6.6.1. *Svārthānumāna and Parārthānumāna*

The most commonly recognized division of inference is one into *svārthānumāna* or the inference for oneself and *parārthānumāna* or the inference for others. In earlier philosophical literature this distinction was observed by Diṅnāga, Praśastapāda and Siddhasenadivākara. In the *Sūtra*-s there is no mention of these forms of inference. In the *Nyāya Sūtra*, for example, this division does not exist, but instead of it three other forms of inference are clearly mentioned. Diṅāga defines *svārthānumāna* as the knowledge of a thing derived from the knowledge of the mark having three characteristics; and *parārthānumāna* is defined by him as the statement in words which communicates to others what has been known through *svārthānumāna*.[54] Praśastapāda uses the term '*svaniścitārtham anumānam*' instead of '*svārthānumānam*', meaning inference for one's own conviction[55] and defines *parārhānumāna* as the demonstration by one with the help of the five-membered syllogism, of a thing that one is convinced of, to others who are ignorant or have a doubtful or wrong knowledge of it.[56] Among the orthodox philosophers

53. SD, pp. 61-63.
54. अनुमानं द्विधा स्वार्थे त्रिरूपाल्लिंगतोऽर्थदृक् ।
    परार्थानुमानं तु स्वदृष्टार्थप्रकाशकम् ॥
55. PDS, p. 206.
56. Ibid., p. 231.

Praśastapāda is the first to observe this distinction. Siddhasena-divākara is the first Jaina thinker to do the same in his *Nyāyāvatāra*. About the question as to who started this distinction nothing can be said decisively except that the answer depends mainly on the relative dates of these thinkers.

In the Mīmāṃsā literature Śabara is either unaware of these two forms of inference or is opposed to them. Kumārila too does not seem to favour the distinction, though he does say that one who wishes to communicate to others what he knows through inference should first mention the *pakṣa*, i.e., that which is to be proved.[57] Umbeka and Sucaritamiśra are definitely opposed to the division of inference into *svārtha* and *parārtha*[58]. Sucaritamiśra says that the Buddhists divide inference into *svārtha* and *parārtha*, but this division is untenable. From this remark it appears that the Buddhists, probably Diṅnāga, were the initiators of this division. Before giving Sucaritamiśra's criticism it may be pointed out that the author of *Mānameyodaya* imports this division in the Bhāṭṭa system also.

Sucaritamiśra says that a person wishing to communicate a conclusion arrived at through inference to others makes a verbal statement and the hearer remembering the meaning of the words arrives at the conclusion by himself, so that the inference on the part of the latter is as much *svārtha* as on the part of the former. Both the speaker and the hearer infer for their own sake. Where, then, is the inference for other's sake? It is true that the statement is for other's sake, but the statement is not inference. When someone learns something from statements made by others the means of knowledge is verbal testimony and it is different from perception, inference and other means. A reliable person is at liberty to communicate to others what he knows from personal experience with or without mentioning the reason why what he knows is as he knows and not otherwise. He may preach that sacrifice leads to heaven with or without saying why it must be so. In case he supports it by an argument his statement will be more convincing, but then it cannot lose its character of being verbal testimony and acquire the character of being a different

57. SV, *Anu.*, 53.
58. TT & KK on Ibid.

pramāṇa, say inference. Inference is defined by the Buddhist as the knowledge of something through a mark having three characteristics. But a statement is neither knowledge, nor does it follow from a mark. How can, then, it be said to be inference? If an inference is called '*parārtha*' in a secondary sense (*upacāra*) simply because the statement which expresses it is meant for the information of others, then a perception too which is communicated to others in words should be called '*parārtha*'. Thus like the two forms of inference perception too must have two forms, viz., *svārthapratyakṣa* and *parārthapratyakṣa*. But neither the Buddhist nor others who uphold the twofold division of inference have recognized this twofold division of perception. The Buddhist may say that perception cannot be *parārtha* because the object of perception is *svalakṣaṇa* which is incommunicable. But this is wrong. If the Buddhist view of perception is correct, then a person making a statement contradictory to what he actually perceives cannot be opposed or corrected. But actually when a person touching a burning coal says that fire is cool, we do oppose him by saying that fire is hot. If the object of perception be inexpressible in words, then this latter statement cannot be explained.

6.6.2. *Viśeṣatodṛṣṭa and Sāmānyatodṛṣṭa*

Śabara recognizes only two other kinds of inference which he calls '*pratyakṣatodṛṣṭasambandha*' and '*sāmānyatodṛṣṭasambandha*'. He does not define these terms. He illustrates them thus: When the form of fire is inferred from the form of smoke the inference is of the first kind. When, seeing that Devadatta's change of position is preceded by his movement, we infer the sun's movement from its change of position in the sky, the inference is of the second kind.[59] The term '*pratyakṣatodṛṣṭasambandha*' literally means inference based on a directly seen relation and the term '*sāmānyatodṛṣṭasambandha*' means inference based on a generally seen or generalized relation.

Kumārila does not approve this terminology and the illustrations given by Śabara. There is no mutual exclusiveness between these two classes of inference. Just as the relation of smoke

59. SB, pp. 100-101

with fire is directly seen, so the relation between change of position and movement also is directly seen. It is true that the relation between the sun's change of position and its movement is not directly seen, but then in a similar way the relation between the hill-smoke and the hill-fire too is not directly seen. If we could observe this latter relation directly, there would be no scope for inference. If it be said that though the relation between smoke and fire on the hill is not directly seen, yet it has been directly seen in such familiar instances as the hearth etc., then it can also be said that the relation between change of position and movement, though not perceived in the case of the sun, is certainly perceived in the case of Devadatta. We directly see the movement of Devadatta. Movement is not always an object of inference. If movement were always imperceptible its inference would be impossible.

Now, just as the term '*pratyakṣatodṛṣṭa*' is applicable to both the illustrations given by Śabara, so the word '*sāmānyatodṛṣṭa*' also is applicable to both. The sun's movement is imperceptible. We have never observed the sun's movement followed by its change of position. We observe the visible movement of moving things, e.g., a man, a cow, a stone etc., and on the basis of this observation we generalize the relation between change of position and movement in the form 'where there is change of position there is movement.' Then we perceive that the sun changes its position in the sky and on the basis of the generalized relation we infer that the sun moves. But the same thing happens in the case of the inference of fire also. We observe the relation of smoke and fire in many instances and generalize it in the form 'where there is smoke there is fire'. Just as the basis of the inference of the sun's movement is the *vyāpti* between change of position in general and movement in general, so the basis of the inference of fire on the hill is the *vyāpti* between smoke in general and fire in general. Thus we see that there is no difference of kind between the two examples given by Śabara.[60]

There must be mutual exclusion (*pratipakṣatva*) among the sub-classes into which a class is divided. But we do not find any such thing between '*pratyakṣatodṛṣṭa*' and '*sāmānyatodṛṣṭa*.' The

60. SV, *Anu.*, 138-40.

opposite of the term '*sāmānya*' is '*viśeṣa*.' It will be shown (in Chap. XIII) that *sāmānya* or general and *viśeṣa* or particular are equally perceptible and the relation between two general things is as much perceptible as one between two particular things. Hence Kumārila rejects the term '*pratyakṣatodṛṣṭa*' and adopts the term '*viśeṣatodṛṣṭa*' in its place. Thus the two kinds of inference according to Kumārila are '*viśeṣatodṛṣṭa*' or specifically seen and '*sāmānyatodṛṣṭa*' or generally seen. The first kind is illustrated thus: A person perceives a particular fire. e,g., the fire produced from dried cow-dung and also its particular effect, the smoke, slightly different in colour and other aspects from other smokes. Next he goes away from the place and returning again after some interval infers the same particular fire from the same particular smoke. This inference is based on an invariable relation between two particulars and hence it is *viśeṣatodṛṣṭa*. It may be objected that though inference may take place in the manner, yet, since the fire is inferred in the same old place in which it was perceived, there is no novelty in it, and hence the inference is not valid. Kumārila answers that though the place of the inference is not new, yet the time is new and hence the inference is valid.[61] Other examples of *viśeṣatodṛṣṭa* are the inference by a father of the presence of his son from his voice and the inference of rise of *Rohiṇī* from the the rise of *Kṛttikā*. The first example is given by Cidānanda[62] and the second by Kumārila himself. Venkataramiah gives one more example in a footnote on page 95 of his translation of SD. The example is the inference of sandal-fire from sandal-scent smoke. This, however, is wrong because 'sandal-fire' and 'sandal-scent smoke' are general terms like 'fire' and 'smoke,' though the particulars denoted by the former two terms are less in number in comparison to those denoted by the latter two terms. The inference of fire from smoke and that of sandal-fire from sandal-scent smoke are both based on a generalized relation. The example of '*sāmānyatodṛṣṭa*' is the familiar inference of fire from smoke on the hill.[63]

Kumārila quotes the authority of Vindhyavāsin in support of his use of the term '*viśeṣatodṛṣṭa*.' The identity of Vindhya-

61. Ibid., 140-143.
62. NTV, p. 140.
63. SV, *Anu.*, 145.

vāsin is not certain. Some try to identify him with Īśvarakṛṣṇa, the author of *Sāṅkhyakārikā*.[64] Īśvarakṛṣṇa, however, mentions three kinds of inference instead of two, without naming them.[65] Gauḍapāda in his Bhāṣya on SK informs that the three kinds of inference are '*pūrvavat*,' '*śeṣavat*' and '*sāmānyatodṛṣṭa*.' The examples of the first two are the inference of the coming rain from clouds and the inference that the remaining sea-water is salty from the fact that a few drops of it have been found to be salty. The third kind is illustrated by two examples, viz., the inference that all the mango trees are in blossom, and the inference that the moon and stars which are seen to reach from one place to another move like Caitra who is known to reach from one place to another after moving. From the first of these latter two examples it appears that *sāmānyatodṛṣṭa* inference is induction based on simple enumeration, i.e., it is an empirical generalization. The second example shows that *sāmānyatodṛṣṭa* is inference based on analogy. It seems more probable that Śabara's *sāmānyatodṛṣṭa* also is inference from analogy. He says:

> As an example of *pratyakṣatodṛṣṭa* we have the cognition of fire following from the cognition of smoke; as an example of *sāmānyatodṛṣṭa* we have the case where finding Devadatta's reaching another place to be preceded by his movement we remember movement on the part of the sun also.

In the example of *pratyakṣatodṛṣṭa* he does not add any qualification like 'finding smoke to be accompanied by fire in the hearth' though in the example of *sāmānyatodṛṣṭa* a qualification like this has been added and the difference is significant. The latter example may be put in logical form thus:

Devadatta changes his position and moves;
The sun resembles Devadatta in changing its position;
∴ It resembles Devadatta in having movement.

This is obviously an argument from analogy. We may now conclude that Śabara divided inference into deductive and

64. See Ramaswami Sastri's Introduction to KK, p. 33.
65. SK, 5.

analogical, and that Kumārila did not accept any inference which is not deductive.

Gautama[66] also divides inference into the above three kinds and this division seems to be the oldest. Vātsyāyana defines *pūrvavat* as the inference of an effect from its cause, e.g., the inference of future rain from clouds. *Śeṣavat* is defined as the inference of a cause from its effect, e.g., the inference of past rain from a swelling river. *Sāmānyatodṛṣṭa* has not been defined by him, but the example given is the same as given by Śabara. According to a second interpretation the first kind of inference is defined as that in which the middle and the major terms have been perceived in the past, e.g., the inference of fire from smoke. The second is defined as the inference based on elimination, e.g., the inference that sound is a quality because it cannot be a substance, an action etc. The third is defined as that in which the relation of the middle and the major terms is imperceptible and the imperceptible major is inferred from the generic unity (*sāmānyāt*) of the middle with some other thing. When we infer the existence of an invisible substance called soul from desire etc. on the ground that desire etc. are qualities and qualities inhere in a substance, it is the inference of this kind. The later commentators offer many oter interpretations in addition. In NS, 2.1.38-39, three examples of inference are given, viz., the inference of past rain from a swelling river, the inference of future rain from the carrying off of eggs by ants, and the inference of the presence of a peacock from its sound. If these examples are intended to correspond to the three kinds of inference mentioned earlier, then *pūrvavat* and *śeṣavat* are inferences based on the relation of succession and *sāmānyatodṛṣṭa* on that of co-existence. The cause-effect relation is a relation of succession and conjunction, inherence and the rest are relations between co-existing things.

Praśastapāda[67] divides inference into two kinds, viz., *dṛṣṭa* and *sāmānyatodṛṣṭa*. He explains their difference in quite unambiguous terms. That inference is called *dṛṣṭa* in which the character of the familiar instances and the character that is

66. NS, 1.1.5.
67. PDS, pp. 205-6.

inferred possess specific unity (*jātyabheda*), i.e., in which the two characters belong to the same species. For example, when from the perception of dewlap alone we infer the presence of a cow the inferred character, viz., cowness is specifically the same as cowness characterising cows seen in the past. *Sāmānyatodṛṣṭa* is defined as that in which the perceived character and the inferred character have generic unity, i.e., they belong to one genus though their species are entirely different (*atyantajātibheda*). For example, when seeing that the actions of a farmer, a merchant etc. lead to some result, we infer that such actions of the four castes as sacrifice etc. must lead to some result, then the result that is inferred, viz., the attainment of heaven, which is non-secular, is of a species totally different from the former result, which is secular.

Prabhākara explains Śabara's division of inference into *pratyakṣatodṛṣṭa* and *sāmānyatodṛṣṭa* differently. He says that this twofold division is based on a twofold division of the objects of inference. The probandum is sometimes one whose specific individuality is perceptible and sometimes one whose specific individuality (*svalakṣaṇa*) is imperceptible. For example, the specific individuality of fire is perceptible whereas that of action or movement and potency (*śakti*) is imperceptible. Accordingly, inference is of two kinds, viz. *dṛṣṭasvalakṣaṇaviṣaya* and *adṛṣṭasvalakṣaṇaviṣaya*. But the difficulty is as to how the relation of that, whose specific individuality cannot be observed, with the probans, i.e., the *vyāpti*, can be established. Prabhākara says that in such cases the *vyāpti* is generally seen, not specifically. For example, we know in a general way that that which has an occasional existence must have some cause. Then, when we observe a thing having conjunction and disjunction (*saṃyoga-vibhāga*) occasionally we infer that there must be some cause which produces them. The substance of the thing cannot be the required cause, since it is present in the presence as well as absence of conjunction and disjunction. Conjunction and disjunction cannot be explained by supposing a change of substance, because we recognize that the same substance persists throughout. Therefore, the cause, which is different from these, must be movement (*karma*). Prabhākara advocates the view that movement cannot be perceived and that what we actually perceive when a thing is in motion is the conjunction and disjunction of the thing with some other thing, e.g., the ground. Potency is inferred in the following way: Fire burns things, but sometimes under the influence of a *mantra* or some herb it does not burn things. Now, the visible form of fire cannot be the cause of burning, because, though it is present when it burns a thing, it is not absent when it does not burn things. Therefore, it is inferred that the cause of burning must be some invisible property of fire, which is present when fire burns things. This invisible property is the potency or burning capacity of fire.[68]

Prabhākara's view that movement is supersensuous is not accepted by other schools, not even by other Mīmāṃsakas. It is true that in some cases movement is not observed, for instance, when it inheres in an invisible thing or when it is too subtle though inhering in a gross, sensible thing, or when it is so slow that it falls below the threshold of sensibility. But it is not always imperceptible. When a stone is hurled into the sky or when Devadatta walks the movement is directly perceived. Prabhākara wrongly thinks that conjunction and disjunction of a thing are perceived and movement which is supposed to be their cause is inferred. A cause is different from its effect. But movement is not different from conjunction and disjunction. The former is identical with the latter. What is inferred is the effort (*prayatna*) on the part of Devadatta, which initiates movement in his legs, and this inference is based on the experience of a relation between movement and effort in one's own case. If movement is inferred from the perception of successive conjunction and disjunction, then we cannot infer the movement inhering in the sun, because we do not perceive conjunction and disjunction of the sun as we perceive them in Devadatta's case. The sun is always seen to be fixed. We see the sun on the eastern horizon in the morning and on the western in the evening, and from this observed change of position we infer that it must have moved from east to west during the interval. Again, if movement is always inferred, Devadatta's movement too is an object of inference just as the sun's movement is, so that it cannot be cited as a known example in corroboration of the latter. If

68. PP, pp. 78 & 81.

discrete conjunction and disjunction are the marks of inferring movement, the present tense in 'this is moving' cannot be explained. When conjunction has already come to an end before disjunction takes place, it has become a thing of the past, so that the inferred movement too must be a thing of the past and its cognition must arise in the form 'this has moved' instead of 'this is moving.' Again, movement should be inferred in the case of a fish also, because, though it be in a fixed position, it has conjunction and disjunction with water constantly flowing to and away from it. In the case of a fixed post also there should be the inference of movement, because it has disjunction from a hawk (when the hawk flies away) as much as the hawk has disjunction from it. If it be said that movement is inferred not from disjunction alone but from conjunction preceded by disjunction, then, when the post has disjoined from one hawk and is conjoined with another hawk, we should infer that the post moves. Again, when Devadatta disjoins from a point of space and conjoins with another point, we must apprehend that he is still moving though actually he has stopped. It will be said that the hawk which has disjoined from the post is seen to come in conjunction with another place and that this fact cannot be explained by movement inhering in the post. This is true, and then let movement be presumed in the hawk too, but so far as the movement of the post is concerned nothing can debar us from inferring it, because the alleged marks of the inference, viz., conjunction and disjunction are present in the post. It is again said by Prabhākara that movement is inferred only when conjunction and disjunction are seen to arise in the place of the moving object, while the hawk is not the place of the post, so that movement of the post cannot be inferred. Let, then, there be no inference of movement in the post, yet this does not affect the case of the fish quoted above, because water is its own place. Prabhākara holds that the sky is invisible, and hence the conjunction and disjunction of a hawk flying in the sky with parts of the sky will also be invisible, so that we cannot infer that the hawk moves. We certainly apprehend the movement of the hawk in the sky, but this cannot be explained by its conjunction and disjunction with parts of light scattered in the sky (if such be the alternative explanation), because when it is dark no such thing can happen. The supposition of conjunction and disjunction with parts of darkness cannot be of any avail, because darkness, according to Prabhākara, is not a positive entity but a mere negation of light and hence it is not capable of having conjunction and disjunction with anything. Potency is imperceptible unlike movement, but it is known through presumption as will be shown later on. Therefore, there being no imperceptible thing to be known through the inference called *adṛṣṭasvalakṣaṇa*, the twofold division of inference suggested by Prabhākara falls to the ground. Really speaking, inference always proceeds from an observed relationship, which cannot be possible unless both the terms of the relationship are perceptible.[69]

6.6.3. *Kevalānvayin, Kevalavyatirekin and Anvaya-vyatirekin*

Uddyotakara[70] mentions three more kinds of inference, viz., *kevalānvayin, kevalavyatirekin* and *anvayavyatirekin* according as the *vyāpti* is derived respectively from uniform agreement in presence alone, or uniform agreement in absence alone, or uniform agreement in presence and absence both. In the first case the *vyāpti* is purely an affirmative proposition, e.g., 'all knowable things are nameable; the pot is a knowable thing; therefore, it is nameable.' In the second case the *vyāpti* is a purely negative proposition, e.g., 'what is not different from the other elements has no smell; the earth has smell, therefore, the earth is different from the other elements'. In the third case the *vyāpti* can be stated in affirmative as well as negative forms. The inference of fire from smoke is of this kind. This inference can be put in two forms, viz., 'all cases of smoke are cases of fire; the hill is a case of smoke; therefore, it is a case of fire' and 'no case of non-fire is a case of smoke; the hill is a case of smoke; therefore, it is a case of fire'. In the inference of the first kind no negative instance can be observed; in that of the second kind no positive instance can be observed; and in that of the third both positive and negative instances are observed.

In the Bhāṭṭa system the second kind is not recognized because it is based on a negative *vyāpti*, while negation, according

69. KK on SV, *Anu.*, 138.
70. NV, 1.1.4.

to Kumārila is the object of an independent *pramāṇa* called '*anupalabdhi.*' The second form of the third kind of inference also is not recognized for the same reason. Though in the inference of fire from smoke the *vyāpti* is derived from the observation of both positive and negative instances, yet logically the conclusion follows from the affirmative form of the *vyāpti* alone. Kumārila's view seems to be correct. One of the general rules of syllogism is that when the conclusion is affirmative both the premises must be affirmative. Accordingly, the conclusion 'the hill has fire' must follow from the affirmative premises, viz., 'whatever has smoke has fire' and 'the hill has smoke'. Thus the Bhāṭṭa recognizes only one form of inference, viz., the mood Barbara in the first figure.[71]

6.7. *Conditions of a Valid Inference*: *Fallacies*

The validity of an inference depends on the validity of its constituent propositions. If any of the constituent propositions is fallacious the whole inference is vitiated. Kumārila classifies the fallacies of inference into the fallacies of conclusion (*pratijñābhāsa*), those of the minor premise (*hetvābhāsa*), and those of the major premise (*dṛṣṭāntābhāsa*).

6.7.1. *Pratijñābhāsa*-s[72]

An inference proceeds from what is already known to what is inferred. All *pramāṇa*-s are characterized by novelty. Hence a valid conclusion should be one which is not previously known in the form in which it is stated (*tādrūpyeṇa gṛhītatvam*) or in a contradictory form (*tadviparyayato'pi vā*). That is, the conclusion must not already be known to be true or false. That which is already known so does not require any proof. When a conclusion is known to be true the inference appearing to prove it becomes superfluous and when it is known to be false the inference has no scope, since it is contradicted as soon as it appears by a quicker (*śīghrabhāvi*) and more convincing *pramāṇa*.

Now, the question arises as to how one *pramāṇa* can contradict another *pramāṇa*. If one *pramāṇa* can contradict another, how

71. MM, p. 56.
72. SV, *Anu.*, 55-75; NR & KK on ibid.

can we have faith in the *pramāṇa*? The answer is that a *pramāṇa* is never contradicted and that which is contradicted is not a *pramāṇa*, but a *pramāṇābhāsa*, i.e., that which bears the deceptive appearance of a *pramāṇa*. A *pramāṇa* is a true and definite knowledge. When a thing is truly and definitely known to have a character it contradicts and resists the appearance of a knowledge pointing to an opposite character. When there is a conflict between two means of knowledge, one which is stronger prevails over the other which is weaker. Though usually perception is seen to be stronger, yet it cannot be generalized that it is always stronger. The strength of a *pramāṇa* lies in its stronger appeal to the intellect, its indubitable character and the ease and quickness with which it arises. Contrarily, a weak *pramāṇa* is slow in its birth and intellectual appeal and is less convincing. Among these characteristics quickness or slowness is not so important as the power of conviction. Perception always arises more quickly than other *pramāṇa*-s, yet sometimes due to distance and other factors it remains doubtful. In such a case it is liable to be contradicted by a more convincing *pramāṇa*, e.g., inference. It is not a rule that a false inference should always be contradicted by preception. It may be contradicted by any of the six recognized *pramāṇa*-s.

The conditions of a valid inference mentioned above are psychological rather than logical. The logical conditions are that the premises must be true and that they must imply the conclusion. They are called by Stebbing the '*constitutive*' conditions of inference. From their violation arise the fallacies called '*hetvābhāsa*-s' and '*dṛṣṭāntābhāsa*-s'. Here we are concened with the fallacies of *pratijñā* or conclusion which arise from the violation of the psychological conditions. The psychological conditions relate to the knowledge of the person who infers. Their non-fulfilment cannot be declared to be a positive disproof of the conclusion. Yet, it is their fulfilment on which depends the value of the conclusion for the inferrer. Stebbing calls them '*epistemic*' conditions.

> Since, inference is a process in which a thinker passes from something known to something inferred, it is clear that we could not say we had inferred 'q' if we had already asserted

'q'. It is, therefore, obvious that 'q' must not be known to be true, and equally obvious that 'q' must not be known to be false. We must also know that 'p' implies 'q'. These conditions are 'epistemic'; they relate to what the thinker who is inferring knows. These conditions depend upon the relation of the thinker to the propositions involved in the process of inference.[73]

The following are the fallacies of conclusion:

6.7.1.1. *Siddhaviśeṣaṇa*

When the conclusion is already well known independently of the inference which seeks to prove it, the fallacy is called '*siddhaviśeṣaṇa*', i.e., conclusion having a well known predicate. For example, when an elephant is directly perceived, the inference of its presence from its trunk involves this fallacy. Another example is the inference proving the conclusion that fire is hot which everybody knows directly through perception.

6.7.1.2. *Bādhita* (*Sublated*)

This fallacy occurs when a conclusion is sublated by another stronger *pramāṇa*. It is primarily of six kinds according as the sublating *pramāṇa* is perception, a more convincing inference, *śabda*, *upamāna*, *arthāpatti* or *anupalabdhi*. Sublation by perception (*pratyakṣabādha*) is exemplified in proving the conclusion that fire is not hot or that sound is imperceptible. We directly perceive through touch that fire is hot and we actually perceive sound.

Sublation by inference (*anumānabādha*) is illustrated in proving that sound is not audible. Diṅnāga cited this example as a case of sublation by perception. But this is wrong. What we mean by audibility is that sound is apprehended by the ear. But we do not perceive this fact, though we have a direct or perceptual knowledge of sound. Audibility is really an object of inference. The perception of sound must have some cause and the cause must be something other than utterance, because in spite of the utterance by the speaker we sometimes fail to apprehend sound. We observe that when the ears are closed or they suffer from some disease, as in the case of a deaf person, there is no perception of sound and

73. *A Modern Introduction to Logic*, p. 215.

that when the ears are not closed or diseased, though the other sense-organs may be diseased, as in the case of a blind man, there is a perception of sound. Thus from this agreement between the ears and the perception of sound in presence as well as absence (*anvayavyatireka*) it is inferred that the ears are the cause of the perception of sound, i.e., that sound is audible. The inference may be put in the following logical form: 'That on whose presence a second thing occurs and in whose absence it does not occur, is the cause of the latter; the ears are the thing in whose presence the perception of sound occurs and in whose absence it does not occur; therefore, the ears are the cause of the perception of sound'. This inference sublates the inference of a person who argues that sound is not audible because it is a quality like colour.

Sublation by *śabda* is of three kinds, viz., sublation by one's words (*pratijñābādha*), sublation by one's previous statement (*pūrvasañjalpabādha*) and sublation by what is generally accepted by peaple (*lokaviruddha*). When a person says, 'I have been silent throughout my life', the statement is contradicted by the mere utterance of it, because as soon as he utters this sentence he gives up his silence. If a person says, 'all statements are false', the predicate 'false' applies to this statement also. If all statements are really false, then the statement embodying this assertion also being a statement must be false. And if this statement is not false, then it cannot be asserted that all statements are false, because then at least one statement will be true. When someone says, 'my mother who gave birth to me is barren', the statement is sublated by the subject 'my mother' which implies that she is not barren. All these statements are self-contradictory. When the Buddhist tries to prove that sound is eternal or indestructible it is contradictory to his own accepted tenet that everything is momentary. Actually which of the two inferences, one proving the eternality of sound and the other its non-eternality, is the sublator and which the sublated depends on the comparative strength of them. However, the accepted theories of a schoo of thought must form a self-consistent system and if there is any inner conflict it is a serious weakness in the logic of the school. Sublation by what is generally accepted is exemplified in the statement of one who says that '*śaśi*' is not a name of the moon.

Sucaritamiśra says that these are not really the examples of sublation by *śabda*. A statement is really sublated by *śabda-pramāṇa* when it is opposed to the scripture. Pārthasārathi says that this fallacy occurs in the following examples: 'The human skull is sacred, because it is a part of body like shell'; 'Sacrifice is not a means of acquiring heaven, because it is an action like the action of eating'; 'Animal sacrifice is a sin, because it is killing like killing a brāhmaṇa'.

Sucaritamiśra says that the above threefold division of the fallacies called *śabdabādha* is in accordance with the view of other logicians. The words of a speaker are not *pramāṇa.* Similarly, *lokaprasiddhi* or tradition is neither *śabda-pramāṇa*, nor any independent *pramāṇa*, but is only one among perception, inference etc., so that opposition to it does not mean opposition to *śabda*. It is, however, difficult to find who the other logicians are, whose view Kumārila has given. The other logicians who enumerate the fallacies of conclusion separately are Praśastapāda and Diṅnāga. Praśastapāda mentions the fallacies called *āgamavirodha*, *svaśāstravirodha* and *svavacana-virodha* separately without including them under one head, viz., *śabdavirodha.*[74] Diṅnāga also mentions *āgamaviruddha*, *loka-viruddha* and *svavacanaviruddha* separately.[75] It seems more probable that Kumārila has given his own view. And there is no inconsistency in it, because Kumārila does not restrict *pramāṇatva* to scriptural statements alone as Prabhākara does. According to him both kinds of statement, scriptural as well as secular, are included in *śabdapramāṇa*.

Sublation by *upamāna* (*upamānabādha*) is exemplified in the statement of a person that cow does not resemble gavaya when he tries to prove it to another person who, having perceived the forms of both a cow and a gavaya knows beyond doubt through *upamāna* that cow resembles gavaya.

When some reliable person reports that Devadatta is fat and does not eat during the day, we presume that he eats at night. Now, if someone states that Devadatta does not eat at all, his statement is sublated by the above *arthāpatti*. If we know that

74. PDS, p. 234.
75. NP, p. 2.

Caitra is alive and we do not find him in his house, then we presume that he must be outside. To state that he is not outside would be another example of sublation by *arthāpatti*. Sublation by *arthāpatti* is of six kinds according to the six kinds of *arthāpatti*. The various kinds of arthāpatti will be described later.

An example of sublation by *anupalabdhi* is the statement that a hare has horns or that fire is cold, since by *anupalabdhi* or non-apprehension we definitely know that a hare has no horns and that fire is not cold.

The fallacies called *bādhita* are classified from another point of view into *dharmadharmisambandhabādha*, *dharmasvarūpabādha*, *dharmaviśeṣabādha*, *dharmisvarūpabādha*, and *dharmiviśeṣabādha*.

The first of these is so called because in it the relation of the subject of the conclusion to the predicate is sublated by a stronger *pramāṇa*. In it the subject and predicate are real by themselves, but their relation is unreal. The examples given above are mostly of this kind.

When a person seeing burnt straws in ice infers that ice contains fire, the conclusion is sublated by perception. In this example the subject 'ice' and the predicate 'fire' both are real, but their relation is sublated. This is, however, cited as an example of *dharmasvarūpabādha*, i.e., one in which the existence of the predicate is sublated. When it is said that ice contains fire it is implied that ice contains heat, though it is not directly stated, and this is cited as an example of *dharmaviśeṣabādha*, i.e., one in which a particular property of the predicate is sublated.

When it is said that a prescribed sin, e.g., animal sacrifice causes pain to the performer, the subject is unreal because it is self-contradictory. That which is prescribed by the scripture cannot be a sin and that which is a sin cannot be prescribed. This is an example of the fallacy called *dharmisvarūpabādha*, i.e., one in which the existence of the subject is sublated. The statement also implies that a prescribed duty causes pain to the performer, and this is cited as an example of *dharmiviśeṣabādha* or one in which a particular property of the subject is sublated.

There may also be a statement in which the existence and some particular properties of both the subject and predicate are sublated. This fallacy is called *ubhayasvarūpaviśeṣabādha.* When it is said by the Buddhist that all cognitions are false, it involves this fallacy. The particular property of the subject sublated is momentariness and the particular property of the predicate sublated is absolute falsehood. The Buddhist equates existence with cognition. Accordingly, cognition = cognition of cognition; falsehood = cognition of falsehood; mementariness = cognition of momentariness; and absolute falsehood = cognition of absolute falsehood. Now, if the statement 'all cognitions are false' is accepted, then all the right-hand members of these equations are false, which is equivalent to the negation of all the left-hand members.

We have noted that some of the given examples are put in wrong classes. If we examine these examples we shall find that they are cases either of contradiction by one's own words or of contradiction by one's previous statements. This classification of the fallacies of conclusion based on the sublation of its subject and predicate is not found in the works of Diṅnāga, Praśastapāda and Dharmakīrti. It appears that Kumārila suggested it as an improvement on older classifications. But actually this classification presents unnecessary complications and seems to be superfluous. This is why the later Bhāṭṭas[76] gave it up.

6.7.2. *Hetvābhāsa*-s

Kumārila's treatment of this class of fallacies is primarily based on the rules of debate. One of such rules is that the premises must be accepted by both the parties in the debate. This is again complicated by the observation that some party may accept a premise doubtfully while the other party may be perfectly convinced of it, and some party, though believing in the truth of a premise, may not give its assent to it in explicit terms. Now a classification based on these considerations is quite possible, but it has little logical value. Probably for this reason Pārthasārathi gives another improved classification. Here we

76. Cp. MM, pp. 67-68.

follow Pārthasārathi's account[77] of the *hetvābhāsa*-s or the fallacies of the minor premise, referring to Kumārila only on controversial issues.

The fallacies are mainly three in number, viz., *asiddha*, *anaikāntika* and *viruddha*, and each is subdivided as follows:

6.7.2.1. *Asiddha or the Non-Established Middle Term*

It is of five kinds: (i) *Svarūpāsiddha* or non-established existence. 'Buddha is the knower of dharma, because he is omniscient'. Here the middle term 'omniscient' is non-established, because omniscience is not found anywere. Omniscience is an imaginary character, not an actual one. (ii) *Sambandhāsiddha* or non-established relation: 'Fire does not burn, because it is cold.' Here the middle term 'cold' is a real character found in other things, but its relation to the minor term 'fire' is unreal. (iii) *Vyatirekāsiddha* or non-establishment elsewhere: 'Cow is an animal having dewlap etc., because it is denoted by the word 'cow'.' Here the middle term 'denoted by the word cow' has no existence apart from the *pakṣa* or minor term. The middle term should be capable of residing in things other than the *pakṣa*. This fallacy is also called '*asādhāraṇa*' or the uncommon middle. According to some it is a variety of the doubtful middle. (iv) *Āśrayāsiddha* or non-established substrate: 'Space is eternal, because it is a substance without parts.' The Sautrāntika denies the reality of space. So, from his point of view the minor term of the inference, which is the substrate of the middle term, is imaginary. (v) *Vyāptyasiddha* or partly non-established: It is also named '*Bhāgāsiddha*' and '*Pakṣaikadeśahetvāsiddha*.' This fallacy occurs when the middle term resides only in a part of the minor term: 'Air and space are non-eternal, because they are tangible.' Here the middle term resides only in air, not in space, because space is not tangible.

6.7.2.2 *Anāikāntika or Non-Conclusive or Doubtful Middle*

It is of two kinds: (i) *Savyabhicāra* or irregular middle: 'Sound is eternal, because it is intangible.' Here intangibility does not regularly accompany eternality. Intangibility is found to characterize eternal things, e.g., soul, as well as non-eternal

77. SD, pp. 64-67.

things, e.g., action. Thus the relation of the middle term with the major as well as its contradictory is a source of doubt, so that the inference of eternality becomes non-conclusive. This fallacy is also called *sādhāraṇa* or the common middle, because it is commonly found in the major and its absence. (ii) *Saprati-sādhana* or *satpratipakṣa*: Kumārila calls it '*viruddhāvyabhicāri*'.[78] It occurs when there are two middle terms leading to conflicting inferences and there is no decision as to which of the two is the real one. 'Air is perceptible, because it possesses finite magnitude and is tangible.' Again, 'air is imperceptible, because it is a substance without colour.' Here there are two middle terms 'having a finite magnitude and tangibility' and 'being a substance without colour,' both leading to conflicting inferences. They appear to be equally cogent and it is difficult to determine whether air is perceptible or imperceptible. Hence it gives rise to doubt.

Prabhākara rejects the second variety of *anaikāntika*. He argues that two contradictory middle terms cannot be equally powerful and cannot be predicated of the minor term simultaneously. If it were not so the resultant doubt could never be removed. In the above examples, Prabhākara says, the first middle term is more powerful and leads to the perceptibility of air. Pārthasārathi's answer to this objection is that cases of *saprati-sādhana* are of a frequent occurrence and the doubt in such cases is removed by some stronger *pramāṇa*. What is said is not that two equally powerful but contradictory middle terms can reside in the some *pakṣa*, but that, though one of them is really stronger than the other, yet it is not discovered at the time as to which one is stronger and which weaker. The result is that doubt arises and continues till a decision is not arrived at by appealing to a stronger *pramāṇa* later on. We have many such instances of doubt in common experience, for example, when a man seeing a branchless tree from a distance doubts whether it is a man or a post. Such a doubt is seen to be temporary. It disappears as soon as the thing is observed closely, and similarly, the doubt produced by a *sapratisādhanahetu* disappears with the help of a stronger *pramāṇa*.

78. SV, *Anu.*, 92.

Kumārila mentions three varieties of *anaikāntika*. In addition to the above two the third is *asādhāraṇa* or the uncommon middle. When someone argues that 'earth is eternal, because it has smell', the middle term 'smell' is a unique property of earth, i.e., it is not found in other elements. Since it is not found in anything which is established to be eternal or non-eternal, except in earth, and since the eternality or non-eternality of earth is yet unknown, the middle term 'smell' cannot lead to any inference.

Now, it is true that this uncommon middle is a source of fallacy, but can it be a source of doubt? The *sādhāraṇa* middle is common to the probandum as well as the absence of the probandum and it is rightly a source of doubt, because it leads to two contradictory cognitions, viz., the cognition of the probandum and that of its absence. But an *asādhāraṇa* middle being found neither in the probandum nor in its absence does not lead to any cognition. How, then, can it be a source of doubt? Kumārila answers that a *sādhāraṇa* middle is concomitant with the probandum, but is not non-concomitant with the absence of the probandum. Intangibility, for instance, is present in eternal things, but is not absent from non-eternal things. Invariable concomitance, which is the ground of inference, depends on *anvaya* and *vyatireka* both while in the case of a *sādhāraṇa* middle there is only *anvaya* but no *vyatireka*. A *sādhāraṇa* middle fulfills only one condition of validity and hence it is a source of doubt. Similarly, an *asādhāraṇa* middle also fulfills only one condition and, hence it too is a source of doubt. To explain, the *asādhāraṇa* middle 'smell' is absent from non-eternal things, e.g , action, cognition etc., and so far it has *vyatireka*, but it being absent even from eternal things, e.g., soul etc. there is no *anvaya*. The point may be explained in a different way thus: A *sādhāraṇa* middle produces doubt not simply because it produces two cognitions but because it produces two contradictory cognitions which cannot be reconciled. The same thing happens in the case of an *asādhāraṇa* middle also. An *asādhāraṇa* middle is found to be absent from the probandum as well as the negation of it and thus leads to two irreconcilable cognitions., viz., the cognition of the absence of the probandum and that of the absence of the negation of it. Smell is not found in eternal things and hence its presence in earth produces the cognition that earth is not eternal.

Again, smell is not found in non-eternal things and hence its presence in earth produces the cognition that earth is not non-eternal. These two cognitions are contradictory and so they give rise to doubt.[79]

Umbeka does not say anything on this point.[80] But Pārthasārathi and Sucaritamiśra say that the above view is not Kumārila's own[81]. Diṅnāga, who precedes Kumārila by some centuries, holds that *asādhāraṇa* middle is a source of doubt.[82] He cites the inference 'sound is eternal because it is audible' as an example of this fallacy. Praśastapāda makes *asādhāraṇa* an independent kind of *hetvābhāsa* and calls it *anadhyavasita*.[83] Sucaritamiśra says that doubt is a mental state in which the mind swings between two extremes and that there are no extremes in the case of an *asādhāraṇa* middle, because such a middle term is not found to be concomitant with anything. Moreover, doubt occurs only when there is a limited number of alternatives, not when the number is infinite. In the case of 'smell', however, there is an infinite number of alternatives, because it is absent from everything other than earth. We cannot restrict the number to two, viz., eternality and non-eternality alone. We can do so only onthe basis of the following inference: Things having an uncommon property are seen to be either eternal or non-eternal; earth is a thing having an uncommon property 'smell'; therefore, it is either eternal or non-eternal. Thus if there is a doubt as to whether earth is eternal or non-eternal, the source of it is not 'smell' which is *asādhāraṇa*, but it is *asādhāraṇatva* or the character of possessing a unique property, which is common to earth and other things of a doubtful character. Therefore, an *asādhāraṇa* middle cannot be a source of doubt. Sucaritamiśra rejects Praśastapāda's view on the ground that *anadhyavasāya* is nothing but an absence of cognition[84] and concludes that an *asādhāraṇa* middle is not a source of doubt but is merely a means of stimulating curiosity (*jijñāsāmātrahetu*). We have already given Pārthasārathi's view,

79. SV, *Anu.*, 86-9.
80. TT on ibid.
81. NR & KK on ibid.
82. NP, p. 3.
83. PDS, p. 239.
84. Vide Ch. III.

who includes this fallacy in *asiddha* under the name *vyatirekāsiddha*, though, it should be noted, this name seems to be improper, because in the case of *asādhāraṇa* not only *vyatireka* but *anvaya* also is non-established. Sucaritamiśra's view seems to be correct, but it is difficult to say that Kumārila has given not his own view but that of his adversary. It is unlikely that one should propound a view which he does not accept and even defend it without expressing his own disapproval.

Kumārila mentions that some logicians try to reduce *sapratisādhana* to one or the other of the two fallacies known as *sādhāraṇa* and *asādhāraṇa*. But his own view is that it is different from both. In *sapratisādhana* there are two inferences proposed by two different parties in a debate and doubt arises in the mind of a third party, viz., the audience. But in *sādhāraṇa* and *asādhāraṇa* each there is only one inference proposed by one party and the doubt arises in the mind of the opposite party, while the audience may not have the doubt. Thus *sapratisādhana* is fundamentally different from *sādhāraṇa* and *asādhāraṇa*.[85]

6.7.2.3 *Viruddha or Contradictory Middle*

It is called *bādhaka* also. A contradictory middle term establishes just the opposite of the desired major term and it is of one kind only. If, however, it be necessary to mention subsidiary divisions, then two only need be mentioned, viz., (i) *dharmasvarūpabādha* or the middle that proves the non-existence of the desired major, and (ii) *dharmaviśeṣabādha* or the middle that proves the non-existence of a particular property of the major. Some mention six varieties adding four more to the above two, (iii) *dharmiśvarūpabādha* or the middle that proves the non-existence of the minor, (iv) *dharmiviśeṣabādha* or one that proves the non-existence of a particular property of the minor, (v) *ubhayasvarūpabādha* or one that proves the non-existence of the major and minor both, and (vi) *ubhayaviśeṣabādha* which is the combination of (ii) and (iv). Others exclude (v) and (vi). 'Sound is eternal because it is a product.' In this inference the middle term 'being a product' is invariably concomitant with non-eternality and hence it really proves the non-existence of eternality

85. SV, *Anu.*, 92-93 & KK.

which is desired to be proved. 'Body and sprouts have a sentient being as their creator, because they are products like a pot'. In this inference the middle term rules out the disembodied character of the creator, because the creator in the case of a pot etc. is always seen to be an embodied being. This is an example of the second variety of *viruddha*, since it proves the non-existence of a desired particular property 'disembodiedness' of the major 'creator'. Though this property is not clearly stated, yet it is implied.

6.7.3. *Dṛṣṭāntābhāsa*-s[86]

These are the fallacies of example. Example is of two kinds, viz., similar example (*sādharmya*) and dissimilar example (*vaidharmya*). When a similar example is stated the middle term should be the subject and the major term the predicate. But when a dissimilar example is stated the negation of the major should be the subject and the negation of the middle the predicate. For example, in the case of the inference of fire from smoke the similar example should be accompanied by the statement 'where there is smoke there is fire', and the dissimilar example should be accompanied by the statement 'where there is no fire there is no smoke'. This should happen when the middle and major terms are of an unequal extension. But when tney are of an equal extension there is no harm in making the negation of the middle the subject and the negation of the major the predicate. The fallacies of similar example are : *sādhyaśūnya*, *hetuśūnya*, *ubhayaśūnya* and *vyāptiśūnya* which arise when the example is devoid respectively of the probandum, the probans, the both and invariable concomitance. 'Sound is eternal because it is formless.' If the example in this inference is 'action', it is devoid of the probandum 'eternal'; if it is 'atom', it is devoid of the probans 'formless'; if it is 'jar', it is devoid of both; and if it is 'ether' it is devoid of *vyāpti* or invariable concomitance, though it is not devoid of the co-existence of the probans and the probandum. It should be noted that *vyāpti* is not a mere co-existence of the middle and major terms. Some people do not believe in the reality of ether. For them the example of ether is an imag-

86. SV, *Anu.*, 108-137.

inary one and thus one more fallacy may be added to the above four: Kumārila calls it *dharmyasiddha* and Nārāyaṇa calls it *āśrayahīna* or devoid of the base.[87]

The dissimilar example is not necessarily to be stated. But when it is stated the following fallacies are to be avoided: 'Whatever is non-eternal has form, like an atom' involves the fallacy called *sādhyābhāvaśūnya*, because an atom is devoid of the negation of eternality. When the example is 'cognition' instead of atom the fallacy is *hetvābhāvaśūnya*, because it is devoid of 'form' which is the negation of 'formlessness'. When the example is 'ether' the fallacy is *ubhayābhāvaśūnya*, because it is devoid of the negations of both eternality and formlessness. It also involves the fallacy of *āśrayahīna* or imaginary example from the Buddhist point of view. When the example is 'jar', the fallacy is *vyāptiśūnya*, because, though there is a co-existence of non-eternality and form in a jar, it cannot be universalized.

87. MM, p. 89.

Chapter VII

VERBAL TESTIMONY (ŚABDA)

Testimony is an important source of knowledge. A major portion of a person's stock of knowledge about the world is acquired from the oral or written testimony of other persons. The importance of testimony becomes obvious when we imagine a person deprived of all contact with other persons and books in which case he would simply be reduced to the level of a brute. Compared with what we know from testimony, the amount of what we know through perception and inference is extremely meagre. Testimony has been recognized as an independent source of knowledge by all Indian philosophers except the Cārvāka, the Buddhists and the Vaiśeṣika. The Cārvāka rejects testimony in general, because, according to him, it does not give valid knowledge, and scriptural testimony in particular, because Vedic knowledge in his opinion is "all fraud, a device of the cunning priests to earn their living by cheating the ignorant masses". The Buddhist and the Vaiśeṣika recognize testimony, but not as an independent means of knowledge. They reduce testimony to inference.

7.1. *The Nature of Verbal Testimony*

Testimony may be verbal or non-verbal. Non-verbal testimony consists of gestures. But it is not important, because it lacks precision. Verbal testimony consists of verbal statements of people intended to express certain facts. Gautama defines verbal testimony as the statement of a reliable person.[1] The reliability of a person making a statement is a condition ensuring the validity of the knowledge derived in this way. This definition is quite acceptable. Kumārila and other Mīmāṃsakas, however,

1. आप्तोपदेशः शब्दः । NS, 1.1.7.

do not accept it for the following reasons: The Nyāya definition presupposes that all verbal statements are made by persons. But the Mīmāṃsaka has reasons to disagree with it. At least in one case, viz., the case of Vedic statements, he holds, there are statements which are not made by any person. According to the Nyāya Vedic statements are statements of God who is a supernatural person. But according to the Mīmāṃsaka there is no God, and hence Vedic statements are impersonal. The Nyāya definition thus is too narrow. Therefore, following Śabara, Kumārila[2] defines verbal testimony as a statement which produces in the mind of the hearer, who knows the meaning of words, a knowledge of facts that lie beyond the range of his perception.[3] Explaining this definition Pārthasārathi says that a verbal statement gives the knowledge of a fact through an understanding of the statement depending on the meaning of words which the statement is composed of and that it is an independent means of valid knowledge in so far as the assertion contained therein is not already known by other means to be true or false.[4] This latter qualification is added because whatever is a *pramāṇa* must give a new knowledge.

Knowledge based on testimony is of two kinds, one arising from the words of a person and the other arising from the words of impersonal origin (*pauruṣeyamapauruṣeyaṃ vā*) according as the testimony is secular or scriptural.[5] Secular testimony is the statement of a trustworthy person, and scriptural testimony is the statement of the Veda. Scriptural sentences are eternal, having no human or divine authorship. A sentence uttered by a trustworthy person issues from a faultless source. There being no defect in the source, both the kinds of sentences are valid. Words are not created by any agency. A *pramāṇa* is invalidated by the defects of its source. The Veda, as it has no author, has no cause or source. Therefore, there is no possibility of its being invalidated by defects of the source.

2. SV, *Śabda*, 52-53.
3. शास्त्रं शब्दविज्ञानादसन्निकृष्टेऽर्थे विज्ञानम् । SB, p. 105.
4. विज्ञाताच्छब्दात् पदार्थाभिधानद्वारेण यद् वाक्यार्थविज्ञानं तच्छब्दं नाम प्रमाणम्; असन्निकृष्टग्रहणं च पूर्ववत्ताद्रूप्यतद्विपर्ययपरिच्छेदनिरासार्थम् । SD, p. 72.
5. SV, *Śabda*, 51.

A sentence either is of two kinds, one which expresses some existing thing (*siddhārthavākya*) and the other which expresses something to be done (*vidhāyakavākya*). The former is the statement of a fact and the latter is that of a command. The former refers to such facts as 'this is a man' and the latter to commands such as 'do this', 'avoid this' etc. We divide factual statements into affirmative, negative, hypothetical, disjunctive etc.

According to Kumārila a word directly denotes a universal or class concept. When a word is not used in a sentence, it means the universal for which it stands, and it does not refer to the existence of the universal, for, a universal is eternal and no question of its existence or non-existence arises. An affirmative factual statement, which contains the verb 'is', refers to the existence of something. But this something is not the universal directly denoted by the subject-word. It rather is the individual qualified by the universal.

Regarding negative factual sentences Kumārila says that they refer to non-existence which also is a fact like existence. The word 'not' occurring in a factual sentence sometimes serves the purpose of differentiating one existing thing from another existing thing. 'A cow is not a horse' means 'a cow is different from a horse'. The function of the word 'not' occurring in a factual statement is to remove ignorance or doubt or to reject a false idea (*ajñātasandigdhaviparītārthavāraṇam*). When a person is ignorant of something, a negative statement removes his ignorance by pointing out that something does not exist. When a person is in doubt about something, as when one is not sure whether a thing is a man or a post, his doubt is removed on hearing a statement negating one of the alternatives. When a person falsely perceives a snake and another person who perceives correctly makes the statement 'this is not a snake', then the falsehood of the former's perception is exposed by the latter's statement. It may be pointed out here that the first two functions of a negative statement are not peculiar to it, since an affirmative statement also removes ignorance and doubt. The third function alone seems to be peculiar. When I make the statement 'this is not P', it may be taken as exposing the falsehood of an actual or possible assertion in the form 'this is P'. Thus my statement is equivalent to the assertion that the assertion 'this is P' is false. There is no need of another person even. I myself might have made the assertion 'this is P' on some earlier occasion and now discover its falsehood. In this case my statement 'this is not P' rejects my own previous cognition as false (*pūrvajñātopamardanam*). In case I or anyone else has never made the assertion 'this is P', even then the negative statement 'this is not P' may be taken as rejecting a mere supposition.

Regarding a disjunctive statement Kumārila says that it refers to a subjective attitude of doubt towards some fact. Reality is not disjunctive. When our knowledge of reality is not definite, we make disjunctive statements like 'this is a man or a post', 'this is moving or stationary'[6] etc.

7.2. *Criticism of the Buddhist and Vaiśeṣika Views*

The Buddhist and the Vaiśeṣika do not accord the status of an independent *pramāṇa* to verbal testimony. The Buddhist maintains that the intention of a speaker finds expression in his statement. The intention is the cause and the statement its effect. When a speaker utters a word, the hearer infers his intention as he infers the presence of fire from its effect, viz., smoke. In this inferential process the speaker is the minor term, his intention is the major term and the word is the middle term.[7] Śrīdhara also remarks:

> Just as the inferential process functions through invariable concomitance, so do words also.... As a matter of fact, we know that a word never denotes anything until it is known for certain that it never fails in its concomitance with such denotation; and when it does denote an object after the unfailing concomitance has been ascertained, it becomes an inferential sign pure and simple.[8]

The Buddhist maintains that when a word is heard the hearer infers the intention of the speaker. But how can one infer the said intention unless he has already understood what the word

6. SV, *Vākya*, 301-21.
7. TH, 1512-22.
8. NK, pp. 213-14.

means? Whatever the intention of the speaker may be, the meaning of the uttered word has already been cognized by the hearer without the help of syllogistic reasoning. The Vaiśeṣika holds that the meaning of a word is cognized through inference, because just as the cognition of fire from smoke depends on a positive and negative experience of smoke-fire relationship, so the cognition of the meaning of a word too depends on the experience of a positive and negative experience of word-object relationship. This experience we have in childhood when adults utter the word 'cow' and a cow is present and when they do not utter this word and the cow is absent.

Kumārila says that when we have already learnt the meaning of a word in the said manner and then afterwards hear that word, the cognition of its meaning arises in our mind through memory and not through inference. Thus the understanding of the word being of the nature of recollection, it is not a *pramāṇa* at all. The Buddhist and Vaiśeṣika attempt to reduce our cognition of meaning on hearing a word to inference is futile, because what constitutes the *pramāṇa* called verbal testimony is not a word but a sentence. Even if the meaning of a word be cognized through inference, the knowledge of a fact on hearing a sentence is not inferential and hence the Buddhist and Vaiśeṣika arguments are irrelevant.[9]

The knowledge of the meaning of a sentence arises through the meaning of words whose relation was not apprehended before. Therefore, even the suspicion that the meaning of a sentence is known through inference is illegitimate. An inference presupposes a knowledge of the invariable relation between the probans and the probandum. In the cognition of sentence-meaning the constituent words may be said to serve as the probans, but there is no *vyāpti*. The relations between words are infinite. It is not possible to know in advance the infinite relations between words. It is an indubitable fact that when somebody talks of distant countries, the particular meaning of the sentences uttered by him are comprehended through word-meaning even though they refer to entirely new and strange things. It shows that sentence-meaning does not depend on a previously

9. SV, *Śabda*, 60 and 104-108.

known relation between the utterance of a sentence and a fact. Therefore, our knowledge of a fact from a sentence is not inferential.[10]

Some people argue that verbal testimony is of the nature of inference, because the validity of a sentence is inferred from the trustworthy character of the speaker. It may be true, but it does not make the knowledge of a fact on hearing a sentence inferential, because the inference of validity takes place only after the meaning of the sentence has already been comprehended. The meaning of a sentence is grasped exactly after it is heard, for which no knowledge of the trustworthy or untrustworthy character of the speaker is needed. Even when the speaker of a sentence is not known at all, the meaning of the sentence is immediately grasped and it is only later that we have a recourse to inference when the validity of his assertion is doubted. Thus verbal testimony is independent of inference.[11]

7.3. *Refutation of Prabhākara's View*

Prabhākara is unwilling to accord the status of *pramāṇa* to human statements, though he recognizes scriptural statement as an independent source of knowledge. He maintains that human statements are apt to be falsified by the inherent defects of men. They are frequently found to be invalid, so that no reliance can be placed on them. They simply convey what the speaker knows through other means of knowledge, and depend for their validity on verification by other means. So they are not recognized as an independent *pramāṇa* in the world too. When a person utters a sentence the hearer infers his intention from the words that are heard. So, because human words lead to the inference of the intention of the speaker, whatever inconsistency there may be it belongs to inference only and not to the words. But if this inconsistency is held to pertain to the words only and not to inference, as is the opinion of the Bhāṭṭa, then words will be intrinsically invalid. The defects of a person, however, cannot contaminate words, since the function of a person is only to manifest words which are eternally there.

10. SD, p. 73.
11. SV, *Vākya*, 243-46.

This view is criticized by Pārthasārathi[12] as follows: If secular statements are not *pramāṇa* in their own capacity, then, how can scriptural statements be so? Both are words; and if one is accepted to be *pramāṇa*, then the other too has to be accepted to be *pramāṇa*. The charge that if inconsistency is held to belong to human statements words will be intrinsically invalid has no foundation. It would be a real charge if it were accepted that a speaker merely gives manifestation to eternally existing words. But such is not the case. Letters and words are eternally there, but, as regards sentences, they are constructed by human beings: they are not eternal. If it be supposed that sentences too are eternal and speakers only manifest them by their speech, then they will become impersonal like scriptural sentences. In that case the intentions behind the sentences will not properly belong to the speaker, just as the intentions behind scriptural sentences do not belong to the chanter of Vedic hymns. As the intentions are not of the speaker's own, their inference from the words will then not be legitimate. It is generally seen that the construction of a sentence is at variance with the intention of the speaker. An individual often fails to express his intentions in language correctly, so that the inference of his intentions from his speech is generally found to be invalid. The conclusion is that if *śabda* is not recognized to be a *pramāṇa* in the empirical sphere on the ground of its proneness to doubts or incoherence, then it will equally apply to the inference of the speaker's intentions too. If secular statements are not *pramāṇa*, then inference of intention too cannot be so. Moreover, the eyes etc. often reveal things not as they actually are, yet they do not cease to yield valid knowledge. Perception sometimes gives wrong knowledge, but it is not discarded on that ground. Similarly, words sometimes are vitiated by the faults of the speaker, but their power to give knowledge cannot be denied for this reason. Therefore, human statements are a means of knowledge as much as perception and inference are. We know the facts of the world as much from statements made by other persons as from the perceptual and inferential processes going on in our minds. It is no doubt true that sometimes the knowledge of facts derived from

12. SD, p. 24.

statements of other persons is not found to be true; but this can be no reason to deny *pramāṇatva* to human statements, because this defect is common to perception and inference also.

7.4. *Conclusion*

The Bhāṭṭa arguments are sound and convincing and hence it has to be recognized that verbal testimony is an independent means of knowledge. The Buddhist wrongly denies the independence of verbal testimony. The argument that verbal testimony is reducible to inference because the hearer infers the intention of the speaker from the latter's words is irrelevant. We can infer anything about the mental state of the speaker or about nis personal life from his speech. But this is not verbal testimony. When someone says that 'flying saucers' come from Mars, the statement is primarily intended to convey the information about the objective fact that there are 'flying saucers' and they come from Mars. I may personally see the fact or infer it from some other knowledge about Mars; and in such a case the source of my knowledge of the fact will be perception or inference. But when I know this fact from the statement of another person the source of my knowledge is quite different. Though my hearing of the statement is auditory perception, yet my knowledge of the fact is not perception, since perceiving the words 'flying saucers come from Mars' is not the same thing as perceiving the objective fact expressed by these words. So far as the objective fact is concerned, my belief, if there be any, in it depends on my suggestibility and not on the intellectual processes involved in deduction, and for this reason my knowledge is non-syllogistic. From this statement I may infer that the speaker knows this fact or that he has seen 'flying saucers' or that he is insane; but these are only secondary things with which the statement is not directly concerned. Again, verbal testimony is reduced to inference on the ground that the validity of human statements is ascertained inferentially. But this is wrong. Sometimes the validity of perception too is ascertained inferentially, but this does not reduce perception to inference. Knowledge of fact and knowledge of validity are two different things. We acquire knowledge of facts from verbal testimony more frequently than by the sense-organs and inference. We acquire from verbal testimony not only a knowledge of facts but also of validity. I preceive something and if I have any doubt about it I judge the validity of my perception by the statements of other perceivers. But this does not reduce perception to verbal testimony. Hence verbal testimony is an independent source of knowledge. It may be said that verbal testimony is not independent, because the speaker's statement depends on his perception or inference. This is true so far as the speaker is concerned. But so far the as hearer is concerned, the speaker's statement is an independent source of knowledge, because the knowledge that he acquires from it is independent of his own perception and inference. The speaker's statement is intended not for his own information, but for the information of others who do not know a fact.

Let us conclude this section with some remarks on the Vaiśeṣika view. The Vaiśeṣika holds that the meaning of a heard word is known inferentially as fire is known from smoke. This is wrong. We have learnt that smoke is always accompanied by fire; then we perceive smoke and infer fire. We have learnt that the word 'cow' means the animal 'cow'; then hear the word 'cow'; but we do not infer the meaning of the heard word. All smokes are particular smokes belonging to a single class 'smoke'. The particular smokes that I have seen and from which I have learnt that smoke is always accompanied by fire, are different from the particular smoke that I see now. But the words 'cow' do not form a class. The words 'cow' that different people utter at different times cannot be called members belonging to a class. When I hear the word 'cow' now I do not perceive a new member of a class as I perceive a new member of the class 'smoke'. I hear the same word 'cow' that I heard in the past for the first time and I already know its meaning. Therefore, my knowledge of its meaning now again is not inference but memory as Kumārila rightly says. Kumārila is again right when he says that a word is not verbal testimony. A fact is stated not in a word but in a sentence. Thus the Bhāṭṭa view of verbal testimony is quite correct. Of course, the view that words are eternal and language does not depend on convention needs to be examined linguistically and should be restated in more acceptable modern terms—a subject by itself enough to deserve independent research.

CHAPTER VIII

UPAMĀNA (COMPARISON)

8.1. *The Nature of Upamāna*

Upamāna as an independent source of valid knowledge has been recognized by Mīmāṃsā, Nyāya and Advaita Vedānta. The Mīmāṃsā and Nyāya views on the nature of *upamāna*, however, are fundamentally different. Between the Prābhākara and Bhāṭṭa schools of Mīmāṃsā there is a minor difference, viz., that *sādṛśya* or similarity, which is the object of *upamāna*, is an independent category, not reducible to substance, quality action, universal etc., according to Prabhākara, while, according to Kumārila, it is nothing but an assemblage of common features. The Advaita Vedānta view[1] is identical with the Bhāṭṭa one.

According to Śabara, "*upamāna* is resemblance which brings about the cognition of an object not in contact with the senses".[2] The subject of this definition is obviously *upamāna*, the means, though in the cases of *pratyakṣa*, *anumāna*, *śabda*, *arthāpatti* and *anupalabdhi* Śabara has defined the result. In the Nyāya system the means is always clearly distinguished from the result. Accordingly, there is a difference between *upamāna* and *upamiti*, the former being the means of cognition (*pramāṇa*) and the latter the result (*pramiti*). Śabara, on the other hand, might have been aware of this difference, yet he uses the same term for the means as well as the result. Consequently, we observe that in his definitions of the *pramāṇa*-s the subject is sometimes the means and sometimes the result. In the present case the subject is the producer of a cognition (cf. *buddhim utpādayati*), i.e., the means.

We have already remarked that the Mīmāṃsā view of *upamāna* is fundamentally different from the Nyāya view. If, however, we take into consideration only the above-quoted part of Śabara's

1. VP, pp. 86-87.
2. उपमानमपि सादृश्यमसन्निकृष्टेऽर्थे बुद्धिमुत्पादयति । SB, p. 107.

statement and leave aside the example of *upamāna* given by him we find that Śabara's definition of *upamāna* is not inconsistent with the Nyāya definition, since, according to the latter too the means of cognition in *upamāna* is a well known resemblance (*prasiddhasādharmya*). A man goes to the forest and perceives an animal resembling the cow. This observed resemblance is the means of knowing something not given by perception, inference and verbal testimony, but by *upamāna*. But, what is the result of *upamāna*? According to Nyāya the result is the cognition of the relation of a name with the named, e.g., in the given case, the cognition that the animal which is found to resemble cow is called '*gavaya*'.

According to Prabhākara, Kumārila and Vedānta the result is the cognition that a cow resembles a gavaya. From Śabara's statement[3] it is not clear whether he means the same thing as is meant by Prabhākara and Kumārila, though it is clear that he does not contribute to the Nyāya view. *Upamāna* is '*sādṛśya*' and in the given example '*gavayadarśana*' is *upamāna*. From this we conclude that the perception of a gavaya qualified by its similarity to a cow (*gosādṛśyaviśiṣṭagavayadarśanam*) is the means, and not the perception of a gavaya in its unrelated character, as the compound '*gavayadarśana*' would literally mean. The result of this means in Śabara's words is '*gosmaraṇa*' which literally means the remembrance of a cow. Now, if the cognition that results from *upamāna* is of the nature of remembrance, then, it is nothing but the revival of a past impression through association, the observation of a similar thing being the stimulus for the revival, in which case *upamāna* ceases to be a *pramāṇa*. Kumārila rejects this interpretation of Śabara's statement, saying that

> the cognition of a thing observed in the past, resulting from the perception of a thing similar to it is memory exactly like the memory of a thing arising from concentration without any external stimulus.

and that

> it is not a *pramāṇa* because unlike recognition the remembered thing in this case has the same old spatio-temporal context.[4]

3. Ibid.
4. SV, *Upamāna*, 4-5.

Probably the word '*smaraṇa*' used by Śabara is not intended to mean an exact reproduction of a past cognition. In giving the example of '*sāmānyatodṛṣṭa*' inference also Śabara uses the word '*smaraṇa*' (*āditye'pi gatismaraṇam*); but the movement of the sun there cannot be an object of remembrance, because it has never been experienced in the past. Hence, it should be concluded that Śabara uses the word '*smaraṇa*' in the sense of a cognition which is partly memory and partly fresh experience. Now, in the case in question the cognition of a cow on perceiving a gavaya definitely involves an element of memory, but it is not as yet certain what the element of experience is.

According to Kumārila's interpretation the result of *upamāna* is the cognition of a remembered thing qualified by its similarity to a perceived thing (*sādṛśyayuktārtha*). A man who has never seen a *gavaya* but has seen a cow goes to the forest and sees a *gavaya* there for the first time. Then he observes that the *gavaya* is similar to a cow. 'The *gavaya* is similar to a cow' is a judgment of perception, because it arises immediately after perceiving the *gavaya*. From this judgment the cognition that next arises in the observer's mind is that the remembered cow is similar to the *gavaya*. This cognition is the result of *upamāna*.[5]

Pārthasārathi defines *upamāna* as the cognition that a formerly perceived object, which is now recollected, bears resemblance to the object which is now perceived.[6] Unlike Śabara, Pārthasārathi here defines *upamiti*, i.e., the result of *upamāna*. Thus *upamāna* is a knowledge of similarity, and *upamiti* too is a knowledge of similarity; but the difference between the two similarities is that the former is a perceptible similarity while the latter is not. In the given example the perceptible similarity to the cow existing in the *gavaya* is the means (*upamāna*) and the similarity to the *gavaya* existing in the cow is the resultant cognition (*upamiti*). The *gavaya* is the subject and cow is the counter-correlate (*pratiyogin*) of the similarity existing in the gavaya.

Sucaritamiśra[7] defines *upamāna* as the cognition, arising from an observed similarity, of the counter-correlate, which is not perceived, as qualified by similarity to the object which is per-

5. Ibid., 15.
6. पूर्वदृष्टे स्मर्यमाणेऽर्थे दृश्यमानार्थसादृश्यज्ञानमुपमानम् । SD, p. 74.
7. KK, on SV, *Upamāna*, 1.

ceived. What is perceived is that the gavaya is similar to the cow and this leads to the cognition that the cow is similar to the gavaya. In the judgment of perception the gavaya is the subject and its similarity to the cow is the predicate, while in the judgment of *upamiti* the cow is the subject and its similarity to the gavaya is the predicate. The latter judgment is neither recollective nor perceptual in nature. It is not recollective because, though the cow is recollected, its similarity to the gavaya is not recollected. Recollection presupposes experience; but as the gavaya is perceived for the first time now, the similarity of the cow to it could not possibly be experienced prior to the perception of the gavaya. It is not perceptual, because the cow which is now known to be similar to the gavaya is not actually in contact with the eyes. Hence, *upamiti* cannot be reduced to memory or perception. Though the cow is recollected and similarity is perceived, yet the knowledge of the cow qualified by the similarity is not given either by memory or by perception. Thus *upamiti* is different from them and is a *pramāṇa* like the inference of fire on the hill, in which too the hill is perceived and fire is remembered, but the knowledge of the hill qualified by fire is not given either by perception alone or memory alone.[8]

Śālikanātha's interpretation of Śabara's view is identical with Kumārila's. He says that *upamāna* is the cognition of similarity brought about by the perception of similarity and exemplified in the cognition of a cow as being similar to a gavaya, arising in the mind of a person who has already perceived a cow in the past and observes now the similarity of the gavaya to it.[9] This is exactly what he says in the following verse of *Ṛjuvimalā*, a commentary on Prabhākara's *Bṛhatī*:

> *sādṛśyāt dṛśyamānād yat pratiyogini jāyate|*
> *sādṛśyaviṣayaṃ jñānam upamānaṃ taducyate||* (RV, p.109)

Dr. Jha, however, has a different opinion. He remarks that

> according to *Ṛjuvimalā*, the meaning of the sentence (i.e., Śabara's statement) is 'the sight of the gavaya' brings about the analogical cognition that 'the animal seen is called gavaya', to the man who has remembered the cow.

8. SV, *Upamāna*, 37-39.
9. PP, p. 110.

He further remarks that

> this is the same as the Nyāya view which has been controverted by the *Ślokavārtika*.[10]

Dr. Jha's view will be found to be entirely mistaken by one who reads the *Ṛjuvimalā*. In the whole section of the *Ṛjuvimalā* dealing with *upamāna* there is not a single word which can directly or indirectly be interpreted as favouring the Nyāya view. On the contrary, Śālikanātha reduces the Naiyāyika's *upamāna* to inference:

> The knowledge that the animal observed to be similar to a cow is called gavaya is *not upamāna but anumāna*.[11]

Śālikanātha certainly criticizes Śabara on the point that he has used the word '*smaraṇa*.'[12] But this criticism does not imply that Śabara accepts the Nyāya view, because in the Nyāya view what is remembered is the name '*gavaya*' instead of the name '*go*.' Really the critic is not Śālikanātha himself but some opponent, because Śālikanātha further says that the compound '*gosmaraṇasya*' does not mean 'of the remembrance of cow' but it means 'of the person who has already seen a cow and remembers it now',[13] thus interpreting it as a *Bahuvṛihi* rather than a *tatpuruṣa* compound.

Here it should also be pointed out that Dr. Jha's rendering of the term '*upamāna*' as '*analogy*' is quite misleading. Analogy is a form of argument in which from a resemblance between two things in some known respect, a further resemblance in some unknown respect is inferred. For instance, when we infer from the known resemblance between the Earth and Mars in such respects as the presence of atmosphere etc., that there is life on Mars as it is there on the Earth, the argument is analogical. But such is not the nature of *upamāna* in the Mīmāṃsā or the Nyāya system. In Mīmāṃsa *upamāna* is a form of immediate inference in which from the similarity of A to B we infer the similarity of B to A. In Nyāya *upamāna* is the means of knowing the denotation of an unfamiliar name and is thus allied to the process of identification.

10. SB, Trans., p. 16.
11. यत्त्वेतस्य गवयशब्दवाच्यतावगतिः सापि गवयशब्दप्रयोगादानुमानिकी। PP, p. 112.
12. गोस्मरणस्येति भाष्यमयुक्तम्; न हि स्मरणस्य बुद्धिरुत्पद्यते। RV, p. 107.
13. Ibid.

8.2. *The Nyāya View of Upamāna*

According to NS, 1.1.6. "upamāna is the knowledge of what is to be known from a well known similarity" (*prasiddhasādharmyāt sādhyasādhanam upamānam*). What is to be known through *upamāna*, i.e. the result of *upamāna*, is according to Vātsyāyana the relation of a name with the named (*saṃjñāsaṃjñisambandha*). There is a difference of opinion about the exact means (*karaṇa*) in *upamāna* between the older and later Naiyāyikas. The older Naiyāyikas define *upamāna*, the *karaṇa*, as the statement (*atideśavākya*) of a reliable person asserting similarity between a known and an unknown thing and resulting in the cognition of the relation between a name and the named. A citizen, having a desire to know what a *gavaya* is, but having not ever seen a *gavaya*, asks a forest-dweller as to what a *gavaya* is like, and the latter informs him that a *gavaya* is like a cow. This statement of the forest-dweller declares that the unknown animal is similar to the well known cow. This is *upamāna*, and it results in the cognition, when the citizen goes to the forest and perceives an animal similar to a cow, that the animal is called *'gavaya.'*

The reason why the statement of the forest-dweller is a different *pramāṇa* instead of verbal testimony in which the statements of reliable persons are generally included, is that the reliable person in the present case points out the means of knowing something and that the hearer does not solely depend on his statement for the required knowledge. In *parārthānumāna* a person having already known the presence of fire on the hill makes the statement that 'the hill is fiery because it is smoky.' The hearer does not cognize the presence of fire on the hill from the mere statement of the speaker but from the presence of smoke which is the *liṅga* or mark of the fire and occurs in the statement. The speaker by drawing the attention of the hearer to the *liṅga*, points out the means of knowing the presence of fire, and the hearer, on hearing the statement, infers for himself. Thus the statement of the speaker is a different *pramāṇa*, viz., inference, though it is a statement like the statements included in verbal testimony, because in it a new principle becomes operative. Similar is the case of *upamāna*. Had the forest-dweller not stated the means of knowing a *gavaya*, his statement would not have been different from verbal testimony. But just as in *parāthānumāna* the speaker states the means of knowing the presence of fire, viz., the *liṅga* 'smoke', so here too the forest-dweller states the means of knowing a *gavaya*, viz., similarity. Hence, *upamāna* is an independent *pramāṇa* like *parārthānumāna* and is different from the latter because similarity is not a *liṅga*.

The later Naiyāyikas define *upamāna*, the means, as the sensuous cognition of a person, who has heard the statement of similarity, that an unfamiliar object bears similarity to a familiar object, which results in the cognition that the unfamiliar object is called by the name mentioned in the statement. Accordingly, the citizen's perception of an animal resembling a cow is *upamāna*. Like the perception of smoke, which is the *liṅga* of fire, the perception of similarity also is a *pramāṇa* different from perception, because both are the means of knowing a thing not revealed by perception, viz., the fire in the case of inference and the relation of the name '*gavaya*' to the animal perceived in the case of *upamāna*. The mere perception of an animal having similarity to a cow does not lead to the cognition that the animal is called *gavaya* unless the perceiver remembers the statement that a *gavaya* is similar to a cow.

Combining both these views we may say that *upamāna*, i.e., the means of *upamiti*, in Nyāya is the perception of similarity together with the remembrance of *atideśavākya* or the statement of similarity. But, it may be asked, is not the relation of a name with the named, which is said to be the result of *upamāna*, known from the *atideśavākya*? If it is not, then the *atideśavākya* serves no purpose; and if it is, then *upamāna* cannot be different from verbal testimony. The Naiyāyika escapes from this dilemma by asserting that, though from the *atideśavākya* the said knowledge is gained, yet the knowledge is not definite for the reason that the *gavaya* is not perceived at the time of hearing the *atideśavākya*. The *atideśavākya* declares that a *gavaya* is similar to a cow, yet, the term *gavaya* being unfamiliar, the meaning of the statement cannot be fully comprehended unless a *gavaya* is directly seen. The statement gives only a general notion of what a *gavaya* is, and the notion becomes well defined only when the hearer actually perceives a *gavaya* in the forest. The hearer receives a second-hand information from the *atideśavākya* and when he actually sees an animal similar to a cow, he directly knows what the denotation of the word '*gavaya*' is. In other words, what we gain from the *atideśavākya* is the knowledge through description and what we gain from the perception of similarity is the knowledge through acquaintance. Thus *upamāna* is different from perception and verbal testimony like inference. In inference the perception of *liṅga* is aided by the memory of *vyāpti*, while in *upamāna* the perception of *sādharmya* is aided by the memory of *atideśavākya*. *Upamāna* is different from inference, because a person recognizes the animal similar to a cow as having the name *gavaya* independently of the knowledge of *vyāpti* between that animal and the name *gavaya*. The knowledge of *vyāpti* depends on the knowledge of *anvaya-vyatireka*, i.e., agreement in presence and agreement in absence, while in the case of *upamāna* there is no knowledge of *anvaya-vyatireka*.[14]

Now, if the result of *upamāna* is a first-hand knowledge of the relation between a name and its denotation, then the application of the term '*upamāna*' should not be restricted to the perception of similarity alone, because we recognize the denotation of a name by other means also. For instance, when a person, not knowing what a horse is, is told that a horse, unlike a cow, hasno cloven hoofs and later, perceiving such an animal, he comes to know that this is what is called a horse, we have a case in which the means of knowing the denotation of an unfamiliar name is the perception of dissimilarity. Sometimes we recognize an unknown object neither from its similarity nor from dissimilarity to another well known object but from its own peculiar characteristics. For instance, one who does not know what a camel is, is told that a camel is an animal having a long neck and drooping lips and feeding on thorns, and later when he comes across an animal of this description he immediately recognizes it as a camel. Thus we see that a statement may contain the description of an unknown object not only in terms of its similarity to a well known object but also in terms of its dissimilarity or peculiar properties and that in all these cases the person who has heard the state-

14. NM, pp. 41-44.

ment, later recognizes the object on finding that it tallies with the given description. Varadarāja, a Naiyāyika belonging to a still later period, unlike his predecessors, includes all the above cases in *upamāna* and accordingly gives a wider definition of *upamāna*. He says that *upamāna* is the recognition through perception, of an object denoted by a name occurring in the statement of an authoritative person, by a person who does not know the meaning of the name.[15] *Upamāna*, then, in this wider sense, is the identification of a previously unknown object from its description given by a reliable person.

8.3. *The Bhāṭṭa Criticism of the Nyāya View*

Kumārila rejects the Nyāya view of *upamāna*. According to him, *upamāna* as viewed by the older Naiyāyikas is not different from verbal testimony. The Naiyāyika defines verbal testimony as the statement of a reliable person (*āptopadeśa*). *Upamāna* too is a statement of a reliable person. A man does not know what a *gavaya* is, but when he is informed that a *gavaya* is an animal similar to a cow, he knows what he did not know previously, believing that the information is correct, just as an ignorant person comes to know what *dharma* is from scriptural statements, or a thirsty person, not knowing where he would get water, knows from another person that he would get it down in the valley.[16] Jayanta says that *upamāna* is different from verbal testimony like *parārthānumāna*, because the reliable person in his statement merely shows the method by which the hearer can discover a thing for himself. This, however, is a weak argument. A person may tell an ignorant person that in order to know a *gavaya* the latter should go to the forest and carefully look out for an animal closely resembling a cow. The ignorant person certainly knows the method of knowing a *gavaya* in this way, yet whatever he knows is based entirely on the statement of a reliable person, so that it cannot be a *pramāṇa* different from *śabda*. The definition of *śabdapramāṇa* does not exclude those cases in which the aim of a statement is to inform about a way or method

15. अव्युत्पन्नपदोपेतवाक्यार्थस्य च संज्ञिनि ।
प्रत्यक्षप्रत्यभिज्ञानमुपमानमिहोच्यते ॥ TR, p. 85.
16. SV, *Upamāna*, 1-3.

instead of an object. A thirsty person is told that he should go ahead, take a right-turn and then he will get water at a distance of half a mile. Can we say that it is a *pramāṇa* different from *śabda* simply because a method has been pointed out here? *Parārthānumāna* has been cited as a parallel case. But, as has been shown in the previous chapter, *parārthānumāna* is not really inference but verbal testimony, differing from ordinary dogmatic statements of authoritative persons insofar as it appeals to suggestibility as well as reason.

According to later Naiyāyikas *upamāna* consists in the perception of similarity by one who has heard an *atideśavākya*. This view also is wrong, because in the given illustration the *gavaya* is known through perception and similarity is remembered. It may be said that, though the *gavaya* and its similarity to a cow are separately known through perception and memory, yet their combination, viz., the *gavaya* qualified by similarity is known neither by perception nor by memory alone but by a different *pramāṇa*, viz., *upamāna*. It may be true. But the Naiyāyika may be asked whether the cognition of similarity does or does not contain some novel feature not contained in the *atideśavākya*. If there is no novelty in it, it cannot be different from memory and, hence, is not a *pramāṇa*. Just as the knowledge of meaning from a word is not a *pramāṇa* because there is no novelty in such a knowledge, so here too the cognition of similarity is not a *pramāṇa* for the same reason. A *gavaya* is perceived as similar to a cow; but this is already known from the *atideśavākya*. If it be said that the novelty in the cognition of similarity consists in its being a specific cognition while from the *atideśavākya* we have only a general cognition, then the novelty can be explained as due to perception alone, so that *upamāna* becomes unnecessary. It may be said that the *gavaya* qualified by its similarity to a cow cannot be an object of perception because a cow is not perceived at the time. But this is wrong. Perception is a cognition which appears when the sense-organs become active and which disappears with the cessation of sense-activity. We know that the present animal is similar to a cow when the eyes are open and we cease to know when the eyes are closed. Therefore, the cognition of the animal qualified by similarity is perceptual. The similarity of the *gavaya* to a cow does not reside partly in the *gavaya* and partly in the cow, and hence the non-perception of the cow cannot be an obstacle to perceiving the similarity. The *gavaya* is perceived, and the similarity, which resides in it in its entirety, also is perceived.

Again, the hearing of the *atideśavākya* is useless, because even those who have not heard it apprehend that the animal which they perceive in the forest resembles the cow which has been perceived in the city. Of course, such persons cannot know that the animal is called *gavaya* unless they have already heard the *atideśavākya*. Yet, there is no harm because *upamāna* in common parlance means similarity and similarity is perceived even without the *atideśavākya.* Let '*upamāna*' be used in the sense of knowledge of the relation between a name and the named, yet the relation is already known from the *atideśavākya*, so that there is no necessity of a new *pramāṇa.* The subsequent cognition arising from the perception of a *gavaya* in the form '*this is called gavaya*' cannot be different from perception, since, though it is mixed with the use of a word, it has been shown in the chapter on perception that such verbalized cognition is a form of determinate perception.[17]

Some critics reduce the Naiyāyika *upamāna* to *anumāna*. *Upamāna* can be reduced to inference thus:

> All animals similar to a cow are *gavayas*;
> This is an animal similar to a cow;
> Therefore, this is a *gavaya*.

This inference differs from the inference of fire from smoke in one respect: The *vyāpti* 'all smoky things ary fiery', which is the ground of the latter inference, is derived from the experience of agreement in presence and agreement in absence (*anvaya-vyatireka*), while the *vyāpti* 'all animals similar to a cow are *gavaya*-s', which is the ground of the former inference, is derived from verbal testimony, viz., the statement of the forest-dweller. We have mentioned that Jayanta refuses to reduce *upamāna* to *anumāna* on the ground of merely this difference. But this is a very weak ground. There is no rule that all *vyāpti*-s must be derived by the person who infers, from his personal experience of *anvaya*-

17. Ibid., 6-15 and KK.

vyatireka. When I see a cobra I cognize that it is poisonous. The *vyāpti* 'all cobras are poisonous' is not the result of my personal investigation. This is a knowledge gained by me from the statements of others. Can, then, it be said that my cognition 'this is poisonous' is not inferential? Pārthasārathi's view (mentioned in a previous chapter) that a *vyāpti* may be derived from any *pramāṇa* and that the evidence on which it rests may be perceptual or non-perceptual is correct. In inference the major premise must be a universal and necessary proposition. This condition is fulfilled in the present case too. Hence, the Naiyāyika's *upamāna* is not different from inference.

8.4. *Can the Bhāṭṭa Upamāna Be Reduced to Anumāna?*

The term '*anumāna*' means inference in a narrower sense, viz., that of syllogistic reosoning only and hence the question asked above means not whether the Bhāṭṭa *upamāna* can be reduced to any form of inference, but whether it can be reduced to the syllogistic form. Kumārila strongly opposes an attempt to reduce *upamāna* to *anumāna*.[18] In the given example of *upamāna* the resultant cognition is in the form of the judgment that the cow which has been observed in the city is similar to the *gavaya* which is observed in the forest. Now, if *upamāna* is not different from *anumāna* this cognition should be the conclusion following from two premises, viz., a *vyāpti* and a *pakṣadharmatā* or a major and a minor premise. The major premise should state a universal relation between some middle term and the predicate of the conclusion in the form 'whatever is so and so is similar to *gavaya*', and the minor premise should state a relation between the subject of the conclusion and the middle term in the form 'a cow is so and so'. But what can be the middle term here? The ground of *upamiti*, i.e., the cognition arising from *upamāna*, is the observed similarity of a *gavaya* to a cow and this could likely be made the middle term in the corresponding syllogism. But we cannot do so, because it cannot be predicated of the minor term 'cow'. The observed similarity to a cow resides in the *gavaya* and hence it is a property of the *gavaya*, while what is required here must be a property of the cow. The similarity to a *gavaya* is

18. SV, *Upamāna*, 43-51.

certainly a property of the cow, but it cannot be made the middle term, since it would otherwise be identical with the major term. The *gavaya* too cannot be the middle term, because it cannot be predicated of the cow, nor can there be an invariable concomitance between the *gavaya* and the probandum, viz., the cow qualified with its similarity to the *gavaya*. Even if there were any invariable concomitance, it could not be known prior to the inference, because the *gavaya* is observed for the first time while the knowledge of invariable concomitance presupposes a frequent observation of the middle and major terms in the past. The property of having horns etc. too cannot be the middle term, because, though we know that a cow possesses this property, its function in the present case ceases with giving rise to the knowledge of the *gavaya* alone. We observe the horns etc. as belonging to the animal in contact with the eyes and not to the cow which is absent. Even if there be the cognition of a cow from the perception of horns etc., it would be a cognition devoid of similarity, i.e. it would simply be a case of memory. We have seen cows with horns frequently in the past, so that the idea of horns and that of a cow have been linked together in our mind and then whenever the idea of horns is revived in the mind the idea of a cow also is revived. In the case in question the cognition of the cow qualified by its similarity to the *gavaya* is not the direct result of the observation of horns etc. From the observation of horns etc. there arises the cognition that the *gavaya* is similar to the cow and then arises the cognition that the cow is similar to the *gavaya*. Thus unlike a middle term which is the immediate cause of inferential cognition 'hornedness' is a remote cause of the cognition of the cow qualified by similarity, so that it cannot be the middle term. Moreover, the observed hornedness is a property of the *gavaya* and not of the cow which is the minor term, while in inference the middle term should be a property of the minor term. Therefore, *upamāna* cannot be reduced to *anumāna*.

Jayanta[19] reduces *upamāna* to the following syllogism:

> Whatever has some points in common with something is similar to that thing;

19. NM, p. 148.

The remembered cow has some points in common with the perceived *gavaya*;
Therefore, the remembered cow is similar to the perceived *gavaya*.

Pārthasārathi puts it in a slightly different form:[20]

Whatever is the *pratiyogin* (counter-correlate) of similarity observed in something is similar to that thing;
The cow is the *pratiyogin* of similarity observed in the *gavaya*;
Therefore, the cow is similar to the *gavaya*.

In both of these syllogisms we have four terms instead of three. In the second syllogism the term 'the *pratiyogin* of similarity observed in something' occurring in the major premise is different from the term 'the *pratiyogin* of similarity observed in the *gavaya*' occurring in the minor premise. The same is the case in the first syllogism. Hence, there being no middle term, the conclusion is fallacious. The conclusion would have been correct if the major premise were in the form 'whatever is the *pratiyogin* of similarity observed in the *gavaya* is similar to the *gavaya*'. But this is not known to the person who has never previously seen a *gavaya*. Nor is it essentially the ground of the knowledge that a cow is similar to a *gavaya*, because a person who has never seen a cow and a *gavaya* together, also has such a knowledge on the first perception of a *gavaya*. Thus the inference becomes superfluous. Pārthasārathi rejects the inference for this reason. He remarks:

yo hi dvāvarthau mithaḥ sadṛśau yugapanna dṛṣṭavān ekāmeva tu gāmupalabhya nagare vane gavayaṃ paśyati so'pi gāṃ gavaya-sādṛśya-viśiṣṭām upaminotyeva, tasmānnānumānam /[21]

Mr. Venkataramiah, however, gives a wrong interpretation of this remark. He says in a footnote:

The point is that the man in whom the *upamiti* arises is not perceiving at the time the *pakṣa*, viz., cow, which is essential for inferential cognition.[22]

As has been shown in a previous chapter, the perception of the minor term is not an essential condition of inference. So, the

20. SD, p. 75.
21. Ibid., p, 76.
22. SD, Trans., p. 99.

difference of *upamāna* from *anumāna* cannot be justified merely on the ground that the cow is not perceived.

The major premise in the syllogism given above, is really the principle according to which the conclusion is drawn. We infer that a cow is similar to a *gavaya* in accordance with the principle that 'whatever is the *pratiyogin* of similarity observed in something is similar to that thing', but not from this as a premise. The difference between a principle and a premise may be illustrated thus: In the mathematical reasoning 'B is equal to C, and A is equal to B; therefore, A is equal to C' the principle that is involved is that 'two things which are equal to the same third thing are equal to each other', while the premises from which the conclusion 'A is equal to C' follows are 'B is equal to C' and 'A is equal to B'. The principle is not one of the premises. The conclusion follows not from the principle but in accordance with it. Thus the conclusion 'the cow is similar to the *gavaya*' follows from a single premise, viz., 'the *gavaya* is similar to the cow' in accordance with the principle pointed out above and hence it cannot be reduced to a syllogistic form.

8.5. *The Bhāṭṭa View of Upamāna Criticized*

Śāntarkṣita, Jayanta and Śrīdhara are unanimous in their opinion that the Mīmāṃsaka's *upamāna* is nothing but memory.[23] Though we have already referred to Kumārila's remark that the similarity to *gavaya* existing in cow was not previously experienced, since the *gavaya* which is the counter-correlate of similarity existing in the cow is perceived now for the first time and that for this reason *upamāna* is different from memory, yet we will reconsider here the question whether *upamāna* is indistinguishable from memory.

Kumārila has said that "similarity resides in its entirety, like the universal, in each of the correlates" and that "for this reason it is perceived in a correlate even though the other correlate is not perceived".[24] All the three critics of Kumārila have quoted this remark in favour of their criticism that *upamāna* is nothing but memory. It is true, they say, that the *gavaya* was not perceived when the cow was perceived in the city, but, since

23. Vide TH, 1551-53; MM, p. 221.
24. SV, *Upamāna*, 35.

the similarity to *gavaya* existed in the cow in its entirety even when the cow alone was perceived, it must have been perceived at the time along with the cow, so that the present cognition that the cow is similar to the *gavaya* cannot be different from memory. This criticism appears to be justified, but when we examine Kumārila's remark it loses all its force.

Similarity has been defined by Kumārila as the existence in two things of a plurality of common properties or parts. When we say that A and B are similar to each other, what we mean is that there are some properties or parts which exist commonly in A as well as B. The objective basis of our notion of similarity between A and B is the presence in A and B of x, y, z and other common features. The feature x does not reside partly in A and partly B, but resides in its entirety in each of them. When Kumārila says that similarity resides in its entirety in each correlate, he means that the objective basis of similarity resides in its entirety in each correlate. Thus the common features x, y, z etc., which we observe in the *gavaya* now, must have been present in the cow when the cow alone was perceived, though there was no idea of the *gavaya*. The awareness, however, that the cow is similar to the *gavaya* could not have appeared prior to the perception of x, y, z etc. in the *gavaya*. Memory is a reproduction of some former experience. But when formerly there has been no awareness of the similarity of cow to *gayay* the question of its reproduction does not arise. Though x, y, z etc. were perceived in the cow, yet the awareness that they exist in the *gavaya* too cannot be possible unless the *gavaya* is perceived, and hence the cognition that the cow is similar to the *gavaya* is not a revival of a past experience, but is a new experience.

The second part of Kumārila's remark, viz., that similarity can be perceived even when the counter-correlate is not perceived, simply means that when the *gavaya* is perceived its similarity to the cow also is perceived, though the counter-correlate, cow, is not physically present along with the *gavaya*. The perception of the counter-correlate is not essential for the appearance of the notion of similarity. But this does not imply that the memory of the counter-correlate also is inessential. The critics, on the other hand, wrongly interpret Kumārila's remark as implying this. What Kumārila intends is merely that a present object can be compared to an absent object provided that the latter is present in the mind, while his critics wrongly interpret him as intending that a present object can be compared to an object whose existence we are absolutely ignorant of.

The second point on which Kumārila is criticized is as follows: If for the cognition that a cow is similar to a *gavaya* we require an independent *pramāṇa*, then in a like manner we require an independent *pramāṇa* for each of the cognitions 'this is dissimilar to that', 'this is larger than that', 'this is posterior to that' etc., so that the total number of *pramāṇa*-s cannot be limited to six only. We see that 'A is dissimilar to B', 'A is shorter than B', 'A is prior to B' etc., and from these we know that 'B is dissimilar to A', 'B is larger than A', 'B is posterior to A' etc. Just as the cognition 'B is similar to A' arising from the perception 'A is similar to B' cannot be reduced to perception, memory, or inference, so these latter cognitions too cannot, and thus the number of *pramāṇa*-s becomes more than six.[25] To the above list we can add such cognitions also as 'B is the father of A', 'B is north of A' etc. arising from such cognitions as 'A is the son of B' etc.

This criticism is quite justified. Kumārila and his commentators have not anticipated it. Nārāyaṇa, who is comparatively a recent author, anticipates the objection that if the cognition of similarity requires an independent *pramāṇa* then the cognition of dissimilarity should require another independent *pramāṇa*; and the answer that he gives is that dissimilarity, being the negation of similarity, is cognized by *anupalabdhi*, the sixth *pramāṇa*.[26] This answer has been anticipated and criticised by Śāntarakṣita who precedes Nārāyaṇa by several centuries. If dissimilarity is equated to the negation of similarity, then similarity can also be equated to the negation of identity. Two things are identical when all the features of one are common to the other, and they are similar when some of the features of one are common to the other though the rest are uncommon. Thus if dissimilarity is cognized by *anupalabdhi* for the reason that it involves negation, then similarity too should be cognised

25. TH, vv. 1557-58.
26. MM, p. 111.

by *anupalabdhi* for the same reason, so that *upamāna* becomes superfluous,[27]

The argument offered by Śāntarakṣita is quite valid. The fact that Nārāyaṇa repeats a reasoning which was refuted several centuries ago, is the sign of stagnation in the Mīmāṃsā system. We can generalize this remark and say that by the time when the later commentators flourished practically every Indian philosophical system had lost its vitality and ceased to be a living and growing one. To return to Śāntarakṣita's criticism, if we include all the above cases of immediate inference in *upamāna* it would not conflict with Kumārila's position, because in all of them we compare a physically absent but ideally present thing to another thing which is physically present.

The third target. of the opponent's criticism is the practical utility of *upamāna* mentioned by Kumārila. In the *Saurya* sacrifice the details of performance are not described. Kumārila says that the required details are known through *upamāna*. The *Saurya* sacrifice is similar to the *Āgneya* sacrifice in the respect that both have a common deity. The details of the performance of the latter are known and on the basis of the similarity they are transferred to the former. Again, when *vrīhi*, which is preserved for oblation, is spoilt or stolen we can use *nīvāra* as its substitute, believing that the result will be similar. This also, according to Kumārila, is a practical utility of *upamāna*, because *nīvāra* becomes a substitute by virtue of its similarity to *vrīhi*.[28]

Criticizing Kumārila's view Jayanta says that there is no agreement between the Bhāṭṭa definition of *upamāna* and the said utility.[29] Through *upamāna* we judge an object to be similar to another object on the basis that the latter is similar to the former. Now, from the cognition that the *Saurya* sacrifice is similar to the *Āgncya* sacrifice what we know through *upamāna* is simply that the *Āgneya* sacrifice is similar to the *Saurya* sacrifice. But this much alone cannot justify the transference of the details of the former to the latter. In the second example too *upamāna* helps us in knowing only that

27. TH, vv. 1559-62.
28. SV, *Upamāna*, 52-53.
29. NM, p. 147.

vrīhi is similar to *nīvāra*. But this does not justify us in treating the latter as a substitute of the former.

Jayanta's criticism is right. I see a woman who looks very much like my wife and then I conclude that my wife is similar to her. On the basis of this knowledge I cannot treat her as my wife's substitute. On a closer examination we find that the said practical utility presupposes analogy rather than *upamāna*. The first example of the said utility presupposes the following reasoning:

The *Saurya* sacrifice resembles the *Āgneya* sacrifice;
The *Āgneya* sacrifice has such and such details of performance;
Therefore, the *Saurya* sacrifice also has the same details.

The second example presupposes the following:

Nīvāra resembles *vrīhi*;
Vrīhi is used for oblation;
Therefore, *nivāra* also is used for oblation.

These are really instances of analogy rather than of *upamāna*, because in them similarity in some unknown respect is inferred from similarity in some known respect.

8.6. *What Is Similarity*?

Kumārila defines similarity as the presence in one class of objects of the universals inhering in a number of parts of the individuals belonging to a different class.[30] The similarity of an individual belonging to the *cow* class to an individual belonging to the *gavaya* class consists in the presence in the former of the universals inhering in a number of such parts of the latter as horns, ears etc. In other words, by the similarity of a cow to a *gavaya* we mean the presence in a cow of a number of features common to a *gavaya*. The word universal' in the definition simply refers to the fact that the parts of one thing in their particular character cannot compose another thing, i.e., that what is common to things cannot be particular but universal. The notion of similarity, e.g., 'A is similar to B', arises when the perception of a number of features in A is accompanied by the

30. भूयोऽवयवसामान्ययोगो जात्यन्तरस्य तत् । SV, *Upamāna*, 18.

consciousness that they are present in the counter-correlate B also. Sometimes similarity is observed not between two individual objects composed of parts (*avayavin*) but between their parts (*avayava*) as, for instance, between the petal of lotus flower and the eye of a beautiful woman. The definition of similarity applies here too, because the two parts that are compared are wholes (*avayavin*) in relation to the parts that they are composed of. Thus the similarity between a lotus-petal and a woman's eye also consists in their having a number of common parts. Whenever similarity is perceived the things that are compared are always divisible into parts. We can go on comparing two wholes, their parts, the parts of their parts and so on till we arrive at the atoms which are not divisible into further parts and at this stage there is no awareness of similarity but of the universal atom-ness alone.[31] We cannot say that the atoms of one thing are similar to the atoms of another thing, because they have no constituent parts. Similarity exists between two composite things alone.

It should, however, be remembered that similarity is not always described in terms of common parts but also in terms of common qualities, relations etc. Sometimes the similarity between two things consists in their common origin. A Brāhmaṇa is said to be similar to fire, because the two have a common origin, viz., the mouth of Prajāpati. Sometimes similarity consists in the possession by two objects of common qualities. For example, the similarity between a drawing and the thing which is represented in it consists in the presence in the two of such common qualities as colour, shape etc. Sometimes similarity can also depend on some common action. An aeroplane is similar to a bird, because the two possess the common action of flying in the sky. In the case of the similarity between a wrestler and Bhīma the common feature is strength. Thus similarity is not confined to those things alone which have common parts. Any two things may be similar to each other in any one or more of the respects enumerated above,[32] but they

31. Ibid., 19, 27-28.
32. Ibid., 20.

should always be complex entities analysable into constituent parts, qualities etc.

From the definition it would appear that similarity can exist between two classes only. But this is not Kumārila's intention. He holds that sometimes similarity is observed between two individuals also, as, for example, in the case of twins. When we say that a cow is similar to a *gavaya* the correlates on the two sides of the comparison are classes, because any member of the class *cow* is similar to any member of the class *gavaya.* In the case of twins, however, the correlates are individuals, and, though they belong to the same class, *human beings*, yet the features common to them are more numerous than the features common to any two human beings.

But if, the opponent may object, similarity between twins is recognized, it would, according to the definition, mean that a number of universals inhering in the one inheres in the other, which implies that such universals would be destroyed with the destruction of the twins and this would conflict with the Bhāṭṭa view that universals are eternal. To this the answer is that neither it is accepted as a rule that universals are eternal nor that there is destruction of universals inhering in twins with the destruction of the latter. Universals are held to be eternal in sense that we cannot think of a time when all the individuals in which a universal inheres are destroyed. There will be a time when the present individual cows will be dead, yet then new substrates of the universal *cow-ness* will be born and the process will continue for ever. Similarly, the universals inhering in twins will not be destroyed when the twins are dead, but will continue so long as the other substrates are there. But, it may again be objected, if there are other substrates in which the universals inhering in twins inhere, then how is it that they are not observed to be similar to twins? The answer is that the universals that explain the similarity existing in twins inhere in them in groups, whereas in other substrates they inhere singly. Let a, b, c etc. be such universals. In each of the twins, X and Y, the set of a, b, c etc. inheres. These universals inhere in other objects too, e.g., a inheres in A, b in B, c in C etc. But A is not so similar to X as X is to Y, because A and X possess only a in common, while X and Y posses a, b, c etc. in common.[33] Similarity is a matter of degrees. The amount of similarity varies with the number of common features. The greater the number of points of comparison, the higher is the degree of similarity. In Kumārila's language the degree of similarity corresponds to the number of universals inhering commonly in the objects compared.

The recognition of similarity between twins shows that it is not necessary that the correlates of similarity should belong to two different classes. But there occurs a verse which creates a different impression. The verse runs as follows:

> In a case where we have the recognition of a single class as belonging to the principal objects themselves (and not to the parts), there we have a notion (of identity) such as 'this is that very thing': and where there is difference, there we have the notion of similarity only.[34]

This verse explicitly says that the notion of similarity arises only when the objects belong to different classes and that when the objects belong to the same class then the notion that appears is one of identity. Umbeka[35] also says that in this verse Kumārila states what is to be excluded by the inclusion of the word '*jātyantara*' in the definition (*adhunā jātyantaragrahaṇasya vyavacchedyaṃ darśayati*). But then we cannot say that twins are similar to each other, because they belong to the same class, *human beings* and for the same reason we cannot say that one cow is similar to another cow. Extending this reasoning, we cannot even say that a cow is similar to *gavaya*, since both belong to the same higher class *animal*.

Kumārila's statement may be interpreted as meaning that the consciousness of identity arises when the essential features of two things are the same, though there may be superficial differences, and that the consciousness of similatity arises when

33. Ibid., 22-26.
34. प्रधानानां तु सामान्यं यत्रैकं संप्रतीयते ।
स एवेति भवेत् तत्र तद्भेदे सदृशत्वधीः ॥ Ibid., 29.
35. TT on Ibid.

the essential features are different though the superficial ones may be the same. But in that case the consciousness of identity or similarity will be relative to the attitude of the observer at the moment, because our conception of what is essential and what is inessential differs from time to time. Thus when we need any horse to ride we do not distinguish between one of Indian breed and one of Arabian breed; but when we are on the polo ground we distinguish between them. In the former case there is a consciousness of identity and in the latter there is a consciousness of similarity.

The other commentators[36] take this verse as an answer to Prabhākhara's objection. Prabhākara says,

> Some people have stated that the universal itself is similarity; but this is wrong because a universal like cowness gives rise to the notion of identity in the form 'this is the same thing'[37]

Pārthasārathi explains Kumārila's answer as follows:

> We do not say that universal is similarity, nor that the presence in one thing of the universal inhering in another thing is similarity. What we say is that the assemblage in one thing of the universals inhering in the constituent parts of another thing is similarity. Thus two things are similar not because the principal universal in each is one and the same, but because a number of universals which are different from the principal universal resides in the constituent parts of one thing and also of the other thing. If the principal universal, e.g., cowness, is the same it gives rise to the notion 'this is the same thing'.[38]

This also shows that in two identical things the unity is in essential respects and the difference is in inessential respects and that in two similar things the unity is in inessential respects and the difference is in essential respects. Thus Kumārila's view of similarity appears to differ from the common-sense view that similarity is partial identity.

36. Vide KK & NR on Ibid.
37. BR, p. 109.
38. NR on SV, *Upamāna*, 29.

CHAPTER IX

ARTHĀPATTI (PRESUMPTION)

9.1. *The Nature and Forms of Arthāpatti*

Śabara defines *arthāpatti* as

> the presumption of something not seen on the ground that a fact already perceived or heard would not be possible without that presumption; for instance, it is found that Devadatta who is alive is not in the house, and this non-existence in the house leads to the presumption that he is somewhere outside the house.[1]

Kumārila elaborates Śabara's view. The element which distinguishes *arthāpatti* from the other *pramāṇa*-s is the presence of inexplicability in some observed or well-ascertained fact. Pārthasārathi says that when we observe that a well-ascertained fact cannot be explained without another fact, we presume the latter in order to account for the former and this presumption is *arthāpatti*.[2] We know with perfect certainty that a man is alive; yet we do not find him in the house. The man exists, yet he does not exist in the house. This fact appears to be conflicting. How can a man exist and not exist at the same time? This conflict cannot be resolved unless it is presumed that he exists outside. The supposition of his existence outside explains his non-existence in the house. The means (*karaṇa*) of such a supposition is the consciousness of an inner contradiction (*anupapatti*); and the result of the supposition is the reconciliation of this contradiction (*upapatti*).

Of course, the contradiction is not real but only apparent. When there is a real contradiction in facts, there cannot be any reconciliation. I perceive silver in a place from a distance and when I come nearer and pick it up I find that there is no silver.

1. अर्थापत्तिरपि दृष्टः श्रुतो वार्थोऽन्यथा नोपपद्यते इत्यर्थकल्पना; यथा जीवतो देवदत्तस्य गृहाभावदर्शनेन बहिर्भावस्यादृष्टस्य परिकल्पना । SB, p. 110.
2. SD, p. 76.

Between the cognitions 'there is silver' and 'there is no silver' there is a real conflict and the conflict can be resolved only by assuming that one of the cognitions is false. Similarly when some person says that there are fruits on the river bank and another one says that there are no fruits on the river bank, the two statements really contradict each other. We cannot accept both the statements. When there is a real conflict the only way of resolving it is the rejection of one of the cognitions as false. But in *arthāpatti* the cognitions are both true, though at first they appear to be conflicting. In such a state there is produced a feeling of tension in the mind, because neither anyone of the cognitions can be accepted nor rejected, nor can they be synthesized together. This tension leads to and is removed by presuming something.[3] The conflict which is the cause of presumption is always between two *pramāṇa*-s. In the example given above the two *pramāṇa*-s are inference and non-apprehension. By inference it is known that a living man exists somewhere and by non-apprehension it is known that Devadatta does not exist in the house where he would be normally expected. What is known by the inference is that Devadatta exists somewhere. There is no specification as to the exact place where Devadatta exists, so that he may also exist in the house. But by non-apprehension he is known not to exist in the house. This conflict between inference and non-apprehension leads to the presumption that Devadatta exists outside. This presumption of existence outside explains Devadatta's non-existence in the house and thus resolves the conflict.[4] The two *pramāṇa*-s which conflict with each other and lead to *arthāpatti* cannot both of them be specific, because, if they were specific, they could not be reconciled with each other, for example, the *pramāṇa*-s 'there is silver' and 'there is no silver' both are specific and hence irreconcilable. Thus one of the conflicting *pramāṇa*-s, which lead to *arthāpatti*, must be general and the other specfic.[5]

The words '*dṛṣṭaḥ śruto vā*' in Śabara's statement do not appear to refer to two different forms of *arthāpatti*, viz., *dṛṣṭārthāpatti*

3. Ibid., p. 78.
4. KK on SV, *Arthāpatti*, 1.
5. सर्वत्र चार्थापत्तौ साधारणासाधारणविरोधः । NTV, p. 158.

or presumption from the seen and *śrutārthāpatti* or presumption from the heard. Śabara has given only one example of *arthāpatti*, but in case he intended two forms of *arthāpatti*, he should have given two instead of one. Kumārila, however, interprets Śabara's words as referring to two main forms of *arthāpatti*. He again sub-divides the first, viz., *dṛṣṭārthāpatti*, into five forms and thus we have six forms of *arthāpatti* in all. The example given above is that of *abhāvapūrvikā arthāpatti*, i.e., presumption based on non-apprehension. Devadatta's non-existence in the house is ascertained by non-apprehension and this is a fact which remains inexplicable without the presumption of Devadatta's existence outside. Here the inexplicability lies in a fact given by non-apprehension. But this is not always the case, since the inexplicability may also lie in a fact given by perception or any other *pramāṇa*. Thus *arthāpatti* is of six forms, viz., that based on perception, based on inference, on verbal testimony, on comparison, on another presumption and on non-apprehension.[6]

The first form of *arthāpatti*, viz., *pratyakṣapūrvikā arthāpatti*, is illustrated in the presumption of burning power in fire. In this kind of *arthāpatti* the inconsistency lies in a perceived fact. We perceive that fire burns things. This fact remains inexplicable without the presumption of burning power in fire. Power is an imperceptible entity and is considered to be a category different from substance, quality, action and universal. Kumārila does not clearly show in what the inexplicability consists that leads to the presumption of burning power. Sucaritamiśra says that the inexplicability consists in the inconsistency of the perceived fact with another *pramāṇa*. By perception it is ascertained that fire burns things. We perceive the form of fire, its conjunction with a thing and then the fact that the thing is burnt. Thus perception reveals that fire is the cause of burning things. But this is found to be inconsistent with the experience that sometimes an object, e.g., a human body, is not burnt when some medicine is applied to it, though at other times it is burnt. The visible form of fire or its conjunction with an object cannot be the cause of burning, because a cause is always followed by an effect while the visible form of fire or its conjunction with an object is not at times followed by the

6. SV, *Arthāpatti*, 2.

effect, viz., burning. Burning, however, being an occasional phenomenon cannot take place without a cause. Thus the inexplicability of the fact of burning consists in the inconsistency between two cognitions, viz., that an effect takes place and that its cause is apparently absent, and this inexplicability leads to the presumption that there is some invisible cause of burning, viz., the burning power of fire. Then, why objects are sometimes burnt by fire and sometimes not becomes fully intelligible on the ground that when the burning power is present burning takes place and when it is destroyed, though the visible form of fire is not destroyed, burning does not take place[7] Here we need not dwell on the arguments for and against power as a distinct category.

In *arthāpatti* based on inference the inconsistency lies in an inferred fact and it is illustrated in the presumption of moving power in the sun. It is known by inference that the sun moves. But how can it move unless it has some means? We generally see that living and moving things possess such limbs as legs etc., but we do not find any such limbs in the case of the sun. Thus there is a conflict between two *pramāṇa*-s, viz., that the sun moves and that it possesses no means of motion. This conflict is resolved by the presumption of moving power in the sun.[8]

Arthāpatti based on *upamāna* is illustrated thus: By *upamāna* it is known that a cow is similar to a gavaya. But there is some inexplicability involved in this cognition of similarity. How can the cognition of the cow's similarity arise now on the perception of the gavaya and not at the time when the cow was actually perceived for the first time? The similarity of the cow to the gavaya consists in the presence in the former of the universals of the limbs of the latter and these universals were present in the cow even when it was perceived for the first time; but the cow was not then cognized to be similar to gavaya. This conflict is resolved by the presumption of some power in the cow which is manifested by the perception of the counter-correlate and gives rise to the cognition of its similarity to the gavaya.[9]

7. KK on SV, *Arthāpatti*, 3.
8. Ibid.
9. Ibid., 4.

Arthāpatti based on *arthāpatti* is illustrated in the presumption of the eternality of words. A word is heard and then the cognition of the object that is denoted by it arises in the mind. From this it is concluded that the word is the cause of the cognition of the corresponding object. But there can be no causality unless there is some action. Thus some action inhering in the word is inferred and this action is known as *abhidhā* or denotation. This denotativeness that inheres in the word becomes inexplicable on the ground that when the word was heard for the first time it was not followed by the cognition of the object. The meaning of a word is known only after its relation to the corresponding object is comprehended. But the relation between a word and an object is not found to be of the nature of such usual relations as conjunction, inherence etc. Thus the inexplicability is resolved by the presumption of a peculiar power residing in the word. The relation between a word and an object is of the nature of a power and the meaning of a word is not understood unless this power is apprehended. This is the denotative power (*abhidhāśakti*) of a word. Again the denotative power of a word cannot be possible without the eternality of the word. This impossibility leads to the presumption of eternality of words. A person orders his servant using the words 'bring the cow' and the servant brings the cow because he understands the meaning of these words, and he understands because he has already comprehended the denotative powers of the words 'cow' and 'bring'. The understanding of the meaning of the word 'cow' cannot be explained otherwise than on the ground that the word 'cow' uttered by the master and heard by the servant now is the same as was heard by the servant on a past occasion when he comprehended its power of denoting the animal cow. Thus it is known through *arthāpatti* that the word 'cow' is eternal.[10]

Śrutārthāpatti differs from the other kinds of *arthāpatti* in the respect that it is based on verbal testimony. But the more important difference is that in it words are presumed while in others some fact is presumed. It is illustrated in the presumption of the sentence 'Caitra eats during the night' on hearing the sentence 'Caitra who is fat does not eat during the day'. The

10. Ibid., 5-7.

sentence that is heard involves an inner incompatibility because fatness is concomitant not with fasting but with feasting. From Caitra's fatness it is gathered that he must be eating voraciously. But contrarily to what is expected the other part of the sentence says that he fasts during the day. The meaning of the sentence appears to be self-cantradictory. Caitra's fatness cannot be explained unless it is presumed that he eats at night. Thus to remove the inconsistency in the meaning of the heard sentence, the sentence 'he eats at night' is imported. *Śrutārthāpatti* is the importation of a sentence or word to complete the sense of a heard sentence. Some person utters 'water'. The word 'water' does not give a complete meaning and the hearer knowing the context in which the word is uttered completes the sentence by importing the word 'bring'. This is another example of *śrutārthāpatti.* The fact that Caitra eats during the night without which Caitra's fatness remains inexplicable is not directly denoted by the sentence that is heard, because the heard sentence does not contain such words as 'night' etc. What is directly denoted by the sentence is the fact that Caitra is fat and does not eat during the day. A sentence gives out only one particular sense. Therefore, 'eats at night' is the meaning of a different sentence not uttered by the speaker but presumed by the hearer,[11]

9.2. *Arthāpatti According to Prabhākara*

Prabhākara[12] begins his discussion with the query as to what *anyathānupapatti* is. The meaning of Śabara's statement is that *arthāpatti* is the presumption of a fact explaining another fact which is otherwise inexplicable. Prabhākara asks as to what this inexplicability is and the answer that he gives is that inexplicability means the impossibility of the existence of a thing without another thing. But if this be the case, then *arthāpatti* is nothing but the inference of a cause from its effect, because the existence of an effect cannot be possible without its cause, and thus it ceases to be a different *pramāṇa*. Prabhākara tentatively says that *arthāpatti* is different from inference on the ground that in interence the conclusion is drawn from a known relation between

11. SV, *Arthāpatti*, 51 & 57-58; SD, p. 80.
12. BR, pp. 110-15.

the probans and the probandum, while in *arthāpatti* there is no knowledge of such a relation, and again rejects this distinction saying that the cognition of inexplicability, i.e., of the fact that this is impossible without that, cannot arise unless we already know a relation between what is not explained and what explains it. Inexplicability is not perceptible. It is known when we already know that one thing (effect) is invariably concomitant with another thing (cause), but actually see only one of them (effect). Thus *arthāpatti* too would be based on the knowledge of a relation like inference. What then is the distinctive element in *arthāpatti*? Prabhākara finally says that in the inference of a cause from its effect the probans, viz., the effect is inexplicable and the cause which is the probandum is what explains, while in *arthāpatti* the probans is that which explains and the probandum is that which is inexplicable without the former. In other words, in inference the movement of thought is from the *anupapanna* to the *upapādaka*, while in *arthāpatti* the movement of thought is from the *upapādaka* to the *anupapanna*.[13] Thus the distinctive element in *arthāpatti* according to Prabhākara is the knowledge of that which is not explained from the knowledge of that which explains it. Accordingly in the given example of *arthāpatti* the fact of Devadatta's non-existence in the house explains the fact of Devadatta's existence outside.

Prabhākara's view is just the reverse of Kumārila's view, because Kumārila says that the fact of Devadatta's non-existence in the house is explained by the presumption of his existence outside. Prabhākara's view is not consistent with Śabara's view even, because Prabhākara says that that which is to be known through *arthāpatti* is unexplained while Śabara says that a seen or heard fact is unexplained and that this inexplicability is the means of knowing what explains it. Prabhākara tries to avoid this inconsistency by changing the order of words in Śabara's statement from "*dṛṣṭaḥ śruto vārtho' nyathā nopapadyate ityarthakalpanā*" to "*dṛṣṭaḥ śruto vārtho' rthakalpanā anyathā nopapadyate iti*", which means that in *arthāpatti* a seen or heard fact is the means of knowing another fact which is inexplicable without the former.[14]

13. इह तु यन्नोपपद्यते तदेवावगम्यते । BR, p. 112.
14. Ibid., p. 113.

Prabhākara's view is wrong, because there can be no cognition of the inexplicable from that of which explains. If such be possible, the cognition of *śiṃśapā*-ness from the perception of tree-ness would be correct, because *śiṃśapā*-ness cannot be explained without tree-ness: *śiṃśapā* cannot be *śiṃśapā* unless it is a tree. But as a matter of fact, we cannot say that a tree is *śiṃśapā* because it is a tree. Therefore, in *arthāpatti* the *upapādaka* is known from the *anupapanna*. In the given example what is known is Devadatta's existence outside and it explains his non-existence in the house.[15] Prabhākara says that the known fact of Devadatta's non-existence in the house is not inexplicable. But then there should be no need of presuming his existence outside, because the known fact is supposed to be intelligible by itself. Prabhākara says that Devadatta's existence outside is inexplicable. But the consciousness of the person who does not see Devadatta in the house is really different. When he is aware of Devadatta's absence what he cognizes is not that Devadatta's presence outside is inexplicable but that Devadatta is out.[16]

Śālikanātha tries to make Prabhākara's position more acceptable in the following way: It is not existence outside that remains inexplicable without non-existence in the house, but it is the existence of Devadatta that remains inexplicable without presuming his stay outside when he is not found in the house. Inexplicability arises when a fact is opposed to some *pramāṇa*. Though Devadatta is known to be alive by some *pramāṇa*, yet it is opposed by the knowledge that he is not present in the house where he is generally seen. This opposition renders the fact of his being alive doubtful. The person who does not find Devadatta in the house doubts if Devadatta is really alive, and the doubt is not dispelled unless it is presumed that Devadatta is outside. There are three steps in the *arthāpatti*, viz., first, there is cognition of non-existence in the house, second, this cognition conflicts with the fact of Devadatta's being alive which is thus rendered doubtful, and third, his existence outside is presumed and this presumption removes the doubt. Thus the cause of in-

15. SD, p. 77.
16. KK on SV, *Arthāpatti*, 1.

explicability is the cognition of non-existence; that which is inexplicable is the fact of Devadatta's being alive; and that which results from the presumption of existence outside is the conviction of Devadatta's being alive.[17] The element that distinguishes *arthāpatti* from inference, according to Śālikanātha, is doubt rather than apparent inconsistency. He says that in inference a well-ascertained and indubitable thing is the producer of cognition, but in *arthāpatti* a doubtful thing is the producer of cognition.[18]

Pārthasārathi criticizes Śālikanātha's view as follows: When Devadatta's life itself has been rendered doubtful, it can never be the ground of his existence outside. How can it be said that since Devadatta is either dead or alive therefore he is outside? When one is in doubt about Devadatta's life, the doubt cannot be removed by presuming that he is outside. A doubt is removed only when its cause is removed or when either of the alternatives is confirmed by a stronger *pramāṇa*. The cause of doubt in the present case is non-existence in the house. Now, when existence outside is presumed it will only confirm the cause of doubt, viz., non-existence in the house, because the fact of outside existence is merely a supposition and is not known independently by a stronger *pramāṇa* like perception or inference. This supposition cannot even confirm anyone of the alternatives. The alternatives are stated in the form 'Devadatta is either alive or dead'. Staying outside is one thing and life or death is a different thing. *Arthāpatti* based on non-existence in the house cannot remove the doubt. It is absurd to say that because Devadatta is not present in the house, therefore he is outside and alive. Devadatta's life, which was first known as certain, was rendered doubtful because of his non-existence in the house. How can the cause of doubt itself be the cause of its removal? The fact is that Devadatta is already known to be alive beyond any shade of doubt. But if for some reason a person happens to entertain doubt about Devadatta's being alive and wishes to dispel it, then he should first approach some reliable person for the correct information. If he is able to ascertain in

17. RV, pp. 112-13.
18. PP, p. 115.

this way that Devadatta is alive, then he can say that because Devadatta is alive and not present in the house therefore he must be out. Thus doubt cannot be the distinguishing factor of *arthāpatti*.[19]

According to Kumārila, the words '*dṛṣṭaḥ śruto vā*' in the *Bhāṣya* refer to two kinds of *arthāpatti*. But Prabhākara interprets the words as meaning the same thing: *Dṛṣṭa* means well known and '*śruta*' is another word meaning the same thing in common usage.[20] Thus according to Prabhākara there is no *śrutārthāpatti* or presumption of a sentence or word. Śālikanātha says that what is presumed on hearing the sentence 'Caitra who is fat does not eat during the day' is the fact of eating at night instead of the sentence 'he eats at night'. The inexplicability that is removed by the presumption consists in the conflict between fatness and fasting, not between the words 'Caitra is fat' and 'he does not eat in the day'. So the conflict between two facts must be resolved by presuming another fact. Even when the words 'eats at night' are uttered after uttering the sentence 'Caitra who is fat does not eat during the day', the conflict arising in the mind of the person on hearing the latter sentence is not resolved if he does not know the meaning of the word 'night'. Therefore, it should be admitted that the immediate cause of resolving a conflict is the presumption of a fact, not of words. It is true that in the case of all who know the use of language determinate (*savikalpaka*) cognitions are always accompanied by the memory of words; and accordingly when a person cognizes the fact that Caitra eats at night his cognition is verbalized, yet this is not an uncommon thing, because even in *dṛṣṭārthāpatti* the cognition of the presumed fact, e.g., Devadatta's existence outside, is verbalized.[21]

The only argument that Kumārila offers in favour of *śrutārthāpatti* is the one refuted by Śālikanātha. Kumārila says that all determinate cognitions (*savikalpaka vijñāna*) are accompanied by the memory of words and the cognition resulting from a verbal inconsistency is a determinate cognition.[22] Śālikanātha

19. SD, p. 77.
20. BR, p. 115.
21. PP, p. 117.
22. SV, *Arthāpatti*, 78.

has exposed the weakness of this argument and Kumārila's commentators admit the point raised by him. Sucaritamiśra offers another argument: It is true that the inconsistency in a heard sentence is primarily an inconsistency in facts and that which is presumed to remove this inconsistency is also primarily a fact, yet the inconsistency of a sentence can be removed only by the presumption of another sentence. An inconsistent sentence is really an incomplete sentence and it can be completed only by importing another appropriate sentence or word. When someone utters the word '*pacati*' (cooks) the hearer expects another word, say, '*odanam*' (rice) and is not satisfied merely with the perception of rice before him. The expectancy is relieved only when the speaker himself adds the word '*odanam*' or when, in case he does not add it, the hearer imports it. Similarly when an incomplete sentence stands in need of another sentence the expectancy thus created can be relieved only by importing that sentence, not merely by presuming the corresponding fact.[28]

9.3. *Arthāpatti According to the Advaita Vedānta*

Dharmarājādhvarīndra defines *arthāpatti* as the presumption of a fact to account for an inexplicable fact. In *arthāpatti* the knowledge of an inexplicable fact is the instrumental cause and the knowledge of the fact that explains is the result. The fact that a person is fat, though he does not eat in the day, cannot be intelligible unless he eats at night. The fatness of the person is to be explained and eating at night explains it. The inexplicability of fatness in the absence of eating in the day is removed by the presumption of eating at night.

Like Kumārila Dharmarāja also distinguishes between two kinds of *arthāpatti*, viz., *dṛṣṭārthāpatti* and *śrutārthāpatti*. A man observes that there is silver in front of him and immediately afterwards he observes that there is no silver at all. The second cognition denies the presence of silver. But this denial cannot be explained if the first cognition 'there is silver' be true. Therefore, it is presumed that the first cognition was false. The perception of silver is a fact and the non-perception of it also is a fact. The fact of non-perception becomes inexplicable if the silver perceived at first be real. This inexplicability is removed

23. KK on ibid.

when it is presumed that the silver was unreal or illusory. This is an example of *dṛṣṭārthāpatti.*

Śrutārthāpatti is of two kinds, viz., one which is due to the failure on the part of a speaker to make a grammatically complete statement (*abhidhānānupapatti*) and one which is due to the unintelligibility of the meaning of a grammatically complete statement (*abhihitānupapatti*). In the former only a part of a sentence is spoken, which does not express the speaker's intention fully and the hearer presumes the missing word or words. When the speaker utters merely the word '*dvāram*' (door), it is incomplete without a verb in the imperative mood and the hearer cannot understand what to do with the door. The speaker knows what the hearer should do, but since he has missed to utter the appropriate word, the hearer cannot follow his command unless he presumes the missing word, say, '*pidhehi*' (close). Similarly when one hears the scriptural command '*viśvajitā yajeta*' ('should perform the *viśvajit* sacrifice') the sentence is found to be grammatically incomplete without a subject and hence the word '*svargakāmaḥ*' ('one who desires heaven') is presumed. In the second kind of *śrutārthāpatti* the inexplicability of the meaning of a sentence leads to the presumption of a fact. For example, the inexplicability of the meaning of the sentence '*svargakāmo jyotiṣṭomena yajeta*' ('one who desires heaven should perform the *jyotiṣṭoma* sacrifice') leads to the presumption of *apūrva*, a potency produced by the performance and abiding in the performer's soul till the attainment of heaven. The performance of the sacrifice is a transitory event while heaven can be attained only after death. If the performance of the said sacrifice is the cause of attaining heaven the latter should follow immediately, since a cause is always followed immediately by its effect. Thus the meaning of the sentence is unintelligible because *jyotiṣṭoma* is said to be the cause of heaven, the effect, though the cause does not immediately produce the effect. This unintelligibility is removed by presuming an intermediary in the form of *apūrva*. Another example is the presumption of the illusory nature of bondage on hearing the scriptural statement '*Tarati śokam ātmavit*' ('the knower of self transcends grief'). Grief is another name of bondage and the statement declares that knowledge is the means of freeing oneself from bondage. But if bondage is a real thing, how can knowledge help? Therefore, in order to avoid this incongruity it is presumed that bondage is not real but illusory. The illusion of rope-snake can be dispelled only by the right knowledge of the rope and similarly the illusion of bondage can be dispelled only by the right knowledge of self.[24]

The Vedāntic account of *arthāpatti* differs from the Bhāṭṭa in three main respects:

9.3.1. *Difference as to the Cause of Inexplicability*

Dharmarāja does not specify the cause of inexplicability while according to the Bhāṭṭa apparent contradiction is the cause. In most of the examples of *arthāpatti* given by Dharmarāja we find that an element of contradiction is involved. But in the example of the first kind of *śrutārthāpatti* we do not find any contradiction, though inexplicability or unintelligibility is there. According to the Bhāṭṭa too, importation of a word in order to complete a sentence is an instance of *śrutārthāpatti*; and hence according to the rule that apparent contradiction is the instrumental cause of presumption, we should expect apparent contradiction here also. But actually there is no contradiction of any sort here. There is contradiction when a known fact conflicts with our past general experience, i.e., when what happens is opposed to what we expect to happen according to our past experience. But when someone utters the word '*dvāram*' there is nothing which happens to conflict with our past experience. What we expect is that the speaker should speak something more while he does not speak more. It would involve contradiction if we expected one additional word appropriate in the context and the speaker uttered a different word. For example, if the speaker says 'close the door' when it is too hot inside, the sentence gives rise to a conflict because the word 'close' cannot be expected in the situation. Of course, in a way the utterance of the word '*dvāram*' also produces conflict insofar as the hearer does not know for the time being whether he should close the door or see it or break it. But this is not a conflict between two cognitions or facts, because it occurs between two or more subjective responses of the hearer aroused by the

24. VP, Chapter V.

word '*dvāram*', while the word itself is not one of the conflicting parties. Therefore, the unintelligibility caused by the utterance of the word '*dvāram*' is not due to its incompatibility with our experience, but due to the failure on the part of the speaker to express his intention fully. The presumption of the word '*pidhehi*' in this case is like framing an hypothesis, and the situation that it seeks to explain is far more complex than the mere utterance of the word '*dvāram*'. The hearer presumes the appropriate word not merely on hearing the word '*dvāram*' but also on perceiving the other details, e.g. the existing state of the door, the weather etc.

9.3.2. *Inconsistency*: *Psychological and Logical*

The contradiction in the example of *dṛṣṭārthāpatti* is between two specific cognitions, viz., 'this is silver' and 'this is not silver' and it is not apparent but real because the two cognitions cannot be simultaneously true. This seems to be inconsistent with the Bhāṭṭa view. According to the Bhāṭṭa view a contradiction can be reconciled through presumption only when one of the conflicting cognitions is general and the other specific, in which case the contradiction is merely apparent. The Bhāṭṭa view that a real contradiction cannot be reconciled seems to be true, because the term 'reconciliation' implies that the claim of the conflicting cognitions to be true is justified through presumption, while in the case of real contradiction one of the cognitions is really false and hence its claim to be true can never be justified. Thus there can be no reconciliation in the proper sense between the cognitions 'this is silver' and 'this is not silver' through the presumption that the first one is false. However, it is wrong to say that the contradiction which leads to presumption lies between two cognitions. The contradiction which is reconcilable primarily lies not between two cognitions but between a fact and our general experience or between two facts whose co-existence seems to be inexplicable. The fact that living Caitra is not present in the house is inconsistent with my general experience that he was found in the house whenever I went to see him. This inconsistency is not logical but psychological. In Dharmarāja's example of *dṛṣṭārthāpatti* the contradiction lies between the facts that silver is perceived from a distance and that on making a closer approach it is not found where it was perceived; and this contradiction is reconciled by presuming that what was perceived from a distance was not real but illusory silver, because if it were real it could not have disappeared so soon without any visible cause. The co-existence of silver and no silver is inexplicable otherwise than on the presumption of the illusory nature of silver.

9.3.3. *Abhidhānānupapatti and Abhihitānupapatti*

In *śrutārthāpatti*, according to the Bhāṭṭa view, there is always the presumption of a word or sentence, while according to the Vedānta view there is sometimes the presumption of a word and sometimes the presumption of a fact. The Vedānta view seems to be a compromise between the Bhāṭṭa and Prābhākara views. When a person utters a grammatically incomplete sentence, i.e., a sentence in which the subject or object or the verb is missing, the hearer always presumes a word or words. It is true that the incompleteness of the sentence is detected by understanding the fact to which the sentence refers, for example, one who hears the word '*dvāram*' discovers that the speaker's statement is incomplete only when he understands the situation that the weather is cold and the door is open. But then the incompleteness is not removed simply by presuming the fact that the door is to be closed. Suppose the speaker utters the word 'door' and makes a gesture to close it or utters the word 'close' and points with his finger towards the door. Yet the expectancy created in the mind of the hearer is not relieved unless the required word is supplied. We actually find that sometimes the hearer himself utters involuntarily the word or words left unuttered by the speaker. This fact favours the Vedānta view. On hearing the word '*dvāram*' the hearer closes the door, but at the same time he feels that the speaker ought to have spoken the complete sentence '*dvāraṃ pidhehi*', and thus he himself supplies the word '*pidhehi*'.

When, however, a sentence is grammatically complete but the sense involves some inconsistency, it is not a word that is presumed but some fact. A man says that Devadatta is fat and does not eat in the day. The statement is grammatically complete. But the hearer who presumes that Devadatta eats at night does not feel that the speaker ought to have spoken the clause 'Devadatta eats at night' in addition. Devadatta's eating at night is really a fact implied in his fatness in the absence of eating in the day. The speaker himself may be ignorant of this implication. How can then the hearer feel that the speaker has missed to utter the said clause? Hence it is more reasonable to say that the object of *arthāpatti* in the present case is a fact rather than a clause. This type of *arthāpatti* is equivalent to drawing the implication of a statement. Thus the Vedānta view of *śrutārthāpatti* is more reasonable than the Bhāṭṭa and Prābhākara views. *Abhidhānānupapatti* leads to the presumption of the word which together with the actually uttered word forms a complete statement; and *abhihitānupapatti* leads to the presumption of a fact which resolves the conflict in the sense of an already complete statement.

9.4. *Arthāpatti Is Different from Anumāna*

Let us take the example of Caitra's presence outside his house and see if it can be satisfactorily explained as a case of *anumāna*. The given fact in this example is Caitra's absence in the house. That which is to be known from this fact can be stated in two forms, viz., 'Caitra is present in outside space' and 'outside space is one in which Caitra is present'. Accordingly the minor term is either Caitra or outside space. But what is the middle term? The middle term is always the property of the minor term. In the present case absence cannot be the middle term since it is not a property either of Caitra or of outside space. Absence is apprehended in the house. Therefore, it can reasonably be the property of the house alone. Can then the house qualified by the absence be the middle term? No, because the house can never be a property of Caitra or of outside space. What is apprehended is the absence and the house. Caitra and outside space are not apprehended at the time. How can then absence in the house be related to Caitra or outside space? However, imperceptibility can be related to Caitra because when the person goes to Caitra's house he does not perceive him there. Can we then make the imperceptibility the middle term and say that Caitra is present in the outside space because he is imperceptible inside the house? No, because imperceptibility is not directly related to the major term, viz., presence outside. From the imperceptibility it is directly ascertained that Caitra is absent from the house. It cannot have the double function of leading simultaneously to two inferences, viz., that Caitra is not in the house and that he is outside. Thus imperceptibility and absence in the house both singly are useless for our purpose, because the former is related to the minor term, Caitra, but is not related to the major term 'presence outside the house', and the latter may be related to the major term but is not related to the minor term. There is another difficulty also. In *anumāna* the minor term is apprehended prior to the major term. It seeks to prove that a formerly unknown property (*dharma*) belongs to a well known property-possessor (*dharmin*). But in the case in question the property-possessor, viz., Caitra or outside space, is not apprehended. So, how can anything be proved about it through *anumāna*?

Here Kumārila anticipates the following objection. From the rise in river-water rain in higher regions is known and this is recognized by all as a case of inference. But according to the above reasoning it cannot be so, since the minor term 'higher regions' is not seen, so that there can be no *pakṣadharmatā*, i.e., the middle term 'rise in river-water' cannot be related to the minor term. Kumārila's answer is that the minor term in the said case is not 'higher regions' but it is the 'region in which the rise in river-water is seen' and then the conclusion of the syllogism will be 'this place is one whose higher regions have rain' instead of 'the higher regions are such as have rain'. But this answer does not seem satisfactory. It is a mere verbal manipulation. In spite of the change in statement the facts are not altered because the rain occurs in the higher regions while the rise in river-water is seen in this place. And if the change in statement can make the syllogism flawless, then in the case of Caitra's presence outside too we can make the house minor term instead of Caitra. Anticipating this objection Kumārila says that the knowledge of rain in the higher regions is not a case of inference but of arthāpatti.[25]

Pārthasārathi says that Kumārila's answer is a sort of sophism (*jātyuttara*). There is no lack of *pakṣadharmatā*, i.e., the relation between the minor term 'Caitra' and the middle term 'absence in

25. SV, *Arthāpatti*, 10-18 & NR and KK on ibid.

the house'. The relation is obvious when we go to Caitra's house and find that he is absent. It is not a condition of inference that the minor term should always be perceived. Though Caitra is not perceived, yet he is remembered. Thus the syllogism 'Caitra is present outside the house because he is absent in the house, and whoever is absent in the house is present outside, like myself', is quite valid and similarly the syllogism which proves the occurrence of rain in the higher regions also is valid. Therefore, either *arthāpatti* is not different from *anumāna* or if it is different the proper reason should be stated.[26]

What follows is the proper argument for the non-inclusion of *arthāpatti* in *anumāna*. Those who attempt to reduce *arthāpatti* to syllogistic form cannot make Caitra's non-existence in the house the middle term, since by itself it is non-conclusive—when a man is not present in the house we cannot say that he is present outside, because he may be dead. Non-existence in the house devoid of Caitra's being alive is not a proof of Caitra's existence outside. The fact of Caitra's being alive too cannot be made the middle term, because it is as much concomitant with his existence in the house as with his existence outside. Therefore, the opponent should say that Caitra's non-existence in the house together with the fact that he is alive is the middle term which proves the major term 'Caitra's existence outside'. This, however, cannot be done. We cannot apprehend the togetherness of the fact of Caitra's non-existence in the house and the fact of his being alive without the knowledge of his existence outside. In a syllogism the knowledge of the major term follows from the knowledge of the middle term and the latter knowledge is independent of the former. For example, the knowledge of the smoke is independent of the knowledge of fire. Smoke is perceived independently of fire. Smoke is the middle term and fire the major term. First we have the cognition of the middle term and subsequently the cognition of the major term. But in the present case we cannot have the cognition of the middle term independently of the cognition of the major term; and as soon as we cognize the middle term, viz, the togetherness of Caitra's non-existence in the house and his being alive, we also cognize simultaneously Caitra's existence outside. Caitra's existence

26. NR on SV, *Arthāpatti*, 18.

(being alive) and non-existence (in the house) cannot be combined together without dragging in or including difference of place. There is an incompatibility between existence and non-existence, so that they cannot be combined together. We cannot make simultaneously the two assertions, viz, that 'Caitra exists' and that 'he does not exist' without implying that he exists in one place and does not exist in other place. Thus the cognition of Caitra's existence in general and his non-existence in the house itself is the cognition of his existence outside the house, so that there remains nothing to be known after knowing the middle term. The minor premise 'Caitra exists and does not exist in the house' cannot be possible unless the fact of Caitra's existence outside is introduced. Caitra's existence outside is presupposed by the fact of his being alive and absent in the house. The former does not follow from the latter. Hence if the former is made the conclusion of a syllogism in which the latter is the minor premise, the syllogism will involve the fallacy of *petitio principii*. *Arthāpatti*, however, is free from this fallacy because it is a syllogistic fallacy, and *arthāpatti* is different from syllogistic reasoning insofar as in the former we proceed from the awareness of a conflict between two well ascertained facts through the presumption of some other fact to the resolution of the conflict, while in the latter we proceed from the cognition of the middle term through the remembrance of its invariable connection with the major term to the cognition of the major term. *Arthāpatti*, unlike syllogism to which it is proposed to be reduced, is not invalid, because the causes of invalidity, viz., doubt, illusion and non-cognition, are absent and the cause of validity, viz., non-contradiction is pesent.[27]

Another reason why *arthāpatti* cannot be included in *anumāna* is that it does not stand in need of the knowledge of *vyāpti* while the latter cannot proceed without it. *Vyāpti* is a generalization based on a frequent and uncontradicted experience of two things together and in *anumāna vyāpti* which constitutes the major premise is known prior to the conclusion. *Arthāpatti*, on the other hand, is independent of the knowledge of *vyāpti*. It is true that there is *vyāpti* between non-existence inside the

27. SV, *Arthāpatti*, 19-29 and KK & NR.

house and existence outside, but it is not known prior to the presumption of Caitra's existence outside, so that is cannot be the cause of the cognition that Caitra is outside. Even one who has never experienced the concomitance of non-existence inside and existence outside presumes that a person who is not inside is present outside. Moreover, the proof of the said concomitance is none other than *arthāpatti*. From the inexplicability of the fact that Caitra exists and does not exist in the house it is presumed that he exists outside and then we become aware of the relation between non-existence inside and existence outside. The conclusion of a syllogism is the result of applying a general empirical rule to a particular case; but in the case in question *arthāpatti* is the means of knowing the general rule. This establishes the distinctness of *arthāpatti* from *anumāna*.[28]

The opponent may object that *arthāpatti* is not the only means of knowing the relation between non-existence in one place and existence elsewhere, because it is just possible for one who stands at the door and perceives Caitra in the garden to know the relation. This is true and in this way there may be no need of *arthāpatti* for knowing the *vyāpti* in the case of some person in some instances. But we cannot do away with *arthāpatti* for ever, because though in some cases *arthāpatti* is an alternative means of knowing the *vyāpti* in others it is the only means. For example, the *vyāpti* between existence in one place and non-existence in all other places cannot be known otherwise than through *arthāpatti*. The relation between existence in one place and non-existence in all other places cannot be established by experience, since, though one of the terms is directly known, the second is not known—we can know Caitra's non-existence in those places only where we actually go and do not find him, but the number of such places is strictly limited. Non-apprehension cannot be the means of knowing the second term, viz., Caitra's non-existence in all places other than the place where he actually exists. The person who perceives Caitra in one place knows through non-apprehension his absence in those places only which are visible to him. But non-apprehension cannot ascertain Caitra's absence in distant places which are not in contact with

28. Ibid., 30-33.

his eyes. To ascertain Caitra's non-existence through non-apprehension the person must go to every place other than where he exists, which, since the number of such places is unlimited, is impracticable. The opponent says that if non-existence is ascertained not merely by non-apprehension but by non-apprehension in a place where one actually goes, then since it is impossible for one to go to all the places where fire does not exist, the proposition 'where there is no fire there is no smoke' cannot be established. The answer is that this fact undermines the position of only those who hold that the *vyāpti* from which an inference is drawn, must be universal and negative in form. It has, however, been already shown that *vyāpti* is affirmative in form and that it is established by a uniform and uncontradicted experience of the coexistence of the probans and the probandum in a limited number of instances, so that there is no necessity of knowing all the instances of the negation of the probandum and the negation of the probans.

Now if, the opponent again objects, the universal relation between smoke and fire can be established through the experience of a limited number of the places where they co-exist, then the relation between existence in one place and non-existence in all other places also can be established through the experience of Caitra's presence in one place and his absence in the adjoining place: We know from the co-existence of smoke and fire in a few places that they co-exist everywhere and likewise we can know from the absence in a few places of Caitra who is known to be present in one particular place that he is absent everywhere else. To this the answer is that the two cases are not parallel. In the case of the *vyāpti* between smoke and fire the terms are of a limited extension and are found to be present in their entirety in the few places in which they are observed together. But in the case of the *vyāpti* between existence in one place and non-existence everywhere else, the latter term of the relation is of an unlimited extension, so that it cannot be known in its entirety in a few experiences, though the first term is known in its entirety.

The opponent again says that we can know Caitra's non-existence through inference as follows: All places are devoid of Caitra, because they are places other than the one in which he is present, like the place in front. But this inference is inconclusive because it can be counter-balanced by the following inference: All places are those which are not devoid of Caitra, because they are places other than the one in front, like the place where Caitra is present. Thus Caitra's non-existence everywhere else can be known neither by non-apprehension nor by inference, so that the *vyāpti* between existence in one place and non-existence in all other places cannot be established in the above ways.[29]

How then is it known that Caitra who exists in one place does not simultaneously exist in other places? Kumārila says that it is known through *arthāpatti*:

> The fact that the man as a whole is found in one place cannot be established otherwise than through the fact that he does not exist in other places, so that the knowledge of his non-existence everywhere else is based on *arthāpatti*.[30]

Sucaritamiśra explains the process of *arthāpatti* involved here as follows: The fact that Caitra as a whole is apprehended in one place would be inexplicable if Caitra existed in some other place also. Existing things are of two kinds, viz., of those having a finite extension and those having an infinite extension. The objects of the latter kind are in contact with every point of space. But Caitra is not of this kind. He has a limited number of parts joined together. If he were partly elsewhere we could not perceive him here as a whole. Therefore, he has a finite extension and thus when he is in one place, it is absurd to think that he is in other places also. Now what is the inexplicability in the fact of Caitra's presence in one place which leads to the presumption of his absence everywhere else? The presence of Caitra as a whole in one place does not appear to be inconsistent with anything, while the source of inexplicability is said to be an apparent inconsistency. Sucaritamiśra's answer is that the presence of Caitra as a whole in one place is inconsistent with the inference of his presence elsewhere and that the presumption of Caitra's absence elsewhere confirms the inference of his

29. Ibid., 33-45.
30. Ibid., 46-47.

absence elsewhere by sublating the inference of his presence elsewhere.[31]

This answer is, however, not at all satisfactory. From Caitra's presence in one place we know that he is absent everywhere else. Caitra's presence in one place is the given fact. There is no inconsistency in it which may be removed by presuming his absence elsewhere. There is an inconsistency between Caitra's simultaneous presence and absence in the same place; but this is not a given fact.

Pārthasārathi explains the process of *arthāpatti* in a different way. It is known through inference that Caitra who has limited dimensions cannot simultaneously reside in different places, and it is known through perception that he resides in the place in contact with the eyes. If Caitra is supposed to be present in other places, then the inference that he cannot exist in two places simultaneously is contradicted; and if he is supposed to be non-existing here then the perception of his presence here is contradicted. To avoid this contradiction it is presumed that Caitra is absent everywhere else.[32]

Pārthasārathi's explanation too is unsatisfactory. The contradiction pointed out by him lies not between the inferred fact and the perceived fact, but between the inferred fact and the perceived fact on the one hand and a mere supposition, viz., presence elsewhere, on the other. As a matter of fact, Caitra's absence everywhere else is a deduction from 'a finite thing existing in one place cannot exist in other places', as the major premise and 'Caitra is a finite thing existing in this place' as the minor premise. It follows not from any opposition between these two, as it should have been if it were a case of *arthāpatti*, but from a cooperation between them, as is the case in *anumāna*. There is one important difference between the explanations offered by Sucaritamiśra and Pārthasārathi. According to the former the relation between existence in one place and non-existence in all other places is given by *arthāpatti*, while according to the latter it is a generalization from the experience of one's own body which, everyone knows, is not in other places when it is in one place.

31. KK on ibid.
32. NR on ibid.

As a matter of fact, this is not a generalization from experiene but is a necessary implication of the notion of finitude. That a finite thing cannot exist in more than one place at a time is a verbal or analytic proposition, i.e., the predicate here is a part of the connotation of the subject. To say that a thing is finite is to mean that it occupies a limited portion of space and that when it is occupying one limited portion of space it cannot occupy other portions, because a portion of space cannot be identical with the whole of it. Thus the universal proposition 'no finite thing can exist in different places at the same time' is not an empirical generalization as Pārthasārathi thinks.

That it is a case of *arthāpatti* is not true, because, according to the definition, there should be some inexplicability in a well ascertained fact, while there is no inexplicability in the perceived fact of the presence of a person in one place, and this has been admitted by Sucaritamiśra also. The fact becomes inexplicable only when Caitra, who is a finite being, is supposed to be present simultaneously in other places also. But this sort of inexplicability is different from the one which leads to *arthāpatti*, e.g., the inexplicability involved in Devadatta's fatness in spite of his fasting during the day. The contradiction in the present case is not real but hypothetical. The assertion that a thing can be present in many places at the same time is inconsistent with the fact that it is finite; therefore, we have to deny it. Thus the said instance is not a case of *arthāpatti*. It is however a case of *arthāpatti* according to an earlier definition which is found in Vātsyāyana's *Bhāṣya* on NS. By *arthāpatti* Vātsyāyana means "apprehending from opposition what is not directly stated in a proposition."[33] From the proposition that a finite thing is present in a particular place at a particular time we apprehend that it is not present in other places at the same time, because the denial of this latter fact is opposed to the notion of finitude. *Arthāpatti* in this sense is implication rather than presumption.

9.5. *Can Anumāna Be Reduced to Arthāpatti?*

Pārthasārathi raises the question whether *anumāna* could be included in *arthāpatti*. Let us consider the case of the inference of

33. वाक्यार्थसम्प्रत्ययेनानभिहितस्यार्थस्य प्रत्यनीकभावाद् ग्रहणमर्थापत्तिः । *Bhāṣya* on NS 2.2.2.

fire on the hill. We know that where there is smoke there is fire and we perceive smoke on the hill. Now if there were no fire on the hill the proposition 'where there is smoke there is fire' would be false or our perception of smoke would be false. This is the element of conflict; and the inference of the presence of fire may be taken as a means of resolving this conflict, in which case the inference is *arthāpatti* only. Pārthasārathi's answer is that though the cognition of fire on the hill arrived at in the aforesaid manner may be *arthāpatti*, yet the cognition that where there is smoke there is fire is not arrived at through *arthāpatti*. The *vyāpti* between smoke and fire is the result of *anumāna* based on the experience of particular instances of smoke and fire. Smoke and fire are seen together in the hearth and this fact does not involve any contradiction if the invariable concomitance between smoke and fire is not recognized. The proposition 'some cases of smoke are cases of fire' is true even though the proposition 'all cases of smoke are cases of fire' be false. Thus there being no contradiction here there is no scope for *arthāpatti*. And as some cases at least of *anumāna* cannot be brought under *arthāpatti*, the two should be admitted to be distinct *pramāṇa*-s. The distinction between the two having been recognized there is no harm if the same cognition arises through *anumāna* or *arthāpatti*. The knowledge of fire on the hill may be arrived at by *anumāna* or *arthāpatti*, yet this does not mean that *anumāna* and *arthāpatti* are not distinct from each other. When the knowledge of fire on the hill arises from the recollection of the *vyāpti* between smoke and fire it is *anumāna*, and when it is preceded by the consciousness of inconsistency it is *arthāpatti*. Thus the processes are different and none can be reduced to the other.[34]

Pārthasārathi's answer, however, is not accepted by the later Bhāṭṭas. It has been shown in the chapter on *anumāna* that Pārthasārathi's view that the knowledge of *vyāpti* is based on *anumāna* is not accepted by others. As a matter of fact, there is no conflict between the knowledge that all cases of smoke are cases of fire and that the hill has smoke. The presence of fire on the hill is inferred from the perception of smoke on it consistently with the knowledge that where there is smoke there is fire.

34. SD, p. 79.

There is no inconsistency here, so that it cannot be a case of *arthāpatti*. Thus the presence of fire on the hill is known through *anumāna*. But when the fire known in this way is not found in the higher regions of the hill its presence in the lower region is presumed to remove the inexplicability of the fact that fire is present though it is not present in the higher regions of the hill.[35]

9.6. *Conclusion*

In the course of our exposition we have also critically examined the various arguments for and against *arthāpatti* and there is no need to repeat the criticisms here. We found the Bhāṭṭa arguments partly confused and wrong. But in spite of this *arthāpatti* may be accepted as a distinct form of knowledge. In inference there is no element of conflict while in *arthāpatti* there is. When the smoke is perceived on the hill there is not felt any conflict between this perception and our previous experiences. We infer the presence of fire in accordance with our past experience of the concomitance of smoke and fire. In inference an unperceived thing is cognized with the help of a *liṅga* consistently with the past knowledge of *vyāpti*. In presumption, on the other hand, something is assumed to remove the conflict of a known fact with our past experience. Thus the one difference between inference and presumption is that while the former does not start from the consciousness of contradiction the latter does. This is because in the former something usual or familiar is apprehended while in the latter something unusual or strange is apprehended: In the former something is cognized which fits in well with the other known facts, while in the latter something is cognized or not cognized which does not fit in with the other known facts. This is the difference between the two in their starting points. There is a difference in their ends also. In inference the process starts from the cognition of one thing and ends in the cognition of an unknown second thing. But in presumption the process starts from a fact as unexplained and ends in the same fact as explained without stopping at the intermediary which is presumed. In the inference of fire on the hill the process starts from the perception of the smoke and ends in the knowledge of fire. But

35. MM, p. 125.

in the presumption of Devadatta's presence outside the house the process starts from his absence in the house which is unaccounted for and through the presumption of his stay outside ends in the absence in the house as fully accounted for. In inference the beginning is different from the end, while in presumption the beginning and the end co-incide with each other, and the process is not complete until there is a return to the starting point. Thus inference and presumption are fundamentally different processes. However, we can test the validity of the presumption by putting it in a syllogistic form. In the end it should be remarked that presumption is not the same thing as disjunctive syllogism. Some modern writers think that presumption is disjunctive syllogism. This is untenable, because there is no element of contradiction in a disjunctive syllogism. It is, however, easier to give presumption the form of a disjunctive syllogism and then judge its validity by the rules of disjunctive reasoning.

CHAPTER X

NEGATION

We frequently use sentences containing the word 'not'. In logic the distinction of affirmative and negative judgments is well known. A judgment may be true or false. It is said to be true or false according as there is or is not a fact corresponding to it. A fact is a thing or a thing having a property or a thing having a certain relation with some other thing. It is a mode of existence. Now so far as a true affirmative judgment is concerned there is some positive fact corresponding to it. But a true negative judgment creates a problem. It would seem proper to assert that as in the case of a true affirmative judgment so in the case of a true negative judgment also there is some corresponding negative fact. But the term 'negative fact' appears to be self-contradictory. Negation is non-existence. 'There is no book on the table' means the non-existence of a book on the table. But a fact is a form of existence. Thus a negative fact would mean that non-existence is a form of existence. The problem of negation has provoked much thought in recent philosophy, and in view of the solutions so far offered it seems to be a hard nut to crack. The problem may be stated in the following forms: Are there negative facts? If there are, what is the source of our knowledge of them? If there are not, what is the explanation of negative judgments? An affirmative answer to the first question will give an objective view of negation and a negative answer will give a subjective view. Contemporary philosophers are generally inclined to favour the subjective view. Bradley and Bergson are some of the important names. Russell is another. According to Russell the word 'not' can safely be eliminated from language. He says,

> ...the question whether there are negative facts...raise difficulties. These niceties, however, are largely linguistic.[1]

1. *Human Knowledge*, p. 159.

The problem of negation was as alive in ancient India as it is today and in the following pages we will see what solution the Indian philosophers offer.

10.1. *Kumārila's View*[2]

Kumārila holds an objective view of negation. Negative facts are classified into four groups, viz., (1) prior negation (*prāgabhāva*), (2) posterior negation (*pradhvaṃsābhāva*), (3) mutual negation (*anyonyābhāva*) and (4) absolute negation (*atyantābhāva*). The negation of an effect, e.g., curds, in its cause, viz., milk, prior to its birth is an instance of prior negation. The child born in 1955 did not exist in 1954. The marks of ink on this paper were absent some moments ago. These are negative facts of the first kind. The negation of a cause in its effect after the production of the latter is an instance of posterior negation. The non-existence of a thing after its destruction is a negative fact. The non-existence of a man after his death is a fact of the second kind. A cow is not a horse and a horse is not a cow. The paper which is blue in colour is not at the same time green, and another which is green is not blue. These are cases of mutual negation. The non-existence of a sky-flower, the absence of horns on a donkey's skull etc. are instances of absolute negation.

We frequently have such negative judgments as 'the soul does not have a shape', 'there is no pot on the ground' etc., and they are found to be valid. This is a sufficient ground for the reality of negation. If there were no negative facts corresponding to our valid negative judgments, the latter would always be false. The falsity of a judgment implies the truth of its contradictory. If negative facts are not recognized, the contradictories of 'there is no milk in curds', 'a cow is not a horse', 'the soul has no form' etc., viz., 'there is milk in the curds', 'a cow is a horse', 'the soul has form' and so on would be true. To avoid such an absurdity we are forced to recognize negative facts. Our discrimination between cause and effect and the differences among things are grounded on the reality of negation. There are four varieties of negation. If negation were unreal it could not have varieties. A sky-flower which is an unreal thing can have no varieties.

2. SV, *Abhāva*.

The knowledge of a negative fact arises in the form of a negative judgment. When there is no jar before me, I judge that 'there is no jar'. This judgment is as primary as the judgment that I make when there is a jar before me. Affirmative and negative judgments are equally primary psychologically as well as logically. I am not conscious of any other judgment from which the negative judgment 'there is no jar' is derived, nor does this judgment stand in need of premises from which it can follow as a conclusion. A thing has a double form, one positive and the other negative. A jar is a jar because it is a jar, and because it is not a cloth or some other thing. It is positive in its own form and negative in the form of other things. Both the positive and the negative forms of it constitute its being and hence they are equally fundamental. Therefore, both the affirmative and negative judgments, which represent the positive and negative aspects of a thing respectively, are equally fundamental. Though a thing possesses a positive as well as a negative form, yet sometimes it reveals one form to our consciousness and sometimes the other. Sometimes we judge that a particular thing is blue and sometimes that it is not green. What determines our judgment is largely our interest at the moment. The moment when we are interested in the positive aspect of a thing that aspect is revealed to us and the negative aspect in which we are not interested remains concealed. Some people hold that a negative judgment presupposes an affirmative one, while an affirmative judgment does not presuppose a negative one. When, for instance, we judge that a thing is not blue our judgment implicitly refers to the affirmative judgment that the thing is green, but when we judge that the thing is green there is no implicit reference to its not being blue. On this ground it is concluded that affirmative judgments are primary and negative ones derivative. It is also said that the positive form of a thing constitutes its being and the negative form is super-imposed on it by thought. But this is wrong. When we say 'this is the same thing', it is implied that it is not some other thing. And when we say 'it is not that thing', it is implied that it is something else. Position and negation are thus complementary to each other. If we describe a thing in terms of what it is our description would not be complete until we describe it in terms of what it is not. Thus the function of the word 'not' is obviously very important and it cannot be eliminated.

Now what is the *pramāṇa* involved in our knowledge of negative facts? The *pramāṇa*, according to Kumārila, is non-apprehension (*anupalabdhi*) and it is a distinct means of cognition. The source of our negative judgments is neither perception nor syllogistic inference. Perception, inference etc. are the means of knowing the positive aspect of things. In perception the object is some positive entity. The sense-organs and *manas* act in some positive way and there is a corresponding modal change in the soul. But when the object concerned is negative, e.g., the absence of a jar on the ground, there is no sense-activity and no corresponding modification of the soul. Whatever sense-activity or modification of the soul there may be, it pertains not to the absent object but to the object that is present instead of the former. Absence of knowledge is thus the means of the knowledge of absence. In knowledge there is a subjective activity corresponding to some objective fact. When the objective fact is positive, the corresponding subjective activity also is positive, and it takes the form of a positive *pramāṇa*, e.g., perception, inference etc. When the objective fact is negative, the corresponding subjective activity in a similar way should be negative. The means of knowing negative facts cannot be perception or inference which are positive means. In perception there is a contact of a sense-organ with an appropriate object. Contact is possible only between two existing things. The eye of the perceiver, and the jar on the ground both are existing things and from the eye-jar contact the perception of the jar arises. But when the jar does not exist on the ground, how can there be any sense-contact? Hence the knowledge of the absence of the jar cannot be perceptual. There is no doubt that we make the judgment 'there is no jar on the ground' validly with our eyes open and fixed on the spot where the jar would he expected. But here the eye-functioning pertains to the ground which is a positive entity. There can be no pure negation. Negation is always of some positive entity in some positive locus. So far as the positive locus of the jar is concerned, the cognition is perceptual and so far as the counter-correlate of negation, viz., the jar, is concerned the knowledge is memory, but the negation itself is known neither through perception nor through memory but purely through the *manas*.[3]

Here we should guard against some possible misinterpretations of Kumārila's view. It is obvious that the words 'purely through the *manas*' cannot mean that the negative judgment is an ideal or intellectual construction, since, otherwise, negation would be deprived of its objective character. The possibility of interpreting the words as meaning that negation is mentally perceived also is ruled out, since only the soul and its qualities such as pleasure, pain etc. are the objects of mental perception. Mental perception is what is generally called introspection. But negation which is supposed to be an objective fact cannot be an object of introspection. The negation of the jar on the ground is a fact belonging to the outside world. How can it be known through introspection? Moreover, when Kumārila says that non-apprehension is different from perception, it is clear that it is different from introspection also which is a form of perception. Hence the remark made by Dr. P. T. Raju, viz.,

> The Mīmāṃsakas, for example, Kumārila, hold that it (negation) is not perceived by our senses but by our mind, though it is real. It is an object of *Mānasapratyakṣa*, not of *indriya-pratyakṣa*.[4]

is not correct.

The absence of sense-functioning in the cognition of negation is proved by the following example. A man goes out in the morning. In the evening somebody asks him if Caitra was in his house in the morning, and he answers that Caitra was not there. Now there is no sense-functioning in this case. And hence it cannot be a case of perception but is a case of non-apprehension. Sucaritamiśra points out that it is not a case of memory even. It cannot be a case of the memory of an earlier perception. In the morning when the man was in his house, the idea of Caitra did not occur to him and so he could not be aware of the absence of Caitra at that time. He becomes aware of Caitra's absence in the evening only. So it cannot be said that he perceived Caitra's absence in the morning and remembers it in the evening.

3. गृहीत्वा वस्तुसद्भावं स्मृत्वा च प्रतियोगिनम् ।
मानसं नास्तिताज्ञानं जायतेऽक्षानपेक्षया ॥ SV, *Abhāva*, 27.
4. *Proceedings of the Indian Philosophical Congress*, 1939, p. 64.

The cognition of negation is not a result of syllogistic reasoning even, since, unlike the latter, it arises immediately without being preceded by the cognition of a middle term and the memory of a *vyāpti*. The belief in the absence of a jar on the ground does not seem to derive its strength from any other belief. In the syllogistic process there must be some middle term. What can in the present case serve as the middle term? Not the jar, since it is not present at the time. The cognition of the absence of the jar arises when its presence is not cognized. But if the jar itself be present to serve as the middle term, there can be no cognition of its absence. The ground too, which is perceived, cannot serve as the middle term, since it is not invariably related to the absence of the jar. The present locus of the absence of something is at times found to be associated with the presence of that thing. Moreover, sometimes we cognize the absence of a thing in a place where we never previously cognized it. Let, for argument's sake, it be admitted that a *vyāpti* between a locus and absence is possible. Now a *vyāpti* between two terms requires a frequent past experience of the terms related, which must be independent of the knowledge of the *vyāpti*. This shows that our first experience of absence cannot be derived through syllogistic reasoning. It may be said that the non-perception of the jar can serve as the middle term: The jar is absent, because it is not perceived. But here, it may be asked, what exactly is the middle term? Is it absence of perception in general or the absence of the perception of the jar in particular? It cannot be the former, since absence of any perception is not concomitant with absence of the jar. It cannot be the latter for the following reasons. The middle term should be the property of the minor term. But if the ground be the minor term, non-perception cannot be related to it, since it is actually perceived. Let, then, the jar itself be the minor term to which non-perception is related. But the jar is not the probandum, i.e., the object to be known through inference. The probandum is always the minor term qualified by the major, so that in the present case it would be the existing jar qualified by some property, while the jar is actually non-existent. The non-perception is related to the non-existence of the jar, but the latter cannot be the minor term, because it is not known, and if it is already known then the inferential process becomes superfluous. The non-perception of the jar cannot be the middle term for the following reason too. A thing which is unknown cannot serve as the middle term. So the non-perception of the jar must be known before it can serve as the middle term. But, since, it too is of the nature of negation and negation, by hypothesis, is known through non-perception as the middle term, so we need another non-perception to know it. The process, however, involves the fallacy of infinite regress. Hence the cognition of negation cannot be syllogistic. Non-perception immediately results in the cognition of negation without the intervention of any other cognition. Therefore, the former is the *pramāṇa* or means of the latter and is different from perception and syllogistic inference. Non-perception has some affinity with perception in two respects, viz., that it is immediate like the latter and that it gives the knowledge of non-existence without itself being known[5] just as sense-activity gives the knowledge of existence without itself being known.

10.2. *Prabhākara's View*[6]

Prabhākara's view is opposed to Kumārila's. He does not recognize negation as a separate category and non-apprehension as a separate *pramāṇa*. Non-existence is nothing over and above existence, and non-perception is nothing over and above perception. Is then a negative judgment, such as 'there is no jar on the ground', invalid? No, it is valid, but there is no reality corresponding to the word 'no'. Reality is always positive, and a negative judgment is a subjective mode of apprehending it. A negative judgment is valid, not because a negative fact corresponds to it, but because it refers indirectly to a positive fact. When we say 'there is no jar on the ground', it does not imply that we cognize non-existence in the same manner as we cognize existence. 'There is a jar' refers to the existence of the jar as a positive fact. But 'there is no jar' refers to the subjective fact that we do not perceive the jar. The knowledge of 'no jar' is not a positive knowledge of a negative entity, but is a negative knowledge of a positive entity and the negative knowledge too is not a mode of

5. N.B. This is implied in Kumārila's criticism of the view that negation is known inferentially.

6. PP, pp. 120-24.

knowledge different from positive knowledge. Non-perception of a jar means perception of the bare ground together with the idea of the jar which could have been perceived if it were present there. A positive entity is perceived in two ways. It is perceived sometimes with another positive entity and sometimes by itself. We perceive the ground sometimes with a jar and sometimes without it. The perception of a positive entity by itself is of two kinds according as the other entity is imperceptible or perceptible. When two things are equally perceptible but we perceive one of them alone, then there arises a valid negative judgment. The ground and the jar are equally perceptible while the ground alone is perceived. This gives rise to the judgment 'there is no jar on the ground.' Here an objection may be raised. We perceive two things, e.g., the jar and the ground, and later on we perceive the ground alone. Now, what is the cause of this difference if not the removal or destruction of the jar? If it is the latter then Prabhākara must admit the reality of negation, since it is what is known as *pradhvaṃsābhāva* or posterior negation. Prabhākara's answer to this objection is that the cause in question is the presence of the jar elsewhere or the two halves or the pieces into which the jar is reduced in case it is destroyed, and these are positive facts, so that there is no need of admitting posterior negation. Thus the cognition 'there is no jar on the ground' is nothing but the cognition of the ground alone in terms of a second thing, viz., the jar which is elsewhere, and this cognition does not stand in need of another *pramāṇa*, because it is self-luminous (*svaprakāśa*).

The Bhāṭṭa view that non-perception gives rise to the knowledge of negation without itself being known is criticized as follows. There is non-perception when a man is in deep sleep, but there is no knowledge of absence. This shows that the knowledge of absence arises only when non-perception itself is known. We do not perceive the jar on the ground and later on, when someone brings it there, we perceive it. Now, if non-perception by its mere existence were the ground of the knowledge of absence there could be no knowledge of the previous absence of the jar now, since it has come to an end by the present perception of the jar. Therefore, it must be admitted that though the previous non-perception has come to an end, yet by remembering it we come to know the previous non-existence of the jar. Thus just as an eye taken off from its socket cannot give the knowledge of presence, so an unknown non-perception cannot give the knowledge of absence. From this what follows is this. To know the absence of a thing we have to know the absence of the corresponding perception, but as this latter too is absence it can be known only by another non-perception which is to be known by a third one and so on ad infinitum. To avoid this infinite regress we should admit that the absence of a thing is nothing except the non-perception of it and the non-perception is nothing except the perception of something else in disguise and that this latter is self-luminous. This satisfactorily explains the existence of negative propositions in language.

10.3. *The Buddhist View*

The Buddhist view of negation is akin to Prabhākara's. The so-called negation is never experienced independently. Negation is always experienced as pertaining to a particular time, a particular place and a particular object which is the counter-correlate of negation, as, in the case of the negation of a jar in this room at this time. Now, there would be no dispute about the reality of negation if it were really related to the particular time, place etc. But as a matter of fact no relation is possible. The relation of conjunction (*saṃyoga*) subsists between two substances, while negation is not a substance. There can be no *samavāya* or inherence, since otherwise the place itself would be non-existent. There can be no relation between negation and its counter-correlate, say, jar, because they are not simultaneous. When there is a jar there is no negation of it. How can there be any relation unless the terms are present at the same time? It may be said that there is the relation of opposition or incompatibility. But what is the meaning of opposition? The negation of jar would be opposed to the jar if it existed prior to the jar and then behaved in a way to drive away the jar. But how can negation behave in any way? Negation is no real entity. An entity possesses a specific nature of its own by virtue of which it differs from other entities; but we do not find any specific nature of negation which may differentiate it from other entities. So negation is featureless (*niḥsvabhāva*) and our linguistic usage, viz., 'it is not so and so' is thus to be somehow explained in terms of position.[7]

When we say 'there is no jar' what we mean is that we do not see the jar, not that we see the negation of the jar. The objective fact which justifies the use of these words is positive. The assertion 'there is no jar' is preceded by an inferential process of which it is the conclusion. Non-apprehension is the reason (*liṅga*) in this process: A thing, which is capable of being apprehended but is not apprehended in the expected place, is non-existent there; the jar which is capable of being apprehended is not apprehended on the ground; therefore, it does not exist there. The reason here is based on identity of nature (*svabhāvahetu*). Non-apprehension is identical with non-existence. And non-apprehension or absence of apprehension is not something different from apprehension. Non-apprehension of a thing is the same as the apprehension of only one of the two things which could have been perceived together. This apprehension of one thing is self-luminous, so that there can be no infinite regress; and it arises from the sense-organs alone. The inference may be stated in the following way as well: The existence of a perceptible thing is invariably accompanied by its perception; the jar which is a perceptible thing is not perceived; therefore, it does not exist.[8]

From the above account it appears that the Buddhist position is self-contradictory. It is said that the negative judgment 'there is no jar' is a perceptual judgment and at the same time that it is a deduction. Dharmottara tries to avoid the inconsistency as follows:

> ...the negative judgment immediately following on the perception of the bare place is a perceptual judgment....However, (the proper function of negation consists in the following step). Objects might not be perceived, but this only gives rise to. doubt (the feeling arises as to which of them might be present) So long as this doubt has not been removed, negation has no practical importance (it cannot guide our purposive actions).

7. NM, pp 54-55 and KK on SV, *Abhāva*, 8-10.
8. NR on SV, *Abhāva*, 38.

(Imagination then steps in and) it is thus that negation, (as a negative deduction) gives practical significance to the idea of a non-Ens. Since the object which I imagine at present is not really perceived, just therefore do I judge that 'it is not there'. Consequently this negation of an imagined presence (is an inference which) gives life to the ready concept of a non-Ens, it does not merely create this concept itself. Thus it is that (the author maintains that) the negative judgment receives its practical significance (through an inference) from challenged imagination, although it is really produced by sense-perception and only applied in life (through the deductive sense-perception whose logical reason consists in the fact of) a negative experience. A negative inference, therefore, guides our steps when we apply in life the idea of a non-Ens.[9]

10.4. *The Nyāya View*[10]

As regards negative facts the Nyāya view is one with the Bhāṭṭa view. But the Nyāya differs so far as it holds that such facts are known primarily not by a distinct *pramāṇa* but by perception. The cognition 'there is no jar on the ground' is a unitary cognition like the cognition 'there is curd in the bowl.' How, then, can there be such distinction as the ground is cognized through the senses while the negation of the jar through a different means? The ground as well as the negation of the jar are cognized when the eyes function. I open my eyes and perceive them. I close my eyes and cease to perceive them. In the cognition of fire on a distant hill, the hill is perceived but not the fire which is inferred. But it is a different case because between the perception of the smoky hill and the inference of fire there is an intermediate cognition, viz., the memory of *vyāpti*. In the present case, however, both the ground and the negation of the jar on it are equally immediately cognized.

It has been said that negation is devoid of shape and colour, and since only things with shape and colour can be the objects of visual perception, it cannot be perceived through the eyes. Again it has been said that the eyes and other sease-organs can

9. NBT in Stcherbatsky's *Buddhist Logic*, Vol. II, p. 85.
10. NM, pp. 51-54.

perceive existent things only with which they can have a contact and that non-existence, in whose case no contact is possible, cannot be perceived. But this is wrong. A thing is said to be perceived by the eyes not because it has colour and shape but becauge its cognition is born of the activity of the visual sense. The atoms possess shape and colour, yet they are not perceived through vision. Contact too is not essential, since ether is in contact with the eyes, yet it is not perceived. It may be said that in case contact is supposed to be inessential in vision we could perceive even such things as are lying on the other side of the globe. To this the answer is that the condition that we can perceive only those things which are in contact with the senses has relevance in the case of existing things only, not in that of non-existence. Or, there is sense-contact in the case of non-existence too, which is termed *saṃyuktaviśeṣaṇatā*. Negation is a qualification of some positive locus. The negation of the jar is adjectival to its locus, viz., the ground. The eye has contact with the negation of the jar through its conjunction with the ground.

Kumārila cites an instance in favour of the non-perceptibility of negation, viz., that of the cognition arising in the mind of a man in the evening in the form 'Caitra was not in the house in the morning', who was ignorant of this fact till he was questioned about Caitra's existence in the morning. Jayanta says that this is a case of the memory of a previously perceived fact. The man perceived in a general way (*mecakabuddhyā*) the absence in the morning of everything that was not in the house and now in the evening he is reminded of a specific fact, viz., Caitra's absence because of the specific question put to him in the form: 'Was Caitra in the house in the morning'? Though he had perceived the absence of all the absent things, yet he could not be expected to remember all, since the revival of a latent impression depends on some appropriate stimulus which in the present case is a specific one in the form of the question. There is no rule that things perceived simultaneously should always be remembered simultaneously, because we find that it is sometimes done in an order of succession. The cognition of negation in a general way is recognized by Kumārila too when he says that the judgment 'this is that thing alone' involves the cognition that 'this is not anything else' meaning 'this is not X', 'this is not Y' etc.

Kumārila argues that a thing is cognized by a *pramāṇa* similar to it, i.e., that all positive facts are cognized by such positive means as perception etc. and all negative facts are cognized by a negative means, viz., non-apprehension. This, however, is wrong. We cognize negative facts sometimes by perception, sometimes by inference, and sometimes by testimony. The cognition of the absence of rain on perceiving dry ground is inferential. The fact that Aśoka did not fight any war after the massacre of Kaliṅga is known from history.

10.5. *Tha Vaiśeṣika View*[11]

Although the Vaiśeṣika view has not been directly criticized by the followers of Kumārila, yet the account given by Śrīdhara appears to have exercised considerable influence on the Bhāṭṭa view of negation as developed by Pārthasārathi. One of the important contributions of Pārthasārathi is that he includes in the *pramāṇa* known as *abhāva* not only non-perception of the perceptible but also non-recollection of that which is capable of being recollected. The difficulty which this view aims to solve is the case cited by Kumārila in which a man who did not note the fact of Caitra's absence in the house when he himself was in the house is questioned about the said absence when he is out and then comes to cognize the fact. Kumārila himself does not analyse the case fully and his earlier commentators, viz., Umbeka and Sucaritamiśra do not do full justice to it. Now Śrīdhara has analysed the case more fully and so does Pārthasārathi. But though Pārthasārathi does not seem to take note of Śrīdhara's view that the cognition of negation in the said case is inference from the non-recollection of that which is capable of being recollected, it is very likely that the latter precedes the former. If this be a fact, then Śrīdhara's influence on Pārthasārathi is quite evident. However, this cannot be proved conclusively, because there occurs a remark in Śrīdhara's work[12] to the effect that those who hold that *smṛtyabhāva* too is *abhāvapramāṇa* contradict the *Bhāṣya* as well as the *Vārtika*. Perhaps this remark refers to Sucaritamiśra who in his commentary on SV, *Abhāva*,

11. NK, pp. 225-28.
12. Ibid., p. 228.

1 says that *smṛtyabhāva* is also a form of *anupalabdhi*. Anyway, Śrīdhara's account is very relevant in the present context and so we give it below.

Negation is real but is not cognized by a distinct means. It is rather cognized by means of inference. One who holds that *abhāva* is cognized by *anupalabdhi* has to recognize the fact that it is not mere *anupalabdhi* that gives the knowledge of negation but is *yogyānupalabdhi*. There is, however, no intrinsic difference between *anupalabdhi* as such and *yogyānupalabdhi*. Therefore, *anupalabdhi* does not produce the knowledge of negation by its own inherent power like a sense-organ. It is *yogyānupalabdhi* which produces such knowledge when it arises in the mind of one who is well aware of the fact that *ayogyānupalabdhi* does not give a correct knowledge of negation while *yogyānupalabdhi* invariably does so. Thus non-perception becomes the reason (*liṅga*) and the knowledge of negation becomes syllogistic in character. The case of *anupalabdhi* cited by Kumārila and referred to above is analysed thus: When the man is asked now whether Caitra was in the house in the morning or not, does he, it may be asked, cognize the past absence of Caitra by the past *anupalabdhi* or the present absence by the present *anupalabdhi*? The latter is not true, because the present *anupalabdhi* is not *yogyānupalabdhi*, for Caitra might have come to the house though he cannot be seen. As regards the first alternative, it can be said that though it can produce the knowledge of Caitra's past absence, yet the state of the man having changed now the past *anupalabdhi* has ceased to be. Thus as an absent *anupalabdhi* cannot produce the knowledge of negation, this latter remains unexplained. It cannot be explained as a case of memory, and Sucaritamiśra[13] has rightly ruled out this possibility. Umbeka[14] says that the past absence of Caitra is cognized through the memory of the past non-apprehension which is quite inconsistent with Kumārila's position. Śrīdhara anticipates one more explanation: A change in the mental state of the man does not destroy his past non-apprehension of Caitra. It can be destroyed only when Caitra is apprehended again. Since the man is outside the house, though

13. KK on SV, *Abhāva*, 28.
14. TT on ibid.

Caitra may be present in the house, therefore his past non-apprehension whose object is the past absence of Caitra still persists and produces in his mind the cognition of Caitra's past absence. Śrīdhara provisionally accepts this explanation. But how, he asks, will the Bhāṭṭa explain the following case? Suppose there is no jar in the room. However, I am not cognisant of the fact at this time because the counter-correlate, jar, does not occur in my thought. A little later the servant brings the jar and then I cognize that it was not in the room previously. This case cannot be explained in the above way, for the past non-apprehension of the jar comes to an end when the jar is apprehended. The Bhāṭṭa says that the past non-apprehension does not come to an end, because the present apprehension brings an end to the present non-apprehension only. But this is entirely wrong. Non-apprehension of the jar means the prior negation of the apprehension of the jar and this comes to an end as soon as the jar is apprehended. What then is the proper explanation?

Śrīdhara says that in these cases too there is involved a syllogistic process. When a thing is capable of being remembered but is not remembered in spite of the desire to remember while its locus is actually remembered, then it must have been absent there. Caitra who is capable of being remembered in the house is not remembered though there is a desire to remember him. Therefore, he must have been absent from the house. If Caitra were in the house he could have been apprehended there. The aggregate of conditions giving rise to the apprehension of Caitra is the same as the aggregate of those giving rise to the apprehension of the house. Now too the aggregate of conditions giving rise to the memory of Caitra if he were apprehended in the house previously is the same as that of the conditions giving rise to the memory of the house. But in spite of this it is the house alone which is remembered now while Caitra is not remembered. From this the conclusion follows that Caitra was absent from the house. The knowledge of negation thus arises syllogistically sometimes from the non-apprehension of the apprehensible and sometimes from the non-recollection of that which is capable of being recollected.

10.6. *The Bhāṭṭa View in its Revised Form*

Kumārila's followers have taken due note of the relevant criticisms offered by the rival schools. They have offered criticisms and counter-criticisms and have developed a highly consistent theory of negation. The following account is based mainly on the *Śāstradīpikā*[15] of Pārthasārathi.

It was said that Prabhākara does not accept the reality of negation and that non-apprehension according to him is not a distinct *pramāṇa.* Now, that we have experiences like 'there is no pot on the ground' is an indubitable fact. How is such an experience to be explained? What is the basis (*ālambana*) of this experience? If it be said that the ground is the basis, then even when the pot is present we should have such an experience, i.e., the ground being there we should be justified in making the assertion that 'there is no pot' even when it is there. Moreover, we also have experiences like 'a cow is not a horse', 'colour is not taste' etc. What is the basis of the cognition that a cow is not a horse? It cannot be cow, because a cow is cognized without any reference to the horse while the cognition 'a cow is not a horse' has reference to the horse. If it be said that the difference from a horse that exists in the cow is the basis, then, what, it may be asked, is this difference? If difference means mutual negation, then negation is implicitly recognized to be real. If difference means a special quality, separateness (*pṛthaktva*), then, since a quality can exist in a substance only, the cognition of difference between two qualities like 'colour is not taste' cannot be accounted for. Thus Prabhākara's theory fails when distinction among qualities is cognized, because a quality cannot inhere in another quality.

Again, because non-apprehension is rejected and it is said that there is no cognition like 'the pot is not here' as different from the cognition of the ground, so the cognition of the ground also should be rejected, as the two cognitions are supposed to be identical. But the rejection of the positive cognition cannot be Prabhākara's intention. Therefore, negative cognition, i.e., non-apprehension, in the form of a subjective reality has to be accepted.

15. SD, pp. 83-87.

It may again be asked as to what is the objective basis of the verbal usage like 'the pot is not on the ground'. The basis according to Prabhākara is the cognition of the bare ground (*bhūtala-mātra*). If it is so, then when there is a cloth on the ground there should not be any such usage, because then the ground is not apprehended as bare ground. If it be said that the apprehension of the ground apart from the pot is the basis, then what is this being 'apart from the pot'? If it is absence of conjunction with the pot (*ghaṭasaṃyogābhāva*), then this is a tacit recognition of the reality of negation. As a matter of fact, the cognition of the bare form of the ground arises when there is no cognition of the pot and its non-existence. Thus the apprehension of the bare ground means the apprehension of the ground minus the apprehension of the pot and its non-existence. Therefore, if apprehension of the bare ground is accepted to be the basis of the above usage, then non-apprehension which is implied in the apprehension of bareness has to be accepted.

Prabhākara tries to defend his position by saying that the basis of such usage is the apprehension of a place when the object, viz., the pot, exists in a different place. But if this be so, then the cowness which exists in a black cow must be apprehended as non-existing when a white cow is apprehended, or a pole resting on two pillars must be apprehended as non-existing on one pillar when it exists on the other. Therefore, existence in a different locality cannot be the basis of the said usage. As a matter of fact, existence in a different place is known after the non-existence in one place is known.

Finally Prabhākara says that the basis of the usage in question is the perception of the ground while the pot is remembered. But this is not a proper explanation, because we say 'the pot is not there' even when the pot is perceived in the proximity. Even when the pot is brought and kept where it was not we make an assertion about the past non-existence of the pot there.

Next we shall see what the Bhāṭṭa explanation of the cognition of past non-existence is. But before we come to it we should clearly understand three points in the Bhāṭṭa theory, viz., that non-apprehension is the cause of the knowledge of negation by its mere existence (*sattayā*); that *yogyatā* or capability of being perceived contributes to such knowledge by its being known (*jñātatayā*); and that non-recollection (*smaraṇābhāva*) also is a means of knowing negation.

10.6.1. *Mere Existence of Anupalabdhi Enough*

Non-apprehension of the apprehensible (*yogyānupalabdhi*) is the means of knowing negation. It has two elements, viz., absence of apprehension and the fitness of the counter-correlate of being perceived. Now, in order to know negation the first element does not stand in need of being known. Here lies the difference between non-apprehension and inference. In inference the cause of knowledge is some probans and an invariable relation between the probans and the probandum, and both of them should be known before the appearance of the knowledge of the probandum. Smoke produces the knowledge of fire not by its mere existence but by its being known. But the non-apprehension of a pot produces the knowledge of negation of the pot by its mere existence. It is not that to have this knowledge we must also be aware of the non-apprehension, for, otherwise there shall be infinite regress as has been explained earlier.

10.6.2. *Knowledge of Yogyatā Essential*

But it may be objected that sometimes there is non-apprehension but no knowledge of negation and sometimes there is no non-apprehension yet the knowledge of negation does appear. A person whose ring has been lost explores the whole of a dark room in which the ring is suspected with his hands and actually has non-apprehension of what could have been apprehended if it was there. But if he is not sure that he has explored the whole room he cannot have a definite knowledge of the absence of the ring. There may be a second man facing the same problem. He explores the room but not completely. But because he is sure that he has explored the whole room, so he knows definitely that the ring is not there. In this case there is no non-apprehension in the proper sense, yet the knowledge of negation appears.

This objection is met as follows. The absence of the knowledge of negation even when there is non-apprehension and the presence of the knowledge of negation even when there is no non-apprehension are due to the ignorance of *yogyatā* or fitness.

For a valid non-apprehension the knowledge of *yogyatā* is essential; mere existence of *yogyatā* is not enough. It is necessary to know that all the conditions in which the apprehension of the object, if it actually existed there, normally takes place, have been fulfilled. In other words *yogyatā* has to be known before a vaild knowledge can arise through non-apprehension. When *yogyatā* is not known absence cannot be ascertained even though there be absence, or it may be falsely ascertained when actually there is no absence. Therefore, for a valid knowledge of negation *anupalabdhi* must be there and *yogyatā* must be actually known.

Śālikanātha, a disciple of Prabhākara, has argued that *anupalabdhi* which merely exists but is not known cannot give the knowledge of negation. For instance, in deep sleep there is *anupalabdhi* but no knowledge of negation. But this is wrong. Negation is always cognized in some positive locus. In deep sleep there is no knowledge of anything. Hence, because there is no knowledge of a positive locus, where could one know negation? Moreover, a person in deep sleep lacks the knowledge of negation not because he does not at the time know his non-apprehension but because he is ignorant of the *yogyatā*, that is to say, he lacks the capacity of knowing the fitness of a thing to be perceived. Śālikanātha cites in favour of his view another example, viz., one in which a man cognizes the previous absence of a jar only when it is brought before him. But this is not a case of non-apprehension of a thing fit to be perceived. It is rather a case of the non-recollection of a thing fit to be recollected, which we take up now.[16]

10.6.3. *Non-recollection*

The knowledge of negation arises when there is absence of a positive means of knowledge. And it also arises when a thing is not remembered though it is fit to be remembered. If recollective cognition of a thing does not appear though it could have appeared in case the thing were present, then we know that the thing was absent. Non-recollection is ultimately derived from non-apprehension. Perception is the cause and later recollection is its effect. Similarly non-perception is the cause

16. KK on SV, *Abhāva*, 1.

and non-recollection its effect. An effect is nothing but the cause in a different guise. So non-recollection is but non-apprehension in a different guise.

Now we come to the Bhāṭṭa explanation of the knowledge of past negation. When the knowledge of the past absence of a pot arises there is no *yogyatā* in the sense that the relation of the pot to the past time is not fit to be perceived at present. Therefore, it cannot be the result of the present non-apprehension. Nor is there any recollection of the past absence of the pot, because at the time of the absence of the pot the absence was not at all cognized and that which is not cognized cannot be remembered. The knowledge of the past absence really arises by means of the non-recollection of what is fit to be recollected. If the pot which is perceived now were present yesterday also, then it would have surely been perceived by me just as I perceived the place. And if it were perceived it could be remembered now. But I do not remember it. Therefore, it was absent yesterday.

Jayanta says that this is a case of memory. In the past the absence was perceived in a general way and now it is remembered in a specific way, i.e., in the past the ground was perceived as devoid of everything other than what was actually present there, and now it is remembered that it was devoid of the pot. But how can there be a specific memory of a general experience? Memory is based on the revival of an impression left by an experience. The impression strictly corresponds to the experience and memory strictly corresponds to the impression. Therefore, we can remember only a general thing or a specific thing according as the original experience was general or specific. A general experience is vague and undefined. How can it produce a specific and definite memory. It sometimes happens that though the original experience was definite, yet when the impression weakens with the lapse of time the memory becomes indefinite. Thus a definite experience may produce an indefinite memory, but an indefinite experience cannot produce a definite memory.[17]

Non-apprehension is not the same thing as perception. It is true that the absence of a pot on the ground is seen not by blind persons, nor by one whose eyes are closed. But this fact

17. KK on SV *Abhāva*, 28.

does not prove that negation is perceived by the eyes. The eyes function only in the cognition of the ground. Moreover, negation is known not merely by non-apprehension but by non-apprehension of a thing fit to be apprehended. A thing is fit to be apprehended when all the conditions, subjective and objective, such as light, eye etc., which are essential for a normal perception of the thing, are present but the thing is absent. I keep my eyes open while cognizing the absence of the jar simply to ascertain the fitness of the jar to be perceived. By so doing I fulfil the conditions of perceptibility. The opening of the eyes is not related to the cognition of absence but to the expected presence of the jar. Jayanta has said that the different elements of the contents of a unitary cognition should as a rule be apprehended by the same *pramāṇa.* But this is wrong. In recognition such as 'this is the man whom I saw yesterday' the element 'this' is perceived but the element 'the man whom I saw yesterday' is remembered. It is a unitary cognition, yet it is the combination of a sensory element and a memory element. Thus it is quite reasonable to say that the ground is cognized by perception and the absence of the jar by non-apprehension. Jayanta has again said that the absence of the jar is a qualification and the ground is the qualified object and that it is impossible that the qualified object should be perceived while the qualification is not perceived. This too is wrong. There can be no relation of qualification and qualified unless there be conjunction or inherence or some kind of interaction between two things. Between the absence and the ground there is none of these as the Buddhist has rightly pointed out. So the former cannot be a qualification of the latter. Even if there be the relation of qualification and the qualified it is not true to say that in order to perceive the qualified object we should necessarily perceive its qualification. The only truth is that in order to know the qualified object we should necessarily know its qualifications. We cannot make the assertion 'this is Dittha' meaning this man has the qualification of being named 'Dittha' unless we know both 'this' and 'Dittha'. But it is not essential that both should be known by the same *pramāṇa*, because in the present case we know 'this' by perception and 'Dittha' by memory. The Naiyāyika says that negation is perceived by the sense-contact named *saṃyukta-viśeṣaṇatā*. But inventing a name does not make an unreal thing real. If it be a real contact, then there is no need of such contacts as *saṃyukta-samavāya* and *samaveta-samavāya* etc. to explain such perceptions as 'the fire is red', 'the sound is loud' etc., because redness is a qualification of fire and loudness a qualification of sound.[18]

The Buddhist view too is not tenable. The usage 'there is no jar' does not mean that we do not perceive the jar. The absence of the jar is an objective fact, while the absence of perception is a subjective fact. How can an objective fact be identical with a subjective fact? 'There is a jar' is not the same thing as 'I perceive a jar'. Similarly 'there is no jar' is not the same thing as 'I do not perceive a jar'. The absence of a jar cannot be identical with my non-perception, because the jar may be present though I do not perceive it. The Buddhist says that absence is inferred from non-perception and that non-perception is self-luminous, the latter assertion being his device to avoid infinite regress. But it has been proved that no cognition is self-luminous. Even if a cognition be self-luminous, non-perception cannot be self-luminous, because it has no content. The Buddhist holds that the cognition 'this is blue' apprehends its own form, viz., blue. But the cognition 'there is no jar' has no form, since 'no jar', according to the Buddhist, is nothing. How can then it apprehend itself when it has no form. The Buddhist says that non-perception of the jar is the reason (*liṅga*) of our knowledge of the absence of the jar and at the same time that non-perception is nothing but the perception of the locus, viz., the ground, and absence of the jar is nothing but the presence of the ground. This would mean that the perception of the ground is the reason of our knowledge of the ground. But in this way we bid good-bye to perception as an independent and the most primary means of knowledge, and inference thus becomes the only genuine means of knowledge. Therefore, the Buddhist view which leads to such an absurd conclusion should be rejected.[19]

18. KK on SV, *Abhāva*, 18, and MM, pp. 132-34.
19. KK on SV, *Abhāva*, 8 & 38.

10.7. *Conclusion*

From the considerations mentioned in the previous section it is quite evident that negation or absence is as primary a fact as position or presence is, and then non-apprehension becomes as distinct and primary as perception. Non-apprehension cannot be reduced to perception or syllogistic reasoning. The Bhāṭṭa criticism of the Nyāya and Buddhist views stands on a firm footing and we need not dwell on it over again. A few words on Śrīdhara's view may be said here. Śrīdhara admits the reality of negation. He also admits the reality of non-apprehension, since, unlike the other thinkers, he does not reduce non-apprehension to perception. Thus his position is practically the same as the Bhāṭṭa position. The main difference between the two positions is that according to the former the movement of thought from non-apprehension to negation is syllogistic, while according to the latter it is non-syllogistic. A minor difference lies in that according to the former the subjective fact of non-apprehension should be known and is actually known through introspection before the knowledge of negation arises, while according to the latter this is not needed. So far as this latter point is concerned introspective evidence is decidedly in favour of the Bhāṭṭa view. As regards the former we can say that just as the movement of thought from perception to the knowledge of a positive fact cannot be regarded to be syllogistic, since otherwise perception would lose its primacy and syllogistic inference would be the only fundamental form of knowing, so the movement of thought from non-apprehension to the knowledge of a negative fact too cannot be regarded as syllogistic. Śrīdhara's argument is that the knowledge of negation is syllogistic, since it is based on an invariable concomitance between non-perception of the perceptible and negation. But this is wrong, because what is based on such a relationship is not our knowledge of negation but the validity of such a knowledge. We can test the validity of a knowledge derived through any means with the help of syllogistic reasoning; but such a process cannot reduce that means of knowledge to syllogistic inference. It is thus plain that the step from non-apprehension to the knowledge of negation does not involve any syllogistic process.

But does it involve the process known as immediate inference? Do we immediately infer negation from non-perception? No, because for it we should be first aware of the premise 'I do not perceive A' and then draw immediately the conclusion 'therefore A is not'. But in fact we are not always self-conscious, though we know the proposition 'A is not'. Therefore, negation is known neither by perception, nor by syllogistic inference, nor by immediate inference.

There, however, remains one more possibility of reducing our knowledge of negation to inference. I see a blue thing and say that it is not red. What is the process here? It may be said that the process is syllogistic: No blue thing is red, this thing is blue, therefore this thing is not red. But then the question arises as to how we know the major premise 'no blue thing is red'. Russell says:

> It might be argued that you know the general proposition 'what is grey is not white', and that from this, together with 'this is grey', you infer 'this is not white'. Or it might be said that you can confront the word 'white' with what you see, and perceive an incompatibility. Either view has difficulties.[20]

Again it may be said that from the proposition 'this is blue' we immediately infer 'this is not red'. Now in immediate inference the conclusion is not based on any empirical generalization but on the *a priori* laws of thought and the *a priori* law in the present case can only be the law of contradiction. But there is no contradiction or logical incompatibility between blue and red. To quote Russell again:

> The incompatibility is not logical. Red and blue are no more logically incompatible than red and round. Nor is the incompatibility a generalization from experience... Some people say the incompatibility is grammatical. I do not deny this, but I am not sure what it means.[21]

All these considerations are sufficient to prove the reasonableness of the Bhāṭṭa view that non-apprehension is an independent *pramāṇa*.

20. *An Enquiry into Meaning and Truth*, p. 81.
21. Ibid., p. 82.

The difference between the ancient Indian and modern treatments of the problem of negation lies mainly in that while the modern philosophers lay more emphasis on the question 'what is negation?', the ancient Indians lay more emphasis on the question 'how is negation known?' The questions 'what is negation?' and 'in what sense is it real?' are treated by the Bhāṭṭa and Naiyāyika rather superficially. They seem to accept negative facts at their face-value. Prabhākara's treatment seems to be more profound and is much similar to the modern treatment. Without going into the details it may be remarked here that the subjective view of negation seems to prevail in modern philosophy. Bradley remarks,

> We might say that, as such, and in its own character, it (negative judgment) is simply subjective: it does not hold good outside my thinking. The reality repels the suggested alteration; but the suggestion is not any movement of the fact, nor in fact does the given subject maintain itself against the actual attack of a discrepant quality. The process takes place in the unsubstantial region of ideal experiment. And the steps of that experiment are not even asserted to exist in the world outside our heads.[22]

A tendency in contemporary thought is to eliminate the word 'no', which presupposes that the problem of negation is only a pseudo-problem. This tendency is well represented in Russell's book *Human Knowledge*. According to Russell a negative judgment, say, 'this is not blue' when it is made at the time of perceiving a red thing, is a judgment of perception, and there are no negative facts.

> Thus when I say truly, 'this is not blue' there is on the subjective side consideration of 'this is blue', followed by rejection, while on the objective side there is some colour differing from blue. In this way, so far as colour judgments are concerned, we escape the need of negative facts as what make negative judgments true.[23]

22. *Principles of Logic*, Book I, Ch. III, Sec. 13.
23. *Human Knowledge*, p. 139.

Russell holds that a negative judgment includes a content which is some positive fact andalso the subjective attitude of disbelief:

> ...when I am said to be believing 'not-P' I am really disbelieving 'P'; that is to say, there is a sentence not containing the word 'not', which denotes a certain content that I may believe or disbelieve, but when the word 'not' is added, the sentence no longer expresses merely a content, but also my attitude towards it.[24]

24. Ibid., p. 144.

PART III

THE PROBLEMS OF SUBSTANCE, SELF AND UNIVERSAL

अथातो द्रव्यादिप्रमेयजिज्ञासा

CHAPTER XI

THE PROBLEM OF SUBSTANCE

In language there are words signifying substances, universals, attributes, relations and actions. One of the main tasks of epistemology is to analyse our conceptions of substance, universal etc. and examine their validity. In this chapter we shall concentrate our attention on the Bhāṭṭa view of substance and the allied problems of whole and parts and identity and change. In the following two chapters the problems of self and universal will be discussed.

Determinate perception apprehends things as qualified by attributes, relations etc. in such forms as 'this is white', 'this is a man with a stick' etc. Now, the question is: What do we mean by 'this', the subject of predication? The possessor of attributes and relations is called 'substance' (*dravya*) and Kumārila says that it is apprehended through vision and touch.[1] Things that are ordinarily perceived are composite. They are composed of parts which are divisible into still smaller parts and ultimately into atoms which are supposed to be indivisible. These atoms possess certain specific properties and they belong to four kinds of primary or ultimate substances, viz., earth, water, fire and air. The Mīmāṃsaka does not believe in a theory of creation, for, according to him, the world is eternal and uncreated and consequently the ultimate substances never exist in their free state, i.e., in the form of disjoined atoms. So Kumārila does not dogmatically stick to the theory of an atomic structure of substances. Whatever belief Kumārila and his followers seem to possess in the existence of atoms is derived from the free particles of matter scattered in space and visible in a sun-beam. These particles are the atoms in the Bhāṭṭa system,[2] while, according

1. SV, 4. 170.
2. MM, p. 164.

to the Nyāya-Vaiśeṣika, atoms are invisible to ordinary people and the entities which are visible in a sun-beam are triads (*tryaṇuka*) composed of three dyads (*dvyaṇuka*) each of which is a combination of two atoms and is invisible. The other substances, viz., space, time, ether, *manas* and soul are not atomic but of an infinite magnitude.

11.1. *Substance and Attributes*

Substance is defined by Nārāyaṇa as the abode of magnitude (*parimāṇaguṇādhāra*). According to Kumārila, however, it is the substratum not only of magnitude but of all the generic and specific properties that are attributed to a thing. The Buddhist denies the existence of substance as an entity different from the attributes of a thing. He asserts that there is no substance over and above the qualities of colour, taste, touch etc., which may possess them as its qualifications. What we call substance is nothing but an aggregate of colour etc. just as a forest is nothing but an aggregate of trees. We do not perceive anything which may be called substance, nor there is any sense-organ which may serve as the instrument of such perception. The five sense-organs give a knowledge of such sensible qualities as colour etc. and their functions are exhausted in apprehending them. The inner sense-organ called *manas* is incapable of giving a knowledge of substance, because it cannot function independently of the external sense-organs in cognizing external objects. Thus, according to the Buddhist, substance is not at all a real entity.

Kumārila says that the existence of substance cannot be denied. Substance is different from qualities. It is the possessor of qualities and gives them unity. A thing is not a particular colour plus a particular taste plus a particular touch, but a substance in which these qualities abide, and we are conscious of it in the form of 'this', to which various qualities are seen to belong. Qualities change from time to time, but substance persists and maintains its identity in spite of the changing qualities. A fruit is now perceived as green and it tastes sour, but after some time it becomes yellow in colour and sweet in taste. In spite of these changes in qualities we recognize it as the same fruit. If there were no substance recognition would be impossible. The qualities of a thing are many in number, yet we say that the thing is one. That which maintains its unitary character amidst the variety of attributes is substance. Kumārila says that substance (*dharmī*) is apprehended through vision and touch prior to the apprehension of attributes.[3] Pārthasārathi comments that what is apprehended in a line of swans in twilight prior to the perception of white colour is an instance of substance. Pārthasārathi's comment suggests that when colour is not perceived no other quality is perceived and Kumārila in quite unambiguous terms says that substance can be apprehended apart from qualities. But it is impossible to apprehend anything without at the same time apprehending some colour or other quality. Perhaps Kumārila identifies the substance of a thing with solidity that offers resistance or that fills a portion of space. It is also possible that by 'the perception of substance before the perception of a thing's qualities' he might have meant that we are immediately conscious of substance as a unity in indeterminate perception before we analyse it into its diverse qualities.

But, how, the Buddhist asks, can sense-organs which are different from one another give a knowledge of unity? It is said that vision and touch give the knowledge of substance. But how can that which is revealed by vision be the same that is revealed by touch? The organs of vision and touch are different and quite in keeping with their difference they give a knowledge of two different qualities, viz., colour and touch. Hence, that which is apprehended as the possessor of colour must be different from that which is apprehended as the possessor of touch. If the substance apprehended by vision and touch is supposed to be the same in spite of the difference in the sense-organs, what is the need of their being two instead of one? Kumārila's answer is that what is apprehended by many sense-organs does not necessarily become many. The colour of a thing is apprehended by eyes belonging to many persons, but it does not become different just because the visual organs are many. A colour may be perceived by different eyes, still it is the same colour. It does not lose its sameness merely because the observers are many. It may be said that the colour is one because the eyes belong to the same class. But if a generic unity of eyes is thus made the ground of

3. तद्धर्मि यत्र वा ज्ञानं प्राग्धर्मग्रहणाद् भवेत् । SV, 4. 152.

the sameness of perceived colour, then, as all sense-organs have a generic unity by virtue of their belonging to the class sense-organ, the thing perceived through them cannot but be the same. As a matter of fact, unity and diversity depend not on the oneness and maniness of apprehending sense-organs but on the consciousness of one and many. Colour, touch etc. are many and different, because there is a consciousness of difference among them; and the substance possessing them is one, because there is a consciousness of unity. Diversity and unity embracing diversity, both are real. A thing may be conceived in two ways, as one from the point of view of substance and as diverse from the point of view of attributes. A substance is neither absolutely different from its attributes nor absolutely non-different. It is different as well as non-different from its attributes. From the co-functioning of senses with reference to substance it is wrong to conclude that their maniness is useless, because when one of them is weak another apprehends it properly. One who is blind or weak in eyes can apprehend things with the help of touch.[4]

11.2. *Whole and Parts*

A substance is a whole (*avayavin*) composed of parts (*avayava*). It is a spatial unity of parts which are many. How are parts unified into one whole? What is the relation of a whole to its parts? Is a whole absolutely different from its parts or identical with them? The Buddhist says that a whole does not really exist. Just as a forest is wrongly seen as a whole while actually there exists a large number of trees at a distance from one another, so an aggregate of atoms is illusorily perceived as a whole while there does not exist any such thing. To this Kumārila answers that a whole really exists. The analogy of forest does not hold good because it is perceived as one whole by mistake caused by distance and such perception is contradicted when we enter the forest, but the perception of a tree as a whole cannot be wrong as it is never contradicted. From a case of illusory perception it is not proper to generalize and say that all perception is illusory.[5]

According to the Vaiśeṣika there is an absolute difference be-

4. SV, 4. 151-59.
5. SV, *Vanavāda*, 53.

tween whole and parts and they are related through a special sort of relation known as *samavāya* or inherence. A whole inheres in its parts and the qualities of parts originate special qualities in the whole. Special qualities are those which inhering in the objects of one class differentiate them from objects of other classes. But according to the Bhāṭṭa the relation between a whole and its parts is that of identity-cum-difference (*bhedābheda*). A whole is identical as well as different from its parts. Cloth is a whole residing in threads. Devadatta is a whole residing in parts such as hands, legs etc. Cloth is not apprehended as distinct from threads. Devadatta is not apprehended as distinct from hands, legs etc. If parts are eliminated one by one the whole also disappears. Thus there is identity between a whole and its parts. Parts themselves appear in the form of a whole. At the same time difference also is manifested insofar as parts such as threads or hands are apprehended as belonging to a whole, viz., cloth or Devadatta. Thus there is identity and difference as is revealed by direct experience. A whole is only a particular arrangement of parts and not a new substance. Parts themselves assume the form of one single substance due to a particular combination (*sanniveśa*). Threads in their cloth-form exhibit unity and as threads they exhibit diversity. Unity and diversity exist together; they are not mutually incompatible.

What has been said by the Vaiśeṣika to the effect that qualities of a causal aggregate originate new qualities in the resultant whole, is wrong, because we do not cognize two sets of qualities, one belonging to threads and another to cloth. What actually happens is that qualities of parts, e.g., whiteness of threads, appear as the qualities of the whole, e.g., whiteness of cloth, when they assume the form of the whole. There is no causal relation between the whiteness of threads and the whiteness of cloth. The latter whiteness is not a different one. Even when the colours of threads are various they themselves are manifested as the colour of cloth. A new colour is not generated therein. The Vaiśeṣika says that in a cloth of variegated colour the colour is cognized as variegated and not as white, blue etc. which are the colours of constituent theads, so that variegated colour has to be accepted as a different and new colour originated by the colours of threads. The Bhāṭṭa answer is that variegated colour is not a new colour. 'Variegated' means having a variety, and there was already present a variety of colours in threads, so that there can be no new variety in cloth. Therefore, a new colour cannot be admitted. A number of colours can inhere in the same piece of cloth through the constituent threads.

A whole resides in its parts, but whether it resides in each part in its entirety or piecemeal is an irrelevant question. A whole is one. There are no many wholes in it so that each may reside in its entirety in each part. A whole has no parts other than those in which it resides. Therefore, the second part of the question too becomes meaningless. A whole resides in all its parts taken together. It is a distinct entity and is different as well as non-different from its parts.[6]

11.3. *Identity and Change*

A thing is a more or less permanent background in which changes occur. The states of a thing change from time to time, but its substance remains the same. In spite of changing states we recognize it as the same. A fruit is unripe and then it becomes ripe, yet it remains the same fruit. Clay is first seen in the form of a lump, then in the form of a jar and then in the form of the pieces of jar. Through these changes of state the thing that changes, i.e., the substance, persists, and we do not fail to recognize it. A man changes from a baby to a youth and then to an old man, still he remains the same man from birth to death. Changes occur in a substratum which itself does not change but maintains its integrity amidst the vicissitudes, and this is substance. Substance endures and its identity is not affected by its changing states. We recognize a thing as the same today as it was yesterday, though it may have suffered many changes during the interval. Substance is the basis of such recognition. The substance of a thing remains the same in spite of the processes of birth, growth and decay until it is completely disintegrated into small particles.

The Buddhist holds that nothing endures in change. Everything is momentary. Things last for one moment only. The next moment they are completely annihilated and absolutely new

6. SD, pp. 106-8.

things are created, which too last for a moment only. The Buddhist argues as follows: That which has being must have causal efficiency (*arthakriyā*). Being and doing are identical. Causal efficiency is the criterion of reality. That which really exists must produce certain effects. If a thing could exist without producing any effects, it would be as good as non-existent. The least effect of a thing is a cognition produced by it in a cognizing mind. Things are the basic cause (*ālambanapratyaya*) of their consciousness in us. There are things of which we are not actually aware, still we are aware of their probable existence and so far they possess causal efficiency. The effects that an existing thing produces must be either simultaneous or successive. If it produces all the effects of which it is capable simultaneously, it becomes devoid of causal efficiency and consequently it ceases to exist in the next moment. And whatever a thing is capable of producing must be produced immediately in the next moment of its birth, because there can be no postponement (*kṣepāyogāt*). For this reason a thing cannot generate its effects successively. If a thing is capable of doing something it must be done instantaneously. It cannot wait for an auxiliary (*sahakāri*) to produce its effects, because, if it is supposed to stand in need of an auxiliary, the causal efficiency would really belong to the modification (*atiśaya*) produced in the thing by the auxiliary. This modification or peculiarity produced in the thing must be different from the thing itself. It cannot be identical with the thing, because, if it were so, it would be as incapable of producing an effect as the thing by itself is. The modification cannot be different from as well as identical with the thing, because difference and identity are mutually contradictory. Thus postponement is incompatible with the causal efficiency of a thing. Therefore, a thing can have only a momentary existence after which it, having become devoid of causal efficiency, must cease to exist.

Another reason for a momentary existence of things is the inevitableness (*dhruvabhāvitva*) of destruction. That which is produced must be perishable. Destruction is inevitable and it does not stand in need of any extraneous cause, because it is natural just as heat which is natural to fire and does not require any extraneous cause for its being. That which is inevitable must take place immediately; destruction is inevitable; therefore, it must take place immediately after the birth of a thing. Things which depend on an extraneous condition, for example, the colour of a piece of cloth, are not inevitable. That which is not inevitable depends on an adventitious cause; destruction is inevitable; therefore, it does not depend on any such cause. Thus as soon as a thing is born it is destroyed and hence the momentary character of things is established.

Destruction is taking place every moment. But it is so subtle that we are unable to apprehend it. A jar is undergoing destruction every moment. The jar of the previous moment is absolutely different from the jar of the succeeding moment. Yet, this difference is not observed by us because of the similarity of the jars of different moments. Consequently we mistakenly think that the jar of this moment is the same as the jar of the previous moment and this mistaken notion of identity persists until the jar is reduced to pieces with a blow. When a jar is crushed with the blow of a stick people think that it is destroyed, while it is really destroyed every moment. Destruction is causeless and a blow cannot be its cause. A blow is really the cause of a series different from the jar-series (*ghaṭasantāna*). With a blow the jar-series comes to an end and a new series (*kapālasantāna*) starts. The destruction of a thing that is apparently caused by some extraneous factor, e.g., a blow, cannot be identical with the thing, because it has a different thing as its cause. And if it were different from the thing the thing would be perceptible as usual even after destruction has taken place, just as when a cloth is produced a jar which is different from it is apprehended as before. Therefore, destruction is inherent in the nature of things and is not caused. This is proved by experience also. Things like a jar preserved with care are observed to perish after some time even without a blow. Their destruction cannot be explained unless a gradual deterioration in their condition from the very moment of birth is accepted. This gradual deterioration is detected in an object even by one who does not know the moment of its birth and this is evident when some person remarks 'this thing is old'. The successive states of growth and decay are many and different and hence they cannot be identical, because identity is incompatible with manifoldness. Therefore, a thing of one moment must be different from things of other moments and consequently nothing can endure for more than one moment. The recognition of identity is illusory like that of a lamp-flame. A lamp-flame changes from moment to moment, still it appears to be the same because of similarity which is confounded with identity. Likewise all apparently enduring things are really momentary.[7]

The doctrine of momentariness was preached for the first time in a systematic way by the Buddhists. But due to its inherent absurdities it could not win followers outside the Buddhist circle. Change is a fact of experience and none can deny it. But change without a comparatively permanent substratum is an absurdity. Change and permanence are relative concepts. We could not talk of change if some sort of stability were not a fact. The consciousness of change is relative to the consciousness of no-change. Change without something which does not change is impossible. There is no proof to establish that all existents are momentary. Perception reveals existence during its own time; it cannot reveal the non-existence of an object in a future moment. Perception cannot apprehend negation. Negation is the object of a different means of cognition, viz., non-apprehension. But non-apprehension too cannot reveal non-existence in the next moment. Non-apprehension gives the knowledge of negation, but of that thing alone which is fit to be perceived at the present moment, while the non-existence of a thing in the next moment is not fit to be perceived now.

The Buddhist tries to establish momentariness by inference. But his reasoning is defective. The premises on which the Buddhist bases his conclusion are all fallacious. He identifies existence with causal efficiency. But this is wrong. Causal efficiency is a property of existence. That which exists possesses causal efficiency—the former is not identical with the latter. It is not a rule that every existent thing must be causally operative. A thing may exist without doing anything. Being is not identical with doing. Nor is it a rule that all existent things must be the basic causes of their respective cognitions.It is just possible that a thing may exist without producing its knowledge in us.

7. SD, pp. 143-44.

Causality belongs only to a present object. In inference and other means of knowledge the object of knowledge cannot be the cause of its knowledge. If causality is attributed to all existing objects with respect to their knowledge, then, their causal efficiency being exhausted by this operation, the whole world shall become a void in the next moment according to the Buddhist himself who rejects the possibility of the appearance of effects in a succession.

The second Buddhist premise that an object cannot produce its effects in an order of succession also is wrong. An object by itself cannot produce its effects. It requires the help of auxiliaries for producing its effects and so it has to wait till such help is available. The modification brought about by an auxiliary in an object may be different from the object or different as well as identical. Seed is the cause of sprout. But it cannot produce a sprout until it comes in contact with earth, water etc. These auxiliaries produce some modification in seed and then the sprout comes out. Thus the order of succession in the effects of a cause which has some stability depends on the operation of auxiliaries. It cannot be said that contact alone is the cause of sprout and not seed, because a sprout is never seen to appear on a mere contact of earth and water. It is the seed qualified by contact that produces sprout and so the causality of seed cannot be denied. The seed is the cause and its contact with earth and water is the auxiliary, and both are essential for the production of sprout. If auxiliaries were not required, a sprout could come out from even a seed lying in the granary.

The Buddhist may say that the seed which comes in contact with earth and water and produces a sprout is different from that which lies in the granary, the difference being that the former has reached its final moment which is sufficient by itself to produce a sprout while the latter has not reached that state. Accordingly the final moment produces a sprout without the aid of auxiliaries. The Buddhist may be asked: Could the seed which comes in contact with earth and water and having reached its final moment produces the sprout produce it if it were still lying in the granary? If 'yes', what is the use of the farmer's effort? Likewise, the effort of people to attain heaven or release for themselves and all instructions of a religious teacher become useless, because people will attain their cherished ends independently of the efforts and instructions when they reach the final moment. Therefore, the aid of auxiliaries is essential and consequently the order of succession in the effects that a causally efficient thing is capable of is justified. This proves the enduring nature of things and disproves their alleged momentariness.

The third Buddhist premise is that destruction is inherent in the nature of things and is not caused by extraneous factors. But is destruction identical with a thing or different from it? If it is identical, then the thing must be imperceptible like destruction. If it is different, then in spite of destruction the thing must be apprehended as before. Thus the Buddhist objection against the non-inherent nature of destruction applies to its inherent nature as well. If to avoid this difficulty it is said that destruction is not anything different or non-different but a non-entity (*abhāva*), then a thing will exist permanently, which is just the opposite of what the Buddhist wants to establish. Thus the Buddhist is obliged to accept that though a thing is different from destruction yet destruction causes it to disappear. That is, destruction is not natural but extraneous, depending on extraneous conditions.

The assertion that there is a change of states from moment to moment may be correct, but it does not prove that the thing which owns these states is destroyed every moment. And the so-called incompatibility between the unitary character of a thing and the manifoldness of states is not really an incompatibility, because different states belong to a thing successively. The difficulty would have been real if various states characterized a thing simultaneously. An orange cannot be ripe and unripe at the same time, but it can quite reasonably be ripe at one time and unripe at a previous time. A thing is born, it decays and is destroyed finally, but all these states are caused by extraneous factors. Just as its birth depends on certain causes, so its destruction too. What is natural to a thing is persistence, but not destruction. When a this is born or destroyed we seek to find out the cause, but nobody is seen to ask why a thing of yesterday persists today. If a thing is left absolutely undisturbed it will continue to exist for ever. A thing may be preserved with care, still the unseen forces of destruction are operative, over which we have no control, and thus the thing is ultimately destroyed.

Recognition is the strongest proof of the enduring nature of things and it is not an illusion. The Buddhist says that what is recognized as the same thing after a lapse of time is not actually the same but similar. But this is wrong. Just as sameness is impossible, so similarity too is impossible for the Buddhist. Similarity consists in some parts or features possessed by two things in common. But, when, according to the Buddhist, destruction is total (*niranvayavināśa*), how can a feature continue to exist in other things? The thing of the past moment was destroyed without leaving a trace behind and the thing of the present moment is an absolutely new product. How, then, can there be any similarity between them? And if there is any similarity between things of the preceding and succeeding moments, then something must continue to exist for more than a moment and thus the doctrine of momentariness becomes refuted.[8]

The theory of total destruction cannot explain the appearance of a thing in the next moment. When a thing is destroyed totally in the present moment, how can it give rise to anything in the next moment? A jar, for instance, is produced by a potter out of clay. But if clay is totally destroyed, how can the potter construct the shape of a jar in the absence of a material cause? The jar of the present moment will be absolutely non-existent in the next moment, still a jar similar to it will appear according to the Buddhist. It would be a miracle if it could appear without the activity of a potter and a material cause ! Construction thus becomes as causeless as destruction is. The following moment is absolutely non-existent at the present moment and hence it cannot have any action towards the construction of the next momentary form of the jar. The present moment too cannot have any such action, because as soon as it is born it is swallowed up by negation. The present moment is destroyed and the following one will be born, but, because the two are independent of each other there cannot be any causal connection between them. The thing which is not yet born cannot serve as an

8. SD, pp. 144-45.

auxiliary to anything, nor can one which is no more, and as for the one which continues to exist, there is no such thing according to the Buddhist. A thing does not become the cause of an effect merely on the ground of its antecedence in time. The previous jar-moment precedes the present jar-moment as well as a cloth-moment. But it cannot be the cause of the cloth-moment because it merely precedes in time and does not operate towards the production of the latter. Similarly it cannot be the cause of the present jar-moment, because the required operation is absent due to its impossibility in the above way. Only such a thing can be a cause as possesses the necessary activity prior to the accomplishment of an effect. The Buddhist cites the instance of lamp-flame to prove his theory. But as a matter of fact, there is no destruction of a lamp-flame every moment. There is a continuous flow of the particles of light in the upward direction. The particles in the region of flame are very close together and hence they appear in the form of a flame. They move upwards and all around and fresh particles take their place. Beyond the region of the flame the particles are scattered wide apart and thus they appear merely as radiance. Still beyond there is no radiance, because the particles are still more scattered. The flame of a lamp is recognized to be the same because of the sameness of arrangement, though every moment some particles of light are moving away and some fresh ones are flowing in. Likewise, a body is recognized to be the same because of the arrangement of its parts, which continues to be the same in spite of the changes of state such as youthfulness, old age etc. Body is not identical with its states and hence it cannot be said that it is destroyed when one of its states comes to an end and is reconstructed when another state appears. Changes are only partial modifications of a thing and in this way they are not incompatible with stability.[9]

9. SV, *Śabdanityatā*, 426-40.

CHAPTER XII

THE PROBLEM OF SELF

Kumārila has not discussed the nature and number of different ultimate substances. The later followers of the Bhāṭṭa system have dealt with the question, but their speculations do not show any striking originality. Even in other Indian systems the discussion of such problems as space, time etc. is not much illuminating. About the nature of self which is said to be a spiritual substance there are many theories. As this question is very relevant to epistemology, it will be discussed here from the Bhāṭṭa point of view.

12.1. *Arguments against the Cārvāka View*

Self, according to Kumārila, is as immaterial substance different from body, sense-organs and cognition. The materialist Cārvāka identifies self with body. He does not believe in any immaterial and supersensuous substance. Consciousness, which is supposed to be the distinctive property of the immaterial substance called self, is nothing but a property of body. The phenomenon of consciousness arises in the body due to a particular combination of the atoms of four elements. Body is a compound of four elements and consciousness is generated in it as the power of intoxication is generated in molasses. Consciousness is not found in the constituent elements of body individually; but this does not prove that it is the property of some invisible substance different from body. We observe that new properties arise when elements are combined in special ways. Red colour is not possessed by a betel leaf, nuts and lime individually. But when all the three are combined together red colour is generated. Consciousness is a by-product of material elements and is destroyed when the body is destroyed.

The attitude of the Cārvāka is naturalistic. Like the nineteenth century scientists he challenged the authority of orthodox religion and refused to go beyond the testimony of the senses. He tried to explain the unfamiliar in terms of the familiar and the complex in terms of the simple. But the consequences implied in his hypothesis were detrimental to religious and moral aspirations of man, and hence it was rejected by the layman equally with the advanced thinker.

Consciousness is a property of living organisms. Life cannot be reduced to a blind play of dead matter. Life and consciousness are fundamentally different from matter. Physical laws cannot explain the phenomena of life and consciousness. The latter exhibit spontaneity and self-determination, while matter by itself lacks them. Matter cannot initiate motion by spontaneous effort. It is always determined externally. Body, being a product of matter, is inert and governed by the laws of matter. When it is living it governs its own processes and is moved by its own effort. The vital and mental processes of a living organism must be governed by some higher and different principle, because these processes disappear at death, though the body is quite intact.

Effort, which is the cause of the functioning of bodily breath (*prāṇana*) and feelings like pleasure and pain cannot be the attributes of body, because they are not seen to last as long as body lasts. After death body is present but effort and feelings are absent. Body possesses such physical qualities as colour, touch, shape, weight etc. and they are not seen to disappear at death. If effort, feeling etc. were the properties of body, there would be no loss of them at death, just as there is no loss of other physical properties. Their loss can be explained only by postulating an invisible substance in which they inhere and which disappears at death. This substance is the self.

The vital functions of body are sustained by the effort of self. Self is the source of energy required for the movements of body, which are visible to an external observer. The qualities of body are perceptible to all. But cognition and feelings cannot be perceived by anyone else except the person to whom they belong. To others they are a matter of inference. From a smiling face the feeling of pleasure is inferred by others. It cannot be said that they are inside the body and hence they are not visible to others. Even when body is torn open nothing is seen inside it except such qualities as colour etc. Thus the subjective phenomena of cognition, feeling etc. are different from the qualities of body and hence they cannot belong to it but to a different substance.

The qualities residing in a substance become the qualities of its product. For example, the colour of clay becomes the colour of the jar produced from it. Body is the product of the atoms of four elementary substances. But consciousness is not a quality of any of them. Therefore, consciousness cannot belong to body but to some conscious substance which is the self.

Self is different not only from body but also from sense-organs. Sense-organs may be destroyed while self continues to exist. Even when a person becomes blind he remembers the colours he perceived in the past, though he is no more able to see colours. The cognizer of colours exists, though he is no more able to see colours. The cognizer of colours exists, though the instruments of colour-perception, viz., the eyes, are destroyed. Sense-organs are many in number, but the cognizing self is one only. The cognizer of colour is recognized as the same person who is the cognizer of touch, while the sense-organs involved in the cognition of colour and touch are different. The perceiving self and the remembering self are recognized as identical. I am now remembering, but I am the same person who perceived. Sense-organs are not conscious. They are unconscious instruments of perception, while self is the nominative or agent in perception. The nominative cannot be identical with the instrumental. Therefore, self is different from sense-organs.[1]

The above arguments have been offered mainly by the Nyāya-Vaiśeṣika and Śabara has accepted them. Our account of them follows Pārthasārathi. But Kumārila, though he refers to them, seems more inclined to accept the Sāṅkhya arguments.[2] He gives his assent to the arguments given by Īśvarakṛṣṇa.[3]

The Nyāya-Vaiśeṣika reasoning appears to be more primitive and less convincing. It says that effort, feeling and cognition

1. SD, pp. 119-20.
2. SV, *Ātm.*, 93-114.
3. SK, 17.

disappear at death, though body itself remains as it was formerly, and makes this the ground of their not being the properties of body. But with the growth of scientific knowledge it is becoming more and more evident that the anatomy and physiology of body is not so simple as it appears to the eye. The vital functions of body are regulated by different chemical substances manufactured inside the body and circulated along with the blood stream. The functions of different cells are so subtle and complicated that it is impossible to observe them through the naked eye, so that it is impossible to assert with surety that after death body remains the same as it was when living. Modern science attributes the phenomena of life to a higher organization of matter and those of consciousness to a still higher organization. In view of the recent developments of science in the conception of matter the Nyāya-Vaiśeṣika arguments lose all force.

12.2. *The Sāṅkhya Arguments*

The Sāṅkhya arguments are based on teleology and stand on a more sound footing. Matter is inert and non-purposive. All material products are subservient to the ends of some purposive being. The existence of material aggregates (*saṅghāta*) is for the sake of another (*parārtha*). They are the objects of enjoyment and the enjoyer is different from them. A bed is not meant for itself, because it has no purpose of its own. It is made for the enjoyment of the sleeper. Similarly, the body and sense-organs too, being material aggregates, are inert and non-purposive, and they presuppose a purposive entity other than themselves. Such purposive entity is the self. Teleological or purposive activity implies intelligence and consciousness and these cannot belong to matter but to self. Thus, however highly organized the mechanism of body may be, it does not function for its own end but for that of a conscious and intelligent self which must be immaterial. If the constituent parts of body were themselves intelligent they could not form an aggregate, because in that case they would be equally important and one could not be subordinated to another as a means to another's end. And if anyone of the constituent elements of body were supposed to be intelligent, the body would be made of that element alone and the help of other elements would be unnecessary.

Epistemological considerations point to the existence of self. The act of knowing presupposes a distinct existence of the knower and the known. The dualism of subject and object in knowledge is ultimate and none of them can be reduced to the other. The body and senses are as much objects of knowledge as other material things are. Hence the knower or subject (*draṣṭā*) of knowledge must be different from them. The body and senses are changeable, while the subject is immutable. Experience presupposes a unitary and self-identical principle in the form of the subject who transcends experience. Matter is subject to temporal changes and the seer of these changes must be beyond them. Therefore, self must be basically different from matter and material products.

Self is inferred as the supervisor (*adhiṣṭhātā*) of bodily activities. It is like a charioteer. Just as a chariot cannot move by itself on the right path without the guidance of a charioteer, so body too cannot move without the guidance of self. Body is a product of matter and hence it is inert. It cannot guide its movements. The activity of matter is blind, because it is non-intelligent. Therefore, the intelligent entity that adapts the movements of body to certain ends of its own and to the environmental conditions is the self.

The religious and moral pursuits of man, his desire for liberation, the feeling of bondage in the association of matter, all prove that the spirit in him is above and beyond matter and everything that is material.

12.3. *The Notion of 'I'*

Self is known fron the notion of 'I' (*ahampratyaya*). Self is directly revealed in self-consciousness. Self-consciousness is the most cogent proof of the existence of self and cannot be denied even by the greatest sceptic. Śaṅkara says that in the very attempt of denying the self asserts itself in the form of the denier.[4] Descartes repeats the same thing when he says that a sceptic can deny everything but not his own self—*cogito ergo sum*. Kumārila says that the word 'I' in the assertion 'I know' refers to the knowing self. Knowership cannot belong to body or sense-

4. य एव हि निराकर्ता तदेव तस्य स्वरूपम् । SBBS, 2.3.7.

organs, because they are material and unconscious. The ego in knowing is other than body and senses, because these are the objects of 'this'-notion (*idaṃkārāspada*)

The difference of self from body and senses is amply revealed by such assertions as 'this is my body', 'this is my eye', 'my mind is tired' etc. 'I' and 'this' are quite opposite in nature and one cannot apply to the other. In Śaṅkara's words they are opposed to each other as light and darkness are (*tamaḥprakāśavad viruddhasvabhāvayoḥ*). The notion of ego cannot have any other object than the cognizing self. We cannot reject the consciousness of self and its difference from body and sense-organs as false. The assertion of identity, on the other hand, between self and body, as 'I am lean', 'I am blind' etc. is false. Leanness, blindness etc. are really the properties of body. Self cannot possess such characteristics, because it is immaterial and formless. These epithets are illusorily transferred to self due to its proximity, just as the redness of a japā flower is superimposed on crystal which lies near it. That leanness, blindness, etc. do not belong to self but to body is revealed by such assertions as 'my body is lean', 'my eyes are blind' etc. In the assertion 'my self' difference is indicated between 'I' and self. But this does not imply that 'I' consciousness and consequently it cannot free itself from the realm of appearance.

But for Kumārila individuality is an ultimate fact and self can in no case lose its individuality. The individual, as Kant says, is an end in itself—it cannot be merely a means to fulfil an alien end. To lose individuality is to lose selfhood. Those who are spiritually advanced or liberated while still remaining in the embodied state certainly give up the false sense of egohood in the body, yet egohood in the form 'I know' is never done away with in their case. If they could do away with this sense of egohood too, they would not be able to instruct their disciples. If there were no consciousness in the form 'I have learnt this' they would have to learn a thing from the very beginning even after having already learnt half of it. In the words of Kant, self is the transcendental unity of apperception. The sense of egohood is false when it arises in connection with such things as are other than self, e.g., when one says, 'I am his father', 'I am his son' etc. Self is eternal, without birth, decay and death. Birth, decay and death really belong to body and are wrongly superimposed on self by ignorant persons. But those who have realized the real nature of self are not deluded in this way. However, the proper sense of egohood is never lost in their case.[5]

12.4. *Refutation of the Buddhist View*

The existence of self is proved by cognition, pleasure, pain etc. which are qualities and which must abide in a substratum different from body. But this is not recognized by the Yogācāra Buddhist. He asserts that cognition, pleasure, pain etc. are not proved to be qualities and hence there is no necessity of postulating a substratum for them in the form of an enduring self. The Buddhist's approach to the problem of self is psychological. Anticipating Hume and other sensationalists he maintains that introspection does not reveal the existence of any enduring entity. What we discover is only a series of ideas appearing and disappearing independently of a soul-substance. Therefore, there is no soul other than a series of momentary ideas. Cognition or idea is the only reality and pleasure etc. are nothing but forms of

5. SV, *Ātm.*, 110-11, 125-35.

cognition. The Buddhist does not maintain like the Cārvāka that cognition is a property of body, because body for him is as much non-existent as other external objects. Like Berkeley he resolves all objects into groups of sensations. Ideas thus become the only reality and accordingly they illusorily appear in the form of the cognizing 'I' and the cognized 'this'.

The phenomena of desire, memory and recognition are cited by others as proving a permanent entity called self. It is said that desire presupposes prior experience. A person has a pleasurable experience of something and he craves for a similar experience in future when he remembers or perceives that thing. This shows that the person who experiences now and desires in future is the same. Similarly memory and recognition also presuppose past perception and prove the continuity and identity of the agent involved in them. Yajñadatta cannot recollect or recognize what was perceived by Devadatta. Momentary ideas cannot explain these facts.

But the Buddhist explains these facts by assuming oneness of a series of ideas (*vijñānasantāna*). The person whom we call Yajñadatta and falsely suppose to be one and identical during different moments of time is nothing but one series of momentary ideas and the person whom we call Devadatta is only a second series of such ideas. Each idea in one series is causally determined by its predecessor. Each gathers all the past impressions from its predecessor, passes them on to its successor and is destroyed completely. A similar process goes on within a second series independently of other series. The ideas of one series are not causally determined by the ideas of other series. The series called Yajñadatta is independent of the series called Devadatta and for this reason the former cannot desire, recollect or recognize what the latter perceived. But in one series what was perceived by a former idea can be desired, recollected and recognized by a later idea on account of the impressions that pass from one to the next. Though the recollecting idea is different from the perceiving one, yet they belong to one series and are related as cause and effect[6].

Kumārila says that the identification of self with a series of

6. Ibid., 102-106 & SD, pp. 120-21.

discrete ideas, that of the cognizer with momentary cognition, is contradicted by the recognition of self as the same in past, present and future. We distinctly recognize the past cognizer as continuing in the present when we say 'I myself knew it formerly and I know it now again'. This recognition of the cognizing self could not be explained if a momentary cognition were the cognizer. A cognition lasts for one moment only while the cognizer is apprehended as permanent without suffering any change through the lapse of time. The object of self-recognition is an enduring entity. If it is a momentary cognition, which cognition is it? Is it the former cognition, the present one or both? If it were the former cognition the recollection 'I knew', i.e., 'the former cognition knew' could be explained on the basis of *vāsanā* or impression, but the consciousness 'I know now' would be false, because the former momentary cognition is no longer present now. If it were the present cognition, the consciousness 'I know' would be true, but the consciousness 'I knew' would be false, because it was not then born. If both the present and the past cognitions be said to be the object of recognition, then both 'I know' and 'I knew' would be false, because the present and the past cognitions could not be simultaneously present in the past or the present moment. The series of cognitions cannot be the object of recognition, because its existence over and above the momentary cognitions is not recognized by the Buddhist. Cognition by an unreal thing is not possible. The Buddhist does not recognize any common element making its appearance in the past and the present moments, which could serve as the required thing. If the recognition is explained on the ground of similarity between the past and present cognitions, then there would be no possibility of recognition when there is dissimilarity. 'I knew a cow formerly and I know a horse now'. Here there is no similarity, because the former cognition had the form of cow and the present one has the form of horse. If the Buddhist says that here the recognition is due to the common character of being a cognition, then, since this character belongs to a cognition in a different series also, this latter too would be recognized as 'I'. Or, a former cognition in the same series would be recognized as 'this' like a cognition in a different series, because both are cognitions, or like an external jar-moment, because a jar-moment and a former cognition are equally external to the present cognition. *Vāsanā* may be the cause of recognition, but it cannot be the cause of apprehending 'this' as 'I', i.e., the not-self as self. The present cognizer, if the cognizer is identical with a momentary cognition, is different from the past one. How can it have the feeling of egohood in that which is not-ego? If such a feeling arises at all it is decidedly false. *Vāsanā* is certainly the cause of recognition. When, for example, an object is recognized as the same as it was some hours ago, it is because the impression of its past experience is still present in the mind and is revived by its present perception. Similarly in the case of self-recognition *vāsanā* is operative. But *vāsanā* cannot be the cause of false recognition. 'This' is always recognized as 'this' and 'I' always as 'I'. The recognition of personal identity is not false, because it is never contradicted[7]. Things must be as they are revealed in uncontradicted experience. Śabara says that we have no right to assume that reality is different from what is revealed in experience, because, otherwise the hare would be unreal and its horn would be real.[8]

12.5. *The Self as a Moral Agent*

The identification of self with cognition is unjustified for another reason also. Self is not only a knower but also a doer (*kartā*) and an enjoyer (*bhoktā*). It is a moral agent engaged in certain actions to realize certain moral purposes and enjoying their good and bad results. Doership and enjoyership would not be possible if it were only a knower. The body, the senses and cognitions are the instruments of accomplishing its moral ends, while the self is different from all these and is eternal. These are the instruments of action and are discarded when they cease to be helpful to the moral progress of self. The self must be eternal, because, if it were perishable, it could not enjoy the results of its actions and others who have not done the actions would enjoy the results. This would result in one's loss of what he has earned and other's gain of what he has not earned (*kṛtanāśākṛtāgamau*), which would not fit in the rational scheme of the universe. If I

7. Ibid., 115-25.
8. शशो नास्ति शशस्य बिषाणमस्ति । SB, p. 232.

were sure that the action I am doing now would not give its fruit to me but to a different person, there would be no motive why I should perform it. And if a different person were sure that he would receive the fruit of my action, he would be foolish to exert himself in doing any action. A motiveless and disinterested action is not possible.

The Buddhist objects that even if the self be granted to be a doer and an enjoyer and eternal, though doership and enjoyership are really incompatible with eterality, it would have no liking for action unless it recognized that the result that it is enjoying now is the effect of such and such an action of his past life. Without such memory as 'I am experiencing the result of that particular good or bad action of mine' there would be no difference between my own enjoyment and that of some other person. And, then a person thinking 'let me perform this action, for at the time of its fruition I will not remember it' will not shun bad works. Thus even when eternality of self is accepted the faults of 'appearance of what is not done' and 'disappearance of what is done' remain practically the same. Therefore, the Buddhist concludes, it is useless to preach the eternality of self.

To this Kumārila answers that the memory of a connection between a particular action and a particular result is not a condition of the enjoyment of the result. A certain action is done and the doer will reap its result whether he remembers or not the action from which it follows. A person may not be convinced from his own experience as to which particular action leads to which particular result, but this is certain that the law of causation operates in the moral sphere as much as in the physical, and, as for the particular modes of its operation, he may learn from persons of superior intelligence and experience. A knowledge of the relation of an act and its result is to some extent desirable for engaging in or avoiding an action (*pravṛtti-nivṛtti*) and such knowledge is available from the scriptures. No sane person can deny that a virtuous deed ultimately results in good results and a vicious deed in bad ones. This much is enough to provide the necessary motivation. From a dull person's inability to establish a connection between particular deeds and corresponding results it is not reasonable to conclude that there is no connection and that what is seen to follow an action immediately is the only result. The moral consequences of actions must accrue to the doer and the resultant enjoyment or suffering in this life or a future one cannot be avoided, enhanced or mitigated by his memory of the action to which it is due. When an action has once been done the *Law of Karma* takes its own course without caring for the like or dislike of the doer. These considerations are sufficient in urging us to act, though we may not remember our acts at the time of enjoyment of their fruits. People are seen to prepare a soft bed to sleep on and are not dissuaded from this act, though at the time of enjoying deep sleep they are unconscious of the fact that their enjoyment is due to the softness of the bed.[9]

12.6. *Change of States Compatible with Identity of Substance*

The Buddhist argues that if the self is eternal and all-pervading, it cannot be modified by pleasure and pain, nor can it be able to act, so that doership and enjoyership cannot belong to it, and conversely if at the time of doing an act and enjoying or suffering the resultant pleasure or pain it leaves its former state it becomes liable to modification and thus ceases to be eternal. According to the Buddhist, permanence and change cannot be reconciled with each other.

But according to Kumārila, there can be no incompatibility between permanence and partial change. The self is eternal, yet it undergoes partial modifications. It remains the same in spite of changes in its state. In activity and enjoyment there is change of its form but its substance remains the same. If by the epithet 'non-eternal' you simply mean modifiable, then there can be no objection to calling the self non-eternal, because there is no total destruction of the self by modification. Just as the sea is not destroyed by the changes occurring on its surface, so the self is not destroyed by engaging in actions and enjoyment. If there were a total destruction of self by a change of state, it would lose the moral consequences of its actions and a different person would enjoy or suffer for what he could not be held responsible. But there is never total destruction of personality. There is only a change in state. A person is seen to remain the same person

9. SV, *Ātma.*, 1-19.

when he attains youth. When a youth attains old age he does not become a different person. Similarly death too is only a change of state and the self continues even after that. People engage in actions and are fully conscious that they will reap the results in another stage of life. They accumulate wealth in youth for enjoying it in old age. If they had no faith in their continuity and thought that they would cease to exist in the next stage of life, all their endeavours would be meaningless.

The states of pleasure and pain, action and inaction appear and disappear, but the self never ceases to be an intelligent substantial entity. If change meant utter destruction, a person who is happy now would be entirely different from the person who was unhappy in the previous moment and if permanence meant no change at all there would be no chance for a person unhappy now to become happy in future. Therefore, absolute change and absolute identity, both the extremes, are to be avoided and the self must be conceived as a substantial unity behind superficial changes.

The changing states of self are like the different positions of a snake. A snake assumes different positions at different times, yet it is the same snake. Similarly the self assumes the states of a cognizer, of an actor, and of an enjoyer at different stages of its existence, yet it remains the same self. One state is destroyed and is replaced by another state, but that to whom the states belong remains the same. Destructibility applies to states only, not to the possessor of the states. This sets aside the Buddhist objection that the state which performs an action being different from the state that enjoys its fruit, there will be *kṛtanāśa* and *akṛtāgama*. As a matter of fact the state of performing an action is not itself the performer and the state of enjoying is not itself the enjoyer. It is the self that performs and enjoys, and, since it remains the same through the changing states, the results of its action do not accrue to a different person. What is meant by the change of a state is not its total destruction but its merger in the substance of self in order to make room for the next one. Different states are mutually exclusive in their individual forms, but the self as an intelligent substance embraces them all equally.[10]

10. Ibid., 20-31.

12.7. *Kumārila and Śaṅkara Compared*

Kumārila follows the middle path. On the one hand, he avoids the extreme view that change alone is real without anything to change and on the other he avoids the extreme view that reality is absolutely static. The two extreme views are held by the Buddhist and Śaṅkara respectively. But both of them are one-sided. Experience reveals two aspects of reality, one static and the other dynamic. But the Buddhist emphasizing the dynamic aspect rejects the other as unreal, while Śaṅkara emphasizing the static aspect rejects the other as unreal. Both take their start from the fact of knowing. The Buddhist resolves reality into momentary cognitions and stops there, because experience does not reveal to him any permanent and unchangeable entity behind cognitions. But Śaṅkara proceeding still further discovers the self which is the pure subject. Cognitions are objects of knowing as other objects are. Hence, logically they presuppose a subject which can never be a content of experience.[11] This transcendental subject is the real self and it must be absolutely unchangeable, otherwise it could not be conscious of change. Thus Śaṅkara conceives self as absolutely static and eternal (*kūṭasthanitya*).

Śaṅkara arrives at this result because he fails to take note of the affective and conative aspects of human personality. The Buddhist also fails to take note of the affective and conative aspects and reduces feelings and actions to the ideas of feelings and actions. They unduly emphasize the cognitive aspect to the neglect of other aspects. Kumārila lays an equal emphasis on all the three aspects. The self is not only a knowing agent but also a feeling and doing one. When Kumārila says that the self is never divested of *caitanya* what he means by the term *caitanya* is intelligence and not merely consciousness. Intelligence implies a conscious pursuit of certain ends. Moral considerations lead him to conceive the self as eternal and at the same time changeable. The self is subject to time, yet it is of an infinite duration. It is not extra-temporal as Śaṅkara holds. The self is *pariṇāminitya* and not *kūṭasthanitya*. It is a dynamic unity underlying changing states. Its states are merely the formal modifications of

11. आत्मा तु प्रमाणादिव्यवहाराश्रयत्वात् प्रागेव प्रमाणादिव्यवहारात् सिध्यति। SBBS, 2.3.7.

its substance. A lump of gold may be given any form without increasing or decreasing its substance: Its form may change but the substance remains constant. Similarly the self may undergo any changes in its state but there is no loss of its substantial character.

Kumārila's view of self appears to be more satisfactory than the views of the Sāṅkhya, Vedānta and Nyāya-Vaiśeṣika. He retains consciousness, purpose and effort to the side of self. The Sāṅkhya transfers purpose and effort to the side of *Prakṛti*. The Vedānta of Śaṅkara transfers them to the side of *Māyā*. According to the Nyāya-Vaiśeṣika and also to Prabhākara consciousness, purpose and effort are just temporary phenomena arising out of the combination of spirit and matter while self is a pure substance devoid of any character.

12.8. *Further Examination of the Buddhist View*

If there were no self as the Cārvāka says, or if it were momentary as the Buddhist says, an individual would know beforehand that either the result of his action will not appear or if it appears at all it will go to a different person and then he would have no inclination to act. The Buddhist identifies self with momentary cognition and yet he believes in rebirth. But as cognitions are devoid of action and omnipresence there can be no possibility of their transference to another body. Even if there be such a possibility the enjoyer would be different from the doer, because a cognition, being momentary, would not continue to enjoy the result of its action. The Buddhist tries to avoid this difficulty by maintaining that just as on the view of a permanent self the states of self are different and impermanent yet the self is one, so there are different momentary cognitions yet they belong to one series, so that the same series is the doer as well as the enjoyer. But if the series be not different from momentary cognitions there would be no one performer of action extending over a long time, and then the disappearance of the result would be out of question, but it would be enjoyed by a different cognition which having never been the performer would not deserve the enjoyment. If the series be identical with momentary cognitions, it is a non-entity and so cannot perform any action. If the series be assumed to be permanent and different from momentary cognitions, it would conflict with the doctrine of universal momentariness and would amount to the acceptance of a permanent self in different words. The assertion that it is the same series which performs an action and enjoys its result, cannot be true unless identity is accepted. But it is difficult to ascertain what sort of identity it is. In a series of air-waves the substance air is identical. In a series of flames light is identical. But in a series of cognitions there can be no common element as each cognition-moment is totally destroyed before the birth of the next moment and does not leave anything behind. The theory of impression (*vāsanā*) cannot be of any help, because there is nothing to be impressed. Thus in the absence of any identity between the performer and the enjoyer the faults of *kṛtanāśa* and *akṛtāgama* become inevitable.

The difference of one series from another also is difficult to maintain. It cannot be said that that is one series in which the preceding and succeeding cognitions are causally related, because it has already been proved that no causal relation can possibly subsist between two momentary entities. Thus the result of the action of one cognition accruing to a different cognition cannot be avoided and consequently the motive behind actions remains unexplained.

The Buddhist says that self-interest is not the only motive behind actions. It is seen that parents are urged to act for the good of their children, forgetting their own good. Similarly, a momentary cognition will engage in action for the good of its successor. And just as the results of the actions of parents done for the good of their own family do not go to the members of another family, so the result of the action of one cognition will not go to the members of another series but to the succeeding members of the same series.

Kumārila refutes this by asserting that there can be no other motive behind one's actions than self-interest. People are certainly led to act out of benevolent considerations, but benevolence derives its strength ultimately from self-interest. Parents nourish and educate children with the conviction that they will be supported by them in old age. They believe that they will continue to live and enjoy the benefits of their children's actions for them when they will have grown too weak to take care of themselves. There is not seen pure benevolence anywhere. People do good to others and expect a return from them. Behind all benevolent actions there lurks the desire for one's own good. People support their family and even if they may not desire any material benefit in return they at least seek self-satisfaction through their benevolent acts. Moreover, family is an instance of self-expansion and the feeling of kinship is but another name of self-love so that an action meant for the benefit of one's children is really meant for one's own self. A person cannot be treated purely as a means for the good of others. If a person sometimes serves as a means to the ends of another person, the latter in turn serves as a means to the ends of the former, and this mutual service presupposes the continuity of both. Among birds and animals there may be no consciousness of their own future good when they support their young. This, however, is a case of instinctive behaviour. Human actions on the other hand are not instinctive but intelligent, and there is an explicit desire for self-benefit. A momentary cognition cannot be actuated for the sake of its own good, because it does not continue to exist till the time of the appearance of result. No support can be found for the Buddhist theory that the cognition A acts for the cognition B, B for C, C for D and so on. Moreover, the result of A's action cannot be enjoyed by anyone, because B for whose sake the action was done commits suicide as soon as it is born. C too cannot derive any benefit out of the actions of A and B because the momentary existence that it is able to enjoy is meant only for the good of its successor D. These difficulties cannot be solved except by postulating a thinking, feeling and doing agent in the form of a permanent self.[12]

Rebirth cannot be possible on the doctrine of momentariness. The Buddhist preaches the doctrine of rebirth while maintaining that there is no permanent self except momentary ideas. But how can a momentary idea leave its abode in a present body and move to another one? The Buddhist compares a series of ideas to a series of flames. Flames, however, being material, are moved from one place to another by the wind. But what can move an idea from one place to another? An idea is immaterial and hence

12. SV, *Ātma.*, 32-58.

it cannot move by itself. If it were movable like a body, then, since the two cannot necessarily have the same velocity there would be a severance of the idea from the body while the latter would be still living.

Some people postulate a subtle body as the vehicle of idea serving as the medium of its transmission from body to body. But there is no proof in support of this theory. A material body is composed of the physical elements and it cannot be other than a gross body perceptible to the senses, so that the assumption of an imperceptible subtle body is purely an imagination. The assumption that a subtle body is suddenly produced at death and suddenly destroyed when an idea takes up a new body is quite unintelligible. Even if the existence of such a body be accepted the transference of an immaterial idea to it and again from it to another gross body is as much unintelligible as its transference from one gross body to another. If the idea of one body were transferred to another body the embryo would already be in possession of it. But the assumption of the presence of idea in the embryo is a sheer contradiction of facts. In the embryo sense-organs are not yet born and hence there can be no consciousness of objects. During the state of swoon too there is no idea, for, there is no sense-functioning at the time. This fact contradicts the Buddhist theory. The theory of a permanent self is not contradicted by it, since, though the self is accepted to be eternally intelligent, it is also accepted that for actual cognitions it depends on sense-functioning. In the embryonic state sense-organs are not yet produced and the mind is still under the influence of previous *karma*-s. Therefore there is no consciousness. The Buddhist cannot say that though cognition is present in the embryonic state it is in the form of a potentiality, because a potentiality cannot exist without a substratum. The Buddhist does not accept any substratum for cognition. And if the gross sense-organs were assumed to be such a substratum, then intelligence would belong to them and in such a case there would be no rebirth as, the sense-organs being destroyed at death, intelligence too would be destroyed. Then, the cause of a cognition would be the sense-organs and not another cognition as the Buddhist holds. Therefore, there can be no other substratum for cognition than the permanent and omnipresent self. Such a self cannot actually move, yet due to its omnipresence it can be easily connected with another body after one is destroyed.[13]

12.9. *The Self as a Conscious Agent, All-pervasive and Non-self-luminous*

Though object-consciousnesses are momentary and dependent on sense-functioning, yet consciousness as such is an eternal and inseparable property of the self. Pure consciousness is one and eternal and the apparent differences in it are due to the difference of objects. The self is eternally conscious just as fire always burns. Fire always possesses the power of burning, but actual burning takes place only when objects are thrown into it. A mirror reflects the image of only that object which is brought in front of it. Similarly, the self is eternally conscious, though actual cognitions take place only when sense-organs bring colour, taste etc. to it. This is how the intelligent character of self continues in the embryonic state, though there are no actual cognitions then[14].

Self is all-pervading and hence actual motion cannot be possible. However, it is the doer of actions because it can initiate action without moving. It is not necessary that movement should inhere always in the doer. Molecular change is not the only form of action as the Vaiśeṣika wrongly supposes. We see that a soldier acts by moving his sword, the commander acts by giving order and the king acts by his mere presence. Molecular changes take place in material bodies alone. But they are not the real doers. The real doer is the self, because the movements of body are guided by it.

The Gītā says that *Prakṛti* is the real doer of actions while self is inactive, but supposes it to be the doer under the delusion of egohood.[15] Kumārila on the other hand thinks that self is the prime-mover of all movements of matter, because matter by itself is motionless. Whatever action and movement is seen in bodies belongs to self, because the end which is realized by them

13. Ibid., 59-73.
14. SV, *Śabdanityatā*, 404-7.
15. प्रकृत्या क्रियमाणानि गुणैः कर्माणि सर्वशः ।
अहंकारविमूढात्मा कर्ताहमिति मन्यते ॥ BG, 3.27.

belongs to self, while material bodies have no end or purpose of their own. Bodies by their movements realize the ends of the selves and thus even behind molecular changes of matter the real agent is the self. The self is the only teleological entity, while matter, being an instrument or means to its ends, is dependent on it for movement. Though body is seen to walk from place to place, yet it derives the power of walking from the determination (*saṅkalpa*) of self. Self is the performer of actions by virtue of its power of determination. The actions of the present body depend on the *karma*-s of self earned in a previous life, the actions of the previous body depend on the *karma*-s of a still previous life, and so on without a limit. Though self is omnipresent and so equally in contact with all bodies, yet it is not the agent in respect of actions done by other bodies, because the actions of other bodies do not fulfil its ends but those of different selves. Thus body is simply a medium of action and not itself the performer of action, while the real agent behind all actions is the self.[16]

The reason why self is conceived as omnipresent lies in its immaterial character. Self being immaterial is immovable and would lose its connection with body when the latter would move. So it must be omnipresent like space. However such a body may move it is not disconnected from space, because space is present everywhere. Similarly there is no disconnection of a body from an omnipresent self. If self were not omnipresent, it would be impossible for it to migrate from one body to another.

Another reason for the all-pervasiveness of self is that it can be neither atomic nor of a medium size. A simultaneous feeling of pain or pleasure in head and foot cannot be explained if it is assumed to be atomic. An atomic self can feel only in that part of body where it resides. The upholders of atomicity try to explain the said simultaneous feeling by ascribing an extremely high speed to self. But this is rejected on the ground that speed is possible only in the case of material things while self is not material. Moreover, this explanation could be accepted if the atomic character of self were proved by some more powerful means. But such a means is not available. The references found

16. SV, *Ātm.*, 74-89.

in the *Upaniṣads* to the atomicity of self should be taken to mean the extremely subtle character of self. Self cannot be of the size of body as is supposed by the Jainas. Body is composed of parts. Its size increases and decreases. If self were coextensive with body it would also have to increase and decrease with body and then it would be perishable like body. Therefore, the only safe course is to assume that self is of an infinite size. Self fills the whole of space and is partless. And though it is omnipresent it manifests itself in only one body at a time, viz., the body that it acquires by its past actions.[17]

Now, if self is infinite in size it can be only one in number. Pārthasārathi argues that if only one self existed in different bodies, the object perceived by Yajñadatta would be recognized by Devadatta. It may be said that there is no such thing because the *manas*-s in different bodies are different. But this is untenable. *Manas* is only a sense-organ like the eye and ear, and just as the difference of cognizing subjects cannot be based on the difference of these sense-organs, so the difference between Yajñadatta and Devadatta cannot be based on the difference of their *manas*-s. There are many sense-organs in a body, yet the cognizer is only one, because it is occupied by one self. There is a plurality of cognizing subjects, because there is a plurality of selves, each occupying one body. If there were no such plurality the whole world would come to an end with the liberation of Devadatta. There do occur in the *Upaniṣads* statements of one self, but they must be taken to emphasize that though there are many selves they are not dissimilar.[18]

The question next arises as to how self is known. Kumārila says that self can be directly known only to itself and in this sense it has been declared in the Veda to be self-luminous (*ātmajyoti*).[19] My self cannot be directly known by others and the selves of other persons cannot be directly known by me. I know other selves through analogy. I compare the movements and gestures of other bodies with my own and then from their similarity with my own movements and gestures I infer that

17. SD, p. 124.
18. Ibid., pp. 124 5.
19. SV, *Ātm.*, 142.

they must have selves as I have. But is one's own self known through perception as other things are known or in some other way? Kumārila says that self is known through the notion of 'I' (*ahaṃpratyaya*) and Pārthasārathi on this basis concludes that self is known through mental perception[20] (*mānasa-pratyakṣa*).

Pārthasārathi rejects the self-luminosity of self. He says that everything is manifested by something else and that there is no instance of any self-luminous thing. The Vedāntin says that self is self-luminous and is of the nature of pure consciousness and bliss. To the objection that there would be self-consciousness during deep sleep also if self were self-luminous, the Vedāntin answers that it is actually so as is revealed by the subsequent recollection 'I slept happily'. But Pārthasārathi says that there is neither self-consciousness nor a consciousness of bliss during dreamless sleep. He cites such common assertions as 'I slept like a dead man and had no consciousness of myself'. He explains the assertion 'I slept happily' as pointing to a mere absence of pain and not to a positive experience of pleasure. Persons of a libidunous nature are seen to regret on waking for not having been able to enjoy sexual pleasure due to an untimely onset of sleep. Had they experienced supreme bliss during deep sleep there should have been no feeling of regret for the loss of an insignificant pleasure. What is called a memory of blissful experience is not a memory but an original experience of no-pain through non-apprehension. Had there been any pain during deep sleep it would have been remembered on waking. But, since that which is fit to be remembered is not remembered, the person thinks that there was no pain. Therefore, the self is neither of the nature of bliss nor is it self-luminous.[21]

20. SD, p. 122.
21. Ibid., pp. 123-4.

CHAPTER XIII

THE PROBLEM OF UNIVERSAL

13.1. *Individuality and Class Character*

Things are perceived as different in some respects and identical in others. An individual cow is perceived as existing in a particular time and occupying a particular place. It stands apart from other objects as an individual existent and can be distinguished from them by its peculiarities. But it is not altogether different. In spite of its peculiar mode of existence it is an existent like other animate and inanimate existents. It is an animal like a horse and a buffalo. It is a cow like other cows. In language we have two kinds of names, proper and common. Proper names denote individual things and common names denote their classes. A proper name is applicable to one individual only, but a common name is applicable to a number of individuals. When an object of perception is determined to be a cow we are conscious of its oneness with other objects which also are known as cows. Cowness is a predicate commonly shared by a number of individual animals. There is a consciousness of difference and also of unity when a number of animals called cows is perceived, and both of them must have corresponding realities as their bases. The objective basis of the consciousness of difference is the mutually exclusive nature of individual things and that of the consciousness of unity is their common nature. Common names refer to this latter. The reality of the common nature of objects cannot be denied. Objects are always conceived in a two-fold way, which would not be possible if they were not of a double nature. The double nature of an object consists in its specific individuality and its class-character.[1] The reality corresponding to our class-concepts is called universal, because it is not confined to this or that particular individual but is

1. SV, *Ākṛti.*, 5.

common to a number of them. There are as many universals as there are class-concepts. Cowness is a universal residing in all past, present and future cows. Similarly, there are such universals as humanity, horseness, redness etc. The universals are of a varying extension according to the number of particulars in which they reside.

The Buddhist denies the reality of universals and holds that only unique particulars (*svalakṣaṇa*) are real. They say that there is nothing common in them. The Vedāntin denies the reality of particulars and says that being (*sattā*) alone is real. Both these views are wrong. The Buddhist cannot explain the consciousness of identity in different particulars. If the universal cow is unreal there is no sense in calling certain animals by the common name 'cow'. And if particulars are unreal, as the Vedāntin says, why should a particular thing be perceived as different from another? As a matter of fact universal and particular are relative to each other, so that a denial of one means a denial of both. There can be no universal unless there are particulars and there can be no particulars unless there is a universal to be particularized. Neither the idea of universal is ever contradicted nor that of particular. Therefore, both of them must be grounded in reality. The Buddhist says that the idea of universal is secondary and that it is derived from the same causal efficiency (*arthakriyā*) possessed by a number of particulars. But why should a number of particular animals, cows, for instance, should possess the same causal efficiency if they are totally different from one another? A functional unity of diverse particulars presupposes their structural identity. The actions of A and B cannot be the same unless they share a common nature. Moreover, if there is no universal at all, how can an action of A be the same as an action of B? And if two different actions can be identical, why should two particuiar cows not be identical? The Buddhist says that particulars and universals are nothing but ideas. But this is wrong. All valid ideas have corresponding real objects as their bases. We have such ideas as 'this is a cow', 'that too is a cow', 'this cow is different from that cow' etc., and all our practical activities are based on such ideas. Therefore, they are valid and universal and particulars must be their objective counterparts.[2]

2. Ibid., 6-9.

13.2. *Is the Word 'Universal' merely a Name?*

The Buddhist says: If there is supposed to be a universal 'cow' on the ground that we call different animals by the name 'cow', then in a similar way there must be a universal 'universal' on the ground that we call different universals, e.g., cow, horse etc. by the name universal. Against this Kumārila asserts that the different universals have nothing in common except the name universal. When we say 'cow is a universal', 'horse is a universal' etc. we designate them by a common name without thinking that there is a corresponding universal embracing all these universals. But the case of the universal cow is different. When we designate different cows as cow there is a common character 'cowness' as the basis of the designation. There is no substantial entity corresponding to the name 'forest' as it is nothing but a collection of trees; but this does not prove that there is no substantial entity corresponding to the name 'tree'. Similarly, from the unreality of the universal 'universal' it cannot be concluded that the universal 'cow' too is unreal. Moreover, the false idea of unity in different universals appears in those alone who know the use of language. But even those who do not know the word 'cow' distinctly recognize all cows as forming one class. Some people say that thingness (*vastutva*) is common to various universals and the name universal refers to this common character. But on this theory we will have to assume an infinite number of universals, because thingness too being a universal will come to possess another thingness and so on ad infinitum. Again, because particular cows and horses too are things and 'universal' is the name of thingness, it will come to apply to them as much as to their classes, which is absurd. Therefore, the different universals have only a verbal identity and not a real one, while corresponding to cowness and horseness there are real identities residing in particular cows and horses respectively.[3]

The point raised by the Buddhist is really very important. Kumārila's answer appears to be unsatisfactory. If the word 'universal' is merely a name without any corresponding reality it should be meaningless. Certainly, there are words, e.g., 'sky-flower' etc. which have no corresponding reality. Yet they have

3. Ibid., 11-24.

meaning and it consists in denoting things which are not actual. Then, should we say that the word 'universal' has a meaning, though the thing denoted by it is not actual? When we say that cowness is a universal, what we mean is that it characterizes many particulars. Similarly horseness characterizes many particulars. Thus the word 'universal' means a common nature. But is common nature not actual? If so, we have to give up the realist theory of universals and adopt conceptualism or nominalism. It may be said that cowness is a common nature and actual, horseness is a common nature and actual, but there is no actual common nature in these common natures. But then we may also say that cowness is actual, horseness is actual but there is no animalness in cowness and horseness and thus the universal 'animal' becomes a mere name. It will be said that animalness is not common to cowness and horseness but to individuals called cows and horses. But then the problem becomes more complicated and the question arises whether cowness and animalness reside side by side in an individual cow or the latter resides in the former.

13.3. *Reality of Universals as the Ground of Inference*

Kumārila says that if the reality of universals were denied inference and verbal testimony would lose their validity and consequently all practical behaviour would come to an end. Inference is based on the knowledge of an invariable relationship between the major and middle terms. The validity of its conclusion depends on the validity of such knowledge. We discover the concomitance of fire with smoke after observing some instances of fire and smoke. But if there were no universals like fire and smoke, i.e., if the observed instances of fire were as different among themselves as a particular fire is from a particular tree and the different instances of smoke as different from one another as they are from a stone, we could have no justification in generalizing the relationship between a particular fire and a particular smoke, or such a generalization would not help in practice because those particular instances would never recur. In that case whenever we spoke 'smoke is always accompanied by fire' the statement would mean only that we have observed in the past some events which we arbitrarily call 'smoke' to have been accompanied by some other events arbitrarily called 'fire'. Actually when we infer fire from smoke we believe that the perceived smoke is essentially the same as we have observed in the past and found to be accompanied by fire and this belief is verified when on making an approach we actually see fire. The sameness of the previous smoke and the present one points to the reality of the universal smoke. Thus the validity of inference depends on the reality of universals. If someone tries to prove the unreality of universals by inference he attempts an impossible thing, because that which is the ground of inference cannot be negated by inference itself. Verbal testimony depends on the reality of universals. If universal were unreal, such words as 'cow', 'horse' etc. would have no meaning and so a person using them would not be understood by others.[4]

The Buddhist says that everything is unique and nothing is common to diverse particulars. But we definitely recognize common features in different particulars. We observe recurrences in nature and our conduct is regulated by them.

> The tailor, cutting out readymade suits, knows the general run of men's sizes; the teacher has a rough idea of the capacities of next year's freshmen; and the mother who believes her baby to be unique, as he certainly is, reads with avidity the nursing book which is written on the assumption that all babies are more or less alike...The same features recur in different individual beings and individual things and we are aware of this fact.[5]

Recurrences imply universals, and the use of general words refers to them. Universals are perceptible as is proved by the appearance of doubt whether a particular animal seen from a distance is a cow or not and the subsequent disappearance of it when the animal approaches.[6]

13.4. *Configuration Theory Rejected*

Now, what is the nature of universal? By a universal is meant an identity existing in numerically different individuals. But what is this identity? What is that which continues to be the same irrespective of differences among particular cows and forms

4. Ibid., 39; SD, p. 99.
5. Aaron, *The Theory of Universals*, pp. 231-2.
6. SV, *Vanavāda*, 25.

the basis of their being called by the same general name 'cow'? Some people reply that the form, shape or configuration (*saṃsthāna*) of all particular cows is the same. But this is wrong. If by a universal we mean a common shape, then how are the universals 'airness' and 'fireness' to be explained? There is no visible shape of air and no definite outline of fire and so there can be no common shape in different airs and fires and still we recognize and speak about the universals 'airness' and 'fireness'. Even in the case of cows, each of which possesses a definite visible outline, we find that there is no agreement in their shapes. No two shapes are found to coincide in nature. How can, then, we speak of a common shape? A shape depends on the arrangement of parts. Sometimes a part is destroyed, as when a cow loses an ear or a leg, and consequently its shape becomes different. But in spite of this change in shape the cow still retains its class-character. If the universal 'cowness' is identified with a common shape, then the same cow without an ear should cease to be a cow. It may be said that the shape is changed, yet the common character 'shapeness' remains. But if 'cowness' is identical with the universal 'shapeness', then a horse also becomes a cow because the latter also possesses a shape. Again, the shape of a picture or a model of cow is also the same as of a living cow; but we never say that the picture or model is a cow. We see that a lump of gold is first given the shape of a ring and then of some other ornament. The shapes of different ornaments are different, yet the character 'goldness' is seen to continue. Therefore, a universal must be different from a shape.[7]

13.5. *Resemblance Theory Untenable*

Others reject the notion of identity as false. They explain general names as based on similarity. Accordingly the word 'cow' denotes a group of numerically different particulars having nothing in common but closely resembling one another. But in what, Kumārila asks, does the similarity between a particular cow A and another particular cow B consist? So far as their particular forms are concerned they are different from each other, one being black and the other red. It may be said that

7. Ibid., 16-23.

the similarity between them is clearly visible. But if so, then when we see B after seeing A we should say 'this is like A' instead of saying 'this is a cow'. It may be said that this latter is illusory. This, however, is wrong, because even if there be an illusion it can at most take the form 'this is A'. The word 'cow' is not a synonym of A. If there were an absolute identity between A and cow, any other individual, however closely it may resemble A, could not be called by the name 'cow', just as it is not called A. Cowness is seen to recur in different individual cows, but A-ness is not. And this is the reason why different cows are called 'cow' but not A. Thus the resemblance theory cannot explain the general name 'cow'. We do not find any individual named 'cow' and so A, B and other particular animals cannot be called cows on the ground of bearing a close resemblance to that.

Plato maintained that universals subsisted in a realm different from the realm of particulars and that particulars were only shadowy copies of universals. This is a mere fancy. Even if it be granted that the name 'cow' belongs to an individual residing in a supersensuous realm, it would be only a proper name A and then calling B by that name would be wholly unjustified. Let it be said that there is no supernatural individual having the name cow and that the first individual of the class 'cow' created by God was cow and the later individuals resembling it are called cows due to the resemblance. But since we do not perceive the first cow now, how can it be ascertained what animals at present resemble it? Moreover, when two similar individuals are perceived the consciousness appears in the form 'this is like that'. So, if the first individual is the cow, then other individuals bearing similarity to it must be apprehended as 'this is like cow' instead of 'this is a cow'. Similarity is a relation between two terms and when it is predicated of one term it has a reference to the other term. When similarity is perceived in A, it invariably refers to B to which it is similar. But a universal is not a relation. When an individual animal is apprehended as cow there is no explicit reference to other individuals. Again, similarity cannot be explained without universals. The ground of similarity is the coexistence in two things of the universals of many parts, qualities or relations. Thus similarity presupposes universal and hence it cannot be made the ground of the latter.[8]

Kumārila says that a universal is perceived and at the same time that it is not a shape. But, then, it is difficult to ascertain what a universal is. When we perceive an individual cow we see a particular shape, a particular colour and such parts as horns, hoofs and dewlap etc. If cowness consists in none of these and yet is a real entity it must be invisible. Kumārila says that by the presence of a dewlap we merely distinguish the universal cowness from such other universals as animalness etc. A number of universals inheres in the same individual, which we distinguish by certain peculiar characteristics.[9] Again he says that dewlap etc. are not the marks from which cowness is inferred, because there is no question of inference when an entity is perceived, and that just as we do no perceive the atoms of a lump of clay yet we perceive its extension so we perceive cowness though we do not distinctly perceive its peculiarities in totality.[10] Thus the perceived cowness is a collective effect on us of the parts of a cow. Kumārila rejects similarity as the ground of universal, because we do not say that one individual animal is like another but that they are cows. The reason behind all these inconsistencies is Kumārila's conception of language, viz., that words are eternal. Words are as much objective as the things signified by them. Facts cannot conflict with one another. The name 'cow' is used from time immemorial. Its usage does not depend on convention started by a particular man and hence it is not influenced by an individual's subjective way of thinking. Therefore, the concepts of a cow, a horse etc. must be valid and as every valid concept has a corresponding real entity there must be a real universal in the form of cow, horse etc.

13.6. *The Buddhist Apoha Theory Rejected*

The Buddhist does not believe in the reality of universals. According to him a universal is a mere figment of imagination. It is a mental construct without any objective basis. He maintains that general names such as cow, horse etc., do not stand

8. SV, *Ākṛti.*, 67-74.
9. SV, *Vanavāda*, 3.
10. Ibid., 4 and 7.

for any positive entity commonly inhering in diverse particulars. There is nothing in common in the individual cows except the name 'cow' with a negative connotation. The ground of the apparent sameness of different particulars is '*apoha*' or the negation of what is different. The different particulars A_1, A_2, A_3 etc. have nothing positive in common except the name 'A' and they are called A's because they all agree in excluding B, C, D etc. which are different from them. 'This is a cow' means 'this is not a non-cow', i.e., 'this is not a horse' etc. Different cows are called cow not because they share a common nature but because all of them agree in being different from a horse, a buffalo etc.

Kumārila says that negation always implies position: A is not B because it has a positive character of its own not shared by B. Now, what, the Buddhist may be asked, is the positive character of A which makes it different from a non-cow? It cannot be the specific form of it, because if it were the basis of being different from a non-cow, the word cow would not apply to B whose specific form is different from that of A. The specific forms of individual cows are different, yet the basis of their being called by the same name, according to the realist, is the universal cowness. The word 'cow' has a positive connotation in the form of cowness which is its meaning. But as the Buddhist does not recognize any such thing the word becomes meaningless. And if any meaning is allowed to it, it will differ from individual to individual just as the meaning of the proper name 'Rama' differs in different cases. An individual cow in specific form cannot be the basis of the negation of non-cows and likewise the collection of all cows too cannot be its basis, because the number of them is infinite and there is no possibility of a simultaneous perception of all past, present and future cows. Since the group of individual cows is not found in one place and they are scattered over different times and places and the connotation of the word 'cow' is not defined in terms of some positive character, it becomes impossible to decide as to which individual is to be included in the group and which to be excluded. Moreover, even if it be possible to demarcate the group of cows from other animals, the name 'cow' would be a collective name like the name 'forest' and would cease to be applied distributively to each individual cow. Therefore, the basis of the concept of cow can be nothing but the positive character 'cowness' common to all cows.[11]

The limits of the application of the word 'cow' cannot be ascertained in the absence of a positive character 'cowness' and again they cannot be ascertained by the particulars excluded by the word 'cow'. The word 'non-jar' has a negative connotation, yet its denotation is easily ascertained because the thing negated (*apohya*), i.e., jar is the name of things possessing a positive character jarness in common. The *apohyas* of the word 'cow', i.e., non-cows, on the other hand, are infinite in number and hence they cannot be conceived by the mind. Horse, elephant etc., which are the *apohyas* of the word 'cow' are themselves universals like cow and thus according to the Buddhist they too are negative entities like the universal cow. To ascertain the denotation of the word 'cow' we have to ascertain the denotation of the word 'horse' and again we have to depend on the ascertainment of the denotation of the word 'elephant' which is one of the *apohyas* of the word 'horse'. In this way we shall be going on ad infinitum without ever knowing the limits of the application of any word. Again, if a cow is nothing but a negation of non-cows, viz., horse, elephant, buffalo etc., then, since the number of these is infinite, the word 'cow' will really have an infinite number of meanings instead of one.[12]

As a matter of fact, when the word 'cow' is uttered we immediately become conscious of a positive character shared by all the individual cows. We never think about a cow in negative terms. When we see a particular individual belonging to the class cow what is apprehended is not of the form of negation, nor are we conscious of non-cows, e.g., horse etc. at that time. A cow is apprehended as a positive entity without implying any reference to other animals excluded by it. The *apoha*-ist also recognizes the positive entity 'cowness', but only indirectly. When we make a denial of a denial the result always is an affirmation. For instance, when it is said 'it is not that there is no jar on the ground', the speaker indirectly asserts that 'there

11. SV, *Apoha.*, 2-10.
12. Ibid., 65, 72, 60.

is a jar on the ground'. Similarly, when the Buddhist says that a cow is the negation of a non-cow (*ago'poha*) he indirectly asserts that it is a cow, and then either it is a tautology or it implies a positive common character.[13]

13.7. *The Relation between Universal and Particular*

About the relation between universal and particular some realists, viz., the Nyāya-Vaiśeṣika and Prabhākara, maintain that they are different from each other and yet they are not apprehended separately because a universal inheres in its various particulars. "Inherence (*samavāya*) is a relation subsisting between two inseparable entities and is the cause of such a notion as 'this is here'." If two entities move independently of one another or have different substrates, they are separable and so cannot be related by way of inherence. Universal and particular are inseparable. There is a relation of inherence not only between universal and particular but also between a substance and its qualities, a whole and its parts and a material cause and its effects.

Kumārila rejects the relation of inherence. Is inherence different or non-different from the terms of the relation? If it is different it must require another inherence to be related with them. Again the same problem arises with regard to the second inherence and to solve this recurrent problem an infinite number of inherences shall have to be postulated. If to avoid this difficulty inherence is assumed to be non-different from the terms related, the postulation of inherence becomes superfluous, because instead of it the terms themselves may be assumed to be non-different from each other.[14] Thus inherence is no real relation and even if it be real it cannot subsist between universal and particular because we never apprehend a universal, e.g., cowness, in the from 'here is cowness' as we should according to the definition of inherence. Consciousness of a universal always occurs in the form 'this is a cow' and never in the form 'here is cowness'. Therefore, universal is not different from particulars but is identical with them.

13. Ibid., 41, 64.
14. SV, 4. 148-9.

From direct experience in the form 'this is a cow' non-difference between the universal 'cow' and the particular 'this' is revealed. However, there is not absolute non-difference. There is difference as well as non-difference between universal and particular. When we say 'this cow is red and this cow is black' the form of cow is apprehended to be common while the form of red and that of black are apprehended to be uncommon. If the universal cowness were absolutely non-different from the form of a particular red cow the latter would recur in another particular cow which is black just as cowness recurs in it, or cowness too would not recur just as red-form does not recur. Therefore, there is difference also. Again, though a particular cow is apprehended as cow, yet 'cow' is not apprehended to be synonymous with 'this'. Therefore, there is non-difference, but not absolute non-difference. The difference and non-difference between universal and particular are not incompatible. When an object is successively perceived as silver and not silver there is incompatibility, because they are two different acts of cognition and the subsequent one cancels the first. But when a particular animal is perceived as cow, identity and difference are apprehended in a single act of consciousness without cancelling one another. The apparent incompatibility between identity and difference ceases when they are viewed from two different points of view. We attribute tallness to one individual when he is compared with one shorter in stature and at the same time we attribute shortness to him in comparison with another who is taller. In the case in question too there are two points of view. When the universal cow is considered as the essential nature of particular cows it is one and identical in all of them, but when it is considered as the embodiment of that nature it is different in different cases. The name 'cow' connotes an essential and common character 'cowness' which does not vary from individual to individual and at the same time it denotes many particulars which are numerically different from one another. The particular cows are the embodiments of the same generic character. They are different so far as they exist at different times and occupy separate bits of space. They also differ in such inessential features as colour, shape, size etc. Identity of nature is not incompatible with numerical difference.

The question whether universal is omnipresent or confined to individuals is answered by asserting that universal is the very self of individual. Being the self of individual how can it be elsewhere? An individual is born from its cause as connected with a universal. The question as to how and whence a universal can come to be connected with an individual in a place where it was not is irrelevant. An individual is born from its cause and the same cause at the same time gives rise to its relation of identity with the universal. The relation of identity springs from its cause just like the relation of conjunction. An object comes from elsewhere and is conjoined with a different place after successively coming in conjunction with different points of space. And, we cannot expect what happens in the case of conjunction to happen in the case of identity also, because the two are different and different things behave in different ways.

The question whether a universal resides in each individual in its entirety or piecemeal is irrelevant. Entirety depends on the possession of parts while a universal is one and devoid of parts. Therefore, only this much can be said that a universal resides in individuals, but to say that it resides wholly in each individual or partly is without any proof. Individuals cannot be said to be parts of universal. A universal is not related to individuals as a whole is related to its parts. A universal resides severally in each individual while a whole resides collectively in all its parts. Universal is a distributive unity while whole is a collective unity. Cowness is apprehended in each individual cow, while a whole, e.g., cloth, is apprehended in the aggregate of threads and not in each individual thread.[15]

13.8. *An Overview*

Kumārila advocates realism. The Buddhist is a nominalist. The Jainas also are realists, but unlike Kumārila who explains general names as signifying an identical essence inhering in many particulars, they explain them as grounded in observable resemblances among individual things. The Nyāya-Vaiśeṣika too advocates realism, but it differs from Kumārila's in maintaining that individual cows are not really 'cow' but externally related to the

15. SD, pp. 100-3.

universal 'cow', though the relation is inseparable, and that the universal 'cow' is all-pervading like space. Kumārila, on the other hand, maintains that a universal is immanent in particulars. Kumārila's view seems to be more reasonable. The Jaina view is defective insofar as it does not recognize any identity. Resemblance is a fact of experience. We perceive two cows and find that they closely resemble each other, though we may not discover any identity between them. So far the Jaina view is correct. But identity also is a fact of direct observation. We perceive things possessing the same shade of blue and are unable to distinguish between them in this respect. If the existence of identical qualities is denied we get involved in grave difficulties. We cannot distinguish the colour of a crow from that of another crow. It will be said that they are not identical but similar. But, then what about the colours of the two wings of the same crow? If they too are similar what is the sense in saying about the colour of that crow in the singular? Again, is the colour of one part of the same wing identical with or similar to that of another part? Thus we may go on repeating the question until we reach the constituent atoms of the same crow. The difficulty cannot be solved unless it is accepted that identical qualities exist. Hence, it should be concluded that some universals, at least universals of some sensible qualities, are based on observable identities. But the question arises: How can a quality of this thing, e.g., the colour of this crow, characterize another thing? The reply can be found in Pārthasārathi's remark that the different tāla trees are identical because they are produced out of the seeds of the same original tāla tree. Things in which identical qualities are observed must have come forth from a common source. If from one single lump of clay a number of jars is constructed the colour of the clay will certainly appear in all of them and thus it must be identical in all of them. The question whether there is a character, like the colour of two crows, identical in all cows is a bit more difficult. Is there any single common and identical character 'cowness' in all cows? Certainly, we do not observe such a thing as we perceive an identical shade of blue in many things. Cowness may be a combination of some identical qualities, but we cannot definitely say what they are. Similarity among different individual cows is an observed fact and this may be the only reason why they are called by the same name. Kumārila says that there can be no similarity without identity in some respects. This, however, is very difficult to prove and could perhaps be traced to the Mīmāṃsā theory that words are eternal and the way in which they are commonly treated is absolutely valid.

Nominalism and conceptualism offer different explanations of universals. Hobbes has been one of the greatest exponents of nominalism. According to him the real is always particular. There is nothing common in things having the same name except the name. On this theory naming becomes an absolutely arbitrary affair. Why this particular animal should be called cow and not horse becomes inexplicable. To call this animal and others closely resembling it by the name 'cow', accordingly, does not stand on any rational ground and is no better than to call each of a group of a book, a bicycle, a whale and a feather by the name, say, X. A child is shown an animal and the name cow is simultaneously uttered. It is useless to instruct the child that this and similar other animals should be called by the name 'cow', for, he cannot follow the instruction. The same process is repeated twice or thrice. Next, the child happens to see an animal closely resembling one which was shown to him and he utters the name cow. If there is nothing objective corresponding to the name 'cow', why should the child call the animal which was not shown to him previously by the name 'cow'?

Conceptualism too does not fare better. According to it a universal is merely an abstraction. It is a concept having an ideal existence. The mind in the process of thinking abstracts certain aspects of things and combines them together. If this theory be correct we should be conscious of a definite idea when such general names as 'cow', 'man' etc. are uttered. But actually introspection does not reveal any such thing, though we know how to apply such names correctly. In most of the cases we are unable to define and specify the meanings of general words. Thinking involves abstraction, but it does not mean that thinking is an ideal manipulation of imaginary things. Aaron says:

> In Berkeley's sense of 'singling', abstraction is necessarily present in the discovery of a common quality. I concentrate

> upon the colour in noticing that three objects have the same colour. In this sense of abstracting, it is true, I abstract even in seeing the colour, for I single it out for observation.[16]

Again he says about abstraction in the sense of imaginative concepts:

> We must admit, too, abstract concepts in the sense of constructed or framed imaginative creations, where the abstraction is more than the sense concentrating on an aspect of our experience, but is also taking it away and joining with it other abstractions to create the classificatory standards we require.[17]

Such universals as mermaid, centaur etc. are of this latter type, but all universals are not of this type. Most of the universals are discovered in the real world. They are not the products of joining in the mind two or more abstracted qualities which are not actually joined in the real world.

16. *The Theory of Universals*, pp. 162-3.
17. Ibid., p. 242.

Chapter XIV

BHĀṬṬA REALISM VERSUS IDEALISM

Kumārila's chief contribution was his refutation of subjective idealism and the restoration of realism to the position from which it had been temporarily deposed by the Buddhist *vijñānavādin.* Idealism of the subjectivist type had prevailed over the ancient Indian realism for centuries and it had become almost irrefutable. The idealists used two types of arguments to support their thesis. Arguments of one type were intended to prove that cognition must be known before the existence of external objects can be established and a knowledge of cognition can be possible only when it has some form, in which case the hypothesis of external objects having a form becomes a gratuitous one and hence it must be given up in the interest of economy of thought. Arguments of the other type were employed by the idealist to prove that as the hypothesis of extra-mental objects involves a number of self-contradictions, it is logically untenable.

When the whole philosophical world was overwhelmed by the idealist's anti-realist arguments, Kumārila came forward to the rescue of realism with his equally bold anti-idealist arguments. It is not the case that prior to Kumārila none came forward to meet the idealist challenge. Several thinkers tried to defend realism and expose the weaknesses of idealism. But the credit of silencing the idealist for ever and bringing about the end of the idealistic tradition in India goes to Kumārila alone. Kumārila's achievement can rightly be compared to that of the Cambridge philosopher G.E. Moore who seems to have brought about the end of subjective idealism in the Western philosophy. Kumārila's refutation of *nirālambanavāda* and Moore's *Refutation of Idealism* (published in 1903) both possess equal historical value. India had attained philosophical maturity of the West so many centuries ahead and it is not strange that she had produced thinkers of intellectual acumen like Kumārila who appear to have dwarfed even the greatest intellects of the West today. Kumārila knocked out the idealist from the philosophical arena. He proved that knowledge of cognition is not a prior condition of knowledge of objects and hence the form that is manifested in cognition belongs to the external object. He further showed that external object is not a matter of assumption but a fact.

Kumārila's keen intellect rightly grasped the root idea from which idealism grew. The idealist assumed that cognition must be known before an object is known. He took it as a self-evident truth. Kumārila proved the untenability of this notion. He went further ahead and proved that cognition is never known directly, because it is a formless and fleeting entity. Cognition is not even self-aware. Its existence is rather presumed to explain the fact of object-manifestation. In this connection Kumārila put forward a unique theory which is known as the theory of cognizedness. What is there in a manifested object that cannot be explained without presuming the cognitive act? It is the manifestedness or cognizedness of the object of cognition that leads to the presumption of cognition. Cognizedness is an objective quality just as blueness etc. are and it is generated in the object of knowledge by the act of cognition just as cookedness is produced in rice by the act of cooking.

Here a word of caution is needed. Kumārila's theory of cognizedness should not be interpreted along the idealistic lines. Idealism in epistemology stands for a number of theories which differ widely among themselves. The highest common factor of the epistemological theories grouped together as idealism is the belief that in the process of knowing the mind modifies reality. Kumārila too believes that the act of cognition modifies reality by generating cognizedness in it. But this resemblance is merely a superficial one. It should not mislead us into thinking that Kumārila was an idealist, for, Kumārila never meant that reality as known becomes different on account of the knowing process from the reality as it is in itself. On the contrary, reality known and reality in itself are identical. Cognizedness is a quality that is added to the known object at a moment subsequent to the object-consciousness. As a matter of fact, the so-called cognizedness is nothing but the feeling of familiarity that is associated with a known object.

Kumārila is an uncompromising realist and like other realists he has to face the problem of error. Error is a universally recognized fact. If cognition apprehends reality without any modification, how does the realist explain the occurrence of error? The presence of error is responsible for the existence of the opposite camp of epistemologists known as idealists and also of the theory known as representationism which is a half-way house between realism and idealism. How does then Kumārila explain error? He does not explain it away like Prabhākara. Nor does he say like Śaṅkara that in the so-called error we cognize a real thing though it belongs to a different order of being. His intellectual honesty makes him declare that error is truly a misapprehension of reality. However, Kumārila saves his realism from passing into idealism by saying that error has all the elements of reality though they are wrongly synthesized under certain abnormal subjective and objective conditions. The given 'this' (rope) is real and 'snake' too is real, though their identity is false. All the elements in the phenomenon of error are objective. It is merely the identity of two objective facts that can be called subjective in error. Kumārila has rejected the idealist theory of cognition having a form and quite consistently with this rejection he also rejects the theory that the 'snake' in rope-snake illusion is a subjective or ideal image. He says that it is merely the relation of identity between two objective facts that is subjective or ideal. Kumārila's explanation of error may not be quite satisfactory. Otherwise, how could his own follower, Sucaritamiśra, contradict him later and say that it is the subjective form of cognition that is superimposed on the given 'this' in error. However, Kumārila's defence of realism should be appreciated for the comparatively high degree of consistency that he has been able to maintain and the minimum of ideality that he has allowed in his explanation of error.

Error has played a very important role in the history of philosophy. Had there been no error there would perhaps have been no rival systems of realism and idealism. Error converts our naively realistic belief in the world of knowledge into a sceptical attitude. If the 'snake' that we 'see' turns out to be a mere piece of rope, then the whole world of knowledge as well may just be a fabrication of our own mind. The Buddhist idealist jumps at this possibility and declares that all knowledge is objectless: No knowledge has any objective basis. All knowledge thus becomes false. This gave rise to the great epistemological controversy over the problem of defining and ascertaining the truth of knowledge. The realist recognizes an independent reality of the external world and it is through knowledge that this world manifests itself to the knower. Then obviously enough correspondence of knowledge to the external world constitutes its truth. Kumārila defines truth in terms of correspondence. But a more important aspect of the controversy about truth in India has been the problem of ascertainment of truth. What is the test of truth? This problem gave rise to two rival theories, viz., those of *svataḥprāmāṇya* and *parataḥprāmāṇya*.

The theory of *parataḥprāmaṇya* declares that truth is an extrinsic property of knowledge, since it depends on the presence of excellences in the causes of knowledge, and that it is known through certain extraneous tests. The more important extraneous tests are coherence and pragmatic efficiency. Kumārila shows the deficiencies of these tests, and declares that truth is intrinsic to knowledge and that knowledge by itself is always known to be true, while its falsehood is manifested by another contradicting knowledge. Coherence lacks finality. Truth once doubted can never be established finally. Logically we can never get rid of doubt, however big the number of corroborating cognitions may be. Pragmatic test also cannot be depended upon. Pragmatic efficiency is merely conative experience which is also a type of knowledge. But when we have once refused intrinsic truth to knowledge in general, why should there be any partiality for a special type of knowledge? Moreover, pragmatic test is not always successful. Experience of pragmatic success is sometimes found to be illusory as is usually the case in dreams. The alternative theory offered by Kumārila, viz., that truth is intrinsic and falsehood extrinsic, seems to be more acceptable. By the intrinsicality of truth Kumārila means that truth is not a property added to knowledge by extraneous factors, but is a property depending solely on the causes that give rise to knowledge and is known by the knowledge itself. By the extrinsicality of falsehood Kumārila does not mean that knowledge born true is made false subsequently by another contradicting cognition, but that a false knowledge is born false and known as such only subsequently when another contradicting knowledge appears. Falsehood is extrinsic in the sense that it depends on the blemishes of the causes, and the blemishes are not natural or necessary features of them but merely accidental ones. None except a perverted intellect could say that some devilish power has installed the faculty of knowledge in us with the intention of misleading us and that reality is just the opposite of what appears in knowledge. Could one say that the hare that we perceive is unreal and the horn that we do not perceive is real? The hypothesis that reality is revealed in knowledge is certainly saner and more rational than the one that reality is just the opposite of what knowledge reveals to us. Kumārila's theory of intrinsic truth may be interpreted along this line. Thus interpreted the theory means that a truthful revelation of reality is the natural function of knowledge, and then falsehood becomes a merely accidental feature of knowledge, which is the meaning of the extrinsicality of falsehood. If this is admitted, realism becomes far less exposed to the attack of idealism. Contrarily, idealism could then be seen as making a mere accidental feature of knowledge, viz., error, the universal and necessary attribute of it. This would be sufficient to put the idealist on the defensive, though refutation of idealism would still be a long way ahead.

BIBLIOGRAPHY

A. Primary Texts and Translations

Arthasaṅgraha of Laugākṣi Bhāskara. Text with English Translation and Introduction, ed. A.B. Gajendragadkar & R. D. Karmarkar, Motilal Banarsidass, 1984.

Brahma Sūtra Śaṃkara Bhāṣyam. Text with Vācaspati Miśra's *Bhāmatī* etc., ed. Jagdish Shastri, Motilal Banarsidass, Delhi.

Bṛhatī of Prabhākara. Edited with Śālikanātha's *Ṛjuvimalā Pañcikā* & *Bhāṣyapariśiṣṭa* by G. K. Ramanatha Sastri, 3 Parts, in Madras University Sanskrit Series 3, 1934. Part 4 edited by S. Subrahmanya Sastri, MUSS, 24, 1962.

Kāśikā of Sucaritamiśra. Trivandrum Sanskrit Series No. 99, 1929.

Mānameyodaya of Nārāyaṇa Bhaṭṭa & Nārāyaṇa Paṇḍita. Edited & translated by C. Kunhan Raja & S. Suryanarayana Sastri, Adyar, 1933.

The Mīmāṃsā Sūtras of Jaimini. 2 Vols. Text with Eng. Trans., Intro. & Notes, M.L. Sandal, Motilal Banarsidass, Delhi.

Nītitattvāvirbhāva of Cidānanda. Edited by P. K. N. Sastri. TSS 168, 1953.

Nyāyabindu of Dharmakīrti. Edited with Dharmottara's Ṭīkā by Th. Stcherbatsky, Bibliotheca Buddhica 7, 1918 & translated by Th. Stcherbatsky in *Buddhist Logic*, Bib. Buddhica 26, 1930-32.

Nyāyakandalī of Śrīdhara. Edited by V. P. Dvivedin, VizSS, 1985. Edited & translated into Hindi by Durgadhara Jha Sharma, Ganganatha Jha Grantha Mala 1, Varanasi, 1963. English translation by G.N. Jha, Reprinted, Banaras, 1916.

Nyāyakośa by B. Jhalakikara. Ed. by V.S. Abhyankar, BSS 49, Poona, 1928.

Nyāyakusumāñjali of Udayana. Edited with *Āmoda*, *Viveka*,

Bodhinī, *Parimala* & *Sāra* by Mahaprabhulal Goswami, Darbhanga, 1972.

Nyāyamañjarī of Jayanta. Edited by S.N. Sukla, KSS 106, 1934-36. Translated by Janakivallabha Bhattacharya, MLBD, 1978.

Nyāya-Praveśa of Dignāga, Part I, Sanskrit Text with Commentaries. Ed. A.B. Dhruva, GOS.

Nyāyaratnākara of Pārthasārathi. Edited by Rama Sastri. ChSS 11, 1898-1899.

Nyāyaratnamālā of Pārthasārathi. Edited by Gangadhara Sastri, ChSS 7. Edited with Rāmānujācārya's *Nyāyaratnākara* by K. S. Ramaswami Sastri, GOS 75, 1937. Edited by A. Subrahmanya Sastri, Varanasi, 1972.

Nyāya Sūtras of Gautama with *Bhāṣya* of Vātsyāyana, *Nyāyavārtika* of Uddyotakara and *Tātparyaṭīkā* of Vācaspati, edited by V.P. Dvivedin, BI 113, 1887-1914. English translation by Ganga Nath Jha, 4 Vols., Motilal Banarsidass, Delhi, 1984.

Nyāyāvatāra of Siddhasenadivākara. Edited with Śāntisūri's *Jainatarkavārtika* by Dalsukh Malvaniya; Sri Bahadur Singh Singhi Jain Series, 20, 1949; also edited & translated by Satkari Mookerjee, Vaishali Institute Research Bulletin 1.

Padārthadharmasaṅgraha of Praśastapāda. Edited with Śrīdhara's *Nyāya-Kandalī* by V.P. Dvivedin, VizSS 6. Edited with Udayana's *Kiraṇāvalī* & *Lakṣaṇāvalī* by J.S. Jatly, GOS 154, 1971.

Parīkṣāmukhasūtra of Māṇikyanandi. Edited with Anantavīrya's *Prameyaratnamālā* and translated by Sarat Chandra Ghoshal, Sacred Books of the Jains 11, 1940; also by Hiralal Jain, Varanasi, 1964.

Prakaraṇapañcikā of Śālikanātha. Edited by Mukunda Sastri, ChSS 17, 1903; by A Subrahmanya Sastri, Banaras, 1963.

Pramāṇanayatattvālokālaṅkāra of Vādi Deva Sūri. Edited by Dharmavijaya Jain, Bombay, 1937. Translated by Harisatya Bhattacharya, Bombay 1967.

Pramāṇasamuccaya of Diṅnāga. Passages edited & translated by H. N. Randle in *Fragments from Dignāga*, London, 1926.

Pratyakṣa Pariccheda translated under the title *Dignāga on Perception* by Masaki Hattori, HOP.

Ṛjuvimalā of Śālikanātha. *Bṛhatī* of Prabhākara edited with *Ṛjuvimalāpañcikā* of Śālikanātha by S. K. Ramanatha Sastri, 3 Parts, in Madras University Sanskrit Series 3, 1934. Part 4, edited by S. Subrahmanya Sastri MUSS 24 1962.

Śabarabhāṣya. See *Mīmāṃsā Sūtras* of Jaimini. English translation by Ganganath Jha, GOS, Baroda.

Sāṃkhyakārikā with *Gauḍapāda Bhāṣya*, edited with Vācaspati Miśra's *Tattvakaumudī* & Editor's Hindi Commentary by Ram Shankar Bhattacharya, Varanasi, 1976. Translated by Gerald James Larson in *Classical Samkhya*, Delhi, 1969.

Sāṅkhyatattvakaumudī of Vācaspati. Edited & Translated into Hindi by Ādya Prasad Misra, Āllahabad 1966, & by Ram Shankar Bhattacharya, Delhi, 1967. Translated by G. J. Larson in *Classical Samkhya*, Delhi, 1969.

Sarvadarśanasaṅgraha of Mādhavācārya. Edited by Ānandasrama Pandits, Ānandasrama Sanskrit Series 51; translated by E.B. Cowell & A.E. Gough 1893, 1894. Reprint available.

Śāstradīpikā of Pārthasārathi. *Tarkapāda* Section edited with Rāmakṛṣṇa's *Yuktisnehaprapūraṇī* by L.S. Dravid, ChSS 43, 1916. Translated by D. Venkataramiah, Gaekwad Oriental Series 89, 1940.

Siddhāntamuktāvalī of Viśvanātha. Translated by S. Madhavananda, Ramakrishna Mission.

Ślokavārtika of Kumārila Bhaṭṭa with the Commentary *Nyāyaratnākara* by Pārthasārathimiśra, ed. Swami Dvarikadasa Sastri, Pracya Bharati Series 10, Banaras, 1978. English translation by Ganga Nath Jha, BI, reprinted by Sri Satguru Publications, Delhi.

Syādvādamañjarī. Eng. translation by F. W. Thomas, Motilal Banarsidass, Delhi.

Tantravārtika of Kumārila Bhaṭṭa. ASS 97, Poona, 1929. English Translation by Ganga Nath Jha, reprinted by Sri Satguru Publications, Delhi.

Tarkasaṅgraha of Annaṃbhaṭṭa. Edited with *Dīpikā* & *Nyāya-*

bodhinī by Y.V. Athalye and translated by M.R. Bodas with Eng. notes, Bombay Sanskrit & Prakrit Series; revised by Pusalkar, 1963.

Tārkikarakṣā of Varadarāja. Edited with Mallinātha Sūri's *Niṣkaṇṭaka* and excerpts from Jñānapūrṇa's *Laghudīpikā* by Arthur Venis in *Pandit* & reprinted, Banaras 1906.

Tātparyaṭīkā of Bhaṭṭombeka. Ed. S. K. Ramanatha Sastri, rev. K. Kunjanni Raja & R. Thangaswami, Madras, 1971.

Tattvabindu with an Introduction by V.A.R. Shastri, Annamalai University Sanskrit Series 3, 1936.

Tattvasaṅgraha of Śāntarakṣita with the Commentary *Pañjikā* by Kamalaśīla, 2 Vols. Ed. Swami Dvarikadas Sastri, Bauddha Bharati Series 2, Varanasi 1968. English translation by Ganga Nath Jha, 2 Vols. GOS, Baroda.

Tattvopaplavasiṃha of Jayarāśi. Ed. by Sukhlalji & Pansikar, Gaekwad Oriental Series 87, 1940.

Vākyapadīya of Bhartṛhari. Edited with Helarāja's *Prakīrṇaprakāśa* and Puṇyarāja's *Prakāśa* by Gangadhara Sastri & Ramachandra Sastri, Banaras Sanskrit Series 5, 1887-1905.

Vaiśesikasūtra of Kaṇāda, edited with Śaṅkara Miśra's *Upaskāra* and Praśastapāda's *Padārthadharmasaṃgraha* by Dhundiraja Sastri, Kashi Sanskrit Series 3, 1923.

Vedāntaparibhāṣā of Dharmarājādhvarīndra. Edited and translated by S. Suryanarayana Sastri, Adyar, 1942; Belur 1963.

B. Secondary Literature

Aaron, R.I.: *The Theory of Universals*, Oxford, 1952.

Bradley, F.H.: *Principles of Logic*, Oxford U.P. 1928.

Chatterjee, S.C.: *The Nyāya Theory of Knowledge*, Calcutta University, 1939.

Datta, D.M.: *The Six Ways of Knowing*, George Allen & Unwin, London, 1932.

Drake & Others: *Essays in Critical Realism*, The Macmillan Company.

Dravid, Raja Ram: *The Problem of Universals in Indian Philosophy*, Motilal Banarsidass, Varanasi, 1972.

D'sa, Francis X: *Śabdaprāmāṇyam in Śabara and Kumārila*, De Nobili Research Library, Vienna, 1980.

Gächter, Othmar: *Hermeneutics and Language in Pūrvamīmāṃsā*, Motilal Banarsidass, Delhi, 1983.

Holt & Others: *The New Realism*, The Macmillan Company.

Jha, Ganganath: *The Prabhākara School of Pūrva Mīmāṃsā*, Motilal Banarsidass, Delhi.

———: *Pūrva Mīmāṃsā in its Sources*, with A Critical Bibliography by Umesh Mishra, Banaras Hindu University, Varanasi.

Joseph, H.W.B.: *An Introduction to Logic*, Oxford, 1916.

Keith, A.B.: *Indian Logic and Atomism*, Oxford, 1921.

———: *The Karma Mimamsa*, The Heritage of India Series, 1921.

Koffey: *Epistemology*.

Maitra, S. K.: *Studies in Philosophy and Religion*, Calcutta, 1941, 1956.

Mill, John Stuart, *A System of Logic*, London, Longmans Green & Co. Ltd.

Moore, G.E.: "Refutation of Idealism", *Mind*, 1903, included in his *Philosophical Studies*, London, Routledge & Kegan Paul, 1922.

Murti, T.R.V.: *Studies in Indian Thought*. Ed. H. Coward, Motilal Banarsidass, Delhi, 1983.

Plott, John C: *Global History of Philosophy*, 5 Vols., Motilal Banarsidass, Delhi.

Potter, Karl H.: *The Encyclopedia of Indian Philosophies*, Vol. I, Bibliography, Motilal Banarsidass, Delhi, 1971.

Radhakrishnan, S. : *Indian Philosophy*, 2 Vols., George Allen & Unwin.

Raja, K. Kunjunni: *Indian Theories of Meaning*, The Adyar Library and Research Centre, 1963, 1977.

Randle, H.N.: *Indian Logic in Early Schools*, Oxford, 1930.

Russell, B.: *An Enquiry into Meaning and Truth*, George Allen & Unwin, 1940.

———: *Human Knowledge*, George Allen & Unwin, 1948.

———: *Our Knowledge of the External World*, George Allen and Unwin, London.

Sastri, S. Kuppuswami: *A Primer of Indian Logic*, Madras, 1951.

Sastry, Gaurinath: *The Philosophy of Word and Meaning*, Calcutta, Sanskrit College Research Series 5, 1959.

Sharma, P.S.: *Anthology of Kumārila Bhaṭṭa's Works*, Selected Texts in Roman Script with an Introduction, Motilal Banarsidass.

Shastri, Gauri Nath: *A Study in the Dialectics of Sphota*, Motilal Banarsidass, Delhi.

Shastri, Pashupati Nath: *Introduction to Purva Mimamsa*, Calcutta, 1923.

Sinha, J.N.: *A History of Indian Philosophy*, Vol. II, Central Book Agency, Calcutta, 1952.

———: *Indian Psychology, Perception*, London 1934, Sinha Publishing House, Calcutta. Reprinted by MLBD.

———: *Indian Realism*, Motilal Banarsidass (Reprint).

Stcherbatsky, Th.: *Buddhist Logic*, 2 Vols., Dover Publication, New York, 1962.

Stebbing, L.S.: *A Modern Introduction to Logic*, Methuen, London, 1950.

Vidyabhusan, S.C.: *History of Indian Logic*, Motilal Banarsidass, Delhi.

INDEX

CORRECTIONS

31/-6,-12:	read	**cognitions**	for	**cognition**
64/-4:	,,	***manas***	,,	***mamas***
100/fn. 58:	,,	**बाधे**	,,	**धाधे**
106/-6:	,,	**and**	,,	**aad**
124/1:	delete	**if**	after	**case**
129/13:	add	**when**	before	**in**
143/3:	read	**प्रमाणजिज्ञासा**	for	**प्रमाण जिज्ञासा**
147/fn. 9/1:	,,	**तत्प्रत्यक्षमनिमित्तं**	,,	**तत्प्रत्क्षमनिमित्तं**
155/9:	,,	**past**	,,	**part**
157/13:	,,	**inference**	,,	**coninfer ence**
157/14:	,,	**consequently**	,,	**sequently**
211/-12:	,,	***vyāpti***	,,	***vyāpi***
212/-19:	,,	***pratijñā***	,,	***prātijñā***
224/-15:	,,	***aupādhika***	,,	***au ādhika***
240/fn. 45/1:	,,	**न्यथात्वे**	,,	**न्यथात्व**
248/-11:	,,	**Diṅnāga**	,,	**Diṅāga**
248/-4:	,,	***parārthānumāna***	,,	***parārhānumāna***
248/fn. 54/1:	,,	**स्वार्थं**	,,	**स्वार्थं**
266/-9:	,,	***...hetvasiddha***	,,	***...hetvāsiddha***
270/-9:	,,	***dharmisva...***	,,	***dharmiśva...***
297/-16:	,,	***gavaya***	,,	***gayay***
371/-5:	,,	**thing**	,,	**this**
378/-9:	,,	**from**	,,	**fron**
383/fn. 8:	,,	**विषाण**	,,	**वि षाण**
388/-5:	,,	**enjoyed**	,,	**enjoved**

N.B. Numbers represent pages and lines (from top) respectively. Minus (-) before a number means that the lines have been counted from the bottom.
fn. = footnote